REVISED AND UPDATED

BECOMING VEGETARIAN

the complete guide to
adopting a healthy vegetarian diet

REVISED AND UPDATED

BECOMING VEGETARIAN

*the complete guide to
adopting a healthy vegetarian diet*

vesanto melina, m.sc., r.d.
brenda davis, r.d.

National Library of Canada Cataloguing in Publication

Melina, Vesanto, 1942-
    Becoming vegetarian : the complete guide to adopting a healthy vegetarian diet / Vesanto Melina, Brenda Davis. -- Rev. ed.

Includes index.
ISBN-13 978-0470-83253-0
ISBN-10 0-470-83253-3

    1. Vegetarianism. 2. Vegetarian cookery. I. Davis, Brenda, 1959-II. Title.

TX392.M45 2003   613.2'62   C2003-900258-6

Production Credits
Cover & interior text design: Interrobang Graphic Design Inc.
Cover photograph: Anthony-Masterson / Getty Images, Canada
Printer: EPAC

Wheat Kernal illustration in Chapter 5 courtesy of the Kansas Wheat Commission

Printed in the United States.
10 9 8 7 6

To our children,

Xoph (Chris) and Kavyo; Leena and Cory.

May your life be a reflection of what you believe,

in the deepest recesses of your heart and soul.

contents

acknowledgments

To everyone who contributed time, attention and energy to this project, we offer our heartfelt appreciation.

Sincere gratitude to those who made this book possible: to our publisher Robert Harris at John Wiley & Sons Canada; our editors Joan Whitman, Elizabeth McCurdy and Valerie Ahwee, and Karen Bryan, Publishing Services Director, for their care and expertise. It was a pleasure and a privilege to work with every one of you, both professionally and personally.

Love and gratefulness to our families and close friends: Cory Davis, for many hours of diligent recipe testing, careful record keeping and amazing presentation of the foods prepared. Also many thanks to Cory for daily beautifully prepared lunches, fresh squeezed juices, back rubs and hugs. Paul Davis for endless support, review of various sections and valuable assistance with charts. Leena Davis, for her advice, understanding and encouragement. Vesanto's wonderful community at Windsong, a source of learning and wisdom about living in harmony, and about vegetarian diplomacy. Ted Armitage, for bits of science and much laughter and joy. Chris and Kavyo; for the time, love, and thoughts we share. Bhora Derry, healer and true friend. Shirley and Al Hunting, our "other home" in Seattle. Victoria Harrison, RD, co-author in the first version of *Becoming Vegetarian* (and now living in Hong Kong) for valued friendship, and work that persists in this edition.

Deepest appreciation to our cherished advisors and those sharing many hours of invaluable insight: Stephen Walsh for his thoughtful review of Chapters 1, 2, 3 and 7 and insights on vitamin B12, Dr. Mark and Virginia Messina, Dr. Reed Mangels and Dr. Suzanne Havala Hobbs who have written such carefully researched materials on vegetarian nutrition and who continue to be an inspiration.

Special thanks to those who contributed to specific chapters, providing thoughtful reviews and suggestions: Kathleen Quinn RD, Sue Firus RD, and other staff at Dial-a-Dietitian, staff at Health Canada, Dr. Paul Appleby, John Robbins, Dilip Barnam, Dr. Tomas Barnard, Dr. Michael Klaper, Ketti Goudey MS, RD, writers Greg McIntyre and Valerie McIntyre for help with analogies, Syd Baumel of www.aquarianonline.com, Dennis Bayomi, Vicki Burns of the Winnipeg Humane Society, Glen Corolick of Hogwatch Manitoba www.hogwatchmanitoba.org; and Paul Pomeroy.

Warm acknowledgement to those who gave of their time and energy to support this project: Dr. Susan Barr, Maureen Butler, Robert Sawatzky, Jenise Sidebotham, Ralph Perkins, Vanessa Clarke, Graham Kerr and Deborah Pageau.

Thanks to those who created delicious recipes, and allowed their use in this book. Joseph Forest, John Borders and his wonderful family—Cindy, Mattie, David and Jack, Francis, and Carol Sue Janes of Seattle's outstanding Café Ambrosia, Ron Pickarski, Joanne Stepaniak, Yves Potvin and Yves Veggie Cuisine.

Special thanks. To artist Ben Hodson for his work on the Vegetarian Food Guide.

introduction

In 1994, when *Becoming Vegetarian* was first released, there were not many books about vegetarian nutrition by registered dietitians. For decades, dietitians had been less than enthusiastic about vegetarian diets, as had the medical community as a whole. Vegetarian diets were often categorized as fad diets, and were considered risky, especially for infants, children and pregnant women. However, the tables were beginning to turn. Studies not only established the safety of vegetarian diets, but also demonstrated clear and consistent health advantages, particularly where disease risk reduction was concerned. To quote Dr. Mervyn Hardinge, a pioneer of vegetarian nutrition who took part in the Harvard University's early human dietary studies on plant protein,

> "Attitudes toward vegetarian diets have progressed from ridicule and scepticism to condescending tolerance, to gradual and sometimes grudging acceptance, and finally to acclaim."

Becoming Vegetarian has added momentum to this shifting paradigm. It has also helped to bridge the gap between the scientific community and grassroots vegetarian organizations, as both welcomed this book as a complete and reliable guide to vegetarian nutrition. The book quickly became a national best seller in Canada, then was published in the United States, translated into French and Portuguese, and distributed in 11 countries. With over 100,000 copies in print, it is considered a classic.

Becoming Vegetarian has been, and continues to be an amazing journey for the authors. While Victoria Harrison was not actively involved in the revised edition (she is now living in Hong Kong), her beautiful, loving energy remains sprinkled throughout its pages. For Vesanto and Brenda, *Becoming Vegetarian* was the beginning of adventurous writing and speaking careers that have taken us across Canada and as far a field as Honolulu, Martinique, Oxford, and Brussels. We have addressed thousands of health professionals at dietetic and medical conferences, including the annual conventions of the Dietitians of Canada and American Dietetic Association. It is an immense privilege to be a part of this movement of reason and compassion, and a great honour to be connected to many amazing and inspirational people.

As dietitians, we were trained to educate consumers about food choices based on personal health—both physical and emotional. *Becoming Vegetarian* is about nutrition, and providing optimal nutrition at every stage of the life cycle. Yet its ultimate message goes beyond personal health. It is about recognizing the profound connection between our food choices and life all around us. The food we choose impacts the lives of those who had a hand in getting that food to our table. Our choices affect vast numbers of animals that are part of our food system; they impact wildlife that may lose habitat due to our abuse of land and water. What we eat has consequences for our rivers, oceans, soil and air. Becoming vegetarian softens our ecological footprint—perhaps more than any other single choice we can make. As people become conscious about these connections, the shift towards a plant-based diet simply happens.

Our goal in writing *Becoming Vegetarian* was to assist people in the task of designing vegetarian diets that are practically foolproof. If vegetarian diets are to be accepted by the mainstream population, it will be because people feel absolutely certain that these diets are safe, adequate, and even optimal for themselves, and for their children. Our dream is that all those who choose a vegetarian diet succeed brilliantly. In this vision, we include near-vegetarians, lacto-ovo-vegetarians and vegans. Our message is meant for those who are just beginning a dietary shift, and for those who wish to fine tune a diet followed for many years.

You may be wondering why a whole new version of *Becoming Vegetarian* was necessary. Whereas the first edition broke fresh ground, in the decade since, the amount of scientific research in this field has increased exponentially. Canadian and U.S. scientists have collaborated to forge new recommendations for our intakes of vitamins, minerals, protein and fats. Vegetarian and especially vegan foods have become among the fastest growing categories in the grocery trade. Mainstream supermarkets now stock a tremendous selection of delicious veggie "meats," tofu and non-dairy beverages; sales of many of these products have tripled over the last four years. All of these advancements needed to be communicated in practical terms to consumers. It was time to revise this book that has been loved by so many people.

How is this edition different than the original? The new *Becoming Vegetarian* is seasoned with experience. It digs deeper; it questions harder. Much of what was considered mere speculation 10 years ago is now accepted fact. We speak with greater confidence, and provide more thorough guidance for readers. Several issues that were not dealt with in the original book are addressed in the new edition. For example, we have included chapters on whole grains, fruits and vegetables, weight management, and the prime of life. Our recipes are refined, and include contributions from outstanding chefs around North America.

Becoming Vegetarian was written for you. It is our hope that it will provide you with all the information you need to construct an exceptional diet—one that will nourish your body and soul. May you move forward with confidence and conviction in your journey towards a gentler, kinder, and healthier world.

Vesanto Melina and Brenda Davis

why be vegetarian?

Why be vegetarian? One and a quarter million Canadians would each have a unique answer. Vegetarians dance to their own music. They have the courage to challenge accepted practices, even those respected as tradition. A good number of vegetarians are health enthusiasts, most have a very big heart when it comes to animals, and many are deeply committed to protecting the environment. It is practically impossible to pick a vegetarian out of a crowd. While some look like bohemians; others look like construction workers, movie stars, business people, hockey players, marathon runners, or grandmas and grandpas. Vegetarians are of various ages and from every walk of life. When you tell someone you are a vegetarian, they usually say something like, "I don't eat much meat either." Being vegetarian is considered a very good thing, something many people aspire to.

Types of Vegetarians

A "vegetarian" is defined as someone who does not eat meat, poultry, or fish. In contrast, those who include both plants and animals in their diet are called "omnivores" or "nonvegetarians." The two most common subclasses of vegetarians are lacto-ovo or vegan.

1. Lacto-ovo Vegetarian

Lacto-ovo vegetarians avoid all animal flesh, but do use eggs (ovo) and dairy products (lacto). Some people are simply lacto-vegetarians, using dairy products but not eggs, and others are ovo-vegetarians, using eggs but not dairy products.

2. Vegan (pronounced vee-gun or vee-gan)

Vegans avoid all products of animal origin, including eggs, dairy foods, gelatin (made from the bones and connective tissue of animals), and honey (the product of bees). Vegans avoid animal products not only in their diet but in every aspect of their lives. They may shun leather goods, wool and silk, tallow soaps, and other products made with animal ingredients.

Variations on "Vegetarian"

Within the two main categories of vegetarian, there are many variations, depending on the motivation, experiences, and unique needs of the individual. When people become vegetarian in an effort to achieve better health, there may be some flexibility in their use of animal products; however, when the choice is made on the basis of ethics or religion, there is a greater tendency toward complete adherence to the diet.

When people first become vegetarian, many of them rely heavily on dairy foods and eggs. As they grow in their knowledge and experience of vegetarian issues, they often begin to shift away from the use of animal products, replacing them with protein-rich plant foods such as soy products, legumes, nuts, and seeds. This natural progression gets easier with each passing year. Convenient and delicious vegetarian options are increasing exponentially. Mainstream grocery stores feature an impressive selection of non-dairy milks, veggie meats, tofu, and other vegetarian favourites. This trend away from the use of animal products is reflected in recent figures that compare the number of vegans to lacto-ovo vegetarians. Ten years ago it was estimated that 5–10 per cent of all vegetarians were vegan and 90–95 per cent were lacto-ovo vegetarian, whereas recent surveys show that 25–40 per cent of all vegetarians are vegan.

While many vegetarians do not quite fit the definition of vegan, they are very close. Some avoid all obvious dairy products and eggs, but are not concerned about traces of animal products in prepared foods. Others eat the occasional pizza slice or ice cream cone, but do not consume these products on a regular basis. This rapidly growing subsection of the vegetarian population is much closer in its dietary practices and nutritional intakes to vegans than to lacto-ovo vegetarians; thus people following this type of diet are often called "*near-vegans*."

We might expect that there is little room for diversity among vegans and near-vegans, but this is clearly not the case. Within the vegan/near-vegan category are many variations, among the most popular of which are health movements such as macrobiotics, natural hygiene, living and raw food consumers, and fruitarians. All of these systems promote dietary regimes based on simple, whole foods. In most cases processed foods, refined sugars, and concentrated fats are shunned and, in many cases, nutritional supplements may be avoided as well. These diets are low in total fat, saturated fat, trans-fatty acids, cholesterol, and refined carbohydrates, minimizing potentially damaging dietary components. They are also rich in protective dietary constituents such as fibre, phytochemicals, and several vitamins and minerals (including folate, vitamins A, C, and K, potassium, and magnesium). However, these whole food regimes are considerably more restrictive than vegan diets, which include the full spectrum of plant foods along with any necessary supplements or fortified foods. These diets may lack vitamin B12 and may be deficient in vitamin D. They may also provide insufficient protein, energy, fat, vitamins, and minerals and be too bulky to meet the needs of infants and young children.

Beyond the two main categories, lacto-ovo vegetarian and vegan, are people who call themselves vegetarian, but do not qualify according to accepted definitions. These near-vegetarians are two to three times the number of those who never eat flesh foods. The explanation, it seems, is that many who eliminate red meat, but include poultry and/or fish consider themselves "vegetarian." In addition, some who eat only a little meat, poultry, and fish also often call themselves "vegetarian." The term sometimes used to describe those folks is "semi-vegetarian," although a more appropriate term is "near-vegetarian."

Deciding Factors:
The Motivation for Becoming Vegetarian

The road to a vegetarian lifestyle is paved with love—for our fellow beings, for the planet, and for ourselves. It matters far less what draws us to this path, or how far along the path we have come, than the fact that we have are heading in a direction that leads to a kinder, more compassionate world.

Sometimes it is a single reason that motivates an individual to embark on this journey. With time and experience, other reasons are often adopted and the conviction to continue is strengthened. The four primary reasons people give for choosing a vegetarian or vegan diet include:

1. To support personal health and healing

2. To promote reverence for life

3. To protect the environment

4. To uphold religious or philosophical principles

Let's briefly consider each of these reasons and their relative significance as deciding factors.

Support Personal Health and Healing

Health is the most commonly cited reason for becoming vegetarian. Most people now recognize that vegetarian diets are not only a healthy choice, but are likely to protect us against disease. The potential health advantages of vegetarian diets include:

- *Less obesity*. Vegetarians are leaner than nonvegetarians. This often translates into better overall health.

- *Reduced risk of chronic disease*. Vegetarians have less heart disease, hypertension, type 2 diabetes, and certain forms of cancer than nonvegetarians. There is also some evidence that vegetarians enjoy protection against renal disease, gallbladder disease, diverticular disease, and rheumatoid arthritis.

- *Improved longevity.* Vegetarians live an estimated seven to nine years longer than nonvegetarians. While many people poke fun at vegetarians, saying "It just feels longer," the reality is that vegetarians tend to be healthier in their senior years.

- *Reduced risk of food-borne diseases.* Risk of contracting E. coli, salmonella, listeria, campylobacter, and other food-borne pathogens is significantly lower for vegetarians.

- *Lower intakes of environmental contaminants.* Exposure to heavy metals, DDT, PCBs, and other environmental contaminants is generally reduced in vegetarian diets, as these substances accumulate as we move up the food chain.

- *Improved nutritional intakes relative to current nutrition recommendations.* When compared with nonvegetarian diets, vegetarian diets provide a balance of protein, carbohydrate, and fat that is closer to current recommendations. Plant-based diets are also lower in saturated fat, cholesterol, animal protein, and possibly trans-fatty acids, and higher in vitamins C and E, carotenoids, folate, fibre, magnesium, and phytochemicals.

The extraordinary reality is that when people make choices that support their own health and well-being, the benefits extend far beyond the individual to other living beings and indeed to the planet as a whole. This is because of the intimate and powerful connection between all beings.

Promote Reverence for Life

For increasing numbers, becoming vegetarian is a strong statement against violence and cruelty toward animals. Every year in North America close to 10 billion animals (not including fish) are slaughtered for food. While many people imagine the lives of these animals as they are described in storybooks, the truth is a stark contrast. The concerns about the lives and deaths of food animals today can be briefly described as follows:

- *Food animals are raised inhumanely.* As our population increases, and our demands for food escalate, incidences of overcrowding, confinement, isolation, and brutality become commonplace.

Food animals are often subjected to surgeries, mutilations, and amputations without anaesthetic. The crowding and/or isolation robs these animals of the opportunity to engage in normal social behaviour, and they are often driven insane.

- *Food animals are transported to slaughter in appalling conditions.* Many food animals experience extreme trauma during transport, often going without food or water for extended periods of time. As a result, millions of animals die each year on route to slaughter.

- *Food animals are slaughtered inhumanely.* Laws and regulations regarding the "humane slaughter" of food animals are in place to ensure that these animals are rendered unconscious by an approved, humane method before being shackled, hoisted, and bled. Unfortunately, a concern with profit means that line speeds increase, as do violations of humane slaughter laws and regulations. Stunning methods are often unreliable, and animals improperly stunned become terrified, frequently fighting for their lives. These animals are sometimes beaten, or worse, dismembered, skinned, and boiled alive.

- *Animals have rights.* Animals are not inanimate objects, but thinking, feeling creatures who deserve to be treated with respect and compassion. While most people treat their pets with love and kindness, many fail to recognize that pet animals and food animals are all intelligent and can feel pain, just as humans do. Indeed, whether an animal is a pet or a food is not always determined by their species, but rather by the human beings who "own" them. To assume that our treatment of food animals is of no moral consequence is absurd. The words of one of the greatest philosophers of all times, Nobel Peace Prize winner, Dr. Albert Schweitzer, truly give us pause for thought:

> The thinking man must oppose all cruel customs no matter how deeply rooted in tradition and surrounded by a halo. When we have a choice, we must avoid bringing torment and injury into the life of another, even the lowliest creature; to do so is to renounce our manhood and shoulder a guilt which nothing justifies.

Protect the Environment

People are beginning to realize that we cannot continue to consume the earth's resources at the current rate if there is to be any hope for future generations. The choice to become vegetarian is a way of reducing our ecological footprint, and this is probably the most effective step any individual can take toward this goal. Albert Einstein (1879–1955) once said, "Nothing will benefit human health and increase the chances for survival of life on earth as much as the evolution to a vegetarian diet." We do have a speck or two of evidence to suggest that this man knew what he was talking about. Choosing a vegetarian diet can help to protect the environment in many ways:

- *It assists in the preservation of water resources*. Animal agriculture demands tremendous amounts of fresh water. It is estimated that almost 50 per cent of all water consumed in the United States is used for the raising of livestock. While water requirements vary according to location and the amount of irrigation required to grow animal feed, on average, it takes about 100 times more water to produce a pound of beef than it does to produce a pound of wheat. It takes less water to produce the food that a vegan needs for one year than to produce the food that a meat eater needs for a month.

- *It helps prevents water pollution*. According to the Environmental Protection Agency (EPA), agriculture is the biggest polluter of America's water systems. It is responsible for 70 per cent of waterway pollution, its damage exceeding that of sewage treatment plants, urban storm sewers, and pollution from contaminants in air. The major offenders are livestock-feeding operations. Manure, traditionally used as a natural fertilizer to enrich soil, cannot generally be returned from immense feedlots to distant farmland. Animals produce about 130 times more manure than humans (e.g., animals produce 59 kilograms/130 pounds of manure for every .50 kilogram/1 pound that humans produce). This waste never sees a sewage system or treatment plant and all too often ends up poisoning rivers, causing severe oxygen depletion, and devastating fish populations. Livestock manure is a breeding ground for dangerous pathogens such as E. coli, giardia, and pfiesteria, which cause sickness and death in people living in regions where factory farms are concentrated. Furthermore, waste from North America's 9 billion chickens and 150 million other farmed animals is permeated with hormones that propel the bird "from egg to fryer in thirty-nine days" and other similar unnatural feats.

- *It helps preserve the planet's most valuable ecosystems.* Tropical rain forests are ecological treasures, housing half of the world's plant and animal species. These precious resources are being destroyed at an alarming rate. According to the Rainforest Action Network, two-thirds of the rain forests in Central America have been cleared primarily for the purpose of raising cheap beef to stock American fast-food establishments. They estimate that for every fast-food burger made from rain forest beef, 16.75 square metres (55 square feet) of tropical rain forest has been cleared. With the trees go twenty to thirty different plant species, 100 different insect species, plus dozens of birds, mammals, and reptile species.

- *It provides powerful protection against desertification.* Overgrazing is considered the leading cause of desertification worldwide. In the western United States, 70 per cent of the entire land mass is used for grazing livestock. When land is overgrazed, the soil is compacted, decreasing its ability to absorb water. When heavy rains fall, topsoil is carried away. Fifteen centimetres (six inches) of topsoil are needed to grow healthy crops. It takes approximately 3,000 years for nature to produce this amount of topsoil. Every twenty-eight years in the United States, every fourteen years in developing countries, and every seven years in China, 2.5 centimetres (1 inch) of topsoil are lost as the result of current intensive farming practices. At this rate, it is estimated that there are as few as forty-five years of farmable soil left on the planet.

- *It may help protect against catastrophic environmental changes.* Intensive animal agriculture is a significant factor in global warming, increasing all major global warming gases: carbon dioxide, methane, nitrous oxides, and chlorofluorocarbons. Carbon dioxide emissions come largely from fossil fuels. Raising livestock requires huge amounts of fossil fuels—for transporting feed, heating shelters (often large buildings), and transporting animals to slaughter and the products to meat-packing plants and stores. According to Worldwatch Institute, 15–20 per cent of all methane emissions come directly from livestock. In addition, the chemical fertilizers used to produce food for grain-fed animals are important contributors to nitrous oxides. Finally, the increased refrigeration necessary to preserve animal products releases chlorofluorocarbons in the atmosphere.

- *It reduces consumption of the earth's dwindling resources.* It is estimated that if every inhabitant on this planet used as many resources to produce his or her food as each American does, we would need three planet earths to sustain the current population. Unfortunately, that is the very direction we are heading. Between 1990 and 1995, China's grain consumption increased by 36,280,000 tonnes (40 million tons). Of this total, 29,931,000 tonnes (33 million tons) were consumed as animal fodder and 6,349,000 tonnes (7 million tons) as food for humans. China, like many other developing countries, is rapidly moving up the food chain. Tragically, more and more of the world's resources are used for raising livestock to provide food for the wealthy, while one in every six people goes hungry every day. Today, our planet is home to nearly 1 billion pigs, 1.3 billion cows, 1.8 billion sheep and goats, and 13.5 billion chickens—more than two chickens for each man, woman, and child. We have altered vast ecosystems and devoted massive resources to support this inefficient way of eating. The world's cattle alone consume a quantity of food equal to the caloric needs of 8.7 billion people—more than the entire human population on earth.

Uphold Religious or Philosophical Principles

Some individuals choose a vegetarian or near-vegetarian diet in keeping with their religion or the philosophy of a particular movement. Major world religions that promote vegetarian and/or vegan diets, to varying degrees, as part of their basic teaching include: Buddhism, Jainism, Taoism, Hinduism, and Seventh-day Adventists (a branch of Christianity). In addition, many religions that do not explicitly promote plant-based diets have subgroups that promote vegetarian lifestyles. Good examples are the Christian Vegetarian Association, Doukhobors, Jewish Vegetarians of North America, the Muslim Vegan/Vegetarian Society, and some Sufis. Although many people become vegetarian as a result of their religious persuasion, the reasons why any given faith would promote a vegetarian diet tend to include one or more of those outlined in the preceding three sections. For example, the Eastern religions base their dietary choice on principles of compassion for all living beings, while the Seventh-day Adventists promote vegetarianism on the basis of its benefits to human health.

Vegetarianism Stands the Test of Time

Vegetarianism has been a dietary option since the dawn of recorded time. Its origins remain somewhat of a mystery, although the mythologies of many cultures tell of a beginning without violence, where people lived off the plants of the earth. One of the most widely recognized records is in the Old Testament where Adam and Eve are told what they are permitted to eat:

> And God said, behold, I have given you every herb-bearing seed, which is upon the face of all the earth, and every tree, in which is the fruit of a tree yielding seed; to you it shall be for meat.
>
> — *Genesis 1:29*

Throughout history, vegetarianism has been a part of cultures around the world. Many of the world's greatest philosophers and intellectuals refused meat when such a choice was contrary to dictates of the ruling class.

Pythagoras, who evidently brought these concepts from the East, is often considered "the father of vegetarianism" in the West. Until the late nineteenth century, when the word "vegetarian" was coined, people who lived on a meatless diet were referred to as "Pythagoreans." Pythagoras, born in approximately 580 b.c, was credited with the discovery of the Pythagorean theorem, many other mathematical and geometrical findings, the idea of planetary motion, and the speculation that the earth moves around the sun. He also founded a society that pursued wisdom, believed in the transmigration of souls, and practised meditation. Among the Pythagoreans, materialism and meat-eating were taboo. Contrary to the general view of the time, women were considered equal to men. Pythagoras also believed that one's maximum philosophical potential could be reached only when the body was an efficient instrument. Thus, a strict exercise regime including gymnastics, running, and wrestling was practised.

Following Pythagoras, many influential thinkers through the centuries promoted a vegetarian diet. The following insightful quotes provide a glimpse of a small selection of these extraordinary human beings:

> But for the sake of some little mouthful of flesh we deprive a soul of the sun and light, and of that proportion of life and time it had been born into the world to enjoy.
>
> — *Plutarch (c.a.d. 46–c.120)*

> Not to hurt our humble brethren is our first duty to them, but to stop there is not enough. We have a higher mission—to be of service to them wherever they require it.
>
> — *St. Francis of Assisi (c.1182–1226)*

> Fast all day,
> kill cows at night,
> here prayers,
> there blood—
> does this please God?
>
> — *Kabir, Islamic mystic and poet (1398–1518)*

> I have from an early age abjured the use of meat, and the time will come when men such as I will look on the murder of animals as they now look on the murder of men.
>
> — *Leonardo da Vinci (1452–1519)*

What is it that should trace the insuperable line?...The question is not, Can they reason? nor Can they talk? but, Can they suffer?

> — *Jeremy Bentham (1748–1832)*

We consume the carcasses of creatures of like appetites, passions and organs with our own, and fill the slaughterhouses daily with screams of pain and fear.

> — *Robert Louis Stevenson (1850–1894)*

Non-violence leads to the highest ethics, which is the goal of all evolution. Until we stop harming all other living beings, we are still savages.

> —*Thomas Edison (1847–1931)*

Flesh foods are not the best nourishment for human beings and were not the food of our primitive ancestors. There is nothing necessary or desirable for human nutrition to be found in meats or flesh foods which is not found in and derived from plant foods.

> — *Dr. J.H. Kellogg (1852–1943)*

The greatness of a nation and its moral progress can be judged by the way its animals are treated.

> — *Mahatma Gandhi (1869–1948)*

Until we have the courage to recognize cruelty for what it is—whether its victim is human or animal—we cannot expect things to be much better in this world. We cannot have peace among men whose hearts delight in killing any living creature. By every act that glorifies or even tolerates such moronic delight in killing we set back the progress of humanity.

> — *Rachel Carson (1907–1964)*

Among the most colourful characters of the historical advocates of vegetarianism was George Bernard Shaw (1856–1950). When Shaw decided to eliminate meat from his diet, it was so contrary to his culture that his physician was alarmed. He cautioned the young Shaw that if he continued to insist on this meat-free diet, he would surely die of malnutrition in short order. Shaw replied that he would sooner die than consume a "corpse." One can appreciate the irony of the situation when, as he approached his eighty-fifth year, Shaw proclaimed:

> The average age (life expectancy) of a meat eater is 63. I am on the verge of 85 and still work as hard as ever. I have lived quite long enough and I am trying to die; but I simply cannot do it. A single beef steak would finish me; but I cannot bring myself to swallow it. I am oppressed with a dread of living forever. That is the only disadvantage of vegetarianism.

Many courageous individuals throughout history have taken a strong stand against the use of animals for human consumption. However, one of the greatest impacts on the vegetarian movement of today was made by a core group of about 140 dedicated individuals in England who banded together for discussion and support. The result was the modern world's first vegetarian society in 1847, which was soon followed by similar societies in Europe and the United States.

Alternatives Go Mainstream

Among twentieth-century vegetarians, a small and growing core felt the need for avoidance of all animal products, and the word "vegan" was added to our vocabularies in 1944. The late 1960s and early 1970s launched a new era for vegetarianism. Peace-loving "counterculture" groups sprang up with a message of ecology and natural living. To many people, vegetarianism became linked with the hippie movement. Health professionals often viewed the vegetarian diet as a dangerous fad that could lead to nutritional deficiencies, while nutritional research explored whether or not these views were well founded.

In 1971, Frances Moore Lappé's book *Diet for a Small Planet* gave a tremendous boost to the vegetarian cause. Her 3 million-copy best-seller drew many toward a plant-based diet, with its love for humanity and our planet, and exposure of the inefficiency of feeding mountains of grain to livestock. John Robbins further strengthened the vegetarian movement with *Diet for a New America* (1987), *May All Be Fed* (1992), and *The Food Revolution* (2001). Robbins's powerful writing style appeals to a mainstream audience, while addressing the connection between our dietary choices and the environment, world hunger, and the diseases of affluence. He is also a strong advocate for animal rights, which profoundly touches people as an idea whose time has come.

During the last decades of the twentieth century, health professionals increasingly recognized the potential advantages of vegetarian diets. After research at Harvard University, Loma Linda University in California, Kingston Hospital in London, and other highly respected centres established the nutritional adequacy of plant-based diets, the emphasis gradually shifted to their health benefits. Long-term studies of large groups of subjects were launched by Dr. Colin Campbell of Cornell University (The China Study), by Oxford's Dr. Tim Key, Dr. M. Thorogood, Paul Appleby, and others (The Oxford Vegetarian Study), by international groups (The EPIC study), and by Seventh-day Adventist research teams (The Adventist Mortality Study and the Adventist Health Study). In prestigious medical journals, Dr. Dean Ornish presented evidence that we can actually reverse coronary artery disease through a combination of a vegetarian diet and lifestyle changes. This alternative to painful surgery and to medications with dreadful side effects, held such appeal that Ornish became a regular on the cover of popular magazines and a sought-after guest on talk shows such as "Oprah."   Health care systems began to recognize that billions of dollars, as well as lives, could be saved by a dietary shift. The Physicians' Committee for Responsible Medicine (www.pcrm.org), headed by Dr. Neal Barnard, began research on the benefits of diets that are free of animal products for various conditions such as diabetes, menstrual pain, PMS, and obesity. Outspoken physicians such as Dr. Michael Klaper, Dr. Benjamin Spock, Dr. Thomas Barnard, Dr. John McDougall, and Dr. Caldwell Esselstyn went public with a message urging a shift toward a vegetarian diet.

The American Dietetic Association, in its position papers on vegetarian nutrition, took a strong stand regarding the adequacy of both vegetarian and vegan diets, stating that such diets could meet our nutritional needs at every stage of the life cycle. Dr. Suzanne Havala-Hobbs, Dr Reed Mangels, Dr. Mark Messina, Virginia Messina, Dr. Winston Craig, and Dr. Joan Sabate, with faculty members at Loma Linda University, wrote books and scientific articles on vegetarian nutrition to support the understanding of health professionals. The International Congresses on Vegetarian Nutrition, held every five years, have attracted scientists from more than 36 countries around the globe.

Tentatively, then with enthusiasm, Canadians, Americans, and Europeans explored new vegetarian foods as they appeared in the marketplace. Tofu was transformed from the object of jokes into a super food. The fortification of soymilk with calcium and vitamin D was permitted in Canada in 1997, and soymilk squeezed its way into dairy cases. In a footnote to the U.S. Food Guide Pyramid, the Dietary Guidelines for Americans 2000 identified fortified soymilk as an acceptable alternative to cow's milk. *The Manual of Clinical Dietetics* (2001) went further and included calcium-set tofu, fortified soyfoods and juices, certain greens, beans, almond butter, and tahini in the "Milk and Milk Alternates" food group. Culinary magazines featured colourful spreads of nutritional giants such as broccoli, kale, garlic, papayas, and blueberries. Canadian sales of veggie "meats" more than tripled to $30 million annually, from 1997 to 2001. While vegetarians welcomed these easy-to-use products, most of the buyers were nonvegetarians. *Food Processing* magazine listed vegetarian items in the "hottest" categories for the future.

The Continuing Survey of Food Intake for 1994 to 1996 reported that 2.6 per cent of Americans describe themselves as vegetarians. Significantly more (4.2 per cent) chose vegetarian fare instead of meat, fish, and poultry at mealtimes, though not necessarily calling themselves vegetarian. In Canada, a 2002 survey showed 4 per cent of adults to be vegetarian in name and practice.

Depending on the wording of questions, various polls indicate that between 20 and 46 per cent of North Americans are cutting back on, or eliminating, red meat.

Other Resources
These Web sites are doorways to a world of resources:

www.vrg.org	Vegetarian Resource Group
www.ivu.org	International Vegetarian Union
www.vegdining.com	For your restaurant and travel needs

The Future Is Bright!

Today we see people of every age and from every walk of life choosing to become vegetarian. An even greater segment of the population is moving in that direction and increasingly incorporating plant foods into more meals. While one in four Americans eat fast foods every day, some franchises now feature veggie burgers. Restaurant menus include one or more "heart-healthy" vegetarian options. The waitress and chef are likely to understand the word "vegan." One of Toronto's favourite fall rituals, the three-day Vegetarian Food Fair, attracts over 10,000 people each September, and Vancouver's Taste of Health attracts about 5,000.

Whether we are near-vegetarian or we entirely avoid animal products, there are common bonds in the caring we express through our dietary choices. For some of us, our caring is centred on creating vibrant good health in our loved ones and ourselves. For some, our caring is inspired by a respect for animals. For others, our caring focuses on planet earth and the environment. Yet for all, our choice of a vegetarian meal is a way to make a statement, to vote consistently in a way that really counts.

The vegetarian alternative offers hope for a brighter future. There is little doubt that the shift toward plant-based diets is gaining momentum and there's no indication that it's going to slow down any time soon. The positive impact of these trends is potentially enormous.

A complete set of references is available online at:
http://www.nutrispeak.com/bvreferences.htm

maximizing the vegetarian advantage

There was a time when people believed that meat and milk were the foundation of a healthy diet. Fifty per cent of the space in national food guides was devoted to these foods. Nutrition education resources explained why meat was necessary for high-quality protein and bioavailable iron, and why dairy products were essential for building and maintaining strong bones. People were thoroughly convinced that without these animal products, otherwise healthy individuals would become weak and sickly, children would not grow properly, and athletes would not achieve their potential. Vegetarians were looked upon as heretics and often ridiculed for their singularity. Vegetarian diets were considered risky, if not downright dangerous for children, pregnant, and lactating women.

This prevailing attitude did not come about by chance. In the early 1900s, food policies were directed toward eliminating deficiency diseases. Food supplies of the less fortunate were often meagre and the variety limited. For these undernourished people, adding meat and milk to the diet made a big difference. In addition, early feeding studies showed that children, especially those who were small for their age, grew faster with more animal products. As a result, these foods were granted special status. Governments offered large subsidies to farmers in an effort to increase production, and supported intensive marketing initiatives and massive nutrition education campaigns to insure increased consumption. Diseases of nutritional deficiency rapidly diminished, and the interests of animal agriculture became deeply entrenched in the economy. It appeared as though the job of improving the health of the nation through nutrition had been brilliantly accomplished.

However, by the middle of the twentieth century, a less favourable health picture emerged. While deficiency diseases were no longer the threat they had once been, heart disease, cancer, type 2 diabetes, and obesity had begun to rise ominously.

Beyond a Reasonable Doubt

Authorities were baffled; scientists could uncover no bacteria or virus on which to blame the surge in these devastating conditions. Experts began to ponder the possibility of an environmental influence, and it was not long before diet became a primary suspect. For the second half of the twentieth century, researchers studied populations, their dietary and lifestyle patterns, and their relative risk of various diseases. They set up clinical trials to compare the effects of dietary changes on groups of individuals, and examined specific foods and nutrients in an effort to determine their effects on health. In 1990, the World Health Organization (WHO) commissioned a panel of nutrition experts from around the world to sift through the existing research and assess the strength of the evidence linking diet to disease. The resulting technical report, entitled "Diet, Nutrition and the Prevention of Chronic Diseases," was strong and clear in its conclusion:

> Medical and scientific research has established clear links between dietary factors and the risk of developing coronary artery disease, hypertension, stroke, several cancers, osteoporosis, diabetes, and other chronic diseases. This knowledge is now sufficiently strong to enable governments to assess national eating patterns, identify risks and then protect their populations through policies that make healthy food choices the easy choices.

With regard to specific dietary patterns, the panel states:

> The population nutrient intakes recommended in this report translate into a diet that is low in fat, and especially saturated fat, and high in complex starchy carbohydrates. Such a diet is characterized by frequent consumption of vegetables, fruits, cereals and legumes, and contrasts sharply with current diets drawing substantial amounts of energy from whole-milk dairy products, fatty meats and refined sugars.

Over the next decade, evidence linking diet to chronic disease continued to mount, prompting numerous health organizations to develop dietary guidelines and recommendations urging a shift toward plant-based diets. What was truly remarkable was how consistent these diverse groups were in their public health messages. In 1999, five of the top health organizations in the United States (the National Institutes of Health, the American Dietetic Association, the American Pediatric Society, the American Cancer Society, and the American Heart Association) joined forces to develop and endorse one set of dietary guidelines. By unifying their message, these organizations hoped to present a stronger voice, one that would alter food choices, ultimately reducing rates of chronic disease. The key message: Choose most of what you eat from plant sources. More specifically, the group recommended that people choose a diet rich in grain products, vegetables, and fruits, one that is low in fat, saturated fat and cholesterol, and moderate in sugar, salt, and alcohol, if used. Richard J. Deckelbaum, M.D, co-author of their report and professor of pediatrics and nutrition at Columbia University in New York City, explains one the most salient points that came out of their work:

> The good news is that we don't need one diet to prevent heart disease, another to decrease cancer risk and yet another to prevent obesity and diabetes. A single healthy diet cuts across disease categories to lower the risk of many chronic conditions.

Today, governments, health organizations, and nutrition authorities are acutely aware of the health benefits of plant-based diets, and their nutrition education materials consistently reflect this knowledge. However, while people are strongly encouraged to increase the amount of plant foods they eat, there is an obvious hesitation to tell people to cut back on their intake of animal products. Instead, we are told to eat less saturated fat and cholesterol. One might wonder why, when animal products are the primary sources of these potentially damaging dietary components, that there would be any reluctance to urge the public to eat less. Marion Nestle, chair of the Department of Nutrition and Food Studies at New York University, in her exceptional exposé, *Food Politics*, provides a thought-provoking explanation:

> The meat industry can live with euphemistic advice to consume diets "low in saturated fat." It is only when that term gets translated into food sources—"animal fat" or "eat less meat"— that industry groups are galvanized into action, and nutrition scientists and educators become uncomfortable and advise "moderation."

There is no denying the political and economic links between governments and agricultural industries. To further complicate matters, health organizations and nutrition authorities are frequently engaged by these industries as allies or partners in wellness initiatives. The end result is a message that is, at best, diluted and, more often, seriously compromised. Fortunately, the population is becoming increasingly savvy when it comes to matters of health and nutrition. Efforts to hide the potentially deleterious effects of high-fat meat and dairy products behind more complex nutrition concepts such as saturated fat and cholesterol are becoming futile.

The Health of Vegetarians

With plant-based diets being so highly valued as protectors against chronic disease, one might imagine all vegetarians dancing until dawn on their ninetieth birthday. While there is little question that vegetarians enjoy some advantages where chronic disease is concerned, quantifying this advantage is no simple task.

First, it is important to understand that becoming vegetarian is no guarantee of a healthful diet. In fact, it is possible to completely blow it as a vegetarian. Think about it. Coconut cream pie, hot-fudge sundaes, jam-filled doughnuts, potato chips, and soda pop all fit the definition of vegetarian foods. And when it comes to comparing vegetarians to nonvegetarians, we find certain limitations that affect the research findings:

- *Vegetarians are not consistently defined.* In some studies, the participants are actually "near-vegetarians" who eat meat less than once a week, rather than true vegetarians. Some have been meat eaters for sixty years and vegetarian for only two years. These individuals would rarely experience the same level of protection afforded to someone who has been a long-term vegetarian, yet they are sometimes lumped into the same category.

- *People's reasons for being vegetarian can place them at different ends of the health spectrum.* Some have adopted a plant-based diet in response to recent, devastating news from their cardiologist or oncologist. Thus, people with serious illnesses may be grouped with long-term health and fitness enthusiasts.

- *Specific food choices are not always considered.* There is tremendous diversity of food choices among individuals, whether vegetarian or nonvegetarian. Some vegetarians are raw food vegans, while others are junk food junkies. Simply comparing vegetarians and nonvegetarians is of limited value if specific dietary choices are not considered.

- *Other lifestyle factors are not always taken into account.* Numerous factors, apart from diet, can affect health. If smoking habits, exercise level, and response to stress are not considered, it becomes difficult to determine what proportion of the risk reduction is due to diet, and how much is due to non-dietary factors.

- *Studies are often too small to accurately reflect the general vegetarian population.* While interesting insights may be gained by observing just a few vegetarians or vegans, these studies do not provide the final answers.

Keeping this in mind, our knowledge regarding the health consequences of vegetarian diets has expanded enormously over the past couple of decades. As a result, the primary research focus has shifted away from the question "Are vegetarian diets safe?" to "How much protection can vegetarian diets afford?" Even our most conservative nutrition organizations, which, for many years, categorized vegetarian eating patterns as fad diets, now recognize their safety and potential benefits. The 2003 American Dietetic Association and Dietitians of Canada position paper on vegetarian diets provides an excellent reflection of the current view on vegetarian diets: "It is the position of the American Dietetic Association and Dietitians of Canada that appropriately planned vegetarian diets are healthful, nutritionally adequate, and provide health benefits in the prevention and treatment of certain diseases."

Today, there is little question that well-constructed vegetarian and vegan diets can provide completely adequate nutrition at every stage of the lifecycle and foster excellent health. While vegetarian diets have been charged with increasing risk of deficiency diseases, what many people fail to realize is that there is at least as much potential for malnutrition ("faulty nutrition") with animal-centred diets as with vegetarian diets, perhaps more. According to the State of the World 2000 (Worldwatch Institute), there are three kinds of malnutrition:

1. **Hunger—a deficiency of calories and protein.** Hunger affects some 1.2 billion people worldwide. In countries with the greatest hunger problems, more than 50 per cent of the population are underweight.

2. **Overconsumption—an excess of calories, often accompanied by deficiency of vitamins and minerals.** Overconsumption also affects 1.2 billion people worldwide. In countries with the greatest amount of overeating, more than 50 per cent of the population are overweight.

3. **Micronutrient deficiency—a deficiency of vitamins and minerals.** This form of malnutrition affects 2.0 billion people worldwide, and overlaps with both hunger and overconsumption. It is the result of insufficient variety in the

diet, and/or an excess of fat and sugar, crowding out foods that would otherwise contribute essential nutrients.

Technically, hunger (protein-calorie malnutrition) need occur only with insufficient access to food. In Western vegetarian populations, hunger is uncommon. It can occur, for example, in rare instances when infants and children are fed extremely low-fat, high-fibre diets, or when calories are restricted to achieve a model-thin slimness. Micronutrient deficiencies can occur among vegetarians when good sources of iron or vitamin B12 are not included in the diet, or when the diet is based on junk foods or refined carbohydrates and lacks vegetables, fruits, legumes, whole grains, nuts, and seeds.

Two types of malnutrition are widespread among nonvegetarians: *overconsumption* and *micronutrient deficiencies*. Overconsumption dramatically increases risk for numerous chronic diseases and is the fastest-growing form of malnutrition in the world. It is most commonly seen in diets centred on animal foods, processed foods, and fast foods. These diets are low in fibre and high in fat, cholesterol, sugar, and salt. In such diets, micronutrient deficiencies are associated with lack of variety (i.e., burgers and fries) or with too much refined food (high-fat, high-sugar foods that squeeze out valuable whole grains, vegetables, fruits, and legumes).

Both vegetarian and nonvegetarian eating patterns have the potential to nourish a population, if appropriately planned—and to be risky, if not.

Overall Health and Longevity of Vegetarians

Vegetarians tend to be a very healthy group of people. Death rates from chronic diseases in vegetarians are about half that of the general population. Some of the advantage can be attributed to non-dietary lifestyle factors. Fewer vegetarians smoke or abuse alcohol, and a higher percentage are very physically active. When vegetarians are compared with similar health-conscious nonvegetarians (e.g., those with similar smoking, drinking, and exercise habits, and who eat plenty of vegetables, fruits, and whole grains), their advantage decreases, yet they still hold an advantage. This suggests that avoiding flesh foods brings its own health benefits.

Scientific studies consistently show that vegetarians are slimmer than nonvegetarians. Within the Seventh-day Adventist (SDA) community, vegetarians are not only leaner than their meat-eating counterparts, but the relative degree of overweight was found to increase with the frequency of meat consumption. In the U.K. and Europe, vegetarians have also been found to be slimmer than non-vegetarians. These differences are noted for men and women, and in all age groups. When meat-eaters, fish-eaters, lacto-ovo vegetarians, and vegans are compared, those who had been vegan for at least five years were the leanest, and meat eaters the most over-weight. Overall, vegetarians are about 5 per cent leaner than non-vegetarians, and vegans are about 5 per cent leaner than lacto-ovo vegetarians. This seemingly small variation leads to remarkable differences in the incidence of obesity. Rates of obesity among meat-eaters are approximately double that of vegetarians and triple that of vegans. Why are vegetarians at such an advantage when it comes to healthy body weights? Researchers suggest that at least some of the advantage stems from the reduced total and animal fat intakes, and increased vegetables and fibre. It is also possible that the advantage is not exclusively due to diet, but may reflect increased levels of activity in the vegetarian population.

Vegetarians also enjoy greater longevity than nonvegetarians. In the Adventist Health study, vegetarian men where found to live an average of nine years longer, and vegetarian women 6.6 years longer than the general population. When compared to similar, health-conscious Adventist nonvegetarians, vegetarians lived one and a half to two years longer.

Rates of Specific Diseases

Let's have a look at the rates of disease in vegetarians compared with nonvegetarians. We will examine the two major killers—heart disease and cancer—and zero in on how vegetarians can maximize the advantage they currently enjoy. We will also consider other major diseases for which there is significant evidence of benefit from vegetarian diets, including diabetes, kidney disease, gastrointestinal diseases, gallstones, rheumatoid arthritis, and dementia.

Heart Disease

Heart disease reigns as the number one killer in North America, accounting for about 40 per cent of all deaths. For many people, a heart attack is the first warning they have of heart disease, and for one in four of these people, it will be their last. Those who survive are often told that they will need coronary bypass surgery to make a detour around the blocked part of the coronary artery, or an angioplasty to widen narrowed arteries. Many assume that surgery will take care of the problem, and they will simply go on with life, being a little more careful not to stress their weak ticker. Unfortunately, they'd be dead wrong. While it is tempting to think that surgery is the answer, 20-40 per cent of patients who are given angioplasty develop another blockage within six months of the procedure, and 40 per cent of bypass surgery patients experience closure of their graft within ten years. Heart disease is rarely a disease of chance; it is more commonly a disease of choice—a product of diet and lifestyle. Unless we make changes in our day-to-day activities and eating habits, the disease will continue its damage, eventually taking our life. The good news is we have the information and technology necessary to prevent it and, in some cases, to reverse it.

Where Do Vegetarians Stand?

Vegetarians have a solid advantage over nonvegetarians when it comes to heart disease. On average, death rates from heart disease in vegetarian men are less than half those of the general population, with somewhat smaller differences seen in women. As with other diseases, some of the benefits are due to differences in lifestyle choices, apart from diet. However, significant advantages remain, even after these factors are taken into consideration. The largest study ever done, comparing the heart disease rates in vegetarians with similar, health-conscious nonvegetarians, was a collaborative study in the United Kingdom, which pooled the results of five large prospective studies (studies that follow large groups of people for long periods of time), with a combined total of 76,000 participants. On average, death from heart disease was 31 per cent lower among vegetarian men compared to nonvegetarian men, and 20 per cent lower among vegetarian women compared to nonvegetarian women. These figures also took into account body mass index (BMI, a measure of body fatness), alcohol use, education level, exercise level, and, in most studies, smoking. Death rates for vegetarians were also lower than for near-vegetarians who ate meat less than once per week.

Examining these studies independently provides further insight. In the Heidelberg Study, after eleven years of follow-up, heart disease risk reduction was nearly 75 per cent for vegetarians and approximately 50 per cent for near-vegetarians relative to the general population. The Oxford Vegetarian Study, after almost eighteen years of follow-up, found a 58 per cent risk reduction in vegetarians compared with the general population, and a 14 per cent risk reduction in vegetarians compared to nonvegetarians making similar lifestyle choices. In the Health Food Shoppers Study, after almost nineteen years of follow-up, vegetarians had a 53 per cent risk reduction compared to the general population, and a 15 per cent risk reduction compared to healthy living nonvegetarians. The Adventist Health Study compares health and death rates of a group of health-conscious people with differing dietary patterns (about 40 per cent of the population being vegetarian). Vegetarian men enjoyed a 37 per cent risk reduction compared with similar nonvegetarian men. This study also found that risk increased with more beef in the diet. Those eating beef up to three times a week had almost twice the risk of heart disease, compared to vegetarians. Those eating beef more than three times a week had well over double the risk. Among the most interesting findings of this study was that nuts reduced the risk of heart disease more than any other food studied. People who eat nuts four or five times a week cut their risk in half, compared with those who eat only one serving of nuts or less a week. The earlier Adventist Mortality Study compared heart disease rates in men who were vegan, lacto-ovo vegetarian, and nonvegetarian. Vegetarians had a 60 per cent risk reduction, and vegans an 80 per cent risk reduction, compared with similar nonvegetarians. However, the collaborative study did not note such a profound advantage for vegans. In fact, in this larger combined analysis, vegans had a 26 per cent risk reduction compared with a 34 per cent in lacto-ovo vegetarians.

This is a surprise, because based on blood cholesterol levels, we would expect vegans to have significantly less heart disease than lacto-ovo vegetarians. In the next section, we will shed light on the possible explanations for this finding.

Why Are Vegetarians at an Advantage?

What is it that protects vegetarians from heart disease? Some assume that vegetarians gain an advantage simply because they are more health conscious—they smoke less, exercise more, and are leaner. While it is true that vegetarians tend to lead healthier lifestyles, the vegetarian diet itself has been shown to reduce risk by about 25 per cent, independently of other factors. So what is it about vegetarian eating patterns that confer this advantage? Examining the various risk factors for heart disease sheds a lot of light on this question.

Heart Disease Risk Factors

Heart disease is rarely the result of a single frailty or stroke of bad luck. Most often, many factors combine to put someone in the danger zone. There are two categories of risk factors—major or "classic" risk factors and contributing or "novel" risk factors.

Major risk factors have been proven to significantly increase risk. They include factors that are diet-related (shown in Table 2.1), factors we cannot change (family history, gender, and age), and factors, apart from diet, that we can change (smoking, physical activity, and stress).

Contributing factors are those for which there is some evidence, but exactly how they act and how much of an impact they have has not yet been determined. These are shown in Table 2.2 and Table 2.3. Table 2.3 features risk factors that may be higher for vegetarians.

In each table (2.1, 2.2, and 2.3) the column on the left lists the risk factors. The second column explains how each factor affects risk and the extent of its impact, when known. The third column compares the risk of vegetarians and nonvegetarians. In the fourth and final column, specific foods and dietary components that affect risk are discussed.

TABLE 2.1 *Major Diet-Related Risk Factors for Heart Disease (HD)*

Major Risk Factor	How It Affects Risk	Vegetarians (V) vs. Nonvegetarians (NV)	Dietary Components Affecting Risk Factor
High total cholesterol (TC) and low-density lipoprotein (LDL) levels	LDL carries cholesterol to your arteries where it forms plaque. LDL is the main part of TC. For every 1% increase in TC, HD risk increases by 2-3%.	TC levels are approximately 14% lower in V and 35% lower in vegans than in NV.	*Risk increased by:* Saturated fat, cholesterol, trans-fatty acids, and animal protein. *Risk decreased by:* Soluble fibre, plant protein (especially soy protein), plant sterols and stanols, several phytochemicals (see box below), and mono- and polyunsaturated fats replacing saturated fats.
Hypertension (high blood pressure [BP])	High BP raises the heart's workload and risk for HD and stroke.	Vegetarians have lower BP (5-10 mm Hg less) than NV. Hypertension rates in V are one-third to half that of NV.	*Risk increased by:* Excess fat and calories, overweight, and excess sodium in some people. *Risk decreased by:* High-fibre intakes, plentiful potassium, magnesium, phytochemicals, and omega-3 fatty acids.
Obesity and overweight	Excess weight in the trunk puts strain on the heart, increases BP, TC, and triglyceride levels, lowers HDL levels, and elevates risk of diabetes.	Rates of obesity are two to three times greater in NV than V.	*Risk increased by:* Overconsumption, excessive intakes of fat and refined carbohydrates. *Risk decreased by:* High-fibre diets, moderate food intake.

TABLE 2.2 *Contributing Diet-Related Risk Factors for Heart Disease (HD)*

Contributing Risk Factor	How It Affects Risk	Vegetarians (V) vs. Nonvegetarians (NV)	Dietary Components Affecting Risk Factor
High triglycerides (TG)	High TG can lead to smaller, denser LDL particles, which are more likely to trigger the obstructions in the blood vessels that lead to heart attacks and strokes (as opposed to lighter, fluffy LDL).	Several studies show similar TG levels in V and NV, although a recent study showed vegan TG levels to be almost 20% lower than NV.	*Risk increased by:* High saturated fat, high cholesterol, refined carbohydrates, simple sugars, alcohol. *Risk decreased by:* Omega-3 fatty acids, soy protein, fibre, replacing saturated fats with mono- and polyunsaturated fats.
Low levels of high-density lipoprotein (HDL)	HDL carries cholesterol from your bloodstream to your liver where it is broken down and then excreted. HDL reduces the oxidation of LDL cholesterol.	Higher levels are protective. Some V have lower HDL levels; however, it is thought to be because they have less cholesterol to be removed from the body.	*Risk increased by:* Trans-fatty acids, refined carbohydrates. *Risk decreased by:* Weight loss. *Risk possibly decreased by:* Joint action of soy protein and isoflavones, fish, monounsaturated fats, and moderate alcohol consumption. *Note:* risk is most profoundly reduced by exercise.
High Lipoprotein a (Lp[a])	Lp(a) is an LDL particle with an abnormal protein called (a) attached. A high level of Lp(a) may trigger plaque formation and increase HD by up to three times.	Some evidence suggests that V eating whole foods diets have lower levels of Lp(a) than V eating processed foods or NV.	*Risk increased by:* Trans-fatty acids, possibly processed food, high-fat, low-fibre diets, possibly powdered soymilk from soy protein isolates. *Risk possibly decreased by:* Low-fat, whole foods, vegetarian diets.

TABLE 2.2 *continued*

Contributing Risk Factor	How It Affects Risk	Vegetarians (V) vs. Nonvegetarians (NV)	Dietary Components Affecting Risk Factor
Elevated C-reactive protein (CRP).	CRP is a body protein that is elevated when there is inflammation of blood vessels, and plaque buildup. Increased CRP may indicate low-grade inflammation, higher risk of cardio vascular disease, and sudden cardiac death.	Several studies have shown reduced CRP levels in whole food vegan diets, although information is limited.	*Risk increased by:* Low magnesium levels, high-fat, processed food diets. *Risk possibly decreased by:* Whole food vegan diets, antioxidants, certain phytochemicals, fruits, and vegetables rich in salicylic acid. *Note:* Bacterial or viral infections such as Chlamydia pneumoniae or Helicobacter pylori, smoking, environmental pollution, and lack of exercise may increase CRP.
Iron overload	Too much iron can act as a pro-oxidant, increasing oxidation of LDL cholesterol and damaging body tissues. We don't yet know if risk is increased with moderately elevated iron levels.	About 12% of the NA population has one gene for enhanced iron absorption and one in 250 have two such genes, markedly increasing their risk for heart disease. V have lower levels iron stores and possibly of oxidative damage from excess iron.	*Risk increased by:* High intakes of iron, especially heme iron (present in meat, poultry, and fish). *Risk decreased by:* Vegetarian diets.

TABLE 2.2 *continued*

Contributing Risk Factor	How It Affects Risk	Vegetarians (V) vs. Nonvegetarians (NV)	Dietary Components Affecting Risk Factor
Oxidized LDL cholesterol	When LDL becomes oxidized, it is extremely damaging to blood vessels. It is a major contributor to plaque formation.	Vegetarians, especially vegans, have higher levels of antioxidants and lower levels of lipid oxidation products in their tissues than NV.	*Risk increased by:* Saturated fat, cholesterol, pro-oxidants such as damaged fats and excess iron. *Risk decreased by:* Antioxidant nutrients (vitamins C, E, carotenoids and selenium) primarily in foods, and phytochemicals.

TABLE 2.3 *Contributing Risk Factors That Are Potentially Higher for Vegetarians*

Contributing Risk Factor	How It Affects Risk	Vegetarians (V) vs. Nonvegetarians (NV)	Dietary Components Affecting Risk Factor
Elevated blood-clotting factors	Heart attacks and strokes are caused by a blood clot resulting in a blockage in blood vessels. When the artery lining is injured, the tendency to clot increases. Platelet aggregation is the process by which platelets stick together at the site of injury within blood vessels, and is the first step in clot formation.	Vegetarians have reduced levels of several clotting factors, including fibrinogen and factor VII, providing protection against heart disease. However, several studies have noted elevated levels of platelet aggregation, which may reduce the protective effect of V diets.	*Risk increased by:* High-fat diets, saturated fat, and trans-fatty acids. *Risk decreased by:* Omega-3 fatty acids, polyunsaturated fat, taurine, soluble fibre, and certain phytochemicals.

TABLE 2.3   *continued*

Contributing Risk Factor	How It Affects Risk	Vegetarians (V) vs. Nonvegetarians (NV)	Dietary Components Affecting Risk Factor
Elevated total homocysteine (tHcy)	High levels of tHcy damage the walls of the arteries, causing plaque to form. Homocysteine is a breakdown product of the amino acid (aa) methionine (a sulphur-containing aa, highest in animal products). Three B-vitamins are needed to reduce tHcy levels—folate, B6, and B12. For every 1% increase in tHcy, heart disease risk increases by 1%.	Close to a dozen studies have shown higher tHcy levels in V, with the highest levels being found in vegans. This is thought to be related to V and vegans not insuring adequate intakes of vitamins B12 (and perhaps B6). Homocysteine levels are normalized with supplemental B12.	*Risk increased by:* Low levels of folate and vitamins B6 and B12. *Risk decreased by:* Dietary and supplemental folate and vitamins B6 and B12. *Note:* High intakes of methionine have not been associated with increased tHcy levels.

Column 4 provides valuable insight into our original question, "Why are vegetarians at an advantage?" Vegetarian diets contain significantly less of the dietary constituents that contribute to heart disease, while being more concentrated in those that offer protection. However, there are a few protective constituents that are either reduced or completely lacking in vegetarian diets, as shown in Table 2.3. These may, to some degree, counteract the benefits of the vegetarian diet, reducing its potential for protection. These may explain why vegans in the collaborative study had higher rates of heart disease than would have been expected, based on their blood cholesterol levels. *If vegetarians are to maximize their risk reduction, they must be aware of these components and include adequate dietary sources.*

Potentially Damaging Dietary Components

The dietary components that have been most consistently associated with promotion of heart disease include:

Saturated Fat: Animal products, like meat and dairy, are the main sources of saturated fat in the diet. Tropical fats are also loaded with saturated fat, but because we eat relatively little of these fats, they don't contribute much to our overall saturated fat intake. Other plant foods are generally low in saturated fat (see page 38 for percentages of saturated fats in a variety of foods). Compared to nonvegetarians, lacto-ovo vegetarians eat about one-third as much saturated fat, and vegans about half as much.

Trans-fatty Acids: Ninety per cent of our trans-fatty acids come from hydrogenated and partially hydrogenated fats in processed foods such as packaged cookies, crackers, snack foods, hydrogenated margarine, shortening, and deep-fried foods. The other 10 per cent comes from meat and milk. (It is naturally produced in animals.) Several studies suggest that vegetarians consume less trans-fatty acids than nonvegetarians, while vegans consume even smaller quantities.

Cholesterol: Cholesterol is found *only* in animal foods, and is particularly concentrated in organ meats and eggs. Even high-fat plants like nuts, seeds, avocados, and olives are cholesterol-free. Lacto-ovo vegetarians vary in the amount of cholesterol they eat, but it is generally less than nonvegetarians (unless they eat a lot of eggs). Vegan diets are completely cholesterol-free.

Refined Carbohydrates: This category includes both complex carbohydrates such as white bread, white rice, and white flour-based baked goods, and simple carbohydrates such as white sugar, brown sugar, syrups, soda pop, and candy. Intakes of refined carbohydrates can be high in any diet, although there is some evidence that vegetarians, especially vegans, consume more whole grains.

Oxidative Stressors: Oxidative stressors include oxidized fats, peroxides, environmental contaminants, and heme iron. Oxidized fats and peroxides are found in fats and oils that have been damaged by heat, light, or oxygen (e.g., excessive cooking temperatures and poor storage). Environmental contaminants tend to move up the food chain, thus being more highly concentrated in animal foods. Heme iron is present exclusively in meat, fish, and poultry. Thus, vegetarians, and especially vegans, consume fewer oxidative stressors than nonvegetarians.

Animal Protein: Animal protein, is, of course, concentrated in meat, poultry, fish, and dairy products, with lean meats, poultry, and fish being especially rich sources. Compared with nonvegetarians, lacto-ovo vegetarians consume much less animal protein, while vegans consume no animal protein at all.

Potentially Protective Dietary Components

The dietary components that have been found to offer the most powerful protection against heart disease are the following.

Fibre (especially soluble fibre): Fibre is found only in plant foods. Legumes, berries, dried fruits, bran cereals, and whole grains are especially high in fibre. Excellent sources of soluble fibre include legumes, flaxseeds, oat bran, and pectin-rich fruits. Vegetarians consume about two to three times as much fibre as nonvegetarians, with vegans having the highest intakes.

Omega-3 Fatty Acids: There several different omega-3 fatty acids, the most significant being alpha-linolenic acid (ALA) and two very important longer-chain fatty acids, eicosapentaenoic acid (EPA) and docosapentaenoic acid (DHA). All of these seem to be protective for heart health, although the longer-chain EPA and DHA seem most effective. Fortunately, we can convert ALA to EPA and DHA in our bodies. ALA is found in flaxseeds and flaxseed oil (our richest sources), hempseeds and hempseed oil, canola oil, walnuts and walnut oil, butternuts, soybeans and soyfoods, and green leafy plants. EPA and DHA are found mainly in fish and seafood. EPA is also present in most seaweed (in very small quantities), and DHA is found in some microalgae and eggs (especially omega-3-rich varieties).

Both vegetarian and nonvegetarian diets tend to be low in omega-3 fatty acids. Vegetarian diets contain very little EPA and DHA. However, in recent years, DHA from microalgae has become available in supplement form. (See Chapter 7 for more information on these omega-3 fatty acids.)

Folate, Vitamin B6, and Vitamin B12: The most concentrated sources of folate are legumes, vegetables (especially leafy greens), fruits (especially citrus fruits), nutritional yeast, sunflower seeds, and whole and folate-enriched grains and grain products. Vitamin B6 is widely distributed throughout the food supply, and is plentiful in several unrefined plant foods and animal foods. Vitamin B12 is found in all animal foods and in vitamin B12-fortified foods. Plant foods are not reliable sources of vitamin B12 unless fortified. Vegetarian diets contain approximately double the folate of nonvegetarian diets, similar amounts of vitamin B6, and lower levels of vitamin B12. Diets of vegans are especially low in vitamin B12 unless they have the good sense to use fortified foods or supplements.

Phytochemicals: Phytochemicals are naturally occurring plant chemicals that give flavour, texture, odour, and the full spectrum of colours to plants. They help regulate growth and defend against attacks by insects or fungi. There are thousands of different phytochemicals, each of which has unique properties, and many of which have been shown to be highly protective to human health.

Antioxidant Nutrients: Vitamins C and E, carotenoids, and selenium are known as "antioxidant nutrients." Vitamin C is found almost exclusively in plant foods, especially in fruits and vegetables. The most concentrated sources of vitamin E are vegetable oils, nuts, seeds, wheat germ, avocado, and sweet potatoes. Our richest sources of carotenoids are deep orange and yellow vegetables and fruits. Selenium is found in both plant and sea foods, and is high in nuts (especially Brazil nuts), seeds, and grains.

Compared with nonvegetarians, vegetarians (especially vegans) have higher tissue levels of many antioxidants: vitamins C, E, and carotenoids. Intakes of vitamins C and carotenoids are close to double those of the general population. Tissue levels of selenium are similar for non-vegetarians and nonvegetarians.

Monounsaturated and Polyunsaturated Fats: Monounsaturated fats are plentiful in nuts and nut oils (except for walnuts), olives and olive oil, avocados, and high-oleic sunflower and safflower oil. The primary sources of polyunsaturated fats are vegetable oils (sunflower, safflower, corn, soy and grapeseed), grains, seeds, and walnuts. Vegetarian diets tend to be higher in unsaturated fats, especially polyunsaturated fats.

Vegetables and fruits are our primary sources of phytochemicals. Blueberries and other berries, kale and other greens, and garlic are especially rich sources. Legumes, whole grains, nuts, seeds,
herbs, and spices also provide an impressive array of these protective plant components. Since these occur only in plants, vegetarian
diets are richer in phytochemicals than nonvegetarian diets.

Plant Protein (especially soy protein): Concentrated sources of
soy protein include tofu, tempeh, veggie "meats," textured vegetable
protein, soy nuts, edamame (green soybeans), soymilk, and soy
yogourt. Other legumes provide abundant protein, while plant
foods, including whole grains, nuts, seeds, and many vegetables are
good sources. Vegetarian diets are naturally rich in plant protein,
and often in soy protein, as numerous popular vegetarian products
are soy-based.

Plant Sterols and Stanols: These naturally occurring plant compounds, similar in structure to cholesterol, block cholesterol absorption from the gut. Fruits, vegetables, nuts, seeds, cereals, and
legumes contain small amounts of these compounds. More concentrated sources are new margarines on the market that have
added sterols and stanols. Vegetarian diets are naturally higher in
plant sterols and stanols than nonvegetarian diets.

Salicylic Acid: It is common knowledge that taking Aspirin may
protect the heart. This is because Aspirin contains acetylsalicylic
acid, which is converted to salicylic acid in our bodies. Salicylic acid
is an anti-inflammatory, and appears to reduce the chronic inflammation involved in heart disease. Salicylic acid is also present in
some plants, helping them to resist infection. It is found in varying
amounts in all fruits, vegetables, herbs, and spices. While the
amounts of salicylic acid in foods are not as high as in Aspirin, they
are high enough to boost blood levels significantly. However, if
you've been advised to take a baby Aspirin every day, don't stop
because you are eating more fruits and vegetables (unless advised
by your doctor). Studies have found that vegetarians have greater
intakes and blood levels of salicylic acid than nonvegetarians.

Maximizing the Vegetarian Advantage

Well-planned vegetarian diets offer highly effective protection against heart disease. For the best results, the diet must be centred on whole plant foods, including a wide variety of legumes, vegetables, whole grains, fruits, nuts, and seeds. Processed foods containing hydrogenated or partially hydrogenated fats and deep-fried foods are best avoided. Refined carbohydrates, such as white flour products and white rice, and animal products, such as cheese and eggs, if used, should be limited. However, it has become evident that even if you are doing all of these things, your protection against heart disease could still be thwarted by ignoring a couple of crucial dietary factors.

CAUTION: Do Not Undermine Heart Disease Advantages!

For maximum protection against heart disease, vegetarians must insure that their diets include reliable sources of:

1. Vitamin B12
2. Omega-3 fatty acids

Some vegetarians, and especially vegans, have diets low in vitamin B12. This is both unfortunate and completely unnecessary. It is unfortunate because a lack of this essential vitamin has numerous negative health consequences, including a significant rise in homocysteine levels, increasing risk of heart disease. It is unnecessary because it is easy for vegetarians and vegans to insure sufficient vitamin B12 intakes with fortified foods or supplements. **It is extremely important that vegetarians, who make such positive diet and lifestyle choices, do not undermine these benefits by ignoring their need for vitamin B12.** (See Chapter 8 for more information on achieving excellent vitamin B12 status).

Long-chain omega-3 fatty acids—EPA and DHA—can help to reduce blood pressure, triglyceride levels, platelet aggregation, inflammation, and cardiac arrhythmias. Long-chain omega-3 fatty acids come mainly from fish. **Vegetarians can improve levels of EPA by consuming sufficient quantities of ALA, the form of omega-3 fatty acids in flaxseed, walnuts, and other plant foods, or by consuming direct sources of DHA (DHA-rich eggs or supplements).** (See Chapter 7 for more information on improving omega-3 fatty acid status.)

Vegetarian Diets in the Treatment of Heart Disease

Are vegetarian diets an effective alternative, or complement, to drugs and surgery? Although studies designed to answer this question are limited in number and small in size, their results are encouraging. In 1990, Dr. Dean Ornish demonstrated that a very low-fat vegetarian diet (less than 10 per cent calories from fat) and lifestyle changes (stress management, aerobic exercise, and group therapy) could not only slow the progression of atherosclerosis, but significantly reverse it. After one year, 82 per cent of the experimental group participants experienced regression of their disease, while in the control group the disease continued to progress. The control group followed a "heart healthy" diet commonly prescribed by physicians that provided less than 30 per cent calories from fat and less than 200 milligrams of cholesterol a day. Over the next four years, people in the experimental group continued to reverse their arterial damage, while those in the control group became steadily worse and had twice as many cardiac events. In 1999, Dr. Caldwell Esselstyn reported on a twelve-year study of eleven patients following a very low-fat vegan diet, coupled with cholesterol-lowering medication. Approximately 70 per cent experienced reversal of their disease. In the eight years prior to the study, these patients experienced a total of forty-eight cardiac events, while in over a decade of the trial, only one non-compliant patient experienced an event.

This might lead us to assume that very low-fat vegetarian diets are "as good as it gets" when it comes to the prevention and treatment of heart disease. However, there is also compelling evidence to support that higher fat plant-based diets, such as Mediterranean-style diets, can be extraordinarily protective and potentially useful in the treatment of heart disease. These diets are centred on relatively unprocessed plant foods, and include about 30-35 per cent of calories as fat, mostly from olive oil. They typically feature small amounts of animal products. One of the largest studies to examine the potential benefits of this type of diet was the Lyon Heart Study, which compared the effects of a Mediterranean-style diet with those of an American "heart healthy," 30 per cent fat diet (605 participants; 302 on the Mediterranean diet, 303 on the heart healthy diet). After two and a half years on a Mediterranean-style diet, patients had an unprecedented 76 per cent lower risk of dying of a heart attack or stroke when compared with patients on the "heart healthy" diet. The study was originally planned to last five years. However, in only half that time, the Mediterranean-style diet was so effective that the study's ethics and safety committee ordered it to be stopped in fairness to the control group participants.

These studies strongly suggest that it is something other than a lack of fat in the very low-fat vegetarian diets or the presence of olive oil in the Mediterranean diet that is responsible for their health benefits. Perhaps the effects are due more to the vegetables, fruits, legumes, and whole grains, which serve as the foundation of these diets, and the abundance of plant protein, fibre, phytochemicals, vitamins, and minerals—all components in foods that are protective to health. Neither eating pattern is high in saturated fat, trans-fatty acids, cholesterol, or animal protein—food constituents that seem to contribute to heart disease.

The question of fat and heart disease was also looked at in the Nurses Health Study and Health Professionals Follow-up Study (more than 80,000 people were followed for several years). Researchers found that rates of heart attacks and deaths from heart disease were more strongly related to types of fats in the diet than total fat intake. They estimated that replacing 5 per cent of total calories from saturated fat with unsaturated fat would reduce the risk of heart attacks and death from heart disease by about 40 per cent. (This is the equivalent of replacing 85 grams (3 ounces) of cheddar cheese with 57 grams (2 ounces) of mixed dry roasted nuts on a 2,400 kilocalorie diet). They also found that replacing only 2 per cent of total calories from trans-fatty acids with unsaturated fats would reduce risk by an astounding 50 per cent. Two per cent of fat as trans-fatty acids would typically be less than 5 grams; this is the amount in 57 grams (2 ounces) of microwave popcorn or a medium order of fries.

It is possible that well-constructed vegetarian diets, which contain sufficient vitamin B12 and omega-3 fatty acids, and include moderate amounts of healthful fats from whole plant foods such as nuts, seeds, olives, and avocados could have even more impressive results than very low-fat vegetarian diets, or traditional, higher fat Mediterranean diets.

The implications for both the prevention and treatment of coronary artery disease are enormous. Well-planned vegetarian diets have one major advantage over drugs and surgery—the side effects are pleasant. You can anticipate some weight loss, a drop in blood pressure, better blood sugar control, improved regularity, and possibly even improvements in immune-inflammatory conditions such as arthritis. It sure beats stomach aches, diarrhea, flushing, nausea, liver damage, cataracts, and gallstones, which many people experience on cholesterol-lowering drugs, or a slow, painful recovery from open-heart surgery.

Cancer

Cancer is the second leading cause of death in the developed world. It strikes one out of every two American men and one out of every three American women at some point during their lifetime, with 80 per cent of the cases appearing in people over the age of fifty-five. Of all the chronic diseases, cancer is the most dreaded and perhaps the least well understood. Many people believe it is a random killer, like an infectious disease. It is not. The American Cancer Society estimates that 75 per cent of all cancers are the product of our environment and lifestyle. Experts estimate that as many as 30-40 per cent of all cancers are caused by diet. When we look at specific cancers, the figure is even higher. An estimated 66-75 per cent of cancers of the stomach, colon, and rectum are preventable by diet, as are 50-75 per cent of esophageal cancers, 33-66 per cent of liver cancers, and 33-50 per cent of cancers of the mouth, throat, nose, pancreas, and breast. Worldwide, every year, over 10 million people in the world develop some form of cancer, and over 6 million die of cancer. Thus, it is estimated that 3 to 4 million cases of cancer could be avoided each year if people made better food choices. Although we are beginning to understand the links between diet and certain forms of cancer, there are many questions yet unanswered. While it doesn't appear that scientists will discover a cure for cancer anytime soon, we are gaining ground in prevention and treatment. Being a vegetarian may just provide the edge that is needed.

Where Do Vegetarians Stand?

Vegetarians experience lower death rates from cancer, compared with the general population, although it is unclear how much of the difference is due to diet and how much to other positive lifestyle choices. Some, but not all, studies have found less risk of cancer among vegetarians when compared with similar health-conscious nonvegetarians.

Among the most useful information we have comes from the largest long-term study to date comparing disease rates of vegetarians and nonvegetarians, the Seventh-day Adventist Health Study (U.S.). After adjusting the data for age, gender, and smoking, the nonvegetarians had an 88 per cent higher risk of colon cancer than vegetarians, and 54 per cent higher risk of prostate cancer. In the Heidelberg Study (Germany), compared to the general population, cancer in vegetarians was only 48 per cent for men and 74 per cent for women. People who had been vegetarian for over twenty years had about half the cancer deaths of the general population. The greatest advantages were seen for cancers of the gastrointestinal system and stomach.

In the Health Shoppers Study (U.K.), cancer death rates were about 70 per cent those of the general population. In this study, cancer rates did not differ significantly between vegetarian health shoppers and similar nonvegetarian health shoppers. In the Oxford Vegetarian Study (U.K.) death rates from cancer in vegetarians were 59 per cent that of nonvegetarians. Although differences were not significant when vegetarians were compared to healthy-living nonvegetarians, rates were about 11 per cent lower in the vegetarians.

Why Are Vegetarians at an Advantage?

Is it the lack of meat or the abundance of vegetables and fruits that gives vegetarians the edge? While it is tempting to assume one simple answer, the reality is that both are likely responsible, along with many related factors. Vegetarian diets can affect metabolism and general physiology in a favourable way, reducing our cancer risk. For example, vegetarians have reduced fecal excretion of cholesterol, its by-products, and bile acids. High excretion of these constituents is linked to increased cancer risk. Vegetarians have lower levels of secondary bile acids, which are possible tumour promoters. In addition, vegetarians have remarkably different bacterial flora, and less cancer-causing substances in their bowels. There is some evidence that vegetarian females are exposed to less estrogen over the course of a lifetime, and their overall balance of sex hormones is protective, compared with nonvegetarians.

Thousands of scientific studies have explored the relationship between diet and cancer, giving us some solid clues as to which factors play the greatest roles in promoting cancer, and which provide the most powerful protection. In 1997, the World Cancer Research Fund (WCRF) and the American Institute of Cancer Research (AICR) commissioned a panel of experts from twenty countries to examine the available evidence on the diet and cancer connection. The resulting 670-page document, *Food, Nutrition and the Prevention of Cancer: A Global Perspective*, provides the most comprehensive analysis of this research to date. The panel, in their discussion of the issue of vegetarian diets and cancer, summaries as follows:

> In conclusion, various studies have shown that groups following lacto-ovo, lacto-vegetarian and vegan diets have decreased incidence of cancers at several specific sites. Plausible biological mechanisms have been identified by which vegetarian diets may specifically reduce the risk of cancers of the colon, breast, and prostate. Any effect of vegetarian diets is likely to be due not only to the exclusion of meat, (which has been judged by the panel to increase the risk probably of colorectal cancer and possibly of cancers of the pancreas, prostate, kidney and breast), but also due to the inclusion of a larger number and wider range of plant foods containing an extensive variety of potential cancer-preventive substances.

When people think about diet and cancer, the first things that generally come to mind are possible carcinogens lurking in the food supply. Yet few are aware of the powerful protectors provided by plant-based diets. The evidence for the many ways in which they reduce cancer risk is both strong and consistent. Let's take a closer look at the dietary components that have been shown to promote cancer, and those that appear to be most protective.

Dietary Components That May Promote Cancer

The dietary components that have been most consistently associated with increased cancer risk are:

Alcohol: There is no doubt that alcohol increases the risk of cancer, especially cancers of the mouth, esophagus, and surrounding areas, and cancer of the liver. There is also substantial evidence that alcohol increases cancers of the colon and rectum (colorectal cancers), and breast cancer. The evidence against alcohol is consistent for all types of alcoholic beverages. The WCRF/AICR panel recommends against alcohol consumption. They add that if alcohol is consumed, it should be limited to less than two drinks per day for men and one for women. Alcohol consumption among vegetarians has been shown to be lower than in the general population.

Total and saturated/animal fat: For many years, experts thought that eating too much fat was a huge contributor to cancer. Today, we understand that while high-fat diets *may* increase risk for some cancers such as endometrial, colorectal, and hormone-related cancers (breast and prostate), it is the *type* of fat that seems to play an even bigger role. For breast cancer, some research suggests that too many calories may be a greater culprit than too much fat. There is reasonable evidence that diets high in saturated and animal fat increase the risk of lung, colorectal, endometrial, ovarian, and hormone-related cancers. In a recent study of 6,689 women, diets high in animal fat increased risk of ovarian cancer by 70 per cent, compared with diets low in animal fat. Another study of 906 women in China found an almost five-fold increased risk of ovarian cancer in those consuming high amounts of animal fat. The WCRF/AICR panel recommends that fatty foods be limited, particularly those of animal origin. Vegetarian intakes of total fat are slightly lower than the general population, while intakes of saturated fat and animal fat are substantially lower than the general population.

Meat: A century ago Todd Ferrier (a health writer and philosopher) wrote: "There is a growing consensus of opinion among the eminent Medical Faculty that the great increase in cancerous growths may be traced to the effete products taken into the system with flesh foods...." While we now know that there are many causes of cancer, these physicians just may have been on to something. Today we have solid evidence that meat, especially red meat, increases risk of colorectal cancer. There is some evidence that suggests it may also increase the risk of cancers of the prostate and kidney. While most of the available evidence implicates only red meat in colon cancer, the SDA Health Study suggests that white meat (poultry and fish) may also be suspect. Compared with vegetarians, people eating red meat at least once a week had a 37 per cent increase in colon cancer, and those eating red meat more than once a week had an 86 per cent increase in risk. Surprisingly, those eating white meat less than once a week had a 50 per cent increase in risk, while those eating it more than once a week had a 200 per cent increase in risk. The WCRF/AICR panel recommends that, if eaten at all, red meat (beef, lamb, and pork) should limited to less than 80 grams (3 ounces) daily. Of course, vegetarians consume no meat.

Cholesterol: Evidence is growing for a link between cholesterol intake and risk of cancers of the lung, pancreas, and endometrium. More than half the research that has studied cholesterol and both lung and pancreatic cancers found increased risk with high cholesterol intakes. Almost all the research on endometrial cancer has confirmed that higher intakes of cholesterol increase risk. Cholesterol is present only in animal products. Lacto-ovo vegetarians tend to consume less cholesterol than the general population, while vegans consume none.

Grilled (broiled) and barbequed meats, poultry, and fish, and fried foods: Evidence that grilling, broiling, and other high-temperature cooking of meats, poultry, and fish increases risk of cancer, particularly colorectal cancer, is rapidly increasing. Frying foods also appears to increase cancer risk. Grilling (broiling) and barbecuing generate two major groups of carcinogens—heterocyclic amines and polyaromatic hydrocarbons. The more intense the heat, the greater their production. Heterocyclic amines and polyaromatic hydrocarbons enter cells, damage DNA, and can trigger the cancer process. The WCRF/AICR panel recommends that charred food be avoided. They suggest that those who eat meat, poultry, and fish should minimize the use of direct flame and avoid burning meat juices. Vegetarians do not eat grilled meat, poultry, or fish, but may consume some fried foods.

Smoked and cured meats, poultry, and fish: These foods may increase risk of colorectal cancer. Some studies also suggest that stomach cancer risk could be increased by cured flesh foods, and cancer of the pancreas by both cured and smoked flesh foods. A recent Chinese study of 189 participants found that intake of smoked foods more than doubled the risk of stomach cancer. Another recent Finnish study found intake of smoked and salted fish increased risk of colon cancer by more than two and a half times (comparing highest eaters with lowest eaters). Cured and smoked foods (such as bacon) are our largest dietary sources of nitrites and preformed N-nitroso compounds (nitrites can also be converted to nitroso compounds in our stomach), which are recognized carcinogens. Vegetarians consume no smoked or cured meats.

Trans-fatty acids: Few studies have examined the impact of trans-fatty acids on cancer risk. However, one recent study showed a very strong positive association with breast cancer. Researchers in Europe investigated the relationship between trans-fatty acids and breast cancer in 698 postmenopausal women. A high intake of trans-fatty acids (as determined by tissue concentrations) was associated with a 40 per cent increase in risk, even when age, BMI, use of hormone supplements, and socio-economic status were taken into account. Further research is needed before any specific recommendations can be made regarding trans-fatty acid intake and cancer risk. Trans-fatty acid intakes appear to be somewhat lower in the vegetarian population than in the general population.

Refined grains: Studies indicate that refined grains may increase risk of cancers of the whole gastrointestinal system—from the mouth to the rectum. There is some indication that vegetarians eat fewer refined grains than nonvegetarians.

Dairy products: A number of studies suggest that milk and dairy products may increase risk of prostate, breast, and kidney cancer. Higher intakes of dairy product have been associated with increased levels of insulin-like growth factor 1 or IGF-1, a hormone important to the growth and function of many organs. Elevated levels of

IGF-1 have been associated with an increased risk of prostate, breast, and other cancers. This association raises the possibility that dairy products could increase cancer risk by increasing levels of IGF-1 in the bloodstream. While the research is provocative, further studies will be needed to determine whether milk consumption is an important factor in cancer. It is important to note that several studies suggest that milk, or perhaps calcium and calcium-rich foods in general, may protect against colon cancer. The amount of dairy products eaten by lacto-ovo vegetarians varies tremendously, as it does in the general population, while vegans consume no dairy products at all. For more information on dairy products and alternative calcium sources, see Chapter 4.

Food additives, pesticides, DDT, PCB's, hormone residues and other chemical contaminants in foods: While most people assume that food additives and contaminants are among the greatest contributors to cancer risk, the evidence is weak, at best. This may be because it's difficult to find groups of people that have not been exposed to additives, pesticides, and contaminants, at least to some degree, to act as a control group! Some food contaminants are highly toxic in large doses, and have been found to be carcinogenic. Although there are few studies on people, there is some evidence that DDT residues may increase risk of breast cancer and PCBs may increase risk of bladder cancer. Some studies have also found increased risk in farm workers with direct exposure. There is little convincing evidence that food additives such as colours and preservatives are significant cancer-causing agents, although there is some question regarding saccharin, cyclamates, and aspartame. Certain chemical residues are known to accumulate in the fat of animals and humans, becoming more concentrated as we move up the food chain. Fish and seafood can be high in such pollutants (especially PCBs, dioxin, and DDT) due to the dumping of environmental contaminants in rivers, lakes, and oceans.

In general, while regular, sprayed fruits and vegetables contribute significantly to overall intake of pesticides, we have strong evidence that intake of these foods is highly protective, even for commercially grown products. The WCRF/AICR panel suggests that when additives, contaminants, and residues are properly regulated, the exposure risk is minimal; however, unregulated or improper use may increase cancer risk. It makes sense to attempt to limit our exposure by making organic choices that support a clean and healthy environment. Levels of chemical contaminants in tissues of vegetarians may somewhat lower than nonvegetarians, while levels in vegans may be substantially reduced.

Dietary Factors That May Protect Against Cancer

The dietary components that have been found to offer the most powerful protection against cancer are:

Vegetables and Fruits: There is substantial evidence that diets high in vegetables and fruits, particularly vegetables, lower risk of cancer. High intakes of fruits and vegetables appear to protect against cancers of the mouth and surrounding areas, esophagus, stomach, and colorectum. In some cases, cancer risk is reduced by 50-60 per cent when those eating high amounts of vegetables and fruits are compared with those eating few vegetables and fruits. There are many components of vegetables and fruits that are thought to be protective. Antioxidant vitamins and minerals, fibre, and phytochemicals all play their part in warding off cancer.

The WCRF/AICR panel estimates that 20 per cent of all cancers could be avoided if people increased their vegetable and fruit intake to at least five servings a day, even if no other dietary changes were made. The panel recommends an intake of five to ten servings of vegetables and fruits per day or 7-14 per cent of calories. This recommendation does not include starchy vegetables and fruits such as tubers and plantains. Vegetarians consistently consume higher amounts of vegetables and fruits than the general population. Whereas the day's vegetable intake for many North Americans consists of a side of fries with ketchup, it's not unusual for vegetarians to eat 900 grams (4 cups) of salad at a meal.

Fibre: Fibre is nature's broom, and among its greatest tasks is keeping the colon healthy, so it comes as no surprise that people who eat lots of fibre have lower rates of colorectal cancers. Based on the results of thirteen large studies, it was estimated that the risk of col-orectal cancers in the United States could be cut by about one-third if people were to increase their intakes of fibre from foods by 13 grams per day (the amount in 250 millilitres/1 cup each of oatmeal and lentil soup). There is also evidence that fibre cuts risk of can-cers of the stomach, pancreas, and breast. A large Swedish study found that the more fibre people ate (mainly cereal fibre), the less likely they were to develop stomach cancer. People who ate the most cereal fibre had less than one-third the risk of those with the lowest intakes. The combined results from twelve studies showed that eating more fibre reduced the risk of breast cancer. Most North American health authorities recommend eating 20-35 grams of fibre per day, which is about double the current intakes. Many experts suggest that optimal intakes are even higher: 40-50 grams per day or more. Vegetarians average about 30-50 grams of fibre per day.

Phytochemicals: Phytochemicals appear to provide powerful pro-tection against all forms of cancer. However, the research is still in such early stages that we have few details about which phytochem-icals are most effective, which cancers they act against, and how much of any plant food we need for maximum protection. The can-cers for which we have the most data regarding protective effects of phytochemicals are the hormone-related cancers, and cancers of the stomach and bladder. Phytochemicals block tumour formation and growth by:

- Reducing cancer cell proliferation (multiplication of cancer cells).

- Supporting enzyme systems that make cancer-causing agents ineffective, and promote their excretion.

- Reducing oxidative damage to tissues and to DNA.

- Acting like antibiotics by killing bacteria that are associated with certain cancers (for example, by destroying of Helicobacter pylori, which is a risk factor for stomach cancer).

- Blocking the cancer-promoting action of estrogens, possibly reducing hormone-related cancers.

Foods that are particularly high in these cancer-blocking phytochemicals are cruciferous vegetables (broccoli, cauliflower, kale, collards, cabbage, turnips, Brussels sprouts, kohlrabi, mustard greens, and turnip greens), umbelliferous vegetables (carrots, parsley, celery, dill, fennel), tomatoes and tomato products, allium vegetables (garlic and onions), berries (especially blueberries), grapes and plums, citrus fruits, certain herbs (turmeric and ginger), and soyfoods.

Although we don't have enough information to suggest specific doses of phytochemical-rich foods, it's clear that eating more plant foods (vegetables, fruits, whole grains, legumes, nuts, and seeds) will reduce our risk of cancer. There is no doubt that vegetarian diets have higher phytochemical concentrations compared with standard North American diets.

Vitamins: There is convincing evidence that folate and foods containing vitamin C and carotenoids reduce cancer risk, and some evidence that vitamin E is protective as well. Vitamin C may protect against numerous cancers, including much of the gastrointestinal system, the lungs, pancreas, and cervix. Carotenoids seem to protect against lung cancer and possibly colon cancer, while folate appears effective against colorectal cancers. Much of the evidence for these vitamins suggests that they provide the greatest protection when they come from foods (rather than supplements), although there is some evidence that vitamin C, folate, and vitamin E could be beneficial even in supplement form. There is no evidence that supplements of beta-carotene are protective. In fact, two large trials reported that participants who took synthetic beta-carotene were 18 per cent and 28 per cent more likely to develop lung cancer than those not taking the supplements. The explanation may be that a wide spectrum of carotenoids is needed to afford protection, and isolating a single carotenoid may interfere with the protective effects of the others. At this point, we don't have enough evidence to recommend using specific amounts of vitamins to reduce risk of cancer. However, everyone should attempt to eat plentiful food sources of vitamin C, carotenoids, folate, and vitamin E. Vitamin C, carotenoids, folate, and vitamin E are all significantly higher in vegetarian diets compared to nonvegetarian diets.

Minerals: Two minerals—selenium and calcium—have been shown to possibly reduce risk, at least for some types of cancer. Low selenium intakes appear to be associated with increased risk of several different cancers. Selenium serves as a co-factor for various enzymes, some acting as antioxidants, and others as detoxifiers of carcinogenic substances. Several studies have shown that cancer risk declines with higher intakes of selenium from foods, although some work indicates a protective role for selenium supplements as well. While the evidence is provocative, further studies are needed before specific recommendations regarding selenium supplementation for cancer prevention or treatment can be made. What we do know is that it makes good sense to meet the recommended intakes for selenium. Great plant sources of selenium include Brazil nuts and other nuts and seeds, whole grains, dairy products, and egg yolks. The calcium story is a little confusing, as it appears to *decrease* risk of colon cancer, while possibly *increasing* risk of prostate cancer. Thus, it would make sense to insure adequate calcium intakes without being excessive. Intakes of selenium and calcium in vegetarians are similar to that of the general population, although calcium intakes are often reduced in vegans.

Whole grains: There is little doubt that whole grains protect people against cancer, especially cancers of the gastrointestinal system (stomach cancer in particular), and hormone-related cancers. Whole grains are rich in fibre and fermentable carbohydrates, as well as antioxidants, trace minerals, and phytochemicals—all protective against cancer. They also help to improve glucose response, which may protect against colon and breast cancer. Vegetarians tend to eat more whole grains than the general population.

How These Protectors Work

Protective substances in our diets can block or suppress the development of cancer in a number of ways at different stages. They can prevent carcinogens from entering the cells and damaging DNA. They can support enzyme systems that make carcinogens ineffective. They can also stop the out-of-control multiplication of cells. Figure 2.1 provides an overview of the many ways components in our diet can serve to thwart the development of colon cancer.

FIGURE 2.1: *The Cancer Process*

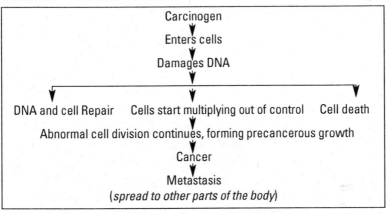

As you can see in Figure 2.1, there are several things that happen in the body before cancer develops. There are many dietry factors that serve to increase cancer risk by initiating or promoting the cancer process. Good examples invlude saturated and animal fat, meat and excess alcohol. Fortunately, there are just as many dietary factors that can interfere with this process or block it completely. Let's consider how specific dietary components work to reduce risk of colon cancer:

- Dietary fibre speeds waste products, and carcinogens, through the colon, not allowing them to stagnate long enough to enter cells and do their damage.

- Cruciferous vegetable such as broccoli or kale contain isothiocyanates, which induce potent detoxifying enzymes, helping to eliminate carcinogens from the body.

- Vitamin E from grains nuts, seeds, and other plant foods prevents damage to cell membranes, keeping them whole and blocking entry by carcinogens.

- Carotenoids and other antioxidants protect DNA from damage by free radicals.

- Organosulfur compounds in garlic help to speed the death of defective cells.

- Vitmin C keeps collagen structures in the body strong, containing cancer and keeping it from spreading.

- Isoflavones in soybeans are powerful inhibitors of enzymes that promote tumor growth and cell proliferation.

Maximizing the Vegetarian Advantage

Making wise food choices can go a long way toward improving our odds of avoiding cancer, and possibly even beating the disease if we are afflicted. We can begin by keeping food intake moderate, consuming just enough calories to support a healthy body weight. We can balance our calories coming in with our energy going out by getting sufficient exercise. Next, we need to make a variety of whole plant foods the foundation of our diet. If anything gets "supersized," it should be vegetables and fruits. Processed foods—especially those made with white flour and added fat, sugar, and salt—should be limited. If animal products are used, it is best to stick to low-fat or non-fat choices. There is simply no doubt about it—building our diet around whole plant foods is our best line of defence against cancer.

For more detailed information about diet and cancer, read the excellent book: *Healthy Eating for Life to Prevent and Treat Cancer* by The Physicians Committee for Responsible Medicine with Vesanto Melina (New York: Wiley and Sons, 2002).

Effects of Vegetarian Diets on Other Diseases

When we consider the profound effects vegetarian diets can have on the risk for and treatment of heart disease and cancer, it is no surprise that plant foods can decrease our risk of other chronic diseases too. Let's briefly review a few of the diseases for which the evidence is most compelling:

Gallstones

There is solid evidence that gallstones are much less common in people eating plant-based diets than in those eating typical high-fat, animal-centred North American-style diets. One study of over 600 nonvegetarian and 130 vegetarian women aged forty to sixty-nine years found that nonvegetarians had two and a half times the risk of developing gallstones, compared to vegetarians. Even after age and body weight were taken into consideration, risk was still double that of vegetarians. Researchers suspect that the advantage enjoyed by vegetarians is primarily due to the lower rates of obesity; reduced intakes of saturated fat, cholesterol, and refined sugars; and the increased consumption of fibre. We can maximize our protection by not overeating, by limiting intakes of saturated fat and cholesterol from eggs and dairy products, by including plenty of whole plant foods in the diet, and by limiting use of refined, processed foods.

Gastrointestinal Diseases

Since fibre, which is found only in plant foods, is so supportive of intestinal health, it's no surprise that vegetarians have fewer gastrointestinal disorders than nonvegetarians, and specifically less constipation and diverticulitis. While such disorders were exceedingly rare 100 years ago, they now affect an estimated 30-40 per cent of people over the age of fifty. One study showed that diverticulitis was 50 per cent lower in vegetarian adults (aged forty-five to fifty-nine years) compared with nonvegetarians. The much higher fibre intakes of vegetarians and vegans compared with nonvegetarians is the most likely explanation for this advantage; however, other dietary factors may also play a role. A number of studies have found links between meat consumption and diverticulosis. One study, conducted in Taiwan, noted a twenty-five-fold difference between the most frequent and least frequent consumers of meat products. A Greek study found a fifty-fold difference in risk between people who ate a lot of vegetables but rarely consumed meat, and those who rarely ate vegetables and frequently consumed meat. Meat's potent damaging effect may be related to its promotion of bacteria that produce a toxic metabolite, which can weaken the walls of the intestine. Too much fat also seems to increase risk. We can minimize our risk of gastrointestinal diseases such as diverticulosis and constipation by eating mainly whole plant foods: plenty of legumes, whole grains, vegetables, and fruits. Processed foods prepared with refined grains should not be dietary staples.

Kidney Disease and Kidney Stones

Research shows vegetarians to be at lower risk for kidney disease and kidney stones than nonvegetarians. Vegetarian diets, once considered inappropriate for people with renal disease, have recently been shown to be useful in the treatment of the disease, in some cases significantly improving kidney function. The protection enjoyed by vegetarians is thought to be due to several factors:

- **Vegetarians consume less protein, especially animal protein.** High-protein diets, especially those rich in animal protein, increase glomerular filtration rate (GFR) and have a negative impact on kidney function in other ways. One study found that plant protein produced less protein in the urine and less kidney damage than animal protein, independent of total protein intake. Another study compared a vegan diet with the low-protein diets that is used in treatment of kidney disease and found similar benefits to GFR and a slower progression of the disease. In addition, the vegan diet lowered cholesterol levels and blood pressure, while the conventional diets did not.

- **Vegetarians consume significantly less saturated fat and cholesterol.** High intakes of saturated fat and cholesterol increase blood cholesterol levels and increase damage to blood vessels in the kidneys.

- **Vegetarians have higher intakes and tissue levels of antioxidants.** Antioxidants help to reduce LDL cholesterol oxidation and preserve kidney function.

- **Vegetarians have a reduced risk of diabetes.** Diabetes is the leading cause of kidney disease in North America. It can cause severe damage to the kidney's blood vessels.

- **Vegetarians have only one-third to one-half as much hypertension.** High blood pressure is the second leading cause of chronic kidney failure in North America. Severe hypertension can cause kidney damage very quickly, while mild hypertension can cause problems over many years.

We can protect our kidneys by keeping protein intake moderate, relying primarily on plant foods as protein sources and maintaining a healthy body weight. Our diet should be built around vegetables, fruits, and other antioxidant-rich foods. Processed foods containing added fat, sugar, and salt should be limited.

Rheumatoid Arthritis

Vegetarian diets may be valuable in both the prevention and treatment of rheumatoid arthritis. In the Adventist Health Study (almost 35,000 participants) vegetarians enjoyed a 50 per cent reduction in rheumatoid arthritis compared to nonvegetarians. Although there are only a few studies looking at the effects of vegetarian or vegan diets on people who have rheumatoid arthritis, the results are quite compelling. One study of twenty-four participants found considerable relief from symptoms of rheumatoid arthritis with a 10 per cent-fat vegan diet for four weeks. Four studies used a period of fasting followed by at least three months on a vegetarian diet. Participants showed significant long-term improvements in joint swelling, pain, morning stiffness, grip strength, and other indicators of overall health. While there are a number of possible explanations for these benefits, experts believe that they may be related to improved intestinal flora (bacteria in the intestines) on vegetarian or vegan diets. People with rheumatoid arthritis have been found to have more antibodies to specific bacteria, compared with people without the disease. Plant-based diets appear to alter flora and the body's response to the bacteria in a positive way. While these results are encouraging, the studies are not large enough to draw any firm conclusions. However, people with rheumatoid arthritis may want to experiment on themselves, using a vegetarian or vegan diet. For those wishing to attempt the more aggressive regime of fasting followed by a vegetarian diet, medical supervision is advised.

Diabetes (Type 2)

A disease of diet and lifestyle, type 2 diabetes is sweeping North America and rising to epidemic proportions. Estimates range from 80-97 per cent of all type 2 diabetes is induced by overconsumption (leading to overweight) and insufficient activity. Risk of diabetes is approximately double for those who are moderately overweight (with a body mass index above 25), and triple for those who are obese (body mass index above 30). So pervasive is this connection that the new term "diabesity" has been coined to describe the type of diabetes brought on by overweight. Most alarmingly is the rise in type 2 diabetes in children and teens. Until recently, the disorder was known as "adult-onset diabetes" because it occurred mostly in people over fifty years of age. Today, it is estimated that approximately one-third of all newly diagnosed diabetes in children and teens in North America is type 2.

While excess body fat plays a strong role in this disease, the way the fat is distributed is perhaps even more significant. Weight concentrated around the abdomen and in the upper part of the body (apple-shaped) increases risk far more than weight that settles around the legs and hips (pear-shaped). In addition, fat accumulated in and around vital organs (visceral fat) is far more damaging than fat that accumulates close to the skin's surface.

The lowest rates of type 2 diabetes occur in populations consuming whole foods and plant-based diets. Some experts believe that is mostly due to their lower body weights, although very high-fibre diets may, in themselves, be protective. When populations such as these adopt high-fat, low-fibre diets, diabetes risk quickly escalates. If they revert back, incidence of diabetes is once again reduced.

Studies show that vegetarians are less likely to develop type 2 diabetes. In the SDA Health Study, rates of type 2 diabetes were 53 per cent lower for male vegetarians, and 55 per cent lower in female vegetarians than in nonvegetarians. People aged fifty to sixty-nine showed the greatest difference in diabetes rates, with 76 per cent less diabetes in vegetarians.

Many dietary factors can help to explain the vegetarian advantage. First, vegetarians are leaner than nonvegetarians. They have significantly higher fibre intakes and lower intakes of saturated fat, both of which may improve insulin sensitivity. There is also some evidence to suggest that the absence of meat, especially processed meat, may provide additional benefit.

We can maximize our protection against type 2 diabetes, or improve its outcome if they already have this condition, by eating just enough calories to achieve and maintain a healthy body weight. A wide variety of unprocessed plant foods should form the foundation of the diet. Legumes ought to be included in our meals every day as they are tremendously helpful in controlling blood sugar levels. Fruits should be the primary source of simple sugars as they offer far more nutritional value and have significantly less impact on blood sugar than refined simple sugars.

Healthy fats should be included, with the best sources being nuts, seeds, olives, and avocados. These foods are high in calories, so quantities must be moderate. Adequate intakes of omega-3 fatty acids are especially important for people with diabetes (aim for at least 2.2 grams/.10 ounces of alpha-linolenic acid per 1,000 calories). People with diabetes are well advised to include a direct source of DHA (see pages 212-213 for more information). Whole grains are a far better choice than refined white flour products.

For a much more comprehensive look at type 2 diabetes and its management, *Defeating Diabetes* by Brenda Davis, Thomas Barnard and Barb Bloomfield (Summertown, TN: The Book Publishing Co., 2003) is a "must read."

Nutrition Recommendations for the Prevention of Chronic Disease

Evidence supporting the beneficial effects of vegetarian diets in both the prevention and treatment of the vast majority of chronic diseases have never been more clearly recognized or embraced. The current view on vegetarian diets is well reflected by the words of Dr. Marion Nestle:

> There's no question that largely vegetarian diets are as healthy as you can get. The evidence is so strong and overwhelming and produced over such a long period of time that it's no longer debatable.

It is reassuring that being vegetarian can bring such powerful health advantages. However, if we are to enjoy the benefits to their fullest, we must construct our diets with some thought, being mindful of the valuable lessons learned thus far. The following guidelines are designed to assist you in this endeavour:

1. **Focus the diet on a wide variety of plant foods.** Plant foods should form the foundation of our diet. Include a wide variety of vegetables, fruits, legumes, whole grains, nuts, and seeds. Select minimally processed foods whenever possible.

2. **Eat seven or more servings of vegetables and fruits per day.** Vegetables and fruits are extraordinarily nutrient and phytochemical-dense foods. Include them with every meal. Aim for a wide variety of colourful vegetables and fruits. While usual recommendations are for five to ten servings per day, evidence suggests that eating more servings may provide further benefits. (Note that a serving is a small quantity, such as 125 millilitres (H cup). It's easy to eat two or three times that amount—and it won't make you fat.)

3. **Select whole grain products, and limit refined starches and sugars.** Whole grains contribute significant amounts of protein, vitamin, mineral, fibre, and phytochemicals. Refined starches such as white flour products, and sugars, such as white or brown sugar, are stripped of the greatest portion of these protective dietary components.

4. **Make plant foods the primary protein sources.** Our best sources of protein are legumes and products made from legumes (like tofu, tempeh, falafels, and hummus.) These protein-rich foods are low in saturated fats, contain no cholesterol, and are free of trans-fatty acids. They are also rich sources of vitamins, minerals, and fibre.

5. **Keep total fat intake moderate, and select healthful fat sources.** While total fat intake may be less important than the type of fat, it is recommended that fat consumption be moderate. Nuts, seeds, soybeans, avocados, olives, and other whole plant foods provide the healthiest types of fat. As an added bonus, the fat in these foods is packaged with many protective components. Nuts, seeds, and soybeans are excellent sources of several trace minerals such as zinc and selenium. If using concentrated fats and oils, select those rich in monounsaturated fats (olive oil) and/or omega-3 fatty acids (flaxseed, walnut, or soybean oil).

6. **Include a reliable source of omega-3 fatty acids in the daily diet.** Plant foods that are rich in omega-3 fatty acids include flaxseeds and flaxseed oil, hempseeds and hempseed oil, canola oil and walnuts. Be sure they are fresh when purchased, and store them in the refrigerator or freezer. Long-chain omega-3 fatty acids can also be obtained from microalgae supplements. (See pages 212-213 in Chapter 7.)

7. **Limit intake of saturated fat, cholesterol, and trans-fatty acids.** Saturated fat and cholesterol are concentrated in animal foods. Trans-fatty acids are found primarily in processed foods. These are our least desirable fat sources. Our main sources of saturated fat are animal products and, to a lesser extent, tropical oils. Animal products are our only sources of cholesterol. If you use animal products such as dairy, select those that are low in fat. Trans-fatty acids are found primarily in processed foods containing hydrogenated fats and, to a lesser extent, in animal products. If using processed foods, select those that avoid or minimize the use of hydrogenated fats.

8. **Use salty foods in moderation.** Too much salt can contribute to hypertension (in some people), osteoporosis, and some forms of cancer. Moderate intake of salty foods, and use of salt in cooking and at the table. Heavily salted foods include salty snack foods, many commercially prepared foods (such as soups, canned pasta products, frozen entrées, packaged pasta, and rice mixes), pickles, and condiments. Tamari, soy sauce, and miso are high in salt, too.

9. **Limit use of smoked, charred, and cured foods.** These methods of food preparation and preservation, especially with animal products, increase our exposure to carcinogens and should therefore be minimized.

10. **Use plant foods grown without the use of pesticides, whenever possible.** Select foods that have been grown without pesticides or with minimal use of pesticides. Look for certified organic products.

11. **Alcohol, if consumed, should be used in moderation.** Frequent use of alcohol takes the place of more nutritious foods and can contribute to degenerative disease. If consumed, limit alcoholic drinks to two drinks a day for men and one for women.

12. **Avoid being underweight or overweight, and get regular physical exercise.** Both overweight and underweight can increase the risk of disease. The safest way to maintain a healthy body weight is to eat a varied, balanced diet and to exercise regularly.

A complete set of references is available online at:
http://www.nutrispeak.com/bvreferences.htm

---

power from plants
legumes, nuts, and seeds

For many, the words "protein" and "meat" are almost interchangeable. People assume that meat is our primary source of protein and iron, and that meat is essential for strong muscles. There is a common belief that animal products outrank plant foods in their value to human health. The seed is planted very early by parents, schoolteachers, and favourite TV shows. When asking "What's for dinner," people are usually referring to the type of meat that will be served, rather than the seemingly inconsequential side dishes like broccoli or rice. The notion that beef, fish, or poultry must be the dominant theme of our meals is powerful and deeply ingrained. This focus on meats often makes people defensive when the "V" word is uttered. It is a stretch for most Canadians to accept that life can be every bit as good, and bodies every bit as strong without consuming a single piece of animal flesh. Four common myths underlie these misconceptions. In this chapter, we will shatter these myths and provide you with the tools needed to set the record straight.

- **Myth #1: We need meat to get enough protein.**

- **Myth #2: Plant protein lacks essential amino acids and is poor quality.**

- **Myth #3: Vegetarians must carefully complement plant proteins at every meal.**

- **Myth #4: Most vegetarians end up with iron-deficiency anemia.**

    None of these statements is true. Each is based on misconceptions from a bygone era. In fact, *no nutrient essential to human life is found in meat that is not also found in diets composed entirely of plant foods.* As we look down the food chain, we see that every one of the nutrients used to build animal and human bodies come from plants and micro-organisms. Protein and iron required for the muscles, blood and bones of large, powerful herbivores such as elephants are derived from plant foods. Even vitamin B12, a nutrient present in animal foods, actually originates from the bacteria and other micro-organisms that grow in animals, in soil, and on plants. Vegetarians can easily ensure that their diets include these and other required nutrients. At the same time, there are several myths in circulation that paint an unrealistically rosy picture of vegetarian diets—as if choosing a "virtuous" eating pattern allows one to ignore the need for some planning!

- **Myth #5: All vegetarian diets provide more than enough protein.**

- **Myth #6: Eating any combination of plant foods will provide you with recommended amounts of zinc and other trace minerals.**

    Whether you are beginning to cut down on the amount of meat in your diet or have made a complete shift from meat, fish, poultry, and other animal products, it's important to examine the facts about our needs for protein, iron, and zinc. In this chapter, we'll help you chart a course, avoid problems, and find simple ways to meet the nutrient needs of you and your family. In the process, you'll learn to harness the power of plant foods.

Protein in Vegetarian Diets

We begin with protein, the essential part of all plant and animal cells, and the myth that we need meat to get enough protein.

    Vegetarians are often asked, "Where will you get your protein?" For a variety of reasons this concern has been overemphasized. As you will recall from Chapter 2 (see page 17), meat and other animal products gained special status in the first half of the 20th century as necessary protein sources when deficiency diseases were our primary nutritional concerns. Farmers were granted subsidizes for raising animals for food, and nutrition education materials emphasized the value of animal products as the primary protein sources in the diet. As a result, the consumption of animal products increased, with average protein intakes being 50 to 100 per cent higher than recommended intakes. Contrary to what many people believe, excessive protein intakes do not lead to bigger muscles. According to the World Health Organization (WHO) Technical Report 797: "There are no known advantages from increasing the proportion of energy derived from protein, and high intakes may have harmful effects in promoting excessive losses of body calcium and perhaps in accelerating age-related decline in renal function."

Protein is essential to build and repair cells throughout our bodies, transport oxygen (as part of the hemoglobin molecule in blood), make protective antibodies, and regulate the balance of water and acids, thus allowing our systems to function smoothly. These proteins are built from a "pool" of amino acids distributed in the fluids throughout our bodies. The amino acids originate from the proteins in our diets. Several concepts are central to understanding why we don't need meat. (In fact, we would do ourselves a favour by relying on plant protein.)

1. **All of the amino acids that we require either originate from plant foods, or can be built in our bodies from other amino acids.** Our cells use an amino acid such as methionine to build muscle fibre and for this purpose, a methionine molecule from a hamburger is no different than a methionine molecule from a soybean. In fact, the amino acids in animal products can be traced back to their plant origins.

2. **Too much protein is not good for you.** We require a certain minimum of dietary protein and specific amino acids. However, excess dietary protein, particularly animal protein, can contribute to heart disease, stroke, colorectal cancer, and osteoporosis; it puts extra stress on the kidneys and liver. After fulfilling the necessary building, repair, and maintenance functions, extra protein becomes a burden on the body. Some can be

used as fuel, but it is not a clean-burning fuel like carbohydrate. Certain waste products (urea) must be eliminated, and this is where the stress comes in.

3. **In meat-centred diets, mounds of saturated fat and cholesterol accompany the bulk of this protein.** With meat, *three* distinct components are linked to increased blood cholesterol and risk of coronary artery disease: dietary cholesterol, animal protein, and saturated fat. Plant foods are entirely free of cholesterol and animal protein, and most are low in saturated fat (with the exception of tropical oils).

4. **Protein-rich plant foods bring us unique benefits not found in meat.** They provide protective phytochemicals found only in plant foods, including the isoflavones present in soy. Beans have a unique ability to level our blood sugar because the protein is combined with fiber. Beans are rich in magnesium. Compared to meat, beans, peas and lentils are lower in sulfur amino acids, resulting in less excretion of calcium and helping us retain the calcium in our bones. Many beans, and to an even greater extent calcium-set tofu, actually *contribute* dietary calcium, whereas meat does not.

More is not always better; this is true of protein and particularly animal protein. In fact, the somewhat lower, yet adequate, protein levels in vegetarian diets are proving to be a health advantage. The quantity of protein in well-designed vegetarian diets is the golden mean, and meets recommended intakes at all ages. Even elite athletes can meet their protein needs without eating a single piece of meat.

Recommended Protein Intakes

How much protein do we need for good health? The exact amount depends on our age, body size, and, to some extent, on the composition of our diet. Protein needs are greater than average for many athletes (especially while building muscle mass) and for people recovering from certain illnesses. Scientists have established recommended intakes that include a considerable margin of safety because people differ metabolically and proteins differ in composition and digestibility. For most individuals, these recommendations are well in excess of real needs.

Recommended protein intakes assume that people are getting enough total calories. If calories are insufficient (for reasons of poverty, illness, extreme weight-loss diets, anorexia nervosa, or unusually high levels of energy output), protein will be used as a fuel rather than being spared for its roles as a building material and regulator of cell function. While protein is not our preferred fuel, we use it if we have to in order to keep our system going!

Because protein is used to build cells, from our toenails to the hair on our heads, our needs are greatly increased during times of growth. Recommended intakes during pregnancy, lactation, and from infancy through adolescence are referred to on pages 258, 269, 277, and 292.

Recommended Protein Intake on the Basis of Body Weight

The RDA (Recommended Dietary Allowance) for protein is 0.8 grams of protein per kilogram of body weight (g/kg). This applies to nonvegetarians and vegetarians alike. For vegetarians, the recommendation assumes a diet that includes variety of plant foods: legumes, grains, nuts and seeds, vegetables, and fruits, as in the Vegetarian Food Guide (pages 241-243 in Chapter 9). The RDA includes a safety margin to cover individual variation in protein requirements. To determine your weight in kilograms, divide your weight in pounds by 2.2. A few examples of recommended protein intakes at different weights are shown in Table 3.1.

TABLE 3.1. *Recommended Minimum Protein Intakes for Different Body Weights*

Weight (lb)	Weight (kg)	Recommended protein (g)
110	50	40
132	60	48
155	75	60
176	80	64

Some experts suggest that recommended protein intakes should be increased 10-20 per cent for vegetarians over fourteen years of age, to compensate for the lower digestibility of some whole plant foods. This increase is thought to be unnecessary for those who eat soy products such as tofu and soymilk, or dairy products and eggs, in addition to a variety of plant foods. This slightly increased protein recommendation is suggested for those who get most of their protein from whole plant foods: legumes, whole grains, nuts, seeds and vegetables. Here is an easy way to estimate these slightly higher recommendations for some vegetarians.

> Easy estimate of protein needs:
> 1 gram of protein per kilogram of body weight.

Using either the guideline of 0.8 g/kg or 1 g/kg, it is not difficult to meet and exceed protein recommendations with a diet that is mainly or entirely plant-based. Menus 3 and 4 of this chapter (pages 92 and 94) show how to nourish even those whose protein needs are particularly high.

Scientific research has supported the adequacy of protein intake from plant-based diets since the classic study by Hardinge and Stare in the 1950s. Figure 3.1 compares intakes of total protein, including plant and animal protein, for adult vegans, lacto-ovo vegetarians, and nonvegetarians. On this chart, protein intakes are expressed as grams per kilogram of body weight, with the total shown at the top of each bar. When we compare the average intake of each group to 1 gram per kilogram of body weight (the darkened line across the middle of Figure 3.1 on next page), we see that all groups easily meet and exceed this amount. For nonvegetarians, approximately two-thirds of the protein was of animal origin (light portion of bar) and one-third of the protein was from plant sources (dark portion of bar). This ratio reflects a pattern similar to the overall protein intake of people in North America and Europe.

FIGURE 3.1 *Protein on Various Diets*

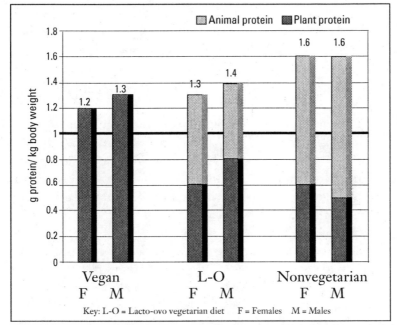

The protein RDA for lacto-ovo vegetarian and for non-vegetarian children has been set at 1.1 grams of protein per kilogram of body weight (g/kg) at age 1-3 years and 0.95 g/kg at age 4-13 years. For youngsters on vegan diets or diets that include primarily whole plant foods, we include an extra margin of safety to compensate for lower digestibility of some of these foods. Table 3.2 shows the protein RDA for these youngsters, including this safety margin of 30 per cent at 1-3 years of age and 20 per cent at 4-13 years of age. The suggested daily protein intake for typical weights is also shown. Note that these intakes are easily achieved.

TABLE 3.2 *Recommended Protein Intake for Vegan Children*

Age (years)	Protein RDA Plus Safety Margin (g per kg body weight)	Typical Weight (kg)	Suggested Protein (g per day)
1-3	1.1 + 30% = 1.4	12	17
4-8	0.95 + 20% = 1.1	20	22
9-13	0.95 + 20% = 1.1	36	40

Protein for Vegetarian Athletes

There is no separate protein RDA for athletes as the scientific review committee that established the RDAs found "a lack of compelling evidence" that those doing resistance or endurance exercise have higher protein needs. For most people who engage in regular exercise, the easy estimate of 1 gram of protein per kilogram of body weight is plenty.

Yet if muscle is being built, more protein may be appropriate. Dietitians of Canada, the American Dietetic Association, and the American College of Sports Medicine in their joint position paper, "Nutrition and Athletic Performance" (on-line at www.eatright.com/adap1200.html) advise endurance athletes to get about 1.2-1.8 grams of protein per kilogram of body weight. For a brief period of time during the early stages of training, when muscle mass is increasing and protein needs are highest, athletes may aim for as much as 2-2.3 grams of protein per kilogram of body weight. Even these increased requirements can easily be met using plant-based diets. This is particularly true since people who are doing a great deal of exercise also consume considerably more calories. The higher intakes of grains, beans, nut butters, tofu, and other soyfoods that are eaten by top vegetarian athletes automatically result in much higher protein intakes. It isn't difficult to meet requirements of competitive athletes who eat big portions of Scrambled Tofu, Hot Tofu with Cool Greens and Shepherd's Pie (pages 389, 414, 421). The most common challenge is learning simple and practical ways to prepare protein-rich foods, such as the shakes and smoothies on pages 390-393 and the entrees on pages 414 to 423. It can take ingenuity to get high-protein vegetarian foods at sports events and while travelling—but it can be done. For more on nutrition for vegetarian athletes, see pages 69-71 and the reference materials listed there.

Action Tips for Vegetarian Athletes

Can vegetarian diets support peak performance in athletes? Both vegetarian and nonvegetarian diets have the potential to enhance or hinder performance, when they are appropriately designed. However, well-constructed vegetarian diets may offer the upper hand where endurance sports are concerned. The following information will assist vegetarian athletes in achieving their maximum potential:

Energy (calories): Energy needs of athletes vary considerably depending on body size, body composition, gender, training, and typical activity pattern. For recreational athletes, caloric needs generally increase only slightly. However, for competitive athletes, caloric needs can shoot up markedly. Physical activity boosts energy expenditure and metabolic rate. Reports suggest that vegetarian diets may further increase energy needs by up to 10-15 per cent. Thus, vegetarian athletes who are struggling with energy levels, or finding it difficult to maintain body weight will need to include plenty of energy-dense vegetarian options such as tofu, nuts and seeds and blender drinks in their diet.

Carbohydrates, Protein and Fat: It is recommended that most athletes distribute their caloric intake among protein, fat and carbohydrates as shown in Table 3.3. The suggested distribution of calories for the general public is shown on page 71.

TABLE 3.3 *Recommended Distribution of Calories for Athletes*

	Protein	**Fat**	**Carbohydrates**
Most Athletes	12-15%	<30%	60-65%
Endurance Athletes	12-15%	<25%	65-70%

High carbohydrate diets are important for athletes as they allow for maximum glycogen stores, helping to improve energy reserves. Increased carbohydrate intake can also help reduce muscle fatigue. Protein needs are increased in athletes, as described above. It is important that athletes do not go overboard on fat restriction (no less than 15 per cent of calories), as sufficient fat makes it easier to meet energy needs. In addition fat is important for nutrient absorption, and for maintaining fats within muscles at an optimal level.

continued

Vitamins and Minerals. Requirements for vitamins and minerals are generally increased in athletes, although needs are usually easily provided by the greater food intakes. Vegetarian athletes need to take special care to insure sufficient intakes of the following vitamins and minerals:

Vitamin B12 – use fortified foods, supplements, or appropriate amounts of dairy products and eggs (see Chapter 8).

Vitamin D – insure sufficient sunshine, and/or fortified foods (see Chapter 4).

Iron – iron-deficiency is common among athletes, especially endurance athletes. Female runners are at the highest risk. It is wise to monitor iron status by having occasional laboratory tests. Insure ample intake of iron rich foods such as legumes, seeds, nuts and fortified veggie meats. Maximize iron enhancers and limit inhibitors (see pages 96-107).

Zinc – zinc needs increase with intense exercise, as this mineral is necessary for metabolism, and is lost in perspiration. To insure sufficient intakes include plenty of legumes, nuts, seeds and whole grains in the diet (see pages 107-112).

Calcium – do not assume weight bearing exercise will rule out osteoporosis. While exercise is very important as a protective measure, osteoporosis is a growing problem in athletes, especially in girls and women who have limited their caloric intake in order to insure very low body weights. For female athletes with amenorrhea, 1500 mg calcium per day is recommended. For most people this means using plenty of fortified soymilk, calcium-set tofu or dairy products, and likely a supplement as well.

Fluids. Keep well hydrated. A sedentary person living in a cool climate loses about 1 H litres of fluid each day. An athlete can lose 2-4 litres in an hour of heavy activity, especially in warm climates. If these fluids are not soon replaced, performance suffers. Water is the preferred fluid, although sports drinks are recommended for endurance events lasting longer than one hour.

Supplements. Well-planned vegetarian diets can provide all of the nutrients necessary for athletes. As on any diet, multi-vitamin mineral supplements can help to insure needs for certain harder-to-get nutrients are met. For those with lower energy intakes, or those eating poorly, these supplements are potentially quite beneficial. For additional information on supplements, see the resources listed on the next page.

For more details on sports nutrition for vegetarians, check out the following resources:

Davis, B. and Melina, V. *Becoming Vegan*, Summertown TN., The Book Publishing Co., 2000.
Dorfman, L. *The Vegetarian Sports Nutrition Guide*. NY., John Wiley and Sons, 1999.
The Veggie Sports Association: www.veggie.org/main/vegetarian.html

Recommended Protein Intake as a Percentage of Total Calories

Another way to look at protein recommendations is to consider the percentage of our total caloric intake from each of three nutrients that provide calories: protein, carbohydrate, and fat. Carbohydrate and protein provide approximately 4 calories per gram, whereas fat, a highly concentrated form of energy, provides 9 calories per gram. Table 3.4 presents recommendations on how those aged 4 years and over can best divide dietary calories among protein, fat and carbohydrates. This summary is based on reports from The World Health Organization's Study Group, and from the Institute of Medicine. Health experts suggest, in the case of fat, that a range of 20-25 per cent of total calories may be best for most of us, for prevention of chronic disease. Optimal protein intake may be in the range of 12 to 15 per cent of calories. For more details on children's diets, see Chapters 7 and 10.

TABLE 3.4 *Recommended Distribution of Calories*

Protein	Fat	Carbohydrate
10-20%	15-35%	50-70%

Do Typical Vegetarian Diets Provide Enough Protein?

The Harvard University research in the 1950s showed that protein intakes of lacto-ovo vegetarians and of vegans meet and exceed recommended intakes (Figure 3.1). Since that time, **studies in Canada, the United States, Australia, Britain, and various parts of Europe have established repeatedly that vegetarian diets provide more than enough protein.**

There are occasional cases of marginal protein intakes, for example with vegan women whose caloric intake is particularly low. But these are cases of consuming insufficient food, and are not characteristic of vegetarian diets. Other examples of insufficient dietary protein (and iron and zinc) occur with the "fries and granola bars" vegetarians, or those who try to live on pasta and bagels. Some of these people might eventually decide that they must be the wrong blood type to be vegetarian, or that being vegetarian just doesn't work for them. In fact, the problem was not their blood type at all. It's just that they didn't keep their fridge stocked up with bean salads or tasty marinated tofu slices from the deli. They never learned how to make something quick, easy, and delicious from lentils, such as the recipe on page 416. They haven't found that a banana, a cup of soymilk, and a handful of strawberries make a fine shake, providing 10 grams of protein. It becomes increasingly easier to meet our protein needs—we now have convenience "natural foods" in mainstream supermarkets, veggie dogs at ball games, and restaurants offering meatless, heart-healthy entrees. It's simple for anyone—whether a restaurant diner, a gourmet cook, or a novice in the kitchen—to get enough protein. It just takes a little know-how.

Protein in Plant Foods

As examples, here's how much protein you get from each of the following:

- 250 millilitres (1 cup) of cooked lentils or beans (black, kidney, cranberry, garbanzo, navy, pinto) provides 14-18 grams protein

- 250 millilitres (1 cup) of cooked soybeans provides 28 grams protein

- 125 millilitres (H cup) of peanuts provides 17 grams protein.

For purposes of comparison, note that a "quarter pounder" (113 grams) hamburger patty provides 19 grams of protein, and a chicken leg 15 grams. In addition to protein, all of these foods listed above provide the minerals, iron, and zinc. (Also see Table 3.10.)

Protein is present in most plant foods, with the notable exceptions of sugar, fats, and oils. Many of us are unaware of the substantial amounts of protein contributed by the plant foods in our diets. Figure 3.1 shows us that even for nonvegetarians, plant protein provides at least half of the recommended protein intake. Although we generally think of meat and other animal products as concentrated sources of protein, an assortment of plant foods provides us with an excellent balance of protein, fat, and carbohydrate. Table 3.5 shows the percentage of calories from protein, fat, and carbohydrate in some common foods. When we compare these with the recommended distribution for our total diet, shown in Table 3.4 and at the bottom of Table 3.5, it becomes clear that a heavy reliance on animal products can easily lead to excessive protein and fat.

What Are Legumes?

Legumes are plants that have their seeds arranged in pods. When removed from the pods, these seeds are the familiar beans (Anasazi, black, cranberry, garbanzo, Great Northern, kidney, lima, mung, navy, pinto, red, soy, white), lentils, and peas. Legumes are the protein power-houses of the plant kingdom. As you can see in Table 3.5, they have approximately twice the protein content of cereal grains. The percentage of calories from protein in lentils, kidney beans, soybeans, and tofu is in the same general range as regular ground beef, cheddar cheese, cow's milk, and eggs. Though their nutritional profile resembles nuts, peanuts are legumes (beans) as well. They grow in pods underground and are called groundnuts in Africa.

Legumes: Beans, Peas, Lentils, and Soyfoods

It's important for vegetarians to become acquainted with these protein powerhouses and to find their special favourites. While soyfoods are excellent, convenient sources of protein, they are not "essential foods" for vegetarians. Within this group are *many* different foods, each with their own appeal and nutritional advantages. We can choose among them to suit our own unique needs and preferences. For those who are keeping an eye on their weight, lentils, split peas, and most beans are extremely low in fat, though high in protein, iron, zinc, and fibre. A lentil or bean soup or stew fills us up and gives us staying power between meals. During the growing

TABLE 3.5 *Percentage of Calories from Protein, Fat, and Carbohydrate in Foods*

	Protein	Fat	Carbohydrate
Legumes: Beans, Peas, Lentils, and Soyfoods			
Anasazi, black, lima, mung, pinto, red, or white beans; black-eyed or split peas	23-27%	2-4%	70-73%
Garbanzo beans (chickpeas)	21%	14%	65%
Kidney beans	28%	1%	71%
Lentils	30%	3%	67%
Peanuts	15%	71%	14%
Soybeans	33%	39%	28%
Soy protein isolate	91%	9%	0%
Tofu, firm	40%	49%	11%
Veggie "meats," low fat	69-85%	1-4%	14-30%
Veggie "meats," higher fat	56-75%	7-17%	18-28%
Nuts, Seeds, and Their Butters			
Almonds	14%	74%	13%
Cashews	10%	68%	21%
Hazelnuts, filberts	9%	81%	10%
Pumpkin or sunflower seeds	17%	71%	12%
Sesame butter (tahini)	11%	75%	14%
Grains			
Amaranth	16%	15%	69%
Barley, corn, rice	9%	4-7%	84-87%
Millet	11%	7%	82%
Oatmeal	17%	16%	67%
Quinoa	13%	15%	72%
Rye	18%	8%	73%
Wheat	15%	5%	80%
Vegetables			
Broccoli	34%	9%	57%
Carrots, yams, baked potatoes	8%	1-3%	89-91%
Kale	22%	11%	67%
Mushrooms	32-50%	0-6%	50-62%
Salad greens	31%	11%	38%
Spinach	40%	11%	49%
Fruits			
Apples	1%	5%	94%
Dates, figs, raisins	3-4%	1-2%	94-96%
Melons	5-9%	2-11%	82-93%
Oranges	7%	2%	91%
Raspberries, strawberries	7%	9-10%	83-84%
Animal Products			
Beef, lean ground	37%	63%	0%
Beef, regular ground	33%	67%	0%
Cheddar cheese, medium	25%	74%	1%
Codfish	92%	8%	0%
Cow's milk, 2%	27%	35%	38%
Eggs	32%	65%	3%
Salmon, sockeye	52%	48%	0%
Other Foods			
Sugar	0%	0%	100%
Oil	0%	100%	0%
Recommended Distribution (from Table 3.4)	10-20%	15-35%*	50-70%

years, our youngsters benefit from tofu and nut butters, which contain healthful, unsaturated plant oils. Athletes appreciate that soy protein has a protein quality (combination of amino acids) comparable to the Amino Acid Scoring Pattern (Tables 3.6, 3.7, and Figure 3.2). The veggie "meats"—burgers, dogs, slices, and other meat alternatives—make life easier for many health-conscious people. These have been shaped into the same convenient sliced, croquette and ground forms into which animal products have been shaped, yet they are free of the saturated fat and cholesterol and most are low in fat. Some brands are fortified with iron, zinc, and vitamin B12. See Table 3.10 for iron, zinc, and protein in a variety of foods.

For people who have bone-building as a priority, calcium-set tofu and fortified soymilk are ideal, as they provide several minerals that support our bone health, along with protein—an important part of bone—and isoflavones. White beans and black turtle beans are significant sources of calcium, too. For prevention of chronic disease and maintaining health, legumes fit right into today's nutritional recommendations. For diabetics, heart disease patients, and those who want to reduce risk of these diseases, legumes have been shown to lower blood cholesterol levels and improve control of our blood sugar.

North American farmers are major producers of about twenty types of legumes and we can truly support our agricultural economy when we use these foods. Adding them to one's diet has elements of taking a world food tour. Think of all the tasty dishes from around the globe. We may have a favourite recipe for pea or lentil soup, enjoy chili at a Mexican restaurant, or have acquired a taste for Middle Eastern or East Indian dishes while travelling. Preparing ethnic foods at home is a wonderful way to begin incorporating more legumes into our diets. Tofu will absorb the flavours of other ingredients in a dish, making it an extremely versatile food. See Chapter 14 for recipe ideas to get you started.

Legumes, Soyfoods, Nuts, and Seeds: Power Foods

Myth: All vegetarian diets provide more than enough protein.

Vegetarians occasionally head down the wrong dietary path when they believe that they can eat any combination of plant foods and get enough protein. While it is not at all difficult to get ample protein entirely from whole plant foods, there are ways of blowing it—for example, if the main choices are chips, sweets, and vegetarian junk foods, or if total caloric intake is insufficient. *The reality is that for vegetarians, legumes, soyfoods, nuts, and seeds are important keys to success in meeting recommended protein intakes.*

Nuts and Seeds

Recent research on nuts and seeds has brought us new appreciation of the nutritional benefits of these often-neglected foods. Here's an example. Among people with otherwise similar lifestyles, those who ate nuts five times a week had just half the risk of heart disease compared with those who ate nuts less than once a week. As shown in Table 3.5, about 75 per cent of calories in nuts are provided by fat. Yet instead of saturated fats and cholesterol, much of this fat is healthful monounsaturated fat or in the case of walnuts and flaxseed, essential omega-3 fatty acids. Nuts contain fibre and protective phytochemicals (such as reservatrol, saponins, phytates and plant sterols) all of which can help to protect us against heart disease.

Nuts and seeds are rich in vitamin E. Without them, people's diets tend to be low in this fat-soluble vitamin that stabilizes cell membranes and acts as an antioxidant. In addition to iron, certain nuts are good sources of one or other of the minerals. A single Brazil nut provides your quota of selenium for the day. These nuts are harvested from the wild in Venezuela and (not surprisingly) Brazil. Almonds, almond butter and sesame seeds (or the seed butter, tahini) provide calcium, and make wonderful spreads for toast and sandwiches. Cashews, which are the seed at the centre of a fruit that looks like an apple, are rich in zinc. They are particularly high in carbohydrate for a nut, and will thicken when ground in a blender and then heated, forming a lovely cream. Seeds are also high in zinc. Seed butters make a flavourful base for salad dressings, replacing all or part of the oil to provide a highly nutritious addition to salads. Not only do nuts provide us with valuable nutrients; their plant oils also help us to absorb minerals, fat-soluble vitamins and phytochemicals.

In food guides, nuts and seeds are included with the protein-rich foods like legumes and meat, though their percentage of calories from protein is somewhat lower. When we eliminate meat, eggs and high-fat dairy products from our diets, our intake of fats drops substantially. Nuts and seeds have a very special place in vegetarian diets. For growing children and for others with high-energy needs, these high-calorie foods balance the low-fat levels of most other plant foods. Even in weight-loss diets, small amounts of nuts and seeds are now being included as the ideal form of fat.

Are nuts and seeds fatty foods to be avoided? That idea came from a lifestyle when peanuts were an added burden of fat, eaten as a TV snack with beer after a big steak dinner. (Actually, nuts were the most healthful part of that whole scenario!) Instead, nuts and seeds are our very best sources of dietary fat because of the type of fat, the protein and other nutritional benefits that accompany this fat. So sprinkle them on salads and casseroles, use them as the basis for creamy sauces, dressings and smoothies, enjoy them in desserts and trail mixes, and spread their butters on your toast.

Grains

Wheat, oats, millet and rice are not often regarded as significant protein foods. Yet grains provide almost half of the world's protein. Certain grains, such as South American amaranth and quinoa, have amino acid patterns similar to those found in animal products (for quinoa see Figure 3.2.). Also compare the grains shown in Table 3.5 with the recommended distribution of calories at the bottom of the table and you will see that the percentage of calories from protein in the grains is in the neighbourhood of 10 to 20 per cent—the precise quantity recommended by health experts as a desired goal for our overall diet. As a bonus, grains are low in fat and provide iron, zinc, B vitamins and fibre. (For more about their health benefits, see Chapter 5.) For a creamy, nourishing and soothing way to introduce more of these foods into your breakfast, desserts and snacks, try the Whole Grain Pudding recipes on pages 387-389.

Vegetables and Fruits

For many North Americans, the total contribution of protein from vegetables is minimal, perhaps just the amount found in fries and ketchup! However, as our diet becomes more plant-centred, the presence of vegetables, and their protein, becomes more significant. This is especially true for raw fooders, whose portions of greens and other veggies become immense! Observe that some vegetables derive 30-40 per cent of their calories from protein (Table 3.5).

Fruits are very high in water, which provides 85-90 per cent of their weight. Of the calories present, most come from the natural sugars that make them so enjoyable. In oranges, berries, and melons, an average of 7 per cent of calories comes from protein, as shown in Table 3.5. Other fruits, such as apples, contain less.

Protein Quality

It's clear that the plant kingdom provides us with some potent protein providers. However here's another myth that you may have heard:

Myth: Plant protein lacks essential amino acids and is poor quality.

This brings us to consider the indispensable amino acids that are the building blocks of protein, and the digestibility of protein in different foods. To meet our needs, which amino acids must be present in dietary protein? Our protein building blocks are twenty-two different amino acids. Of these, nine must be supplied ready-made from the protein in foods we eat. These nine are known as the indispensable amino acids (IAAs); they were formerly known as essential amino acids. Though present in animal products too, every one of the IAAs actually originates from plants. Animals get theirs from plants, either directly or from a plant-eating animal further down the food chain. These IAAs are listed in Table 3.6. All the other amino acids we need can be formed in our bodies from the IAAs and other dietary components. Each protein that we build, which may be hundreds of amino acids in length, has an exact sequence, combination, and arrangement of these twenty-two building blocks, and these determine whether this protein will function as insulin, a growth hormone, an enzyme, or another vital worker in the body.

Clearly, to build our body proteins we need adequate amounts of the raw materials (IAAs). Yet in the mid-twentieth century, for several decades we got off on the wrong track about our required amounts of these building blocks. The reasons behind this are understandable. When protein quality was first studied in controlled laboratory situations, single foods were used as the sole protein source. The research focused on how well a food would support growth, generally in baby rats. Young rats grow very quickly, compared to humans; for example, they double their birth weight in six days. Rats need a specific pattern of indispensable amino acids, including large amounts of the sulphur-containing amino acids (cysteine and methionine) to grow quickly and to build proteins for the fur that covers their bodies. For example, rats need 50 per cent more methionine than humans do. Lacking fur, humans thrive on far less. In fact when we consume excessive amounts of cysteine and methionine, these sulphur amino acids can make us excrete too much calcium in the urine.

When a single animal or plant food was given one at a time as the only food available to the animal, it was found that animal proteins, being more concentrated in total protein and in sulphur-containing amino acids, were well suited to the needs of rats. The scientists conducting the animal studies designated the proteins from plants as "incomplete proteins" because, when used as sole protein sources, they were less suited to the fast growth of furry little rodents.

The conclusions from these animal studies have limited relevance for two obvious reasons:

1. **Humans are not big versions of baby rats.** The protein and amino acid needs of growing rats are far different from those of humans at any age.

2. **Humans do not live on any single food.** Research using single foods as protein sources, rather than the combinations that would be freely chosen by humans, provides little practical information about what works best for people.

We now recognize that a varied diet of plant foods suits human protein needs very well. By using animal studies, the value of plant protein had been underestimated.

As we gained understanding of human protein requirements, a new way to measure the value of various proteins has come to be accepted. This is the Amino Acid Scoring Pattern that was presented in 2002 by the Food and Nutrition Board/Institute of Medicine (FNB/IOM) along with the protein RDA. This Scoring Pattern, shown in Table 3.6, is based on human needs and shows the relative amounts of the IAAs (in milligrams) that we require per gram of "ideal" food protein. We can use this Pattern as a gauge against which to measure the IAAs in specific foods and in our overall diets. (Note that for infants, the scoring pattern is based on the amino acid composition of breast milk.)

TABLE 3.6   *Amino Acid Scoring Pattern for Humans Aged 1 Year and Older*

Indispensable Amino Acid (IAA)	Requirement (mg per g of protein)
Tryptophan	7
Histidine	18
Total sulphur amino acids (Methionine + Cysteine)*	25
Isoleucine	25
Threonine	27
Valine	32
Lysine	51
Total Phenylalanine + Tyrosine*	47
Leucine	55

*Some of our requirement for the IAA methionine can be filled by cysteine, and some of our requirement for the IAA phenlyalanine can be filled by tyrosine. Thus cysteine and tyronsine are listed in addition to the IAAs.

To evaluate a particular protein, there are three steps. First, the amount of each IAA in 1 gram of food protein is determined. Second, these are corrected for digestibility by multiplying by a number representing the "true digestibility." Third, for each IAA—and especially for the IAA in shortest supply—the product is compared to the concentration of that IAA in the Amino Acid Scoring Pattern. This results in a score with a very cumbersome name—the Protein Digestibility Corrected Amino Acid Score (PDCAAS). If 1 gram of food protein provides enough of each IAA to meet the Pattern, then the protein is given a score of 1 (or 100 per cent). As way of illustrating this, Table 3.7 shows calculations for soy protein. Next to the name of each IAA is the amount, in milligrams, present in 1 gram of soy protein. In the middle column, this number is multiplied by the digestibility factor for soy protein, which is 92 per cent. (Note that there can be some variability in digestibility between amino acids.)

TABLE 3.7 *Comparison of IAAs in Soy Protein with Amino Acid Scoring Pattern from Table 3.6*

IAA	IAA in Soy Protein (mg/g protein)	IAA × 92% (mg/g protein)	Amino Acid Scoring Pattern (mg/g protein)
Tryptophan	16	15	7
Histidine	29	27	18
Methionine + Cysteine*	27	25	25
Isoleucine	50	46	25
Threonine	41	38	27
Valine	50	46	32
Lysine	66	61	51
Phenylalanine + Cysteine*	82	75	47
Leucine	76	70	55

Reading across for each IAA, compare the digestibility-corrected amount in soy protein (middle column) with the corresponding figure in the Amino Acid Scoring Pattern (right column).

As you can see by following the shaded row in Table 3.7, the amount of methionine + cysteine, corrected for digestibility, matches the Amino Acid Scoring Pattern (25 milligrams per gram of protein). Amounts for all other IAAs exceed the Pattern. Thus, soy protein meets the Pattern and has a PDCAAS of 1 (100 per cent). In practical terms, this means that if we consume enough soy protein to exactly meet our recommended protein intake (0.8 gram soy protein per kilogram of our body weight), and no other dietary protein at all, this soy protein will provide all the IAAs we need. We wouldn't need to eat any other dietary protein at all. Milk and eggs also have scores of 1 (100 per cent); beef has a score of 0.92 (92 per cent). This example illustrates the PDCAAS scoring system. In reality, most foods have PDCAAS scores of less than 1. Generally, soy products are rated between 90-100 per cent, with soy protein concentrate isolates having particularly high scores (depending on the manufacturing process used.). If a protein has a PDCAAS of 0.9 (90 per cent) or more, as most soy foods do, you can consume the recommended grams, plus 10 per cent, and you'll get the recommended quantity of every essential amino acid.

Theoretically, it's possible to meet one's protein needs from a "mono diet," in which most of the protein comes from one food, and plenty of it. In human feeding experiments, such as the five-week Michigan State University Bread Study, adults maintained nitrogen balance with 90-95 per cent of the dietary protein from wheat, the remainder coming from fruits and vegetables. But who would want to do this for long? And even more important, in order to function, our bodies require at least thirteen vitamins, more than seventeen minerals, plus carbohydrates, essential fatty acids, water, and fibre. To get these, we need variety in our foods. In practice, meeting needs for all essential amino acids (along with everything else) is better accomplished with a variety of plant foods.

Digestibility of Protein

The extent to which we digest and absorb proteins varies from one food to another and changes depending on how the food is prepared or processed. For example, cooked soybeans are far more digestible than raw beans and, as the Chinese discovered centuries ago, tofu is better still. Soy protein isolate (used to make veggie "meats," and sold as a sports supplement) is highly digestible. Sprouting or germinating beans before they are cooked increases their digestibility. Clearly there can be nutritional advantages to the cooking and processing of foods. It can increase the amount of protein (as well as minerals and phytochemicals such as lycopene) that we derive from foods.

The digestibility of proteins in tofu, soy protein isolate, meat analogs, and refined grains is in the same general range as that in eggs, dairy products, and meat. Recent research summarized by the FNB/IOM indicates "that true digestibility exceeds 90 per cent for many common foods such as milk, cereals, soy, and other legumes." Many of the "convenience" vegetarian foods, soyfoods and grain products also provide plenty of easily digested, top quality protein. Proteins in whole grains, some legumes, and vegetables tend to be somewhat less digestible. At the same time, these "whole" plant foods have such a tremendous range of health benefits, including an abundance of fibre, phytochemicals, trace minerals, and vitamins that they are highly important parts of our diets. The reduced digestibility of many plant proteins simply means that protein requirements of vegans and people on "whole food" diets may be increased, say by 10-15 per cent, as by using the 1 gram of protein per kilogram of body weight guideline. These levels are easily reached as long calories are sufficient and protein-free items such as sugar and fat are limited. See Menus 2, 3, and 4 on pages 91-94 for 2,000-calorie and 2,800-calorie vegetarian menus that provide plenty of protein.

FIGURE 3.2   *Indispensable Amino Acids (IAAs): Scoring Pattern and Patterns in Foods*

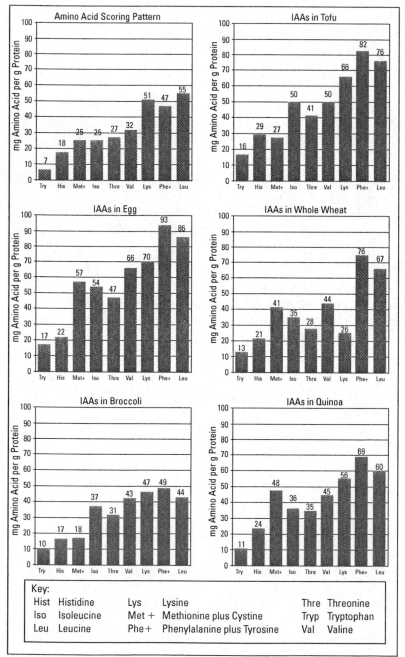

Key:

Hist	Histidine	Lys	Lysine		Thre	Threonine
Iso	Isoleucine	Met +	Methionine plus Cystine		Tryp	Tryptophan
Leu	Leucine	Phe+	Phenylalanine plus Tyrosine		Val	Valine

Do Plant Foods Lack Certain Indispensable Amino Acids?

There has been a widely held misconception that plant proteins "lack something" or are missing indispensable amino acids when compared with animal proteins. This has led many people to undervalue plant protein. Figure 3.2 shows the Amino Acid Scoring Pattern. This is the same "ideal" Pattern from Table 3.6, shown in chart form and stated in milligrams of amino acid per gram of dietary protein. The names of the nine IAAs are shown in the key at the bottom of Figure 3.2. When you look at the relative amounts of IAAs in the protein of tofu, eggs, wheat, broccoli, and quinoa (a South American grain), you can see that the patterns for tofu and eggs meet and exceed the Amino Acid Scoring Pattern in Figure 3.2. The Pattern for eggs has long been held as the "gold standard" for protein quality. The amino acid patterns for wheat, broccoli, and quinoa compare very favourably with the Scoring Pattern.

The Concept of the Limiting Amino Acid

As you can see, the patterns of IAAs differ from food to food. When we compare the IAAs in any food to the Amino Acid Scoring Pattern, one amino acid may be present in relatively small amounts. For example, quinoa is a little short in lysine and wheat even more so. In this situation, lysine is called the "limiting amino acid." In theory, intake of that food could simply be increased to provide higher-than-recommended amounts of protein and, in the process, enough lysine. In practice, this is of great importance *only* when the total quantity of protein in the diet is barely adequate, as is true for some children in developing countries for whom wheat or rice is the main dietary staple.

Meeting All Amino Acid Requirements with Plant Foods

Yet where people have access to a variety and abundance of plant foods, as we fortunate people do, we must use a different perspective. Every food has strengths and weaknesses in its amino acid pattern when compared with human requirements and these naturally complement each other. During the process of digestion, dietary protein is broken down to form a common "pool" of amino acids in muscle and other body tissues, and can be drawn on over the course of the day. For example, soybeans, pinto beans, other legumes, and many other foods in vegetarian diets contribute relatively large amounts of lysine. Though we may not think of broccoli as a protein provider, its amino acid pattern has more lysine than wheat. The variety of amino acids in vegetables can be important for vegetarians who dine on immense salads and colourful entrees from their gardens. When we choose a diverse selection of plant foods, we automatically end up with the entire range of amino acids necessary to meet our protein-building needs.

Protein Complementation Update

In the early 1970s, the concept of protein complementation became widely accepted as the basis for planning vegetarian meals. This concept stressed the need for including specific quantities of grains and legumes (or nuts and seeds) at the same meal. Some people were left with the impression that one needed to spend hours with scales and calculator in hand before getting dinner ready.

Myth: Vegetarians must carefully complement plant proteins at every meal.

Research has established that all whole plant foods contribute IAAs to varying degrees, and that commonly eaten combinations provide an assortment of the amino acids we need. The assortment of foods can be eaten over the course of a day; complementary proteins do not need to be consumed at the same meal. To quote the World Health Organization Study Group, in tracing our evolving understanding:

> "Progressively, it was realized that even in totally vegetarian diets containing a diversity of foods, plant sources tended to complement each other in amino acid supply. If the energy needs of the child or adult are met by these diets, then so are the protein needs."

The concept that all plant foods lack indispensable amino acids is outdated and inaccurate. We do not have to carefully combine grains with legumes at every meal. In practice, we can simply follow the "Vegetarian Food Guide" (page 241-243). For young children, see the guides on pages 285 and 291. These will help meet needs for all minerals and vitamins as well as the indispensable amino acids. Beyond this, planned complementation of plant foods is not necessary.

It's nice to know that we don't have to worry about it, but the fact is that people generally like to eat combinations of grains with legumes, in which the amino acid patterns complement each other. Ethnic dishes based on centuries-old combinations of grains and legumes, or grains and nuts, are increasingly popular and available. We enjoy pea soup with a freshly baked, crusty loaf of bread; baked beans with aromatic cornbread; chili with tortillas; hummus with pita bread and scrambled tofu with toast; many of these include vegetables that further enrich the combination. Here and around the world, delicious, flavourful meals such as these provide a complete range of the necessary amino acids in more than adequate quantities.

Protein in Various Menus

Over the next pages, we show four 2,000-calorie menus that are typical of different spots on a continuum. At one end of the continuum is Menu #1 for a nonvegetarian who eats a varied diet that includes meats, yet who has adopted a number of "healthy eating" guidelines. Menu #2 is typical of many vegetarians who have substituted dairy products and eggs for meat, poultry, and fish. Next is Menu #3, for a vegetarian who has integrated legumes, veggie "meats," and nuts into the diet, and is keeping the overall fat content low. Last on the continuum is Menu #4 for a vegan. It provides more protein, iron and zinc than necessary, but gives an idea how nutrient-rich a plant-based menu can be. Each menu is accompanied by comments and nutritional analysis (showing protein, iron, zinc, calcium, fibre, vitamin B12, and the balance of protein, fat, and carbohydrate). There are also adaptations that bring the menu up to 2,800 calories for a larger or more active person. Further discussion on the fibre provided by each menu is given on page 166, and on the fats present (page 200). Note that in all of these menus there is a focus on healthful choices, and though there are desserts and snacks, these too make a nutritional contribution.

MENU #1   *Nonvegetarian, 2,000 Calories*

Breakfast	Protein (g)	Iron (mg)	Zinc (mg)
Orange juice, 175 mL (I cup)	1.3	0.2	0.1
Cornflakes, 250 mL (1 cup)	1.8	8.7	0.2
Milk, 2%, 250 mL (1 cup)	8	0	0.4
Toast, whole wheat, 1 slice	2.7	0.9	0.6
Butter, 1 pat (5 g)	0	0	0
Jam, 15 mL (1 tbsp)	0	0	0
Non-caloric beverage	0	0	0
Breakfast total (471 calories)	*13.8*	*9.8*	*1.3*
Lunch			
Roast beef sandwich:			
Bread, white, 2 slices	4.9	1.8	0.4
Beef, round lean, 57 g (2 oz)	16.4	1.1	2.7
Margarine, 5 mL (1 tsp)	0	0	0
Mayonnaise, 5 mL (1 tsp)	0	0	0
Lettuce, 1 leaf	0.1	0.1	0
Carrot sticks, 1 carrot	1	0	0.2
Low-fat fruit yogourt, 175 mL (I cup)	7	0	0.6
Apple, 1	0.3	0.3	0.1
Non-caloric beverage	0	0	0
Lunch total (600 calories)	*29.7*	*3.3*	*4.0*
Supper			
Chicken, roasted, 100 g (3.5 oz)	29.5	1.1	1.0
Potato, scalloped, 125 mL (H cup)	3.5	0.7	0.5
Green peas, 125 mL (H cup)	4.1	1.3	0.8
Dinner roll, white, 1	2.4	0.9	0.2
Butter, 2 pats (10 g)	0.1	0	0
Non-caloric beverage	0	0	0
Supper total (519 calories)	*39.6*	*4*	*2.5*
Snack or Dessert			
Cherry cheesecake, 1/12 pie (142 g/5 oz)	7.1	1.8	0.6
Snacks or dessert total (410 calories)	*7.1*	*1.8*	*0.6*
Total for day (2,000 calories)	**90.2**	**18.9**	**8.4**

Nutrient: Recommended amount	Amount in menu		
Iron: women 18 mg; men 8 mg	18.9 mg		
Zinc: women 8 mg; men 11 mg	8.4 mg		
Calcium (age 19-50): 1,000 mg	839 mg		
Vitamin B12: 2.4 mcg	3.1 mcg		
Fibre: 30-62 g	19 g		
Percentage of calories	Protein	Fat	Carbohydrate
	18%	33%	49%

Comments on Menu #1: Nonvegetarian, 2,000 Calories

Our nonvegetarian has made some noteworthy efforts in the direction of healthy eating. She or he:

- uses lean meats, keeps portions small and avoids the skin on chicken
- chooses low-fat milk and yogourt
- strives to eat recommended number of servings from each food group
- avoids "junk" foods

Of the 90 grams of protein in this menu half (45.9 g) comes from beef and chicken, and half from the other foods on the menu. Twelve per cent of the iron comes from beef and chicken, and since dairy products don't contribute iron, the rest is from plant foods. In this menu, animal products are important contributors of zinc: 44 per cent comes from the meats, another 21 per cent from dairy, and the remaining one-third of the zinc from plant foods. Zinc intakes are borderline or low in the diets of many North Americans, and we see this situation reflected here. Though the menu includes 250 millilitres (1 cup) of milk, plus the equivalent of a second cup in the yogourt, scalloped potato, and cheesecake, the total calcium is lower than the recommended amount; little calcium comes from non-dairy sources of calcium, such as those listed on page 245. The fibre intake is significantly lower than recommended, though higher than that of many North Americans.

Nonvegetarian, 2,800-Calorie Menu

We can increase this to a 2,800-calorie menu by adding an extra slice of toast, butter, and jam, an extra half sandwich, 60 grams (2 ounces) of chicken, a large muffin and 250 millilitres (1 cup) of juice. This brings the protein to 126 grams.

MENU #2　*Lacto-ovo Vegetarian, 2,000 Calories*

Breakfast	Protein (g)	Iron (mg)	Zinc (mg)
Orange juice, 175 mL (I cup)	1.3	0.2	0.1
Multigrain cooked or dry cereal, 250 mL (1 cup)	6.1	1.6	1.2
Milk, 2%, 250 mL (1 cup)	8	0	0.4
Toast, whole wheat, 1 slice	2.7	0.9	0.6
Butter, 1 pat (5 g)	0	0	0
Jam, 15 mL (1 tbsp)	0	0	0
Non-caloric beverage	0	0	0
Breakfast total (559 calories)	*18.1*	*2.7*	*2.3*
Lunch			
Egg salad sandwich:			
Bread, whole wheat, 2 slices	5.4	1.9	1.1
Hard boiled egg, 1 extra large	7.3	0.8	0.6
Margarine, 10 mL (2 tsp)	0.1	0	0
Mayonnaise, 10 mL (2 tsp)	0	0	0
Lettuce, 1 leaf	0.1	0.1	0
Carrot sticks, 1 carrot	1	0	0.2
Apple, 1	0.3	0.3	0.1
Non-caloric beverage	0	0	0
Lunch total (478 calories)	*14.2*	*3.1*	*2.0*
Supper			
Vegetarian cheese lasagna, 250 g (8 oz)	16.6	2.5	1.9
Green salad, 375 mL (1 H cup)	2.7	2.0	0.6
Italian dressing, 15 mL (1 tbsp)	0	0	0
Garlic bread with butter, 1 slice (47 g/1.5 oz)	5.0	3.6	0.3
Non-caloric beverage	0	0	0
Supper total (638 calories)	*24.3*	*8.1*	*2.8*
Snack or Dessert			
Cherry pie, J pie, 125 g (4 oz)	2.5	0.6	0.2
Snacks or dessert total (87 calories)	*2.5*	*0.6*	*0.2*
Total for day (2,000 calories)	**58.4**	**14.6**	**7.5**
Nutrient: Recommended amount	**Amount in menu**		
Iron: women 32 mg; men 14.4 mg*	14.5 mg		
Zinc: women 8 mg; men 11 mg	7.3 mg		
Calcium (age 19-50): 1,000 mg	827 mg		
Vitamin B12: 2.4 mcg	1.9 mcg		
Fibre: 30-62 g	24 g		
Percentage of calories	Protein	Fat	Carbohydrate
	11%	35%	54%

*Recommended iron intakes for vegetarians are 1.8 times those of nonvegetarians.

Comments on Menu #2: Lacto-ovo Vegetarian, 2,000 Calories

This vegetarian has found it simple to replace meat, fish, and poultry with eggs and dairy products, and discovered plenty of lacto-ovo vegetarian options at restaurants, in the freezer section of supermarkets, and with easy-to-prepare homemade foods like grilled cheese sandwiches, egg dishes, and Italian entrées. Breakfast choices include variations of Whole Grain Cereal (recipes on page 387 and 388), oatmeal, or ready-to-eat cereals. Getting enough protein is simple; however, the fat content can mount up with some of these choices. In this menu, intakes of iron (for a woman), zinc (for a man), calcium, vitamin B12, and fibre are a little below recommended levels. This menu would benefit with the addition of some legumes, soyfoods, nuts, and seeds as providers of protein, along with minerals and fibre. For example, replacing butter on the toast with 15 milligrams (1 tbsp) of almond butter would add 2.4 grams of protein, 0.6 milligrams of iron and 0.5 milligrams of zinc. Nut butters are proving to have many health benefits, and can be used in place of foods that are high in cholesterol and saturated fats. It would also be good to include more vitamin B12. Replacing the egg sandwich with one containing B-12 fortified veggie "meat," (along with lettuce and slices of tomato) is one way of increasing the B12. In any lasagna, tofu can be added or used instead of some of the cheese, increasing intake of iron and zinc. When a calcium-set tofu is used, this adds to the calcium, as well. These lunch and supper choices could reduce the saturated fat and cholesterol.

Lacto-ovo Vegetarian, 2,800-Calorie Menu

We can increase this to a 2,800-calorie menu by adding an extra slice of toast, butter, and jam, an extra half sandwich, 60 grams (2 ounces) of lasagna, a large muffin, and 125 millilitres (4 ounces) of juice. This brings the protein to 81 grams.

MENU #3:   *Lacto-ovo Vegetarian with More Legumes*

Breakfast	Protein (g)	Iron (mg)	Zinc (mg)
Calcium-fortified orange juice, 175 mL (I cup)	0.8	0.2	0.1
Cream of wheat cereal, 250 mL (1 cup)	4.3	12	0.4
Milk, 125 mL (H cup)	4	0.1	0.5
Toast, whole wheat, 1 slice	2.7	0.9	0.6
Almond butter, 15 mL (1 tbsp)	2.4	0.6	0.5
Jam, 15 mL (1 tbsp)	0	0.1	0
Non-caloric beverage	0	0	0
Breakfast total (524 calories)	*14.2*	*13.9*	*2.1*
Lunch			
Hummus, 175 mL (I cup)	14.8	4.6	3.4
Pita bread, whole wheat, 1	6.3	2	1
Cherry tomatoes, 5	0.7	0.4	0.1
Carrot sticks, 1 carrot	1	0	0.2
Oat bran muffin, 57 g (2 oz)	4	2.4	1
Non-caloric beverage	0	0	0
Lunch total (688 calories)	*26.8*	*9.4*	*5.7*
Supper			
Spaghetti, whole wheat, 250-375 mL (1-H cups)	11.2	2.2	1.7
Chunky Red Lentil Tomato Sauce, 250-410 mL (1-O cup) (recipe, page 416)	14.4	4.8	0.9
Red Star Vegetarian Support Formula nutritional yeast, 5 mL (1 tsp)	1	0.1	0.4
Mixed salad with kale, 625 mL (2H cups)	4.7	3.2	0.9
Liquid gold dressing 15 mL (1 tbsp)	2	0.4	0.7
Non-caloric beverage	0	0	0
Supper total (671 calories)	*33.3*	*10.7*	*4.6*
Snack or Dessert			
Non-fat frozen yogourt, 100 g (3H oz)	3.5	0	0.7
Snacks or dessert total (117 calories)	*3.5*	*0*	*0.7*
Total for day (2,000 calories)	**77.8 g**	**34**	**13.1**

Nutrient: Recommended amount	Amount in menu		
Iron: women 32 mg; men 14.4 mg	34 mg		
Zinc: women 8 mg; men 11 mg	13.1 mg		
Calcium (age 19-50): 1,000 mg	1,260 mg		
Vitamin B12: 2.4 mcg	3.5 mcg		
Fibre: 30-62 g	55 g		
Percentage of calories	Protein	Fat	Carbohydrate
	15%	21%	64%

Comments on Menu #3: Lacto-Ovo Vegetarian, 2,000 Calories with More Legumes

This vegetarian is using some dairy products, yet including other calcium-rich foods: fortified orange juice, almond butter on toast, beans, broccoli in the pasta sauce, 125 millilitres (H cup) of finely chopped kale in the salad (and on some days, fortified soymilk replaces cow's milk). Choosing Cream of Wheat (or a fortified dry breakfast cereal), or veggie "meats" in a sandwich boosts intake of iron (check labels). Using some fortified foods means that the nutrient content can be high, while fat content is relatively low (21 per cent calories from fat.) The fat in this menu comes from excellent sources, such as sesame tahini and olive oil in the hummus, flaxseed oil in the liquid gold dressing, and almond butter (for more on fats, see pages 73-75).

Menu #3 contains plenty of whole grain products; these contribute zinc, selenium, chromium, magnesium, fibre, and phytochemicals that are stripped from refined grains. Chickpeas and lentils (in the hummus and pasta sauce respectively) add minerals, protein, and fibre. The Red Star brand of nutritional yeast, sprinkled on the pasta and in the dressing, provides most of the vitamin B12. This menu is almost enitrely plan based, and can easily be made vegan by using fortfied soymilk and soy yogourt. The protein is high enough to meet the needs of growing teens and athletes.

Lacto-Ovo Vegetarian, 2,800-Calorie Menu with More Legumes

We can increase this to a 2,800-calorie menu by adding an extra slice of toast, butter, and jam, an extra pita bread, and 60 millilitres (1/4 cup) of hummus, increasing the tomato sauce and pasta each by 125 millilitres (H cup), and including one more muffin. This brings the protein to 108 grams. This is *far* more than most people need, however it gives an idea how it could be done.

MENU #4: *Vegan, 2000 Calories*

Breakfast	Protein (g)	Iron (mg)	Zinc (mg)
Blueberries, 250 mL (1 cup)	1.0	0.2	0.2
Basic Whole Grain Pudding, 250 mL (1 cup) (recipe, page 387)	5.7	1.8	1.2
Wheat germ, 30 mL (2 tbsp)	1.7	0.4	0.9
Fortified soymilk, 250 mL (1 cup)	7.0	1.8	0.6
Toast, whole wheat, 1 slice	2.7	0.9	0.6
Sesame butter, tahini, 7.5 mL (H tbsp)	1.3	0.3	0.4
Blackstrap molasses, 5 mL (1 tsp)	0	1.2	0.1
Non-caloric beverage	0	0	0
Breakfast total (586 calories)	*19.4*	*6.6*	*4.0*
Lunch			
Lentil soup, 375 mL (1 H cup)	11.7	4.0	1.6
Brown rice cakes, 3	2.2	0.4	0.8
Carrot sticks, 1 carrot	1	0	0.2
Celery sticks, 1 stalk	0.5	0.2	0.1
Trail mix: pumpkin seeds, raisins, dried cranberries, and apricots 60 mL (G cup)	1.3	0.8	0.5
Apple grape juice, 250 mL (1 cup)	0.6	0.8	0.1
Non-caloric beverage	0	0	0
Lunch total (558 calories)	*17.3*	*6.2*	*3.3*
Supper			
Hot Tofu, 1 serving (recipe, page 414)	33.9	6-18	3.3
Cool greens (green salad with peppers and sprouts), 750 mL (3 cups)	3.5	2.0	0.8
Flaxseed oil, 10 mL (2 tsp)	0	0	0
Lemon juice, wine vinegar, and herbs	0.1	0.1	0
Steamed asparagus, 10 spears	3.1	1.1	0.6
Whole wheat roll, 1	2.5	0.7	0.6
Non-caloric beverage	0	0	0
Supper total (683 calories)	*43.1*	*9.9-21.9*	*5.3*
Snack or Dessert			
Chocolate mint nut bars, 2 (recipe, page 430)	2.8	0.7	0.4
Snacks or dessert total (173 calories)	*2.8*	*0.7*	*0.4*
Total for day (2,000 calories)	**82.6**	**23.4-35.4**	**13**

Nutrient: Recommended amount	Amount in menu		
Iron: women 32 mg; men 14.4 mg	23.4-35.4 mg		
Zinc: women 8 mg; men 11 mg	13 mg		
Calcium (age 19-50): 1,000 mg	768-1707 mg		
Vitamin B12: 2.4 mcg	4.9 mcg		
Fibre: 30-62 g	42 g		

Percentage of calories	Protein	Fat	Carbohydrate
	16%	28%	56%

Comments on Menu #4: Vegan, 2,000 Calories

Our vegan tries to use plenty of whole foods, while keeping things simple at the same time. A batch of Whole Grain Pudding (recipes, pages 387-388) lasts for several days, making a great breakfast, or an occasional evening snack. A thin layer of tahini and blackstrap molasses taste wonderful on toast; they provide calcium, too. At work, a nearby restaurant makes great lentil soups; (alternatively, there are excellent canned and packaged lentil, pea and bean soups that can be warmed in a microwave). Nuts and seeds provide highly nutritious plant oils, along with minerals and phytochemicals. These are used in several ways: as a spread for toast, as a trail mix at noon, and in the dessert square. The delicious and filling tofu and salad at supper provide a wealth of protein and minerals. Most of your week's menus wouldn't be this high in protein, but it gives an idea of the range possible. (This dish uses calcium-set tofu; the ranges are shown because amounts of calcium and iron can vary considerably from brand to brand.) Vitamin B12 comes from fortified soymilk and nutritional yeast. The main sources of zinc are tofu, lentils, wheat germ, whole grains, soymilk, seed butter (tahini), pumpkin seeds, and asparagus. See page 200 for a discussion of fats in this menu.

Vegan, 2,800-Calorie Menu

We can increase this to a 2,800-calorie menu by adding an extra slice of toast, butter, and jam and a half cup of cereal, increasing the soup by 125 millilitres (H cup), adding a little more salad dressing and a roll at supper, and including a Cliff Bar as a snack. This brings the protein to 100 grams, more than enough for a growing teenage boy and most athletes.

Plant sources of protein, consumed throughout the day, make a tremendous difference in sustaining your energy levels as they release calories in a gradual manner. As we will see in the next sections, the legumes, whole grains and seeds are among our richest sources of iron and zinc.

Iron in Vegetarian Diets

Once you've convinced your family, friends, and colleagues that vegetarians can get enough protein, they'll very likely attempt to stump you with the iron issue. After all, iron is viewed as "the mineral from red meat," an association fostered by the meat industry and its advertising. Athletes and "real men" are conditioned to link their performance with steaks and burgers. In this section we will examine facts about the iron in our bodies and our food supply.

The Roles of Iron in the Body

The mineral iron is the crown jewel in the centre of a chiefly protein molecule, hemoglobin, in red blood cells that continually circulate throughout our bodies. Iron has a remarkable ability to attach itself to, and to let go of, oxygen and carbon dioxide. Thus it is central to the breath of life. Iron is also present in muscle tissue, where it helps to store oxygen for future use. Small amounts of iron help us regulate cell metabolism and resist infection.

We require more of this mineral when blood volume is increasing during pregnancy and during the growth spurts of childhood and adolescence. Women need more iron than men because iron is lost each month during menstruation. Endurance athletes require extra iron because of high oxygen transport demands, iron losses in perspiration, and destruction of red blood cells during high-impact exercise. One or two out of every ten North American women who are in the child-bearing years becomes iron-deficient, and children, athletes, and the elderly (whose diets may be limited) tend to be low in this mineral.

Iron Deficiency Anemia

In the "developed" countries, many deficiency diseases have been eliminated, yet insufficient iron remains a problem for a small but significant number of people. Its effects include small, pale red blood cells, fatigue, a weakened immune system, and reduced ability to concentrate. Shortage of this mineral can affect children's learning abilities at school.

Recommended Intakes of Iron

Our bodies efficiently recycle iron, but we need to replace that lost in perspiration and in cells sloughed off from our skin, the intestinal lining, and during menstruation. This amounts to less than 1.5 milligrams of iron per day for women who menstruate and 1 milligram for older women and for men. Because we absorb only a small proportion of the iron present in foods, and particularly plant foods, the recommended iron intakes for adults are considerably higher than this, especially for vegetarians.

Recommendations by Health Canada and by the Food and Nutrition Board in the United States have set intakes for nonvegetarians at 18 milligrams for women aged nineteen to fifty years, and 10 milligrams for older women and for men. These figures are based on typical requirements for a day; they include an added safety factor and should be regarded as the average intake over a period of time, such as a week. The iron recommendations for vegetarians are multiplied by a factor of 1.8 to account for lower absorption from plant foods and are shown below.

TABLE 3.8 *Recommended Iron Intake for Vegetarians*

Gender and Age	Recommended Iron Intake (mg)
Women, 19-50 years	32.4
Women over 50 years	18
Men, all ages	18
Other ages	See Table 15.2 in the Appendix section, page 438.

Are Iron Recommendations for Vegetarians Set Too High?

Not all experts agree with these greatly increased recommendations for vegetarians. They were based largely on one study that compared meat-based diets with vegetarian diets, and this study may not reflect how most vegetarians really eat. As you will see in the section "nonheme iron and our power to affect absorption" (page 100), the preparation and overall composition of a meal affects how iron from plant foods is absorbed. In contrast to the study conditions, vegetarians tend to eat plenty of fruits and vegetables, have diets high in vitamin C, and many do not drink coffee or tea at every meal. They often prepare foods in ways that increase iron absorption and it appears that their levels of iron absorption and retention may adapt and become higher. Thus, vegetarians who adopt many of these practices can probably maintain excellent iron status with total intakes that are somewhat lower than current recommendations for vegetarians. (If you'd like feedback on how well you're doing, request a blood test at your next medical examination.) However, vegetarians can meet even these high recommendations, as you can see in Menus #3 and #4 and Table 3.9.

How Much Iron Do Vegetarians Get?

Many studies show that vegetarians have higher iron intakes than nonvegetarians, and that vegetarian men are likely to meet their iron recommendations. But like nonvegetarian women, many vegetarian women have intakes that fall short of recommendations. Since they don't eat meat, do vegetarians get sufficient dietary iron? This brings us to examine another myth: .

Myth: Most vegetarians end up with iron deficiency anemia.

Iron Status of Vegetarians

We can determine whether vegetarians are getting enough iron by looking at various measures of iron status, such as levels of hemoglobin, transferrin (an indicator of the iron transportation system), and stored iron (ferritin). Studies in Canada, the United States, Australia, and other parts of the world have shown vegetarians to have similar levels of iron in the blood and transport systems, compared with nonvegetarians. Thus vegetarians have as much iron travelling around in their systems, doing its job, and no higher rates of iron deficiency anemia than nonvegetarians.

At the same time, the iron stores (ferritin) of vegetarians tend to be lower than those for nonvegetarians. The average nonvegetarian man has about 1,000 milligrams of stored iron, which could supply his iron needs for about three years and nonvegetarian women have about 300 milligrams, enough to meet their iron needs for six months. Average iron stores in vegetarians are about half that level, 480 milligrams for men and 160 milligrams for pre-menopausal women. What does this mean? Unless you are under-going a period of starvation, high iron stores do not provide any particular advantage. In fact, having a lot of iron stored in your body may be a disadvantage. Iron is a pro-oxidant—it promotes the oxidative damage that is linked to many chronic diseases. Excess iron stores are linked to higher risk of heart disease and cancers, particularly colorectal cancer. Iron stores in vegetarians seem to be sufficient, and the fact that they are lower may be protective.

Iron in Foods

Iron is a crucial part of oxygen transport for humans and animals. It plays key roles in the respiration of plants, and in their enzyme systems, photosynthesis, and chlorophyll formation. Not surpris-ingly, iron is abundant in plant foods. Plants get this mineral from the earth, and animals get their iron from plant foods that they eat. It's the same mineral, which we can adapt for our various uses. We do not require flesh foods as our iron sources.

As you can see from Table 3.11 on page 108, the amounts of iron in plant foods compare very favourably with those in animal products. Since we tend to eat more servings and larger quantities of the plant foods, by making good choices we can reach even the high levels of intake that have been recommended. The four menus in this chapter show the results with different choices.

Levels of iron in the 2,000-calorie, lacto-ovo vegetarian Menu #2 are somewhat low. When people stop eating meat, they often replace it with familiar dairy-based dishes, such as pizza, macaroni and cheese, grilled cheese sandwiches, cream soups, and cheese lasagna. To a certain extent, this pattern is reflected in Menu #2. Unfortunately, dairy foods are poor sources of iron, and to make matters worse, they actually inhibit iron absorption. For these rea-sons, it is a good idea to replace meat not with dairy products but with legumes and other meat alternatives that are good iron sources (see Table 3.11).

When the emphasis shifts to legumes, nuts, seeds, plenty of vegetables, and other iron sources, intakes increase significantly. Menu #3 includes iron-fortified cereal, and there is quite a range in how that can affect total intake.

TABLE 3.9   *Iron in 2,000 Calorie and 2,800 Calorie Menus*

Menu and Page	Calories	Iron (mg)	Calories	Iron (mg)
#1 Nonvegetarian, page 88	2,000	18.9	2,800	26.3
#2 Lacto-ovo Vegetarian, page 91	2,000	14.5	2,800	22.6
#3 Lacto-ovo Vegetarian with More Legumes, page 92	2,000	33	2,800	44.7
#4 Vegan, page 94	2,000	23.4-35.4	2,800	30.7-42.7

Heme and Nonheme Iron

There are two forms of iron present in foods: heme iron and nonheme iron. Forty per cent of the iron in meat, and a lesser amount in fish and poultry, is called heme iron. It is present in animal flesh in the form of muscle myoglobin and blood hemoglobin. People usually absorb 15-35 per cent of the heme iron from foods. The remainder of the iron in meat and all of the iron in plant foods and eggs is called nonheme iron.

Factors That Influence Iron Absorption

Nonheme Iron

Nonheme iron is absorbed differently from heme iron and is much more sensitive to dietary factors that decrease or increase iron absorption. Understanding this difference can help all of us make the most of our dietary iron, since all of the iron in vegetarian diets is in the nonheme form, and more than 85 per cent of that in nonvegetarian Western diets is nonheme iron. The proportion of nonheme iron that is absorbed varies from 2-20 per cent or more, depending in part on foods and beverages eaten at the same time. Accompanying foods do not affect the absorption of heme iron in the same ways.

Beverages with Meals

If you're concerned about iron absorption, it makes a difference which beverage you choose to have with meals. Inhibitors include dairy products, black tea, some herb teas (peppermint, camomile, vervain, lime flower, pennyroyal), coffee, and cocoa. In contrast, citrus, tomato, and vitamin C-enriched juices will help you absorb iron from your cereal, sandwich, soup, or salad.

Phytates and Fibre

There has long been a concern that two beneficial components of whole grains and legumes, fibre and phytate, can also inhibit iron absorption. (Phytate is a form of phosphorus in plants.) Yet it turns out that the effects of fibre and phytate on iron status of vegetarians are somewhat less than we might expect. This situation can give us insights into Nature's wisdom and the balances that are in place. First, vitamin C and other organic acids found in fruits and vegetables can reduce the effects of phytate—and vegetarian diets tend to be high in these. Second, food preparation techniques, such as the soaking and sprouting of beans, grains, and seeds, and the leavening of breads reduce the phytate fraction that binds minerals, reducing absorption. These techniques, commonly used by vegetarians, can make a big difference. Third, the effects of fibre appear to be minor. Fourth, foods that are high in phytate also tend to be high in iron, and the actions of phytate may help us strike the right balance and protect us from iron overload.

Vitamin C

Foods rich in vitamin C work wonders with the iron from plants. Breakfast can be a great time to boost your iron intake. For example, studies have shown that the amount of absorbed iron from cereal or toast doubles or triples when eaten with a large orange or a glass of juice providing 75-100 milligrams of vitamin C. In one study, papaya accompanying a grain meal increased iron absorption up to six times. Fruits and vegetables with smaller amounts of vitamin C also enhance the absorption of nonheme iron, but to a lesser extent. Note that this contradicts popular ideas of food combining, which dictate that fruits be eaten separately from other foods. If you want to do your hemoglobin a favour, include a vegetable or fruit high in vitamin C along with iron-rich foods. Fruits and vegetables provide the maximum amount of vitamin C when they are raw, although cooked foods (for example, onion or tomatoes in a soup or casserole) can also be effective.

Cast Iron Cookware

Another sure way to increase iron intake is to use cast iron cookware. Use of these heavy pots and pans have been shown to significantly increase the amounts of bioavailable iron in foods, especially when we cook acidic foods such as tomato sauce or sweet and sour sauce in them. Use of steel woks has also been shown to add to the amount of iron in food.

Oxalates

Sorry, Popeye, but spinach isn't really the best source of iron, after all. Although his example was widely used to inspire children to eat their greens, the iron in spinach is bound with oxalates, making it largely unavailable. Oxalates are acids found in spinach, beet greens, rhubarb, Swiss chard, and chocolate. In contrast, the low-oxalate greens, broccoli, kale, collards, Chinese cabbage, okra, and bok choy provide abundant iron that is readily absorbed.

In summary, although the iron in plant foods tends to be less well absorbed than the heme iron that makes up some of the iron in meat, this tends to be offset by the increased quantities of iron and by vegetarian dietary choices that support absorption.

Challenges to Iron Out: Common Errors and Solutions

The following situations illustrate potential pitfalls that could lead to low iron intakes for those shifting toward plant-based diets:

- A vegetarian teen eats just the non-meat portion of family meals, and snacks on fries, shakes, and granola bars.

- A busy parent finds cheese to be such a convenient source of protein that it becomes a mainstay for many quick meals.

- A business executive eats many meals at restaurants, often ordering many pasta and cheese-laden entrées, with black tea as the beverage.

For each of these people, iron status may decline over time and their energy level may drop. Each might become uncertain that a vegetarian diet is adequate to meet his or her nutritional needs. Yet simple changes will solve their problems:

- The teen needs to explore the wonderful world of vegetarian convenience foods. Burgers, luncheon slices, instant bean soups, and frozen entrées all make meals more interesting and higher in iron. Youngsters can easily learn to make hummus and keep it handy at the front of the fridge for a quick after-school snack. Families with members whose dietary patterns differ—and there are more of these all the time—can still enjoy tacos together, with optional vegetarian chili (cooked in a cast iron pot) or meat filling. The increased availability of veggie "meats," soy dogs and burgers, and delicious flavours of marinated tofu make things easier every year. Peanut butter is highly nutritious (and try the African Stew, page 419)

- The busy parent could prepare a delicious tofu or lentil dish in minutes after work. Some good examples are Hot Tofu and Cool Greens (recipe, page 414) or Easiest Ever Curried Lentils (page 422). Calcium-set tofu is rich in three minerals—iron, zinc, and calcium—in addition to protein. This parent can buy a bean salad from a deli or stock up on the convenience foods listed above for the teen. An economical solution is to have a cooking spree once a week and stock the freezer with meal-sized portions of entrées, soups, or stews based on beans, lentils, split peas, or tofu. Almond butter, or a thin layer of tahini and molasses, makes a mineral-rich spread for toast in the morning. Fortified dry cereals or cream of wheat also add iron.

- The restaurant eater may frequent ethnic or vegetarian restaurants and order Asian tofu dishes, bean curries, burritos, and lentil or split pea soups; the accompanying vegetables will increase iron absorption. When travelling out of town, he or she could check www.vegdining.com for vegetarian restaurants en route and at the destination. It is also wise for those who are concerned about iron status to drink juice or water in place of tannin-containing teas with meals

TABLE 3.10   *Iron, Zinc, and Protein in Foods*

Food and Category	Amount (serving)	Iron (mg per serving)	Zinc (mg per serving)	Protein (g per serving)
Legumes (cooked)				
Aduki beans	250 mL (1 cup)	4.6	4.1	17.3
Black beans	250 mL (1 cup)	3.6-5.3	1.4-1.9	15.2
Cranberry beans	250 mL (1 cup)	3.7	2.0	16.5
Garbanzo beans/ chickpeas	250 mL (1 cup)	4.7	2.5	14.5
Lentils	250 mL (1 cup)	6.6	2.5	17.9
Navy Beans	250 mL (1 cup)	4.5	1.9	15.8
Kidney beans	250 mL (1 cup)	5.2	1.9	15.4
Pinto beans	250 mL (1 cup)	4.5	1.9	14.0
Soy foods				
Green soybeans	250 mL (1 cup)	4.5	1.6	22.2
Miso	15 mL (1 tbsp)	0.5	0.6	2.0
Natto	15 mL (1 tbsp)	0.9	0.33	1.6-1.9
Soybeans, cooked	250 mL (1 cup)	8.8	2.0	28.2
Tofu, firm (see label)	125 mL (H cup)	1.8-13.2	1.3-2.0	10.1-20.0
Tofu, silken firm	125 mL (H cup)	1.3	0.8	8.7
Tempeh	125 mL (H cup)	2.2-3.2	1.0	15.3-24.0
Veggie "Meats"				
Yves deli slices (fortified)	4 (60 g/2 oz)	1.5	1.2	14.5
Yves wieners/dog (fortified)	1 (46 g/1.5 oz)	2.48	1.1	11.0
Garden vegan burger	1 (60 g/2 oz)	1.1	0.4	11.0
Yves Good Burger (fortified)	1 (75 g/2.5 oz)	4.1	4.7	12.0
Veggie Ground Round (fortified)	60 g (2 oz)	3.9	5.9	12.4-13.1
Nuts, Seeds, and Their Butters				
Almonds	60 mL (G cup)	1.4	1.2	7.5
Cashew nuts	60 mL (G cup)	2.1	1.9	5.2
Flaxseeds	30 mL (2 tbsp)	1.9	0.4	3.7
Hazelnuts	60 mL (G cup)	1.6	0.8	5.1
Pecan halves	60 mL (G cup)	0.7	1.2	2.5
Pine nuts	60 mL (G cup)	3.1	1.4	8.2

TABLE 3.10 *continued*

Food and Category	Amount (serving)	Iron (mg per serving)	Zinc (mg per serving)	Protein (g per serving)
Pistachios	60 mL (G cup)	1.4	0.7	6.6
Pumpkin seeds	60 mL (G cup)	5.2	2.6	8.5
Sunflower seeds	60 mL (G cup)	2.7	1.8	8.1
Sesame tahini	45 mL (3 tbsp)	1.2-2.9	2.1-4.7	7.8-8.8
Non-dairy Milks				
Soy milks (see label)	125 mL (H cup)	0.4-0.9	0.3-0.5	3.2-5.0
Rice milks	125 mL (H cup)	0.2-0.5	0-0.4	0.5-1.6
Grains and Grain Products				
Barley, pearled, cooked	125 mL (H cup)	1.0	0.6	1.8
Barley, whole, cooked	125 mL (H cup)	1.0	0.8	3.7
Millet, cooked	125 mL (H cup)	0.8	1.1	4.2
Oatmeal, cooked	125 mL (H cup)	0.8	0.6	3.0
Quinoa, cooked	125 mL (H cup)	2.1	0.8	3.0
Rice, brown, cooked	125 mL (H cup)	0.5	0.6	2.3
Rice, white, enriched, cooked	125 mL (H cup)	1.0	0.4	2.1
Rye flour*	60 mL (G cup)	0.5-2.1	0.5-1.8	2.1-4.5
Whole wheat flour	60 mL (G cup)	1.2	0.9	4.1
Wheat germ	30 mL (2 tbsp)	0.9	1.8	3.3
Fortified dry cereals (see labels)	30 g (1 oz)	2-5	4	4.2
Vegetables				
Mung bean sprouts, raw	250 mL (1 cup)	1.0	0.4	3.2
Broccoli, raw	250 mL (1 cup)	0.8	0.4	2.6
Carrot, raw, 7.5 long	1	0.4	0.1	0.7
Cauliflower, cooked	125 mL (H cup)	0.2	0.1	1.1
Corn, cooked	125 mL (H cup)	0.5	0.4	2.7
Green/yellow beans, cooked	125 mL (H cup)	0.8	0.2	1.2
Eggplant, cooked	125 mL (H cup)	0.2	0.1	0.4
Kale, raw	250 mL (1 cup)	1.1	0.3	2.2
Mushroom pieces, cooked	125 mL (H cup)	1.4	0.7	1.7
Okra, cooked	125 mL (H cup)	0.4	0.4	1.5
Potato, baked, medium	1 (122 g/4 oz)	1.7	0.4	2.8
Romaine lettuce, raw	250 mL (1 cup)	0.6	0.1	0.9
Spinach, raw	250 mL (1 cup)	0.8**	0.2	0.9
Sweet potato, baked, medium	1 (114 g/4 oz)	0.5	0.3	2.0
Turnip, cooked and mashed	125 mL (H cup)	0.2	0.2	0.8
Winter squash, cooked	125 mL (H cup)	0.3-0.7	0.1-0.3	0.8-1.8
Fruits				
Apple, medium	1	0.2	0.1	0.3

TABLE 3.10 *continued*

Food and Category	Amount (serving)	Iron (mg per serving)	Zinc (mg per serving)	Protein (g per serving)
Apricot halves, dried	8 (60 mL/G cup)	1.3	0.2	1.0
Banana, medium	1	0.4	0.2	1.2
Cantaloupe or honeydew,	G melon	0.2-0.3	0.2	1.2-1.5
Figs, dried	5 (90 g/3 oz)	2.1	0.5	2.9
Strawberries	125 mL (H cup)	0.3	0.1	0.4
Orange, medium	1	0.1	0.1	1.2
Prunes	7 (60 mL/G cup)	1.5	0.3	1.5
Raisins	60 mL (G cup)	1.1	0.1	1.0
Other				
Blackstrap molasses	15 mL (1 tbsp)	3.6	0.2	0
Sugar	15 mL (1 tbsp)	0	0	0
Oil	15 mL (1 tbsp)	0	0	0
Dairy Products and Eggs				
Cow's milk, 2%	125 mL (H cup)	0.1	0.5	4.1
Cheese, cheddar	21 g (0.75 oz)	0.1	0.6	5.2
Yogourt, low-fat	125 mL (H cup)	0.1	1.1	6.4
Egg, large	1 (50 g/ 1.75 oz)	0.6	0.5	6.3
Animal Products (for comparison)				
Ground beef	60 g (2 oz)	1.1	2.3	10.6
Chicken, roasted	60 g (2 oz)	0.6	0.6	17.9
Cod, baked/broiled	60 g (2 oz)	0.3	0.4	13.7
Salmon, baked/broiled	60 g (2 oz)	0.3	0.3	13.4

*Amounts of iron, zinc, and protein are highest with dark rye flour.

**Don't count spinach as an iron source; it's high in oxalates that inhibit absorption of iron (and calcium), as are Swiss chard, beet greens, and rhubarb.

Iron-Clad Rules

Here are tips to help vegetarians increase iron intakes.

1. **Build meals around iron-rich foods.** Follow the Vegetarian Food Guide on page 241, and every one of the food groups will contribute iron. Don't waste many calories on junk foods (high in fat, high in sugar, lacking in iron).

2. **Help your body absorb the iron you do take in.** Eat vitamin C-rich fruits and vegetables at meals. Avoid consuming black tea or wheat bran with your iron sources. Use foods that are yeasted (such as bread), sprouted (such as bean sprouts), roasted (such as nuts), and fermented (such as tempeh).

3. **Use cast iron cookware.**

4. **If in doubt, have your iron status checked to see how you are doing while you get used to a new plant-food way of eating.**

Time to Think About Zinc

While it is unlikely that you will be faced with questions about zinc, it is one nutrient that does present a challenge for vegetarians, as it does for nonvegetarians. Zinc is less well studied than iron; there are unanswered questions regarding the many ways in which it supports our health, exactly how much we need, and whether North American intakes are sufficient.

Zinc in the Body

Zinc plays crucial roles in metabolism from our first moments of conception. It is required for the activity of nearly 100 enzyme systems and affects fundamental processes of life. It is essential for reproduction, growth, sexual maturation, wound healing, and a strong immune system. It helps to protect against the destructive action of free radicals. It enables us to build molecules that are fundamental to our existence and to use carbohydrates as a source of energy. Zinc has a role in our ability to taste; some seniors who have lost the sense of taste are actually zinc-deficient. Infants and children whose diets are short of zinc will have slower physical growth and poor appetites. For those with anorexia nervosa, zinc deficiency could worsen the condition by promoting a true loss of appetite.

How Do We Know If We're Getting Enough Zinc?

There is not a single specific and sensitive way to assess zinc status; instead a combination of tests is used, such as determination of the amounts in plasma and the activity of enzymes that depend on zinc. Testing is expensive and is not done on a routine basis. As a result, we have limited feedback about our zinc status. Our best plan is to aim for recommended dietary intakes.

TABLE 3.11   *Recommended Zinc Intakes*

Gender	Recommended Zinc Intake (mg)
Women, 19 years and over	8
Men, 19 years and over	11

Recommended Zinc Intakes

Zinc recommendations are based on average requirements plus a safety factor. The safety factor has been set to cover the wide range in people's requirements and differences in availability of zinc from different diets.

One reason that men need zinc is that they lose an estimated 0.6 milligrams of zinc with each seminal emission. Ardent vegetarians might be well advised to keep a bowl of cashews on the bedside table. (We absorb about 20 per cent or more of what we consume, and 90 ml or just over N cup of these nuts provides 3 milligrams of zinc.) Pumpkin seeds are another good choice.

Intakes and Nutrient Status

Studies show that the average zinc intake of nonvegetarians is about 11.1 milligrams per day and fall well below recommendations for many people. The average for lacto-ovo vegetarians is even lower at about 9.1 milligrams per day. Intakes of vegans can be worse still. A typical example of someone with a low intake is a young woman on a low-calorie vegetarian diet who eats salads and refined pasta, but avoid nuts, seeds, and tofu in an effort to cut out dietary fat. (In fact, these mineral-rich foods are the best choices one can make for fat sources.)

One popular misconception among some vegetarians is that any diet that based on plant foods will automatically provide all the nutrients necessary for good health.

Myth: All plant-based diets easily deliver trace minerals like zinc. We don't even need to think about it.

Not so. With good planning, vegetarians can get plenty of zinc. But it doesn't happen automatically. Have a look at the zinc column in Table 3.12 and you'll see some powerful sources of this mineral that can be added to your diet. Many of these foods have been integrated into Menus #3 and #4 in ways that are simple and very tasty.

TABLE 3.12 *Zinc in 2,000 Calorie and 2,800-Calorie Menus*

Menu and page	Calories	Zinc (mg)	Calories	Zinc (mg)
#1 Nonvegetarian, page 88	2,000	8.4	2,800	13.9
#2 Lacto-ovo Vegetarian, page 91	2,000	7.3	2,800	12.6
#3 Lacto-ovo Vegetarian with More Legumes, page 92	2,000	13.1	2,800	18.2
#4 Vegan, page 94	2,000	13	2,800	13.9

In the nonvegetarian Menu #1, almost half the zinc was provided by beef and chicken, with peas being the next most important source. Refined flour in the white roll and bread has lost most of its zinc. In Menu #2, the main sources are dairy products, whole grains, and egg. Thus, when the use of animal products is decreased, people may think zinc intake must be insufficient. Yet in Menus # 3 and #4, legumes, plentiful amounts of whole grain products, and frequent use of nuts and seeds all contribute significant amounts of zinc. Other zinc-rich foods are wheat germ and asparagus.

Factors That Increase or Decrease Zinc Absorption

The amount of zinc we absorb can vary greatly, from an average of about 20-30 per cent to as much as 50 per cent from the readily available zinc that infants receive in breast milk. Some of the zinc in our bodies is excreted into the intestine, for example, in pancreatic juices, and a variable amount of this is reabsorbed. We seem to be able to adapt to lower zinc intakes by absorbing more from our food, and by reabsorbing more of the zinc that is secreted. Though more studies would help us understand the intricacies of zinc balance, research has shown that vegetarians have less zinc intake, but also lose less, thus keeping the same overall balance as nonvegetarians.

Phytate-Calcium-Zinc Combinations

The compound phytate, present in whole grains and legumes, and very concentrated in wheat bran, can bind zinc and lower the amount we absorb, especially when calcium is present. This phytate-calcium-zinc combination can result from a meal of whole grain cereal, plus wheat bran, plus cow's milk or fortified soymilk. Naturally, we want to consume adequate intakes of calcium. So what's the solution? While there is no need to avoid the occasional delicious muffin, vegetarians should not add bran to their foods; they already get plenty of fibre. (Wheat *germ* is quite different; it is low in phytate and is an excellent source of zinc.) Also, it's best to take any calcium supplement at a different time than when eating zinc-rich whole grains and legumes, and not in combination with wheat bran.

Reducing Phytate Action with Food Preparation

When we soak or sprout seeds, nuts, grains, or legumes, we decrease the amount of phytate and increase the amount of zinc we absorb from these foods. Many vegetarians soak nuts overnight before use, and legumes are generally presoaked before cooking. Sprouted brown, green, and French lentils are mineral-rich, high-protein additions to salads (see page 408 for details).

The yeasting of bread increases the availability of zinc from whole grain flours (in contrast to unleavened breads). The moist action of fermentation in foods such as tempeh can also increase zinc availability. Scientists are just beginning to understand some advantages of food preparation methods that long-term vegetarians have used for years to ensure good nutrition.

Dietary Fats

Dietary fats are important as they help us absorb zinc (plus other minerals, phytochemicals, and fat-soluble vitamins). On an extremely low-fat diet, absorption can be decreased.

Choose a Good Multivitamin-Mineral Supplement over Single Mineral Supplements

Don't rush out and buy zinc pills. Zinc, iron, copper, and calcium all interact with one another, and large intakes of one of these minerals can interfere with your utilization of one of the others. If you wish to use supplements, choose a multivitamin-mineral complex in the general range of recommended (rather than higher) mineral levels. Check that the supplement you use contains zinc; many do not. Supplements that are below recommended levels are fine too, because your diet should be supplying most of your needs. If you use a separate calcium supplement, take it at a different time than when eating zinc-rich foods.

Guidelines for Maximizing Zinc Intake

For optimum zinc intake, follow these guidelines.

1. **Consume a variety of zinc-rich foods.** Eat zinc sources throughout the day, including whole grains, wheat germ, tofu, tempeh, miso, legumes, nuts, and seeds. Lacto-ovo vegetarians can add eggs and dairy products. Zinc-fortified cereals and veggie "meats" can significantly increase your intake.

2. **Make the most of the zinc in your diet.** Use yeasted breads, sprouts, roasted or soaked nuts, and presoaked legumes.

3. **Eat foods that retain the mineral wealth that nature gave them, rather than refined foods.** White flour and products made from white flour, white rice, and other refined grains have lost most of their zinc.

4. **Wheat bran, added to a diet high in whole grains and legumes, is not only unnecessary, but can interfere with mineral absorption.**

Our best sources of zinc also tend to be rich in iron and protein too, so choosing these is a win-win-win situation—and more! Here are examples of how nuts, seeds, beans, and whole grains can enrich your meals at breakfast, lunch, supper, and for snacks.

TABLE 3.13   *Putting Protein, Iron, and Zinc into All Your Meals*

Breakfast	Almond butter, sesame tahini, or peanut butter on toast; cereal with soy milk; wheat germ; granola with nuts; veggie back bacon or ham, Banana Walnut Pancakes; Cashew French Toast; Marvelous Morning Muesli; Whole Grain Pudding; Scrambled Tofu with whole grain toast (see recipe section)
Lunch or Supper	Nuts or seeds on a salad; sesame tahini in place of salad oil in dressing; hummus and pita bread; pea soup with French bread; lentil soup with a whole grain roll, baked beans with cornbread; marinated tofu with rice; peanut butter with bread, vegetarian chili with tortillas; soy burger or dog with a bun; dahl with chapatis; red beans with rice; falafel (garbanzo beans with pita bread); pasta with pine nuts; Black Bean Soup or Stew; Zucchini Chedda Soup; Hazelnut Paté; Angelic Tofu Filling; Muenster Uncheese; Veggie Clubhouse; African Stew; Easiest-Ever Curried Lentils; Hot Tofu with Cool Greens; Timesaving Tacos; Shepherd's Pie; Chunky Red Lentil Tomato Sauce with whole grain pasta (see recipe section)
Desserts and Snacks	Muscle Muffins; Nutty Date Cookies; Chocolate Mint Nut Bars (see recipe section); Trail mix; soy nuts; pumpkin seeds
Beverages	Chocolate Shake; Hazelnut Paté (see recipe section)

It is clear that meat, fish, and poultry can be replaced by a wealth of alternatives. These meet your needs for protein, iron, and zinc while giving you the benefit of lower intakes of saturated fat and cholesterol. Generally, these nutrients are not as concentrated in plant foods as they are in animal foods, but we don't need such concentrated sources. In fact, as we'll see in the next chapter, more moderate protein intakes can help our calcium balance.

**A complete set of references is available online at:
http://www.nutrispeak.com/bvreferences.htm**

bone boosters
milks, greens, and other calcium champions

Go into a Grade 3 classroom and ask the children why we need calcium. What will they say? "To build strong bones, of course." Everyone knows that. Some may even tell you that if you don't eat enough calcium, you'll get osteoporosis when you are old. Ask the children where we get our calcium. They will not hesitate to tell you that it comes from milk. Some will even mention cheese, yogourt, or other dairy products. There is no doubt about it; few nutrition messages are more strongly promoted than this one. Yet, despite the best efforts of the government and the dairy industry, most North Americans fail to meet calcium recommendations. In addition, 50 per cent of North American women are expected to have at least one osteoporosis-related fracture in their lifetime. The answer seems so simple—drink more milk. While we know that milk is a rich source of calcium, could there be something missing in this nutrition education message?

In this chapter we will explore the many ways in which calcium, a mineral that is fifth in abundance in the earth's crust, can become part of our diets. In the process, we will challenge several myths—some widely held by the general population, others prevalent among some vegetarians.

- **Myth #1: It is virtually impossible to get enough calcium in our diets without dairy products.**

- **Myth #2: Vegetarians need much less calcium than meat-eaters.**

- **Myth #3: Due to its high protein content, milk actually drains our bodies of calcium.**

- **Myth #4: If we get enough calcium, we'll have all we need to build strong bones.**

We will also look at how we get vitamin D, which is a key player in bone metabolism and essential for our absorption of calcium:

- **Myth #5: Vitamin D is not a concern; everyone gets plenty from sunshine.**

Finally, we'll discover our various dietary sources of riboflavin, a vitamin present in milk and many plant foods.

Calcium

Calcium in the Body

Ninety-nine per cent of our body's calcium is found in bones and teeth. Bones are living systems permeated by blood vessels and fluid. The minerals that harden bones are in a state of constant turnover throughout our lives, remodelling up to 15 per cent of the bone mass annually, with about 700 milligrams of calcium entering and leaving bone every day. Though just 1 per cent of our calcium is present in blood and soft tissues, its functions here are so vital that we retrieve calcium from bone to perform them if dietary sources are insufficient. Calcium is a part of all cell membranes, allowing substances to enter and leave, and is involved with muscle contraction and relaxation, blood clotting, the transmission of nerve impulses, and enzyme activity.

Calcium Balance

No matter how much calcium is in our diets, our bodies maintain optimal levels of calcium in blood and inside cells with a complex system of checks and balances. Even as you read this, your body is adjusting the amount of calcium in your blood. To support this fine-tuning, we have some ability to control the proportion absorbed from foods, to alter the quantity of calcium lost in urine, and, if necessary, to draw on calcium in bone. The relationship between calcium intake and calcium losses from the body is known as calcium balance.

We achieve our maximum or peak bone mass in our early thirties. We gain 45 per cent of this bone mass during our first eight years of life and another 45 per cent during the next eight years. As adults, the total calcium in our bodies amounts to between 1 and 1.5 kilograms (2.2 and 3.3 pounds). Through the growing years, we need to maintain a positive calcium balance by taking in much more calcium than we lose. Attaining good bone mass during our first few decades of life is extremely important for long-term bone health. Generally, at stages when we most need calcium, we absorb the highest percentage from our diet. Absorption is greatest during pregnancy, lactation, and the growing years. Thus, children may absorb up to 75 per cent of dietary calcium, as compared with rates of 20–40 per cent in young adults, and 15–20 per cent in most adults.

When intake and output (losses) are roughly equal, we are in calcium balance. This is a good goal during our adult years. Beyond about forty-five years, bone mass typically declines as much as 0.5 per cent each year. In the decade before and after menopause, women's calcium losses accelerates to as much as 2–5 per cent loss of total bone mass in a single year, and then it slows. Our diet and lifestyle choices through the years can help keep our bones strong by maximizing absorption, minimizing losses, and helping us retain the calcium we have. This is of prime importance after menopause and in the later years.

Factors Contributing to Calcium Balance

Though adequate intake is important, it is just one part of the rather complex equation of calcium balance. A study of hundreds of women looked at how calcium balance is determined, and showed that 11 per cent was determined by calcium intake, 15 per cent by absorption, and 51 per cent by urinary excretion. Most people are very aware of the importance of calcium intake for bone health, as a great deal of advertising is directed toward this message. On the other hand, calcium absorption and excretion are seldom recognized. Yet these are also extremely important for long-term bone health. Ignoring excretion is like trying to fill your bathtub without putting in the plug!

Calcium Absorption

For adults, about 15–20 per cent of the calcium from our food and beverages is absorbed from the intestine and into the bloodstream. There can be a great deal of variation. For example, infants, whose bones are growing, absorb as much as 75 per cent of the calcium from breast milk. When our needs increase, vitamin D steps into action and absorption also increases. Vitamin D has a key role in helping us to absorb and keep calcium (see page 136).

We absorb more efficiently when small amounts of calcium are eaten throughout the day, rather than when we consume the total amount at one sitting. For example, we absorb more calcium when we have four 125-millilitre (H-cup) servings of fortified soymilk or cow's milk (with 150 milligrams calcium in each) at different times of the day, compared with drinking the 500 millilitres (2 cups) of either milk (containing 600 milligrams of calcium) all at once.

Certain substances in foods, particularly oxalates (present in spinach, Swiss chard, rhubarb, and beet greens) can bind calcium, so that we absorb only about 5 per cent of the calcium from these foods. Contrast this with 40–70 per cent absorption from kale, broccoli, and turnip greens, which we can rely on as calcium sources because they have negligible amounts of oxalate. Collards are very high in calcium, along with a small amount of oxalates. To a lesser extent, phytates can reduce calcium absorption (wheat bran is a concentrated source of phytates).

Calcium Excretion

Every day, about 8,000 milligrams of calcium passes through our kidneys' filter, and we reabsorb about 98 per cent of the mineral.

Our overall diet has a big impact on the acidity and composition of the urine, which in turn determines how much calcium is lost. There are two major "calcium thieves," protein and sodium, plus several minor ones.

Protein. Research has shown that for every gram of dietary protein above 47 grams per day, we lose about 0.5 milligrams of calcium through the urine. This happens because a by-product of protein breakdown combines with calcium and carries it out of the body. The by-product is sulphate from the sulphur-containing amino acids. (These were discussed in Chapter 3, pages 78 and 79.) Sulphates make our blood more acidic than is optimal, and we restore pH balance by drawing on calcium reserves—which are our bones—or with calcium from our diet. All dietary protein contributes to urinary calcium losses; however, meat, fish, poultry, and eggs are particularly high in protein, and in the sulphur-containing amino acids. Thus, their impact can be particularly strong, causing more calcium to be excreted. Dairy products, legumes, and grains contain moderate amounts of protein and sulphur-containing amino acids, while fruits and vegetables contain even less. These foods have less impact on urinary calcium excretion. Protein is essential for building body tissues (including bone) and meeting recommended allowances is important. At the same time, too much protein can have a negative effect on calcium balance, *especially where calcium intakes are low*.

People with diets high in animal protein are likely to need more calcium than those with plant-based diets. (Exactly how much more is difficult to determine, as there are so many variables that interact.) Thus, excess protein is an important factor in the epidemic of osteoporosis among affluent North Americans. Two other primary factors are high salt intakes and lack of exercise.

Sodium. The amount of sodium we require each day is very low, about 500 milligrams. Intakes of North Americans tend to be about five to ten times that amount. The average intakes from foods alone are over 4 grams (4,000 milligrams) for men and almost 3 grams (3,000 milligrams) for women. Total intakes are even higher because salt added at the table, and that present in our drinking water, are not included in these values. High sodium intakes decrease our kidneys' ability to reabsorb the calcium that passes through. For every 1,000 milligrams (1 gram) of sodium in our diets, we lose about 20–40 milligrams of calcium. Five millilitres (1 level teaspoon) of salt provides 2,400 milligrams sodium; this is also the amount that many experts suggest as our maximum for the day.

TABLE 4.1   *Sodium in Foods*

Food	Amount	Sodium (mg)
Bread, slice	1	100–180
Canned tomatoes	250 mL (1 cup)	24–504
Corn chips	85 g (3 oz)	182–869
Dill pickle, medium	1	900
Doughnut	1	210–380
Kraft Dinner, prepared	250 mL (1 cup)	1,460
Miso	5 mL (1 tsp)	209
Peanut butter	30 mL (2 tbsp)	80–150
Potato chips	85 g (3 oz)	360–660
Pretzel	30 g (1 oz)	450
Ready-to-eat cereal	250 mL (1 cup)	200–350
Salsa	125 mL (H cup)	450–1,300
Soup, commercial	250 mL (1 cup)	700–1,100
Table salt or sea salt	1 mL (G tsp)	581
Tamari or soy sauce	5 mL (1 tsp)	335
Tomato sauce	250 mL (1 cup)	40–1,680
Veggie "meats"	85 g (3 oz)	114–1,148
Suggested maximum intake per day		**2,400**

Generally, we meet our basic sodium requirements through the sodium that is naturally present in foods and water, without added salt. Though few of us would shake 5 millilitres (1 teaspoon) of salt onto our meals at the table over the course of a day, we may add that much to a recipe, and then eat a sizable portion of the dish. Yet only 15 per cent of our salt intake comes from salt added to cooking and at the table. An even bigger calcium drain comes from the processed foods in our diets, which have masses of salt added to appeal to our taste buds. Seventy-five per cent of North Americans' sodium intake comes via processed foods such as salad dressings, soups, pickles, fast foods, and snacks. Some examples are shown in Table 4.1. Note the wide ranges for many products; it helps to read labels!

There's one more bit of math that may convey the impact salt can have. Above, we said, "For every 1,000 milligrams (1 gram) of sodium in our diets, we lose about 20–40 milligrams of calcium." When this occurs, we're losing 20–40 milligrams of calcium *that has been absorbed*. If we absorb only 15–20 per cent of our dietary calcium, this means that each extra gram of sodium in our diets should be counterbalanced by about 100–267 milligrams of dietary calcium. At average levels of sodium intakes (about 4 grams per day), that would amount to an increased dietory requirement of about 400 to 1068 milligrams of calcium lost per day due to sodium consumption. Scientists have calculated that in adult women, each extra gram (1,000 milligrams) of sodium in our daily diet could produce an additional rate of bone loss of 1 per cent per year if all of the calcium loss comes from the skeleton. Research on postmenopausal women supports these results.

To protect our bones as we age, we should check amounts of sodium on labels of our favourite foods, and replace some of the salt in our cooking with other seasonings. Aim for about 2,400 milligrams of sodium or less per day.

Coffee. If we have 500 or 750 millilitres (2 or 3 cups) of coffee per day or less, the effect on calcium balance appears to be negligible, as long as our diet meets recommended calcium intakes. However studies have shown that even 500 millilitres (2 cups) of coffee can encourage bone loss in women whose calcium intake is less than 800 milligrams per day.

Phosphoric acid. Some of the most popular sodas (cola beverages) contain phosphoric acid to balance their sweetness and to inhibit the growth of micro-organisms. Phosphoric acid can increase calcium excretion, although the effects are considered relatively minor. However, if these beverages become a primary fluid, it can be more of a problem.

Calcium Retention

Several lifestyle factors affect bone health, two prime examples being hormonal balance and exercise.

Hormonal balance. Our hormonal balance plays a part. Estrogen appears to aid in calcium absorption and help our bones retain calcium. Vegetarians tend to have lower lifelong serum estrogen. This is thought to be due to the later age of menarche, lower fat intakes, and increased fecal output of estrogen (due to higher fibre diets). The reduced estrogen levels, while an advantage when it comes to cancer, may increase risk of osteoporosis. For about five years around menopause, women may lose as much as 3 per cent of their total bone mass each year. Hormone-replacement therapy has been used by post-menopausal women to prevent calcium loss; however, there can be unwanted side effects. New research is exploring the gentler effects of similar plant estrogens derived from soyfoods (isoflavones) and flaxseeds (lignans). Regular consumption of tofu and other soyfoods may have helped the bone health of Chinese and Japanese women in past centuries, and this practice is being adopted by increasing numbers of North Americans today.

Exercise

The importance of exercise to bone health cannot be overemphasized. Exercise communicates a powerful message to the bones to preserve calcium and keep bones strong. Apart from diet, there is nothing we can do that is more valuable for our bones than to exercise. Taking part in forty-five minutes to an hour of weight-bearing exercise (such as walking, running, cycling, or dancing) three to five times a week, plus a session with free weights, exercise machines, or life activities that provide similar resistance exercise two to three times a week, are our best ways to help our bones retain calcium. Bones appreciate being used!

Calcium Deficiency

Our bodies carefully control the calcium levels in blood and other fluids, maintaining these levels even if dietary calcium is low. So we can't determine the adequacy of our diet over recent months by doing a simple blood test, as we can with iron. If blood levels of calcium drop, we simply make a withdrawal from the bone calcium bank account. Eventually, of course, repeated withdrawals result in fragile bones. During periods of high needs, low intake, or increased excretion, output exceeds intake, so we are in negative calcium balance.

Osteoporosis has been called "a disease of childhood that manifests in old age." The description conveys how this complex condition can reflect years of diet and lifestyle choices that affect calcium balance. This includes many other nutrients that make up or affect our bones. Decades later, we learn the outcome of our choices. For more on osteoporosis, and the many factors that lead to it, see page 137.

Recommended Intakes of Calcium

Establishing recommended intakes for calcium is a tricky business. In *Nutrition Recommendations*, Health Canada's Scientific Review Committee has said "Defining the adult requirement, upon which a recommended intake is usually based, has proved to be one of the most difficult problems in the history of human nutrition." Because blood levels are maintained whether our diets are adequate or not, and because the feedback, in terms of bone density, comes decades later, and because there are so many variables that interact in the equation of calcium balance, it's difficult to determine exactly how much we need. However, combining the wisdom of scientists in Canada, the United States, and other countries, these amounts have been set as Acceptable Intakes (a sort of "best guess") for various ages.

TABLE 4.2 *Acceptable Intakes for Calcium*

Age (years)	Acceptable Intakes for Calcium (mg)
1–3	500
4–8	800
9–18	1,300
19–50	1,000
51 and over	1,200

Upper limits have also been set, and are called "Tolerable Upper Intake Levels." We are advised not to consume more than 2,500 milligrams of calcium daily on an ongoing basis. Generally this would occur only with supplement use. Excessive calcium intakes can lead to kidney stones; this can be a particular problem when plenty of high-oxalate plant foods such as spinach, Swiss chard, beet greens, and rhubarb are consumed. High calcium intakes may also interfere with our absorption and use of other minerals: iron, zinc, magnesium, and phosphorus.

How Much Calcium Do Nonvegetarians, Lacto-Vegetarians, and Vegans Get?

On any of the diets just listed, average intakes of North Americans fall short of these recommendations after about nine years of age. U.S. national surveys show calcium intakes of teenage girls and women to be about 60 per cent of recommended levels. Diets of men come a little closer to recommendations, providing a daily average of about 900 milligrams of calcium until the age of fifty, when intakes drop off to 700 milligrams. For both sexes, intakes of lacto-vegetarians are similar to those of nonvegetarians, or even a little higher. Vegan diets tend to be lower in calcium, providing about two-thirds of recommended levels for men, and half of the recommended levels for women. All in all, it's not enough!

Do Vegetarians (Including Vegans) Need This Much Calcium?

It is well known that many people in less developed countries, whose diets are mainly plant based, have strong bones despite calcium intakes that are far below the adult intakes recommended in Table 4.2. We also know that excessive intakes of animal protein increase urinary calcium losses, and that requirements could theoretically be lower when these excesses are avoided. This combination of fact and theory has led some vegetarians to assume that they don't need to worry about calcium and can manage very well on intakes of 400 or 500 milligrams per day.

Myth: Vegetarians need much less calcium than meat-eaters.

It's important to recognize that people in other cultures, who manage on these low calcium intakes, often lead lives that are far different from ours in North America. Their main mode of transportation may be walking outdoors, in the sunshine. Carrying heavy loads such as children, water, and food is a part of everyday life. Our lives are often very sedentary. We may be indoors much of the time, sitting at a desk during the day, and watching TV at night. Even when we exercise, we drive to the gym, or use a golf cart. When we are outside, we often smear on the sunscreen. Some of us also live at northern latitudes. These factors, including those that determine vitamin D levels, affect our calcium retention.

Vegetarians, including vegans, should meet the calcium intakes recommended for their age group. This can be accomplished by following the Vegetarian Food Guide (page 241). Many people find it easier to meet recommended calcium levels if fortified foods or supplements are included as part of the day's intake.

Taking part in weight-bearing exercise, avoiding excess salt, and avoiding the extremes of insufficient or far too much protein are habits that work to your advantage. One good predictor of our bone health may be the ratio between our calcium and protein intakes. As shown in Table 4.3, the ideal ratio appears to be 16 milligrams of calcium for every gram of protein in our diet. Lacto-ovo vegetarians fit this pattern very closely. The ratios for nonvegetarians and vegans are fairly similar and lower—between 9 and 12 milligrams calcium for each gram of protein in the diet. Vegans have the advantage of less excessive protein intakes, but this is countered by lower calcium intakes.

TABLE 4.3 *Ratios of Calcium to Protein on Various Diets, and Average Sodium Intake*

	Ratio of Calcium to Protein (mg:g)	Sodium (mg)
Ideal	16:1	Less than 2,400
Lacto-ovo Vegetarians	15 to 17:1	2,000–3,800
Nonvegetarians	10 to 12:1	2,000–3,600
Vegans	9 to 12:1	1,800–2,800

Vegetarians may also have lower amounts of estrogen in their bodies over a lifespan. This carries certain anti-cancer health benefits, but could possibly have a negative impact on bone health. Overall, while some vegetarians undoubtedly have lower calcium needs than the general population, we do not have evidence, based on differences in lifelong bone health, that the vegetarian population as a whole needs less calcium than is generally recommended. Some studies have shown that vegetarians and nonvegetarians lose the same amounts of urinary calcium when their calcium intakes are similar. Until we have actual clinical studies showing that vegetarians can have healthy bones with lower calcium intakes, the goal for vegetarians, including vegans, should certainly be to meet calcium recommendations.

Availability of calcium-fortified beverages (such as soymilk and orange juice) and foods (such as calcium-set tofu) has improved immensely in recent years. Most studies of vegan dietary patterns were done before excellent fortified products appeared in the marketplace. Though kale, calcium-set tofu, and other non-dairy sources of calcium (see page 127) are not yet listed on national food guides, our range of choices is becoming more widely known. Vegans, and people whose intakes fall short of recommendations, would be well advised to take advantage of the many calcium sources available to them!

Myth: Due to its high protein content, milk actually drains our bodies of calcium.

Cow's milk and products. Rumours circulate among vegetarians that cow's milk is not a good source of calcium and even that it depletes us of calcium. Is this true? No. Cow's milk has an excellent calcium-to-protein ratio, which is reflected in the diets of lacto-ovo vegetarians. The proportion of calcium that is absorbed is respectable, about 32 per cent. While it's not as high as the calcium from low-oxalate greens, it is comparable to that in tofu (see Table 4.5). Including dairy products in our diets can certainly help us achieve recommended calcium intakes. On average, Americans drink 500 millilitres (2 cups) of cow's milk per day, and Canadians 400 millilitres (1.6 cups).

There are many reasons why people choose to avoid dairy products. These include health reasons (such as saturated fat, and the hormone known as IGF-1 or insulin-like growth factor, which has been shown to accelerate tumour growth); reasons related to the environmental impact of animal agriculture (such as manure's widespread effects); and compassion for animals (the abbreviated lives of veal calves and their mothers, the dairy cows). Intolerances and allergies to milk's sugar and several of its proteins are widespread. These topics are discussed in more detail in *Becoming Vegan* by B. Davis and V. Melina (The Book Publishing Company, 2000) and *Dairy-free and Delicious* by B. Davis, J.B. Clark Grogan, and J. Stepaniak (The Book Publishing Company, 2002). The second book includes excellent recipes.

Calcium-Rich Plant Foods: Plenty of Options

Our culture teaches us that milk and its products are an essential food group; government publications tell us that we must eat foods from each group to be healthy. Children learn that if they don't drink their milk, they won't grow strong bones. Adults get the impression that the best way to prevent, or even cure, osteoporosis is to drink more milk. While milk is a key source of calcium for people consuming animal-centred diets, it is not essential to human health. As it turns out, there are a great many ways for the calcium that originates in the earth's crust to become part of our bones. Cow's milk is just one. Many people, dairy consumers or not, will benefit by knowing some of the plant foods that provide this mineral.

Table 4.4 shows a variety of these foods, along with the amount of calcium they contain. Amounts listed are those in the Vegetarian Food Guide, page 241. Calcium content in plants can be expected to vary somewhat from one crop to another. There can also be great differences between brands of tofu, so check labels. When labels state that a serving provides 10 per cent of the Recommended Daily Intake, this is based on 1,100 milligrams of calcium as 100 per cent. Ten per cent of the Dietary Value (DV) is based on 1,000 milligrams of calcium as 100 per cent. Table 4.5 takes this one step further and combines the research on availability, or of how well we absorb calcium (where this is known) with amounts in various foods.

Greens: Broccoli, Chinese Greens, Collards, Kale, Okra, and Mustard and Turnip Greens

Because calcium is an important structural component in the cell walls of leaves and many other parts of plants, various veggies can easily become important calcium contributors in our diets. In some plants (see box below), the calcium is tightly bound by plant acids called oxalates and little of it is available to us. In contrast, many other greens are low in oxalate and are good sources of easily absorbed calcium; examples are bok choy, broccoli, collards, kale, many Chinese greens (apart from Chinese spinach), okra, and mustard and turnip greens. The proportion of calcium we absorb from these low-oxalate greens is somewhat higher than that from cow's milk.

Greens are among our best bone-builders for reasons beyond their unbeatable calcium absorption. They're high in vitamin K—the darker the leaf, the better. Vitamin K plays a mysterious but essential role in helping our bone-building cells perform their task. Consuming 100 grams (3.5 ounces) per day of vegetables like kale provides enough vitamin K to halve our risk of fracture. Greens also contribute plenty of potassium to the bone-building team. Kale is a hardy crop that Canadian gardeners can grow for much of the year. It's well worth finding out how to prepare it and other greens in delicious ways (see recipes on page 403 and 405).

High-Oxalate Greens: Good Foods, But Not for Calcium

Spinach, Swiss chard, beet greens, and rhubarb contain plenty of calcium. Unfortunately, the calcium is tightly bound by plant acids called oxalates, thus we can absorb only a small proportion of the calcium from these foods (only about 5–8 per cent), so they can't be counted as calcium sources (see Table 4.5). We need not avoid these high-oxalate greens, as they are rich in very important nutrients such as folate and phytochemicals. In fact, scientists observe that oxalates could actually protect us from calcium overload.

TABLE 4.4 *Calcium in Foods*

Food and Amount	Calcium (mg)
Green Vegetables	
Bok choy, raw, 500 mL (2 cups)	147
Bok choy, cooked, 250 mL (1 cup)	178
Broccoli, raw, 500 mL (2 cups)	84
Broccoli, cooked, 250 mL (1 cup)	70–94
Chinese broccoli, cooked, 250 mL (1 cup)	88
Chinese (Pe-Tsai/Nappa) cabbage, raw, 500 mL (2 cups)	117
Chinese (Pe-Tsai/Nappa) cabbage, cooked, 250 mL (1 cup)	158
Chinese cabbage flower leaves, cooked, 250 mL (1 cup)	478
Chinese mustard greens, cooked, 250 mL (1 cup)	424
Chinese (luffa/loofah) okra, 250 mL (1 cup)	112
Collard greens, cooked, 250 mL (1 cup)	226
Kale, raw, 500 mL (2 cups)	181
Kale, cooked, 250 mL (1 cup)	94–179
Mustard greens, 250 mL (1 cup)	128
Okra, 250 mL (1 cup)	101
Romaine lettuce, raw, 500 mL (2 cups)	40
Seaweed, hijiki or arame, dry, 125 mL (H cup; 10 g/.35 oz)	100–140
Turnip greens, 500 mL (2 cups)	209
Legumes and Soyfoods	
Black turtle beans, cooked, 250 mL (1 cup)	46–120
Cranberry beans, cooked, 250 mL (1 cup)	94
Garbanzo/chickpeas, cooked, 250 mL (1 cup)	80
Kidney beans, cooked, 250 mL (1 cup)	50
Lentils, cooked, 250 mL (1 cup)	38
Navy beans, cooked, 250 mL (1 cup)	127
Pinto beans, cooked, 250 mL (1 cup)	82
Red beans, cooked, 250 mL (1 cup)	81–85
White beans, cooked, 250 mL (1 cup)	226
Green soybeans, 250 mL (1 cup)	185
Soybeans, cooked, 250 mL (1 cup)	175
Soy nuts, 60 g (2 oz)	113
Tofu, firm (made with calcium), 125 mL (H cup)	152–336
Tofu, silken firm, 125 mL (H cup)	40

TABLE 4.4 *Continued*

Food and Amount	Calcium (mg)
Tempeh, 125 mL (H cup)	92
Yves Veggie Ground Round, 90 g (3 oz)	62
Non-dairy "Milks"	
Fortified soy and grain milks, 125 mL (H cup)	100–150
Unfortified soy and grain milks, 125 mL (H cup)	5–10
Fruits and Juices	
Figs, 5 (95 g/3 oz)	137–197
Orange, 1 medium	52
Fortified orange juice, 125 mL (H cup)	150–154
Nuts, Seeds, and Butters	
Almonds, 60 mL (G cup)	115
Almond butter, 45 mL (3 tbsp)	130
Flaxseed, 30 mL (2 tbsp)	47
Hazelnuts, 60 mL (G cup)	38
Sesame tahini, 45 mL (3 tbsp)	50–63
Other	
Blackstrap molasses, 15 mL (1 tbsp)	176
Dairy Products	
Cow's milk, non-fat, 2% or whole, 125 mL (H cup)	143–153
Cheese, cheddar, 21 g (.75 oz)	151
Yogourt, 125 mL (H cup)	156–200

Sea Vegetables

Vegetables from the sea, more commonly known as seaweeds, are commonly used in Japan and are packed with minerals. Hijiki (also known as hiziki) and arame are particularly high in calcium; wakame contains calcium, too. In North America, these are available in dried form in health food stores and at far less expense in Asian markets. They can be rehydrated and added to soups, salads, and stir-fries.

Calcium-set Tofu

Tofu is made from soymilk that is allowed to set by adding a coagulant. Traditional methods in Japan involved adding a seaweed extract called nigari. Today, either calcium or magnesium salts are commonly added in amounts that vary considerably from one brand or variety to another (check nutrition panel). Calcium-set tofu can be one of the most significant sources of calcium in our diet.

Tempeh, a fermented, highly digestible, soyfood originating from Indonesia, also contains calcium, though less than tofu (see Table 4.4).

White Beans, Black Turtle Beans, and Soybeans

Although all beans contain calcium, some have more than others. Two hundred-fifty millilitres (1 cup) of white beans contain as much calcium as 175 millilitres (I cup) of milk (see Table 4.4). Black turtle beans provide this mineral. So do soybeans, which we can eat as the mineral-packed green soybeans or as soy nuts (see Table 4.4).

Figs

Although considered a fruit, the fig is actually a flower that is inverted onto itself. Break a fig open, fold it back and you will see all the seeds. The tree upon which they grow is a member of the mulberry family; one grew in the Garden of Eden and figs are mentioned throughout the history of many cultures. Figs were a favorite of the prophet Mohammed. This sweet fruit was a training food for early Olympic athletes. In Rome, Pliny, (ad 52–113) wrote, "Figs are restorative. They increase the strength of young people, preserve the elderly in better health and make them look younger with fewer wrinkles." Certainly dried figs are an excellent treat to carry in our backpack, glove compartment or purse; they give us an energy boost, complete with plenty of calcium, iron, potassium and fiber. Two-thirds of a cup of figs, or five dried figs, contains as much calcium as a half cup of milk.

Calcium-Fortified Beverages

Soymilk, rice milk, and orange juice are all available in calcium-fortified versions, generally containing the same amount of calcium per cup as cow's milk. In soymilk and rice milk calcium is accompanied by vitamin D (which helps us absorb calcium). Check labels for the words "fortified" or "enriched"; read the ingredient list for a calcium salt (such as calcium gluconate, calcium citrate malate, or tricalcium phosphate) or see if the Nutrition Information panel says, for example, "Calcium...28%," which means that there is 308 milligrams of calcium per cup (per 250 millilitre) serving (28 per cent of 1,100 milligrams), approximately the same amount as cow's milk. It may also say 30 per cent of DV, which means 300 milligrams of calcium. The calcium tends to settle to the bottom of the container rather than stay in suspension, so if we want to end up with the calcium inside us, we need to shake the closed container well.

Almonds, Sesame Seeds, and Their Butters

Almonds are a good choice for our high-calcium trail mix. Different nuts have different nutritional features; almonds are particularly rich in calcium. Almond milk made from ground almonds is tasty, but is not a suitable calcium-rich beverage for children; it has nowhere near the 300 milligrams per cup (per 250 millilitres) in fortified soymilk or cow's milk. Almond butter makes an excellent spread for your toast. The sesame seed butter (known as tahini) has less calcium than almond butter, but significantly more than peanut butter or most other nut or seed butters.

Blackstrap Molasses

You've likely heard that white sugar has been stripped of everything but refined carbohydrate. Where do the nutrients go when the sugar cane plant is converted to this nutritionally barren white powder? They end up in a by-product of the sugar refining industry known as blackstrap molasses, a rich concentrate of the minerals that were in the original plants. If you make baked beans, use blackstrap (not regular) molasses for calcium. (The beans contribute calcium, too). Molasses can be concentrated in pesticides that were sprayed on the cane and chemical residues, so organic brands are a great option. (Barbados molasses and sorghum molasses are far less concentrated and have less than one-third the mineral content.)

Fortified Cereals

Cereals such as Nature's Path Optimum Slim and Kellogg's Vector contain calcium that has been added to the formulation.

Foods Falsely Assumed to Be Calcium-Rich

Soy yogourt, cheese substitutes, and soy ice creams are often thought to provide similar amounts of calcium as their dairy counterparts, but they are generally much lower in calcium. Check labels. Some new soy yogurts contain added calcium.

Estimated Absorbable Calcium

Dr. Connie Weaver of Purdue University and others have done excellent studies that give us an idea of how much calcium we can absorb from an assortment of plant foods (Table 4.5). Research of this type has not been done on all the plant sources of calcium available to us; however, it is clear that we can readily absorb calcium from many foods, not just from dairy products.

TABLE 4.5 *Calcium from Foods, Estimated Absorption*

Food	Calcium (mg)	Percentage Absorption*	Estimated Absorbable Calcium (mg)
Beans and Products			
Tofu with calcium, 125 mL (H cup)	258	31%	80
White beans, cooked, 125 mL (H cup)	113	22%	25
Pinto beans, 125 mL (H cup)	45	27%	12
Red beans, 125 mL (H cup)	41	24%	10
Fortified Beverage			
Fruit punch with calcium citrate malate, 250 mL (1 cup)	300	52%	156
Low-Oxalate Greens			
Bok choy, cooked, 125 mL (H cup)	79	53%	42
Broccoli, cooked, 125 mL (H cup)	35	61%	21
Chinese cabbage flower leaves, cooked, 125 mL (H cup)	239	40%	95
Chinese mustard greens, cooked, 125 mL (H cup)	212	40%	85
Kale, cooked, 125 mL (H cup)	61	49%	30
Mustard greens, cooked, 125 mL (H c)	64	58%	37
Turnip greens, cooked, 125 mL (H cup)	99	52%	51
High-Oxalate Foods			
Chinese spinach, cooked, 125 mL (H c)	347	8%	29
Spinach, cooked, 125 mL (H cup)	115	5%	6
Rhubarb, cooked, 125 mL (H cup)	174	8.5%	15
Nuts and Seeds			
Almonds, dry roasted, 30 g (1 oz)	80	21%	18
Sesame seeds, without hulls, 30 g (1 oz)	37	21%	8
Dairy Products			
Cow's milk, 250 mL (1 cup)	300	32%	96
Cheddar cheese, 42 g (1.5 oz)	303	32%	97
Dairy yogourt, 250 mL (1 cup)	300	32%	96

* Note that absorption varies with serving size, and from one crop to another.

Calcium in Our Menus

It is clear from tables 4.4 and 4.5 that we have *many* options when it comes to calcium-rich foods. Here are amounts of this mineral provided by the four menus in the protein section of the last chapter (page 88). As we move from #1 to #4, there is more reliance on the plant sources of calcium. In Menu #1, 80 per cent of the calcium comes from dairy products, and little use is made of non-dairy sources of calcium. In Menu #2, 66 per cent comes from dairy products, and Whole Grain Pudding (recipe on page 387), green salad and breads add a little. If 175 millilitres (I cup) of calcium-fortified orange juice were used instead of the regular variety, that would increase the calcium by 205 milligrams, bringing the total in the 2,000-calorie menu up to 1,036 milligrams. Menu #3 contains 265 milligrams of calcium from dairy products, just over one-quarter of the day's total. All calcium in Menu #4 comes from plant foods; the range depends on the type of tofu chosen. Some brands are extremely high in calcium, and the Hot Tofu with Cool Greens recipe (page 414) gives a hefty serving of tofu. In addition, 480 milligrams come from other calcium sources.

TABLE 4.6 *Calcium in 2,000-Calorie and 2,800-Calorie Menus*

Menu and Page	Calories	Calcium (mg)	Calories	Calcium (mg)
#1 Nonvegetarian, page 88	2,000	839	2,800	1,098
#2 Lacto-ovo Vegetarian, page 91	2,000	827	2,800	1,177
#3 Lacto-ovo Vegetarian with More Legumes, page 92	2,000	1047	2,800	1,239
#4 Vegan, page 94	2,000	768–1,707	2,800	964–1,913

Boosting Calcium from Dawn to Dusk

Here are some ways we can increase our calcium intakes at meals and snacks throughout the day.

Breakfast

• Cook porridge in fortified soy, rice, or cow's milk instead of water.

• Spread toast with almond butter or tahini, and a thin layer of blackstrap molasses.

• Add fortified soy, rice, or cow's milk to a smoothie.

• Choose the calcium-fortified variety of orange juice.

• Scramble some tofu (the type made with calcium).

• Munch on Marvellous Morning Muesli (page 386).

• Top fruit salad with yogourt and granola.

• Use blackstrap molasses as the sweetener in muffins, on porridge, and on toast.

• Add milk powder (fortified soy or cow's) to muffins, pancakes, waffles, or porridge.

Lunch

• Make a sandwich of marinated tofu or Angelic Tofu Sandwich Filling (page 396), using the calcium-rich kind of tofu.

• Pack raw broccoli florets along with the carrot sticks.

• Eat your vegetables with hummus or a yogourt-based dip.

• Bring a thermos of black or white bean soup.

• Use fortified soymilk or cow's milk in cream soups.

• Make a salad with calcium-rich greens, and top with marinated tofu and toasted almonds.

Supper

- Make a huge marinated salad with broccoli, many other vegetables, edamame (fresh green soybeans), and white or black beans.

- Use calcium-set tofu, a variety of Chinese greens, and toasted almonds in a stir-fry.

- Dine on Hot Tofu with Cool Greens (page 414).

- Add white or black beans to stews and chili.

- Turn World's Greatest Greens into a family favourite (page 403).

- Enjoy the Go-for-the-Green Salad (page 405).

- Serve yogourt or puddings made with fortified soy or rice milk, or cow's milk for dessert.

Snacks and Desserts

- Keep a bag of dried figs and almonds in your glove compartment, desk drawer, or backpack.

- Spread a bagel or bread with almond butter.

- Snack on soy nuts or edamame (green soybeans in the shell).

- Use calcium-rich ingredients such as tahini, blackstrap molasses, fortified soymilk, or cow's milk, almonds, and almond butter in making treats such as cookies, squares, or muffins.

- Freeze yogourt in popsicle trays to make frozen yogourt treats.

- Eat the whole German Chocolate Cake (recipe, page 427). Just kidding!

Beverages

- Combine 250 millilitres (1 cup) of calcium-fortified orange juice, 115 grams (4 ounces) of calcium-set tofu, and a ripe banana to make a smoothie.

- Drink calcium-fortified soymilk, rice milk, or cow's milk as a cold beverage or in cocoa.

What About Supplements?

The diets of many people fall short of recommended intakes for calcium, and supplements can help to assure that our needs are met.
U.S. surveys show one in five adults take a supplement that contains
calcium and one in four takes a supplement that contains vitamin
D. The amount of calcium in a multivitamin-mineral supplement
is often about 150 milligrams, which may be enough. (Adding as
much as 1,000 milligrams of calcium to a tablet would make it very
bulky. Chewable multivitamin-mineral supplements can be a little
larger, and may contain as much as 250 milligrams of calcium.) If
we're using a "single mineral" supplement, such as calcium with
vitamin D, the directions may suggest that we take several tablets
for the day's recommended intake, but this much is not likely necessary as our diet can provide most of our calcium needs. The proportion we absorb is much less from amounts above 500 milligrams.
If you take more than one tablet in a day, or use a liquid form, note
that several small doses of calcium are absorbed much more efficiently than the same total amount, taken all at once.

What Kind of Calcium Supplement?

Research on the absorption of different forms of calcium shows as
many differing results as there are studies. Should you get calcium carbonate, calcium citrate, calcium-citrate-malate, or chelates?
In truth, these are all well absorbed, and differences are relatively
small as long as the pill breaks up and doesn't just pass through
your system. (Vegetarians should be aware that hydroxyapatite is
made from the bones of cows, and that oyster shell supplements
are really made from oyster shells!) Physical response to various
formulations may be personal. Some people find that calcium carbonate causes constipation; others find it relaxing when taken
before bedtime. What can make a difference to your overall bone
health (and health in general) is to make sure you have a source of
vitamin D (sun or supplement) to help absorb calcium and an
assortment of trace minerals: boron, vanadium, fluoride, and others. Vegetarians generally don't need much in the way of added
magnesium, as plant foods are high in this mineral—it is a part of
the green pigment chlorophyll.

What About Mineral Interactions?

High calcium intakes can interfere with iron absorption, so if you're short of iron, it's best to take a high-dosage calcium supplement separately from iron-containing supplements and from iron-rich meals. This is because minerals can compete, and calcium could hinder iron absorption. The lower amounts of calcium in a multivitamin-mineral supplement are closer to amounts in a typical meal, and at these levels, minerals are well absorbed.

Building a Strong Defence Against Osteoporosis

North American rates of osteoporosis are among the highest in the world. One in four Canadian women and one in eight men over the age of fifty has osteoporosis. Because women have slightly smaller bones than men, their risk of fracture is higher. Our best protection is to build up to a good bone density early in life, and then maintain what we have with adequate nutrition and exercise. Studies have shown that even in our later years, we can increase bone density and even repair some osteoporotic damage. Exactly how do we do this? Is the solution calcium, calcium, and more calcium?

Myth : Getting enough calcium ensures strong bones.

If we trust advertising, we may get the impression that the way to avoid osteoporosis is to load up on calcium. However, relying on just that one mineral to prevent osteoporosis is like trying to play baseball with only a pitcher on your team. In truth, we need other team members on bases, behind the plate, and in key spots out in the field. Bone health involves a similar team of players, including calcium, vitamin D, protein, magnesium, boron, copper, zinc, manganese, fluoride, and vitamins K, C, B12, B6, and folic acid. Physical activity, which is so vital, would no doubt take the position of "team coach." Bone health is a complex interplay of many lifestyle factors. Thousands of milligrams of calcium will not do us much good if our diet is generally unbalanced, and if we ignore commonsense rules of healthy living.

Here are a few examples of roles played by the members of the bone team. Vitamin C, found in fruits and vegetables, helps build cross-links between molecules of collagen, a protein in bone. Vitamin K, from leafy greens, binds calcium to three types of protein that make up bone structure. Boron, a mineral in apples and other fruits, flaxseeds, nuts, vegetables, and legumes, plays a role in preventing calcium loss and seems to support the action of vitamin D.

Vitamin D for Dull Days

When we expose our hands or face to warm sunlight, even for just a few minutes, our skin cells form vitamin D. Vitamin D is also added to two types of foods: milks (fortified soy, rice, and dairy) and margarine. These two very different sources—sunlight and fortified foods, or supplements—are how we get vitamin D, which we must have.

The importance of sunlight to the sturdiness of the skeleton was referred to even in ancient times. More recently, folk wisdom recognized the importance of time spent in the sun, especially for children. In the twentieth century, we found that certain ultraviolet rays in sunlight would help our bodies create vitamin D. It was also discovered that vitamin D could be taken orally, in foods or supplements, and that both sources were equally effective treatments for a once common disease called rickets.

The Role of Vitamin D in the Body

Vitamin D is essential for the proper formation of the skeleton. If we have too little vitamin D, the skeleton will be inadequately mineralized, leading to a condition called rickets in children and osteomalacia in adults. One of the best-known roles of vitamin D is to maintain blood calcium at exactly the right level. It does this by regulating the movements of calcium in three places: absorption in the intestine, losses through the urine, and storage in the bones. Vitamin D also affects the process of cell division in a manner that may protect against cancer.

Rickets: The First Air Pollution Disease

In past, sunlight was the major provider of vitamin D for most of the world's population, as it still is for many people. For those who ventured to northern regions where there was little ultraviolet light in winter months, fish liver oils were a lifesaver, centuries before their vitamin D content was identified.

With the Industrial Revolution, things changed. From the seventeenth to the early twentieth century, rickets plagued children who played in narrow, dark city streets, or who worked indoors. Very little sunlight made its way through the coal smoke from factories and down between closely packed buildings. In 1900, four out of five children in some smoggy urban areas of North America and Europe had rickets, a crippling disease that resulted in bowed legs, knock knees, and misshapen skeletons. These children grew, yet with insufficient vitamin D, their bones did not adequately mineralize or harden. Instead of being strong and straight, their legs bent in inward or outward arcs under the weight of the body.

By 1925, scientists had recognized the effectiveness of both sunlight and the vitamin from fish liver oil in preventing and treating rickets. Across North America in the 1930s, cow's milk was chosen as a vehicle to distribute vitamin D to the entire population and to children in particular. This public health measure proved to be tremendously effective. With mandatory fortification of cow's milk, along with nutrition education that promoted milk-drinking, rickets became a rarity. With time, several other ways to deliver vitamin D through the food supply have been added, including fortified soymilk, rice milk, and margarine.

A few cases of rickets continue to be reported in hospitals across Canada and in many American cities. Each year, the Toronto Hospital for Sick Children may see three or four children with rickets. Typically, these toddlers are under three years of age and have not received vitamin D in a supplement or fortified beverage. Often they are children with darker skin, meaning that they require somewhat more sun exposure to develop vitamin D. In Manitoba and at many northern latitudes, some children with darker skin are more susceptible to rickets. Occasional cases have occurred with vegan children, especially before the vitamin D fortification of soymilk was permitted in Canada in 1997, and with macrobiotic children if their parents are opposed to the use of supplements.

The Sunshine Vitamin

People who are regularly exposed to adequate amounts of sunlight do not need vitamin D from foods or supplements. When our skin is exposed to ultraviolet light, we can make vitamin D out of a cholesterol compound that is naturally present in the skin. These ultraviolet light rays don't pass through glass, so we can't get the beneficial effects of sunlight through a window. To determine whether an individual is getting enough sun for adequate vitamin D production, a number of factors must be taken into consideration.

Age

As we age, the capacity of our skin to produce vitamin D drops to 25–50 per cent that of young adults, yet we continue to need the vitamin to help us absorb and use calcium, and to ward off osteoporosis. Thus, supplements and fortified foods, in addition to some sun exposure, can become important in our later years.

Skin Colour

People with dark skin require substantially more exposure to sunlight for vitamin D production. Whereas light-skinned people need ten to fifteen minutes of sunlight a day on the face, hands, and forearms, people with increasingly darker skin need from thirty minutes to three hours daily. The melanin pigment in dark skin absorbs some of the ultraviolet radiation. This appears to be a protective adaptation developed by people in sunny climates. It has been suggested that over the evolution of humankind, as people moved to northern latitudes, skin pigmentation decreased to allow for adequate production of vitamin D. Have you ever wondered about those blond, light-skinned Scandinavians in the North and the darker-skinned people close to the Equator? These differences probably developed partly because of our need for vitamin D!

Use of Sunscreen

Sunscreen protection factors (SPF) of 8 and above will prevent vitamin D synthesis. Note that most people apply far less sunscreen than manufacturers recommend, so the blocking effect may be only partial. Our need for vitamin D must be balanced with the obvious need for protection from overexposure to the sun, especially during the hot hours of the day. For vitamin D synthesis, mid-morning to late afternoon sun is fine.

Amount of Clothing Worn

Vitamin D production varies with the amount of clothing worn and the total surface area of skin exposed. For example, the attire of some Middle Eastern women covers the head and face, preventing vitamin D production. The elderly tend to cover more of their skin with clothing. The people on "Baywatch" likely get their vitamin D supply in a minute or so!

Sunlamps

Sunlamps can be used to produce vitamin D in the skin. Like overexposure to sunlight, sunlamps can cause skin damage, so use caution or controlled ultraviolet light chambers.

Time of Year and Geographical Location

Vitamin D production in skin differs seasonally and according to the latitude at which we live, as these factors affect the amount of ultraviolet radiation. On a cloudy summer day, even the "skyshine" will stimulate some vitamin D production. It has been estimated that the amount of ultraviolet radiation received even on sunny days in winter is sixteen times less than in summer. At latitudes above 40 degrees north (and in the southern hemisphere at latitudes above 40 degrees south), we experience "vitamin D winter." In other words, for three or four months, little or no vitamin D production occurs in skin. "Vitamin D winter" is longer the closer we get to the poles. In Los Angeles (34 degrees north) there is no vitamin D winter, while in Boston (42 degrees north) people do not produce vitamin D between November and February. Vitamin D winter lasts longer still, from about October to March, in Edmonton (52 degrees north).

We have the ability to store vitamin D, so to a certain extent we can get more sun in the summer and less in the winter. For populations living along the forty-ninth parallel, adults can expect their serum levels of the vitamin to drop to the lower end of the normal range, or even below, during winter months. Many of us will fare better with a supplement added to whatever sun exposure we get while taking out the trash or walking a few blocks. Infants and children have limited vitamin D reserves, so they need a supplement or fortified food source at latitudes in Canada and in the northern states.

In young men who remained in a submarine for three months with no vitamin D-fortified foods or supplements, serum vitamin D dropped to less than two-thirds of normal levels after a month and a half. Levels shot back up again when they returned to the surface and were able to get regular sun exposure for a month. This situation has relevance for older and younger people who are institutionalized, bedridden, or who remain indoors for some other reason.

As you might have guessed, making a recommendation for the minimum sunlight exposure necessary for vitamin D production can be complicated by all of the above factors. However, the following guidelines will help you meet your vitamin D needs.

Getting Enough Vitamin D from Sun Exposure

A general guideline for North Americans is an average of ten to fifteen minutes of sun daily, mid-morning to late afternoon, on the face and hands, for light-skinned people. Darker-skinned people need more (thirty minutes to three hours daily, depending on skin colour). At the same time, we need to take care to avoid overexposure, which can increase risk of skin cancer; moderate sun exposure seems the wisest course.

In Canada, infants and children cannot depend on adequate skin exposure to sunlight for vitamin D synthesis due to our northern latitudes, especially between November and March.

Researchers found that a total of three hours of sun exposure per week improved calcium balance in a group of elderly people (whose average age was eighty-three years) in Stockholm, which is at a latitude of 59 degrees.

There are many circumstances in which our exposure to ultraviolet light is insufficient for optimal production of vitamin D. We cover ourselves with clothing, stay indoors, live in smoggy cities amid tall buildings that shield us from sunlight, use sunscreens that block ultraviolet rays, and live in geographical regions that do not receive adequate sunlight. Thus, dietary sources of the vitamin become important, particularly true during winter months. We can choose sunlight, fortified foods, supplements, or a combination.

Recommended Intakes from Foods or Supplements

Guidelines set in 1998 advise that if we do not have adequate exposure to sunlight, our intake should be 5 micrograms of vitamin D per day up to the age of fifty-one, and then double that amount until the age of seventy-one when it increases again. Requirements increase as we get older because our skin production drops. Vitamin D supplementation has proven to be effective in preventing bone loss and is deemed especially necessary after seventy years of age.

Amounts are stated in micrograms (also listed as mcg or μ), and as international units or IU (1 mcg is equivalent to 40 IU). Labels on supplements may list vitamin D in either way.

TABLE 4.7 *Recommended Vitamin D Intakes*

Age	Vitamin D3 (mcg)	Vitamin D3 (IU)
Birth–50	5 mcg	200 IU
51–70	10 mcg	400 IU
71 and over	15 mcg	600 IU

Forms of Vitamin D

There are two forms of vitamin D, vitamin D2 (ergocalciferol, generally made from yeast) and vitamin D3 (cholecalciferol, from the skins of sheep, cows, and pigs, and from sheep's wool). Our bodies can use either form.

Researchers have found vitamin D2 to be about 60 per cent as effective as vitamin D3 in raising serum vitamin D levels. It makes sense for vegetarians, who prefer to use the form that is not of animal origin (vitamin D2), to increase their intakes accordingly (multiply by 1.7). This means our intake up to fifty years of age will be 8.5 micrograms of vitamin D2; from fifty-one to seventy years will be 17 micrograms, and after the age of seventy will be 25.5 micrograms.

D-Bulletin for Babies

All breast-fed babies and toddlers should receive vitamin D drops. These are available at pharmacies, sometimes behind the counter so that you must ask for them. The recommended dose is 200 international units (IU) per day. If you have questions about how to measure the dose, ask a community health nurse or pharmacist. It should be given just before or after a feeding. Keep giving the vitamin D drops until your toddler is drinking 500 millilitres (2 cups) of infant formula or fortified soymilk or whole cow's milk every day. Five hundred millilitres (2 cups) of any of these contain a suitable amount of vitamin D. (Breast milk generally cannot be relied on as a source.)

Your breast-fed infant especially needs vitamin D drops if, while pregnant, you did not get vitamin D from fortified cow's milk or soy milk, or from a prenatal supplement, or if you wore sunscreen whenever you were outside. Vitamin D is also especially important for babies born in spring and early summer, born early or with a birth weight less than 1,500 grams (53 ounces). Our youngsters don't get a chance to make vitamin D from sunlight during the wintertime, or when faces and hands are covered with scarves, gloves, pram covers, or sunscreen. If our skin, or that of our baby, has lots of skin pigmentation (dark skin), we require longer sun exposure to make vitamin D.

Your baby's skin production of vitamin D is good when his or her uncovered hands and face, with no sunscreen, are exposed to ten minutes of sunlight a day between the months of April and September (with darker skin, allow more time). For skin safety, avoid the sun between 11 AM and 3 PM.

Beware of Excess Vitamin D

Whereas a little vitamin D is a good thing, too much is toxic. Three to five times the recommended intake of vitamin D over an extended period can cause hypercalcemia (too much calcium in the blood). This is a serious condition in which calcium is deposited in soft tissues, resulting in possible heart and kidney damage. An upper limit has been set, and that is 25 micrograms of vitamin D per day for infants up to one year of age and 50 micrograms after that. Care must be taken not to leave supplements within the reach of infants and children. Getting too much sunlight will not lead to vitamin D toxicity, though it can result in a sunburn.

Natural Sources of Vitamin D

For those growing up in the mid-twentieth century, doses of cod-liver oil were a daily feature of childhood—though the practice never gained popularity among the children involved.

The livers of oily fish, particularly cod and halibut, are among the few food items that are naturally high in this vitamin. The skins of animals (sheep, pigs, and cows) contain vitamin D3. As in humans, their skin is a production centre for the vitamin, and vitamin D3 extracted from skins and wool is used to fortify cow's milk and margarine. Eggs provide small amounts of vitamin D if the chickens have been fed a high-vitamin D diet. Vitamin D is present in a few plants; however, we do not rely on these as food sources. When exposed to ultraviolet light, certain seaweeds, mushrooms, and yeasts can produce a form of vitamin D (vitamin D2). Yeast, irradiated by light, is the source of the vitamin D2 in many vegetarian foods and supplements.

Our Current Sources of Vitamin D

North Americans generally get vitamin D from sunlight, fortified foods, and supplements.

Food sources include fortified soymilk, rice milk, and cow's milk, margarines, and infant formula. Among non-dairy beverages, some use the word "enriched," others "fortified," and some say "Plus" or "Extra" on the label. Because excess vitamin D can be toxic, the range of foods that are allowed to add vitamin D is limited by legislation.

TABLE 4.8   *Vitamin D in Foods*

Food and Amount	Vitamin D (mcg)
Beverages	
Fortified cow's milk	2.5
Enriched Soy Dream or Rice Dream, 250 mL (1 cup)	2.5
Fortified So Nice, Silk or Westsoy Plus, 250 mL (1 cup)	2.5
Vitasoy Enriched, 250 mL (1 cup)	2
Edensoy Extra, 250 mL (1 cup)	1
Breakfast Cereals	
Vector cereal, 250 mL (1 cup)	0.5
Fats	
Fortified Margarine, 5 mL (1 tsp)	0.5–0.75
For Comparison	
Cod-liver oil, 5 mL (1 tsp)	11

Riboflavin

There has been occasional concern that plant-based diets could be low in riboflavin, a vitamin also known as vitamin B2. This is because one half of North American intakes typically come from dairy products, and meat, poultry, fish, and eggs are also important contributors. Yet there are good riboflavin sources in the plant world. Grains, both whole and enriched, provide about 30 per cent of riboflavin intakes. Leafy greens also contain riboflavin, and there are other food sources in Table 4.9.

Like other B-vitamins, riboflavin is involved with energy metabolism and is active in every cell in the body. It also helps to maintain body tissues, including skin, and mucous membranes such as those in the mouth and eyes. Riboflavin deficiencies, although rare, show up as cracks at the corner of the mouth and changes in the tongue and mucous membranes of the mouth. It is a fluorescent yellow vitamin that often shows up in the urine after we take a multivitamin supplement. (That's the extra we didn't need!) Apart from the bright yellow urine, extra riboflavin doesn't seem to cause any problems.

A few studies have shown vegetarian (or vegan) intakes of riboflavin to be low or borderline. This is both surprising and unnecessary because riboflavin is plentiful in many plant foods. Table 4.9 shows several foods that provide 15 per cent or more of the daily recommended intake.

TABLE 4.9 *Riboflavin in Foods*

Food	Riboflavin (mg)
Almonds, 60 mL (G cup)	0.3
Avocado, 1 medium	0.2
Beans, assorted, 250 mL (1 cup)	0.1–0.2
Cereal, ready-to-eat, fortified, 30 g (1 oz)	0.2–0.3
Cow's milk, whole, 2% or skim, 125 mL (H cup)	0.2
Egg, large, 1 (50 g/1.75 oz)	0.6
Fortified instant oatmeal, 1 packet	0.3
Lotus root, 10 slices, 81 g (3 oz)	0.2
Marmite or Vegemite yeast spread, 5 mL (1 tsp)	0.7
Mushrooms, raw or cooked, 125 mL (H cup)	0.2
Nutritional yeast mini-flakes, 15 mL (1 tbsp)	1.9
Soymilk, fortified, 125 mL (H cup)	0.2
Spinach, cooked 125 mL (H cup)	0.2
Sweet potato, 125 mL (H cup)	0.2
Yogourt, 125 mL (H cup)	0.2

Note: Foods providing smaller amounts of riboflavin (0.1 milligrams of riboflavin per serving) include alfalfa sprouts, asparagus, bananas, broccoli, figs, kale, lentils and their sprouts, mung bean sprouts, peas, raspberries, seeds, sesame tahini, tofu, tempeh, wheat germ, and whole grain bread, and enriched bread and pasta.

Recommended Intakes of Riboflavin

Recommended intakes are 1.1 milligrams for women and 1.3 milligrams for men. Canadian and American vegetarians and nonvegetarians generally get about one and a half times the recommended daily intakes. Although some research suggests that vegans consume slightly less, they are still well within recommended levels.

Amounts in Menus

Menus #1 and #2 in Chapter 3 (pages 88, 91) each provide about one and a half times the recommended intake of riboflavin. Menus #3 and #4 provide more than twice the recommended intake, with a big boost from nutritional yeast in the Liquid Gold Dressing and in the Hot Tofu with Cool Greens (see recipe section). To raise your riboflavin intake also try the Scrambled Tofu (page 389). In a vegan diet, one-third of the riboflavin may come from vegetables and fruits, a quarter from legumes, nuts, and seeds, and the rest from grains. Vegans often include good sources that are not commonly used by nonvegetarians, such as nutritional yeast, yeast extracts, spreads like Marmite and Vegemite, wheat germ, and sprouts. A desire to meet riboflavin intakes may inspire us to try a few new foods!

We'll easily meet recommended intakes by including a variety of riboflavin-rich foods and by following the Vegetarian Food Guide (page 241).

Steps for Strong Bones

This chapter has focused on the many ways to meet our need for the nutrients needed to build and maintain strong bones. There is little evidence that bone mineral density differs between Western nonvegetarians and lacto-ovo vegetarians, though the latter may have some advantages. There have been too few lifelong vegans, and the diets in use have undergone so much transition as new products came on the market, so it's hard to give reliable data on the bone health of North American vegans, especially those using calcium-fortified beverages and soyfoods. Studies suggest that bone health is poorer among vegan women with marginal protein and calorie intakes (perhaps due to continual "dieting"). Since we require vitamin D for calcium absorption, adequate intakes of this vitamin D are essential. Certain features of vegetarian diets may help to maximize bone health, such as higher intakes of magnesium, potassium, and vitamin K. We have evidence that soy protein, rich in isoflavones, can help post-menopausal women retain bone in their spinal column.

Here are ten tips for strong bones:

1. **Follow the Vegetarian Food Guide.** Learn which foods are in the "Milks and Alternates" group.

2. **Eat dark green vegetables daily.** Include broccoli, kale, collards, bok choy, and Chinese cabbage on your regular shopping list. Find an Asian grocery store, grow greens in your garden or on your balcony, or arrange for these to be delivered weekly to your door. Learn delicious ways to prepare greens. Some minerals (and vitamins) are lost in the cooking water, so steam vegetables or use the mineral-rich cooking water in soups or in grain preparation.

3. **Use calcium-set tofu.** For those people who haven't tried tofu, realize that, like flour, it is an ingredient. You wouldn't want to eat a bowl of flour, though you may love many baked goods. Tofu is unusually versatile; it can be made into everything from soup to dessert, so it can be used often without your menus becoming repetitious.

4. **Take advantage of the calcium-fortified beverages.** Fortified non-dairy milks and juices can can help raise your total calcium intake to recommended levels.

5. **Make almonds, almond butter, sesame tahini, and blackstrap molasses a part of your meals and snacks.** Every time you replace 30 millilitres (2 tablespoons) of peanut butter with an equal amount of almond butter, you increase your calcium intake by 73 milligrams. By replacing 15 millilitres (1 tablespoon) of jam with the equivalent of molasses, you gain a surprising 168 milligrams of calcium. These wonderfully flavourful options not only provide a boost in calcium, but add iron and zinc as well!

6. **Don't keep company with the calcium thieves.** Avoid high intakes of salt, alcohol, and caffeine, excessive amounts of animal protein, and a sedentary lifestyle.

7. **When you go out for dinner, frequent Japanese, Chinese, Middle Eastern, and vegetarian restaurants.** These cuisines do a masterful job of teaching us about the many wonderful sources of calcium that are seldom recognized in the Western world. You may learn delicious ways to use sea vegetables, such as hijiki, in stir-fries and soups. You'll discover flavourful dishes made with tofu, greens, beans, and tahini.

8. **Build strong bones during the growing years.** Emphasize a broad spectrum of calcium-rich foods, along with a balanced, varied diet for children. Infants need breast milk or commercial infant formula; as children get older, they can switch to fortified soymilk or cow's milk (see Chapter 10).

9. **Add some sunshine to your day.** Take the opportunity to stretch your legs and walk around the block on your lunch break. You'll not only feel good, but ten minutes (for Caucasians) to thirty minutes (for dark-skinned people) of sunlight helps achieve your vitamin D quota for the day.

10. **Exercise!** Walking, jogging, dancing, ballgames, hiking, step exercises, or other weight-bearing exercise is essential for lifelong bone health. Even in the elderly, these activities strengthen bones. With bones, it's a case of use 'em or lose 'em.

A complete set of references is available online at:
http://www.nutrispeak.com/bvreferences.htm

energy plus
goodness from grains

When you hear the word "grains" what comes to mind? Perhaps you imagine fields of golden wheat, freshly baked bread, steamed rice, or piping hot porridge. Most people regard grains as healthful foods, the kind that sticks to your ribs. Governments and health authorities encourage the use of grains as staples in the diet. Grains have been awarded prime positions in food guides around the world. In Canada, grains occupy the largest arc of the rainbow; in the United States and the Philippines, they form the foundation of the pyramid; in Germany they claim the largest wedge of a dinner plate; in Australia they are featured as the biggest section of a circle; and in China and Korea they serve as the base of the pagoda. Yet, despite all the positive press grains have received from health authorities, many of the most popular diet books on the market urge consumers to cut grains and other carbohydrate-rich foods, claiming that they are the root of almost every disease that plagues the Western world. All of this leaves consumers wondering whether grains are truly friend or foe. This chapter explores the myths and realities regarding grains as food staples, and provides practical tools to help us select the kind of grains that best support health.

What Are Grains?

Grains or "cereal grains" are the seeds of a specific group of grasses. Worldwide, the grains people most commonly use are varieties selected for cultivation because of their high yields. These include wheat, spelt, kamut, oats, corn, rye, rice, millet, triticale, Job's tears (barley), sorghum, and teff. While sweet corn is eaten fresh as a vegetable, all varieties of corn are technically grains. Two common, highly nutritious seeds, quinoa and amaranth, are often mistakenly classified as cereal grains. However, they actually come from non-grass species, thus are sometimes referred to as "pseudocereal." Quinoa is a member of the "goosefoot family," along with common lambsquarters, beets, chard, and spinach. Amaranth is in the "amaranth family" along with pigweed. Buckwheat, also incorrectly thought of as a cereal grain, is a member of the "buckwheat family," as is rhubarb. While quinoa, amaranth, and buckwheat are not grains in the true sense, we will include them as such for practical purposes, as that is how they are used.

There are three parts to any grain: the bran (outer layer containing most of the fibre), the germ (core containing much of the protein, vitamins, minerals, and fat), and the endosperm (large middle mass, which is mainly pure starch). Intact grains are also known

FIGURE 5.1   *Picture of a wheat kernal*

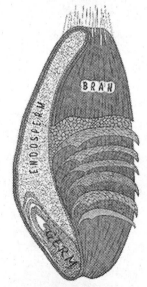

as "whole grains." The whole grain can be rolled (e.g., rolled oats), cut (e.g., cracked wheat), or ground into flour (e.g., whole wheat or whole rye flour) for use in "whole grain" breads, cereals, pasta, and other prepared products.

Are "Whole Grains" Nutritious Foods?

Absolutely—whole grains are little nutrition powerhouses. They are excellent sources of carbohydrates and a number of valuable vitamins and minerals, including many B-vitamins, vitamin E, selenium, zinc, copper, magnesium, manganese, iron, potassium, and chromium. They are also great sources of fibre, plant sterols, and numerous phytochemicals such as phenolic compounds and, in some cases, phytoestrogens.

Nutritional Composition of Whole Grains

The nutritional composition of whole grains is noteworthy. The following list, while it does not cover each and every nutrient found in whole grains, gives us a clear picture of their goodness. For the vitamins and minerals listed, the contribution provided by six servings of whole grains is given, relative to our daily needs. The six grains included in the analysis are a mix of those commonly selected. They include three servings of whole wheat products, and one serving each of oats, barley, and brown rice. The products selected for our analysis are not fortified with additional nutrients. Quinoa and amaranth were not included in this particular analysis as they are less commonly chosen. However, their nutrient makeup is even more impressive than that of true grains.

Energy-Giving Nutrients

Protein. The contribution made by grains to the world's protein intake is far higher than most people imagine. Close to 50 per cent of our protein comes from grains. Typically 10–15 per cent of the calories in grains are provided by protein, although it is even higher for some. While grains are low in lysine relative to the ideal pattern for humans, normal combinations of plant foods easily balance this out, and their contribution to total amino acid intakes is very significant. Quinoa and amaranth provide about twice as much lysine as true cereal grains.

Fat. Grains are low in fat, with about 5–15 per cent of total calories coming from fat. Most of this is polyunsaturated, from the omega-6 family. Levels of saturated and monounsaturated fats are generally under 20 per cent each of total fat content.

Carbohydrates. Approximately 70–85 per cent of the calories in grains come from carbohydrates; making grains the world's most important source of food energy. For many years carbohydrates were divided into two categories: *simple carbohydrates* (single sugars or two sugars bound together) and *complex carbohydrates* (starches and fibre made of chains of many sugars). Traditionally, this division was used to distinguish unhealthy carbohydrates (simple sugars such as white sugar, brown sugar, and other concentrated sweets) from healthy carbohydrates (starches and fibre found in whole plant foods such as grains and beans). However, these terms are becoming obsolete as we recognize that many foods rich in simple carbohydrates can be very healthy, while others rich in complex carbohydrates can be quite unhealthy. For example, super-healthy vegetables and fruits, such as red peppers and blueberries, are generally low in starches and contain mostly "simple sugars." Other far less nourishing foods, such as potato chips and doughnuts, are high in "complex carbohydrates." Thus, rather than focusing on simple carbohydrates as "bad guys" and complex carbohydrates as "good guys," experts are now encouraging us to look at the whole food in terms of its overall nutritional value. Whole grains stand out as excellent carbohydrate sources, providing a wonderful balance of starches and fibre, in addition to many other nutrients and protective components.

Vitamins

Grains are valuable sources of several vitamins, including the B-vitamins, and vitamin E.

B-vitamins. Grains are a treasure trove of B-vitamins, including thiamin, riboflavin, niacin, vitamin B6, pantothenic acid, biotin, and folate. The only B-vitamin not present is vitamin B12. Although each has unique and varied functions, the B-vitamins work as a team to convert carbohydrates, protein, and fat to energy. They are also important for maintaining healthy skin, and for nervous and digestive function. In addition, folate is needed for building new cells, pantothenic acid for building synthesizing hemoglobin, and riboflavin for maintaining healthy vision. Relative to total B-vitamin requirements, consuming six servings of whole grains daily would provide about half of our thiamin, niacin, B6, and biotin, 25 per cent of our riboflavin and pantothenic acid, and 15 per cent of our folate.

Vitamin E. Although not our most concentrated sources of vitamin E (nuts, seeds, and oils are higher), grains do make a significant contribution. Vitamin E helps to stabilize cell membranes, and is a powerful antioxidant. Including six servings of whole grains provides approximately 10 per cent of our daily requirements. This figure would be considerably higher if we added wheat germ, which is where vitamin E is stored in wheat.

Minerals

Grains contribute to our intakes of many minerals, including some of the trace minerals that tend to be lacking in the diet.

Chromium. A valuable trace mineral, often low in today's highly processed diets, chromium is essential for the metabolism of sugar (glucose). It is also a component of glucose tolerance factor (GTF), a compound that works with insulin to move glucose into cells where it can be used to produce energy. Eating six servings of whole grains provides roughly 50–100 per cent of our daily chromium needs.

Copper. As a critical part of a number of body enzymes, copper plays a role in energy production, connective tissue formation, iron metabolism, as well as brain and nervous system function. Six servings of whole grains each day provide about half of our total copper needs. Quinoa and amaranth have about five to eight times more copper than true grains.

Iron. As an essential component of hundreds of proteins and enzymes, iron is necessary for oxygen transport and storage, electron transport, energy metabolism, and DNA synthesis. Whole grains provide a significant contribution to overall iron intake. Six servings a day provides about 6 milligrams of iron or about 20–40 per cent of recommended intakes for most vegetarian adults. Quinoa and amaranth are about four to six times more concentrated in iron than true grains.

Magnesium. Magnesium is necessary in more than 300 essential metabolic reactions, including energy production; synthesis of DNA, RNA, and glutathione (a potent antioxidant); and transport of ions such as potassium and calcium across cell membranes. It is also an integral part of the structure of bones, cell membranes, and chromosomes. Whole grains are an important source of magnesium, with six servings providing approximately one half of our daily requirements.

Manganese. Manganese is a constituent of some enzymes and an activator of others. It serves as an antioxidant to the mitochondria of cells, components highly susceptible to oxidative damage. Manganese is also important in the formation of healthy bones, cartilage, and collagen. Six servings of whole grains give us all the manganese we need for the day.

Potassium. Both an essential mineral and an electrolyte, potassium is indispensable to every cell in our body. It is the main positively charged ion in the fluid of cells; it is critical for nerve impulse transmission, muscle contractions, and every beat of your heart. Potassium is also required for the activity of certain enzymes important to carbohydrate metabolism. When we think of potassium, bananas and perhaps potatoes, or other vegetables and fruits generally spring to mind. Few people would imagine that whole grains are significant contributors to our potassium intakes, with six servings providing about 30 per cent of our daily needs.

Selenium. Selenium is required for the function of at least eleven selenium-dependent enzymes, also known as selenoproteins. Most of these function as powerful antioxidants, reducing potentially damaging free radicals. One selenoprotein is necessary for the activation of thyroid hormones, making selenium necessary for normal growth and development, while another plays a role in muscle metabolism. The selenium content of foods varies considerably, depending on the selenium content of the soil. The richest known plant sources of selenium are Brazil nuts, a single nut containing 110 micrograms, approximately double our daily requirement. Other rich sources include nuts, seeds, and grains. Vegetables and fruits generally contribute little selenium. Six servings of whole grains provide about 90 per cent of our daily selenium needs.

Zinc. The functions of zinc in the human body are numerous and varied. Zinc plays central roles in growth and development, the immune response, neurological function, and reproduction. Nearly 100 different enzymes are dependent on zinc for their function. Whole grains can contribute significantly to overall zinc intake, with 30–45 per cent of recommended intakes in six servings. (See Figure 5.1 on page 152.) Quinoa and amaranth provide about three to six times more zinc than true grains.

Other Protective Components

The value of whole grains does not end with the energy-giving nutrients, vitamins, and minerals. They also contain appreciable amounts of fibre, phytochemicals, and plant sterols. While not currently considered nutrients, these valuable components are found exclusively in plants.

Fibre. Required for the healthy functioning of the digestive system, fibre also helps to keep blood lipids and blood sugar under control (for more on fibre, see pages 164–170). Whole grains are important sources of fibre, with six servings providing about 12–20 grams, or about one-third to one half of the 30–50 grams recommended.

Phytochemicals. Whole grains, like all plant foods, provide a unique mix of phytochemicals, with a remarkable array of protective activities in people. Those most plentiful in grains include phenolic acids such as ferulic acid, p-coumaric acid, and caffeic acids

(which have antioxidant and anti-cancer activity), lignans (phytoestrogens that may cut risk of estrogen-related cancers), and
tocotrienols (forms of vitamin E with antioxidant activity).

Plant sterols. Another important group of health protectors in
grains are the plant sterols or "phytosterols." These compounds are
similar to cholesterol in structure, but they have remarkably different effects on the body. Plant sterols appear to compete with dietary
cholesterol, reducing its absorption from the gut. Studies suggest
that sterols can reduce our blood cholesterol levels; improve blood
sugar control; inhibit breast, prostate, and colon cancer cell growth;
and reduce inflammation.

The Great Grain Robbery

Many people marvel at the rich and diverse nutrient contributions
of grains. The obvious question that arises is: If grains are so full of
goodness, why are they so viciously maligned? The sad truth is that
we humans do something that defies logic: before eating grains we
generally refine them to get rid of their two most nutrition-packed
parts—the bran and the germ. What is left is endosperm, otherwise
known as starch. To make matters worse, we often further undermine their value by adding damaging components such as hydrogenated fats, sugar, and salt. Not surprisingly, in this transformation,
grains shift from being health promoters to potentially damaging
foods. Figure 5.1 helps to quantify the magnitude of this nutritional loss.

FIGURE 5.2 *Percent of Nutrients Lost in White Flour Compared to Whole Wheat Flour.*

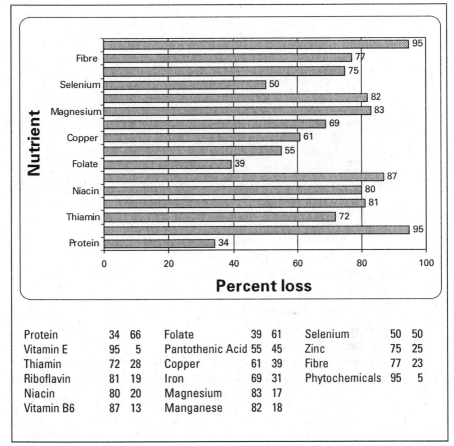

As you can see, the losses (grey area) are staggering. Gone are approximately 95 per cent of the phytochemicals, 80 per cent of the fibre, and 70 per cent of the vitamins and minerals. Sometimes several nutrients are added back to white flour in an effort to prevent nutritional deficiency diseases. This process is called enrichment, and the laws regarding this practice vary tremendously from country to country. While some governments prohibit the addition of nutrients to refined flour, the majority allow for voluntary enrichment. Canada's legislation makes the enrichment of white flour mandatory. The Canadian government requires all refined white flour to have thiamin, riboflavin, niacin, and iron added back. It also allows for the voluntary addition of folate, pantothenic acid, vitamin B6, and magnesium, though the latter three are seldom present. While these regulations help to compensate for some losses of a small portion of the nutrients in Figure 5.1, they seem like a drop in the bucket when compared to the wide array of vitamins, minerals, fibre, and phytochemicals originally present in the whole grain.

Unfortunately, close to 95 per cent of all grains in the North American diet are eaten as refined grains, which leave a scant 5 per cent of total grain intake as whole grains. These refined grains (usually white flour) used to produce many favourite foods: bread, pasta, cereals, crackers, pretzels, cookies, and other baked goods. There is substantial evidence to suggest that this reliance on refined grains as dietary staple has significant negative repercussions for health.

Do Whole Grains Provide Protection Against Disease?

The evidence that whole grains provide protection against diseases such as heart disease, type 2 diabetes, and certain cancers is hard to ignore. In fact, it is so strong that recommendations to increase whole grain consumption have become a standard part of health recommendations from governments and health organizations around the world. The Iowa Women's Health Study showed that women who increased their consumption of whole grains reduced their risk of death from all causes. Let's consider the evidence as it currently stands in relation to these diseases.

Heart Disease

The evidence linking our intake of whole grains with reduced rates of heart disease is very strong. Eating higher amounts reduces our blood cholesterol and blood pressure levels. While experts are not certain how whole grains work their magic, the presence of phytochemicals, fibre, plant sterols, and vitamin E are thought to be key. Some of the most convincing data are provided in the following studies:

- The Nurses' Health Study, which observed the diets of close to 70,000 women, found that those eating the most whole grains had a 23 per cent risk reduction relative to those eating the least. The fibre in grains was found to be even more protective than fibre from other foods. For every 5 gram increase in cereal fibre (the amount in a bowl of multigrain cereal), the risk of heart disease dropped by 37 per cent.

- The Iowa Women's Health Study, which examined the diets of nearly 35,000 women, also showed that eating whole grains reduced risk of heart disease. This study suggested that components other than fibre are most responsible for their benefits.

- The Health Professionals' Study, which involved almost 44,000 men, found that those eating the highest amounts of fibre (average of 29 grams per day) had a 41 per cent lower risk of heart attacks compared with men eating the lowest amounts (average of 12 grams per day). The fibre from grains appeared to be even more effective than that from vegetables and fruits in providing this protection.

- In a Finnish study, which assessed the diets of 22,000 men, those eating approximately 35 grams of fibre a day (mostly from whole grain rye bread) enjoyed a 31 per cent lower risk of heart disease, compared with those eating only 16 grams of fibre a day.

- A Korean study of seventy-six men with heart disease examined the effects of switching from white rice to whole grains and powdered legumes for a period of sixteen weeks. Significant beneficial effects on blood sugar, insulin secretion, and homocysteine levels were noted, along with less free radical damage to body fats.

Cancer

There is solid evidence that high intakes of whole grains can protect against cancer. Experts speculate that the protective effects of whole grains may be due to the phytochemicals and antioxidants they contain, both of which reduce free radical damage to body tissues and DNA. Fibre also protects against colorectal cancer. Two large reviews have confirmed this beneficial effect:

- One large report reviewing forty different studies that looked at intakes of whole grains and cancer risk found an average 34 per cent risk reduction in cancer when comparing the highest and lowest intakes of whole grains. The benefits of whole grains were confirmed in over 95 per cent of the investigations examined.

- A second large review showed that a high intake of whole grains reduced the risk of cancer at almost every site. Those eating the most whole grains cut their risk of cancer by 70–80 per cent for the upper digestive tract, and by 50 per cent for the stomach, colon, and gallbladder cancers compared to those eating the fewest whole grains.

How Dangerous Is Acrylamide in Grains?

Acrylamide is a chemical used in the manufacture of plastics. It is a known carcinogen (cancer-causing substance) that produces nerve damage in animals. It was first discovered in certain foods in a Swedish study in April 2002. Researchers discovered the formation of acrylamide when starch-containing foods such as rice, potatoes, and bread are heated. Higher temperatures seem to further increase their formations. An expert consultation on the implications of acrylamide in food, hosted by the World Health Organization (WHO) and the United Nations Food and Agriculture Organization (FAO), was assembled following the release of this study. The experts agreed that while acrylamide appears to have a similar potency to aromatic hydrocarbons formed in meat when cooked at high temperatures, the intake of acrylamide is likely to be higher. Clearly this is cause for concern.

At this point, we have more questions than answers about acrylamide. We don't know how much acrylamide it takes to cause cancer in humans. We don't even know what fraction of acrylamide in the body actually comes from starch-based foods. Other foods and environmental contaminants such as cigarette smoke may also increase exposure. We have known for some time that high-temperature cooking can create damaging by-products, for example, in grilled meats and deep-fried foods. We are now seeing that the effects of high-temperature cooking may extend to other products that were thought to be safe. While we don't really know enough to make specific recommendations, it makes some sense to be moderate in the amount of starchy foods we eat that have been cooked at high temperatures. In practical terms, this means eating fewer highly processed foods such as French Fries, potato chips, and doughnuts.

Type 2 Diabetes

Whole grains have more favourable effects on blood sugar and insulin response than refined grains. There are important components in whole grains that ward off diabetes, including fibre, phytochemicals, and trace minerals such as chromium, magnesium, and zinc. Some of the most compelling studies are described below:

- In a study of close to 3,000 middle-aged adults, whole grains were associated with improved insulin sensitivity. Insulin, the body's key blood sugar-regulating hormone, tends to be higher in those at risk of type 2 diabetes. People who were overweight or obese had the highest insulin levels and consumed the least whole grain foods.

- The Health Professionals Follow-up Study, which looked at almost 43,000 men, found that the risk of developing type 2 diabetes was 42 per cent lower in those consuming the highest amounts of whole grains compared with those consuming the least. Benefits were linked mostly with the cereal fibre and magnesium in whole grains

- In a six-year U.S. study of over 65,000 healthy people, 915 cases of type 2 diabetes were reported. The researchers found that diets with a high glycemic index and glycemic load increased risk of diabetes, while those high in cereal fibre reduced risk. The combination of high glycemic load and low cereal fibre intake made things even worse, increasing risk of diabetes by two and a half times. The researchers concluded that grains should be eaten in a "minimally refined form" to reduce the risk of diabetes. (*Note*: Glycemic index is a measure of how much a food affects blood sugar. The higher the glycemic index, the greater the effect. Glycemic load is a measure of insulin demand, which takes into account the glycemic index and the amount of carbohydrates eaten.)

• In a small controlled experiment with eleven participants, researchers compared insulin sensitivity using similar diets (55 per cent carbohydrate, 30 per cent fat; six to ten servings per day of breakfast cereal, bread, rice, pasta, muffins, cookies, and snacks). Half the participants received whole grain products and the other half refined products. After six weeks, the diets were reversed so each person received both diets. Fasting insulin levels were 10 per cent lower and insulin sensitivity improved while people were on the whole grain diet.

Fibre Fundamentals

Whole grains contribute more dietary fibre than any other group of foods. Fibre is the part of plants that we cannot digest. All plant foods contain fibre, as it gives plants their structure. In contrast, animals get structure from bones and are fibre-free. Fibre is often divided into two categories based on whether or not it dissolves in water.

Structural fibres, such as celluloses, some hemicelluloses, and lignins, are *insoluble*. Wheat bran is an example of a food rich in insoluble fibre. When it is mixed with water, it absorbs the water, but does not dissolve or become gluey. Almost all whole plant foods are good sources of insoluble fibre.

Gel-forming fibres, such as pectins, gums, and mucilages, are *soluble*. Oat bran is a rich source of soluble fibre. When mixed with water, it becomes sticky. Other good sources of soluble fibre are beans, peas, several fruits (such as canned plums), barley, some vegetables (such as okra), flaxseeds, and psyllium (used in some cereals and bulk fibre laxatives). Most plant foods contain a mixture of insoluble and soluble fibre; generally two-thirds to three-quarters of the total is insoluble fibre.

Fibre Functions

Both soluble and insoluble fibre are valuable to health. Some of the greatest benefits are listed below:

- **They keep our gastro-intestinal system clean and healthy.** This effect comes largely from insoluble fibre, which adds bulk to the stools and ensures that foods pass quickly and easily through the intestinal tract. This helps to protect us against diverticular disease, constipation, hemorrhoids, and anal fissures. It may also help protect us against colorectal cancers, duodenal ulcers, gallstones, and irritable bowel diseases.

- **They control blood cholesterol, triglyceride, and blood sugar levels.** Soluble fibre is mainly responsible for these benefits. The most effective types of soluble fibre are those that are stickiest, as they help to remove bile acids that digest fat. Soluble fibre coats the gut's lining and slows stomach emptying. As a result, it can slow sugar absorption and may reduce insulin needs. Soluble fibre is thought to improve blood sugar control in people with diabetes and to reduce risk of heart disease.

- **They increase satiety or feelings of fullness after eating.** Fibre is bulky, thus making us feel full, and possibly helping to control total food intake. As a result, high-fibre intakes are linked to healthier body weights.

Recommended and Actual Fibre Intakes

Unfortunately, most Canadians eat far too little fibre to enjoy these tremendous health benefits, with average intakes about 15 grams per day. The World Health Organization recommends that we include 15–22 grams of fibre per day per 1,000 calories. For those who eat between 2,000 and 2,500 calories a day, this works out to about 30–50 grams of fibre. An upper intake of 54 grams per day is recommended for adults. It is interesting to note that, on average, lacto-ovo vegetarians consume approximately 30–40 grams of fibre a day, and vegans about 40–50 grams a day. Of course, the amount of fibre in any diet depends on the way the diet is constructed. Eating patterns rich in legumes, whole grains, and high-fibre vegetables and fruits will be far higher in fibre than those built more on refined foods.

This is well illustrated by the menus on pages 88, 91, 92, 94 (Table 5.1 lists the fibre content of each menu). In the nonvegetarian menu (Menu #1), the fibre content is slightly higher than the average intake of 15 grams. Almost two-thirds of the fibre in this menu comes from vegetables and fruit (peas, potatoes, carrots, and apple), while an additional 10 per cent comes from the slice of whole wheat bread. The first lacto-ovo vegetarian menu (Menu #2) is lower in fibre than typical lacto-ovo vegetarian diets because more processed foods are eaten. In this menu 40 per cent of the fibre comes from whole grains, while about a third comes from fruits and vegetables. The second lacto-ovo menu (Menu #3) contains more than double the fibre of the previous menu. This menu contains more whole foods, including legumes, which are especially high in fibre. In this menu, about a third of the fibre comes from legumes, a third from whole grains, and a third from vegetables and fruits. In the vegan menu (Menu #4), the total fibre is slightly lower than the legume-rich lacto-ovo menu because a greater proportion of the legumes used are in a processed form (where much of the fibre has been removed) as tofu and soymilk. About 40 per cent of the fibre comes from whole grains, a third from vegetables and fruits, and only about 10 per cent from legumes.

TABLE 5.1   *Fibre in 2,000-Calorie Menus*

Menu and Page	Fibre (g)
#1 Nonvegetarian, page 88	19
#2 Lacto-ovo Vegetarian, page 91	24
#3 Lacto-ovo Vegetarian with More Legumes, page 92	55
#4 Vegan, page 94	43

What Are Our Best Sources of Fibre?

The richest sources of fibre in the plant kingdom are legumes, the coarse part of grains, dried fruits, berries, and other fruits and vegetables. Table 5.2 provides a list of the fibre content of foods.

TABLE 5.2 *Fibre in Selected Foods*

Amount of Fibre (rounded to the nearest gram)	Food/Serving Size (all grains and legumes are cooked; all serving sizes are 250 mL/1 cup unless otherwise noted)
Ultra high-fibre foods 12–20 g	• Most legumes, green peas • High-fibre bran cereals (e.g., All Bran, Bran Buds with Psyllium), 125 mL (H cup)
Very high-fibre foods 8–11 g	• Lima beans, soybeans, black-eyed peas • Grains (bulgar, buckwheat groats) • Dried fruits (4 figs or pears, 7 peaches, 20 apricots) • Pea soup • Cereals (Raisin Bran and other bran-enriched cereals) • Berries (raspberries, blackberries)
High-fibre foods 5–7 g	• Grains (barley, cornmeal, whole wheat pasta, oatbran) • Cereal (whole grain e.g., shredded wheat) • Cereal (grape nuts, granola), 125 mL (H cup) • Bread, high-fibre whole grain, 2 slices • Potatoes, regular or sweet, 1 medium, baked • Vegetables, (broccoli, Brussels sprouts, squash, eggplant, okra, dark greens, parsnips, carrots) • Artichoke, 1 medium • Berries (strawberries, blueberries), fresh • Fruit (papayas, Asian pears, avocado), 1 medium • Flaxseeds, ground, 30 mL (2 tbsp)
Moderate fibre foods 2–4 g	• Grains (oats, millet, brown rice) • Pasta, white • Bread, whole grain, 2 slices (read label)

TABLE 5.2   *continued*

Amount of Fibre (rounded to the nearest gram)	Food/Serving Size (all grains and legumes are cooked; all serving sizes are 250 mL/1 cup unless otherwise noted)
	• Fruit, most, 1 medium, 2 small, or 250 mL (1 cup) • Vegetables (cabbage, cauliflower, green beans, asparagus, turnips, mushrooms, peppers, leeks, celery), 250 mL (1 cup) cooked; 250–500 mL (1–2 cups) raw • Nuts and seeds, most, 60 mL (G cup) • Popcorn, 750 mL (3 cups)
Low-fibre foods 1 g or less	• Refined grains (white rice, cream of wheat cereal) • White bread, two slices • Baked white flour products (crackers, cookies, cakes, pastries, etc.), 1 serving • Cereals (Cornflakes, Rice Krispies, and other refined grain cereals—read labels) • Fruits (melon) • Fruit juice, all varieties • Vegetables (lettuce, iceberg or bib, cabbage), raw • Potato chips, 30 g (1 oz)
Fibre-free foods Zero fibre	• Meat, poultry, fish • Eggs • Milk, cheese, ice cream, and other dairy products • Fats and oils

Can Too Much Fibre Be Harmful?

Yes, it is possible to get too much of a good thing! Too much fibre can reduce the absorption of certain minerals such as calcium, iron, and zinc. Yet when compared to refined foods, high-fibre whole foods provide enough extra minerals to more than compensate for any losses incurred. The upper limit suggested by the World Health

Organization is based on the maintenance of mineral balance. When fibre does bind minerals, a significant proportion is freed by the action of bacteria in the large bowel. Short-chain fatty acids (also products of fermentation) help to facilitate their absorption from the large bowel. As a general rule, eating a wide variety of whole plant foods will not result in excessive intakes of fibre. It is important to note, however, that problems with mineral absorption can occur if concentrated fibre foods such as wheat bran or fibre supplements are added to a plant-based diet that is already rich in fibre. While these fibre boosters can help people eating low-fibre animal-centred diets, they are both unnecessary and potentially damaging to those eating high-fibre plant-based diets.

Won't Eating This Much Fibre Cause a Lot of Gas?

Gas production is a normal, healthy function of our intestines. It is the result of bacteria in the large intestine using undigested carbohydrates (fibre) and releasing its by-products (hydrogen, carbon dioxide, methane, water, and short-chain fatty acids). It may come as a surprise that this process can protect the colon against damage. However, excessive gas production can create bloating and painful cramping unless, of course, we choose to pass the gas and risk the social consequences.

Fortunately, there are a number of steps you can take to live happily with a high-fibre diet. There are two distinct causes of gas production: fermentation of carbohydrates that reach the large intestine, and swallowing of air. You can reduce the amount of air you swallow by eating more slowly, avoiding carbonated beverages and beer, and not chewing gum or sucking on candy. If you wear dentures, make sure they fit properly so you chew more thoroughly. As for reducing the fermentation of carbohydrates, here are a few simple tips:

- Increase your intake of high-fibre foods gradually so your gastrointestinal system has time to adapt.

- Eat beans and other fibrous foods regularly. This will encourage the growth of bacteria that are more efficient at completely digesting bean sugars (thereby reducing gas production).

- Moderate your intake of foods that are especially problematic, especially at first. Among the worst offenders are the oligosaccharides in beans, and vegetables of the cabbage family.

- Watch for combinations that offend. Some people avoid eating sugar or fruits along with more slowly digested foods.

- Try dahl or other small legumes rather than larger beans, which seem to cause more problems.

- Don't overeat. Overeating increases the amount of food that ends up undigested in the colon.

- Take enzymes designed to break down the undigestible carbohydrates before they reach the colon.

Recommended and Actual Intakes of Grains

Recommended Intakes

Canada's Food Guide to Healthy Eating recommends that five to twelve servings of grains be eaten each day. Consumers are guided to select whole grain and enriched products. The U.S. Food Guide Pyramid recommends that six to eleven servings of grains be eaten each day. The Food Pyramid educational materials suggest that *at least* half (or three) of these servings should be whole grains. As a result, nutrition education materials often suggest a minimum intake of three servings of whole grains a day. Most experts agree that as total number of servings increase, so should the number of servings of whole grains.

Actual Intakes

Food consumption surveys suggest that North Americans eat five to seven servings of grains a day, with slightly lower intakes in Canada than in the United States. Only 13 per cent of North Americans consume one or more servings of whole grains each day. Only 5 per cent of the grains eaten are whole grains, and these are primarily in the form of breakfast cereals. There is some evidence that vegetarians consume a greater proportion of whole grains or grains that have been minimally processed.

Great Gains in Grains: Practical Guidelines

Increasing your intake of whole grains is a valuable step toward a healthier diet. The following practical suggestions will help make great grains a natural part of your day:

- **Replace refined grains with whole grains.** Begin by doing an inventory of your grain intake. What grains and grain products do you eat at breakfast, lunch, dinner, and between meals? How many of these foods are refined grains and how many are whole grains? Decide which of the refined grains you would be willing to replace with whole grains. To start, at *least* half of all the grain products you choose should be whole grains. For example, if you eat an average of eight grain servings a day, (see the Vegetarian Food Guide, page 241 for serving sizes) at least four of these should be whole grains. Some people are willing to eat whole grain breakfast cereals and whole grain breads, but prefer refined pasta and white rice. Others may be happy to eat brown rice and kamut pasta, but couldn't bear to give up their crispy rice cereal and poppy seed bagels. The choice is entirely yours. In time, you can work your way up to a point where all, or almost all, of your grain intake is whole grains.

- **Not all whole grains are created equal.** The following list places whole grain foods into one of five categories from the very best to the least desirable choices. The top category is awarded a five-star rating, while the final category receives a single star. Attempt to gradually shift your choices up from mostly one- and two-star choices, to mostly three-, four-, and five-star choices:

***** **Best choices.** The best possible way to eat your grains is intact—without removing a thing. Whole grains such as brown rice, barley, millet, kamut, wheat or spelt berries, oat groats, and quinoa can be cooked as a breakfast cereal (see recipes for Basic Whole Grain Cereal and Your Very Own Whole Grain Cereal on pages 387 and 388), used in casseroles, soups, stews (see recipe for African Stew on page 419), or as pilafs. Instructions for cooking grains are provided on page 410. Many grains can be sprouted or soaked. (Raw food cookbooks provide excellent recipes and ideas for using uncooked grains.)

**** Great choices. Other great choices are grains that have been "minimally processed" such as those that are cut or rolled or stone ground, with little or nothing added or removed. These methods of processing do little damage to the grain. Examples include rolled oats (see recipe for Marvellous Morning Muesli on page 386), cracked wheat, mixed-grain cooked cereals, muesli, sprouted wheat breads, manna bread, and heavy German rye breads with whole grain seeds.

*** Good choices. Whole grains that are more highly processed can still be good choices. The damage caused by grinding (as in making stone-ground whole wheat flour) is only slightly higher than for rolling or cutting. A little more damage occurs with flaking (as in making flaked cereals), although much of the original value can be retained. To identify foods made with whole wheat, look for "whole wheat flour" as the first ingredient, rather than "wheat flour" or "unbleached wheat flour," both of which are refined flours. Whole grain products such as pancakes, muffins, and other prepared items may have healthful additions such as nuts, seeds, nut butters, dried fruits, and small amounts of nonhydrogenated oils or sweeteners (see recipes for Muscle Muffins on page 424, Banana-Walnut Pancakes on page 384, Lemon Teasecake on page 425, and Nutty Date Cookies on page 429). Examples of good choices are whole wheat or whole grain breads, whole rye crispbreads, flaked whole grain cereals, shredded wheat, whole wheat, spelt, kamut, brown rice, or quinoa pasta.

** Fair choices. These include whole grain products that have undergone considerable processing, products with higher amounts of fat and sugar added, and those with small amounts of hydrogenated fats. Products that contain a portion of flour as whole grain would also qualify as "fair choices." Examples of fair choices include most whole grain cookies, cakes and baked treats, whole grain breads containing hydrogenated fats, 50/50 breads and pastas (half white flour, half whole wheat flour), and puffed cereals (see recipe for German Chocolate Cake and Chocolate Mint Nut Bars on pages 427 and 430).

* **Less desirable choices.** Among the "whole grain" products, the poorest choices are those with large amounts of potentially harmful additions such as hydrogenated fats and sugar. Examples are whole grain crackers made with hydrogenated vegetable oil, whole grain pie crust made with shortening, whole wheat cinnamon buns loaded with butter and sugar, and grain or corn chips.

A complete set of references is available online at:
http://www.nutrispeak.com/bvreferences.htm

perfect protectors

vegetables and fruits

Getting kids to eat their vegetables and fruits is a part of every parent's job description. Moms and dads don't need to go to school to learn how to do this; it comes through a sort of divine intervention with the birth of their first child. The words, "Eat your vegetables" naturally flow off their lips at dinner tables everywhere. It is quite beautiful and perhaps one way the universe is trying to preserve our species.

Though people have recognized vegetables and fruits as being extraordinarily healthful for centuries, their status has been getting progressively stronger. This is because scientists are learning more about the specific protective components these foods contain, their mechanisms of action, and the potential strength of their effects.

What Separates Vegetables from Fruits?

Have you ever heard that tomatoes are actually a fruit, not a vegetable? While botanically this is true, legally in the United States it is not. Back in 1893, in a case of conflict about the true nature of tomatoes, a U.S. Supreme Court judge ruled that a tomato is legally a vegetable. The justification for this decision was that fruits tend to be relatively sweet and are more of a dessert food, while vegetables tend to be savoury and more main course foods. Most of us continue to use the "savoury versus sweet" or "main course versus dessert" method to distinguish vegetables from fruits. *Webster's New World Dictionary* (Second Edition) concurs. It defines a vegetable as a plant that is eaten whole or in part, raw or cooked, generally with a main entrée or in a salad but not as a dessert. Botanists look at things a little differently. They define fruit as the matured ovary of a flower containing the seed. What we eat is the fleshy part surrounding the seed or seeds. Almost any vegetable that contains seeds is botanically a fruit, including tomatoes, okra, squash, cucumbers, bean and pea pods, peppers, and eggplant. A "botanical" vegetable includes the edible "non-fruit" part of a plant. True vegetables include the following edible parts of plants (with examples):

• Roots (beets, turnips, sweet potatoes, and parsnips)

• Tubers (swollen sections of underground stems) (potatoes, Jerusalem artichoke, and yams)

• Leaves and leafy heads (Swiss chard, spinach, cabbage, kale, collards, turnip greens, lettuce, parsley, and Brussels sprouts)

• Immature flower clusters (broccoli, cauliflower, and broccoflower)

• Stems (celery, rhubarb, bamboo shoots, kohlrabi, and asparagus)

• Bulbs (onion, garlic, and chives)

• Corm (modified stem) (taro, dasheen, and water chestnut)

• Rhizomes (underground stem) (ginger)

In the grand scheme of things, whether we call these foods vegetables or fruits matters far less than whether or not we eat them. For practical purposes, we will stick to gastronomical definitions of vegetables and fruit rather than botanical ones.

The Nutritional Value of Vegetables and Fruits

Vegetables and fruits provide people with a unique and marvellous complement of nutrients. In their natural state, it is hard to find fault with any of them. With the exception of a few, such as avocado and olives, vegetables and fruits are very low in fat. All are cholesterol-free. Vegetables and fruits are outstanding sources of several vitamins and minerals, and provide most of the vitamin C and the plant form of vitamin A in our diet. They are also our primary sources of folate and potassium. If that wasn't enough, vegetables and fruits come packaged with fibre, and are the most concentrated sources of protective phytochemicals. With a few exceptions, such as potatoes, most vegetables are lower in calories and higher in protein and trace minerals than fruits. Compared to other foods, vegetables (and fruits to a lesser extent) have very high nutrient densities.

What Is Nutrient Density?

Nutrient density is a measure of the amount of nutrients a food has relative to the number of calories. For simplicity, we often compare the nutrients per 100 calories of food. A food with high nutrient density is one that provides a lot of nutrients for a minimum number of calories. Vegetables (except tubers) are well known to be the most nutrient-dense foods in the diet. In other words, vegetables provide more nutrients per 100 calories than most other foods. When a food is particularly nutrient dense, it means that we can eat large portions of the food without getting a lot of calories. If we eat tiny portions, the nutrient contribution from the food will be relatively small. When it comes to vegetables, we'd be well advised to take a lesson from our raw food friends and supersize our servings! For example, per 100 calories, romaine lettuce provides 257 milligrams of calcium, while 2 per cent milk provides 243 milligrams of calcium. Thus, where calcium is concerned, romaine lettuce is more nutrient dense than 2 per cent milk. However, one hundred calories' worth of romaine lettuce amounts to 3.125-litre (12.5-cups). By comparison, we would get 100 calories in only 200 millilitres (4/5 cup) of 2 per cent milk.

In addition to comparing different types of foods, we can compare the nutrient density of a food that has been prepared in various ways. For example, a baked potato is more nutrient dense than French fries, and an apple more nutrient dense than apple pie. Table 6.1 provides the nutrient densities of several vegetables and fruits, along with a range of other foods, including prepared foods and animal products. As you can see, unprocessed vegetables and fruits have remarkable nutrient densities. Dark green vegetables are the most nutrient dense of all.

TABLE 6.1: *Nutrient Density of Selected Foods*

Food	Nutrient Density Nutrients per 100 Calories							Amount of Food Equivalent to 100 Calories
Vegetables	Protein (g)	Iron (mg)	Calcium (mg)	Potassium (mg)	Vitamin A (RAE*)	Vitamin C (mg)	Folate (meg)	
Broccoli, raw	10.4	3	169	1,144	271	328	250	1 L (4 cups), chopped
Kale, raw	6.6	3.4	270	900	894	241	58.2	750 mL (3 cups), chopped
Romaine lettuce	12	7.8	270	2,030	910	168	952	3.125 L (12.5 cups), chopped
Mushrooms, cooked	8.1	6.5	22	1,330	0	15	66	600 mL (2.4 cups), sliced[
Sweet potato, baked	0.9	0.2	14	177	556	126	12	1 small (100 g/3.5 oz)
White potato, baked	2.2	0.7	11	578	1	13.3	40	1 small (100 g/3.5 oz)
French fries	1.2	0.2	4	199	0	3	11	30 g (1 oz) (N small order)
Fruits								
Apple	0.3	0.3	12	196	5	9.6	5	1 large (170 g/6 oz)
Apple pie	0.8	0.2	5	28	12	1	2	H4th of pie
Orange	2	0.2	85	382	21	112	63	2 small
Watermelon	2	0.5	25	364	57	31	6	500 mL (2 cups), diced
Blueberries	1.2	0.3	11	159	9	23	10	310 mL (1 G cups)
Other Foods								
Oatmeal	4.2	1.1	13	92	0	0	7	175 mL (I cup)
Navy beans	6.1	1.7	48	254	0	1	97	80 mL (1N cup)
Pumpkin seeds	6.4	2.9	9	156	4	0	11	15 mL (1 heaping tbsp)
Eggs	8	0.8	33	82	127	0	31	2 small or 1 jumbo
Milk, 2%	6.6	0.1	243	308	112	0	10	175 mL (I cup)
Fish, cod, baked	21	0.5	13	232	13	1	8	100 g (3.5 oz)
Hamburger, lean	10.5	1.1	8.5	148	0	0	3	42 g (1.5 oz)

*RAE = retinol activity equivalency

Key Vitamins in Vegetables and Fruits

Vegetables and fruits contain almost every vitamin we need, with two exceptions: vitamins B12 and D. While it is possible to get a tiny amount of vitamin B12 (from dirt clinging to vegetables) and some vitamin D (from certain seaweeds and mushrooms), vegetables and fruits are not reliable sources of these nutrients. The vitamins that vegetables and fruits are most noted for are: vitamin A (present as provitamin A carotenoids), vitamin C, vitamin K, and folate (a B-vitamin). Let's consider each of these nutrients and the importance of vegetables and fruits in supplying these nutrients.

Vitamin A

Vitamin A is widely recognized as the "vision vitamin," with deficiency being the leading cause of blindness in children throughout the world. Few people are aware that vitamin A is important for much more than good eyesight. It helps us fight off infection, and supports reproduction, growth, and the production of red blood cells and many proteins.

Vitamin A is an umbrella term for two main categories of compounds. The first is preformed vitamin A. This is the active form of vitamin A, and is present in animal products such as liver, fish, eggs, and dairy products, but is not found in plant foods. Preformed vitamin A has no antioxidant activity. The second category of vitamin A compounds are called provitamin A carotenoids. These are carotenoids that can be converted by the body into the active form of vitamin A. While plants make over 600 different carotenoids, only about 10 per cent of these can be converted to vitamin A. Brightly coloured orange, yellow, and green fruits and vegetables, such as carrots, sweet potatoes, and dark greens, are the richest sources of provitamin A carotenoids. These components serve as important antioxidants for the body.

Measuring vitamin A activity from carotenoids. The way we measure the vitamin A activity from various carotenoids is by looking at their *retinol activity equivalency (RAE)*. One microgram of *preformed vitamin A* equals 1 microgram RAE. Provitamin A carotenoids are less easily absorbed than preformed vitamin A, and must be converted to the active form of vitamin A by the body. Thus, we need greater amounts of beta-carotene and other carotenoids to provide the same vitamin A activity as preformed vitamin A. It takes 12 micrograms of beta-carotene, and about 24 micrograms of other provitamin A carotenoids to make 1 microgram RAE.

Recommended intakes. The recommended dietary allowance (RDA) for vitamin A is 700 micrograms RAE a day for women and 900 micrograms RAE a day for men. The upper limit (UL) that is advised for vitamin A is 3,000 micrograms of preformed vitamin A per day. The upper limit has been set based on three primary adverse effects of excess vitamin A: liver damage, reduced bone mineral density, and birth defects in infants. While large amounts of provitamin A carotenoids (for example, from litres of carrot juice) can make your skin orange, it is not toxic and does not contribute to the damaging effects of excess preformed vitamin A.

Current intakes. Average intakes of vitamin A range from about 750-800 micrograms RAE in men, and 550-700 micrograms RAE in women. In the general population, approximately 25-35 per cent of these intakes come from provitamin A carotenoids, while in vegetarians the proportion would be higher. In vegans, provitamin A carotenoids contribute all of the vitamin A unless vitamin A fortified foods are used.

Meeting recommended intakes. By eating five to ten servings of vegetables and fruits each day, vegetarians and vegans can easily meet the RDA for vitamin A. A single carrot provides enough provitamin A carotenoids to meet daily vitamin A needs. (For other sources, see Table 6.2 on page 184.) It is wise to eat deep green, yellow, or orange vegetables or fruits for at least three of your servings of vegetables and fruits. While many people assume that our best sources of vitamin A are raw foods, it turns out that cooking can increase absorption. We can also increase the absorption of provitamin A carotenoids in vegetables and fruits by eating some fat with them or by pureeing or finely chopping them.

Vitamin A supplements. Vitamin supplements containing more than 3,000 micrograms of preformed vitamin A are not recommended as they exceed the upper limit of safe intake. Taken over several months or years, these high doses can cause a condition called hypervitaminosis A (due only to excesses of preformed vitamin A; cannot be caused by carotenoids). Multivitamin/mineral supplements generally contain a mix of preformed vitamin A and provitamin A carotenoids; however, the amounts are almost always within a safe range.

Vitamin C

Vitamin C is most well known as the vitamin that prevents scurvy, the scourge of the navy that sent countless sailors to the bottom of the ocean centuries ago when they were deprived of fresh produce for months on end. Ascorbic acid, one of the active forms of vitamin C, literally means "no scurvy." We need vitamin C in order to produce collagen, an important structural component of our blood vessels, tendons, ligaments, and bone. Vitamin C also helps us to fight infection. An effective antioxidant, vitamin C can protect proteins, fats, carbohydrates, DNA, and RNA from damage by free radicals. While most mammals can make their own vitamin C, humans cannot, so we must get it through our diet.

Current intakes. Canadian adults consume an average of 70 milligrams of vitamin C a day. Vegetarians consume about 150 milligrams of vitamin C per day, or about double that of nonvegetarians, with vegan intakes being higher still.

Recommended intakes. The RDA for vitamin C is 75 milligrams a day for women and 90 milligrams a day for men. This is considerably higher than the previous recommendation, which was 30 milligrams per day for women and 40 milligrams for men. A new, separate RDA for smokers has also been set at 35 milligrams per day above non-smoker requirements (125 milligrams for men; 110 milligrams for women). The upper limit (UL) for vitamin C is 2 grams a day, based on adverse effects including diarrhoea and gastrointestinal disturbances.

Vitamin C sources. About 90 per cent of our vitamin C comes from vegetables and fruits. Our richest sources include citrus fruits and other tropical fruits, some berries and melons, and several vegetables, including peppers, leafy greens, cruciferous vegetables (e.g., broccoli, cabbage, cauliflower), and potatoes (see Table 6.2 for the vitamin C content of selected vegetables and fruits).

Vitamin K

Vitamin K gets its name from the word for coagulation (*koagulation*), as it is spelled in Denmark and Germany. Once recognized only for its role in building proteins that help us coagulate and clot blood, vitamin K is now in the spotlight. Recent evidence suggests that it plays a key role in bone health by making the proteins needed for bone metabolism. Since recommended intakes are set mainly on the basis of healthy blood clotting, some experts believe that higher levels may be needed for optimal bone health.

Current intakes. Research suggests average vitamin K intakes range from about 80-120 micrograms a day, although some studies have shown lower intakes of 70-80 micrograms per day. While there is very little research on vitamin K intakes in vegetarians, there is some evidence that intakes are higher than in nonvegetarians.

Recommended intakes. The RDA for vitamin K is 90 micrograms a day for women and 120 micrograms for men. However for bone health, we may need as much as 150-200 micrograms a day.

Vitamin K sources. The most concentrated sources of vitamin K are green leafy vegetables. Some vegetable oils (soybean, cottonseed and canola), and other vegetables and fruits also provide significant amounts, with lesser amounts distributed throughout the food supply. Early analyses overestimated the vitamin K content of foods, particularly of animal foods such as liver, cheese, and eggs. Now we know that these animal foods are poor sources of this nutrient.

Folate

The terms "folic acid" and "folate" are two different forms of the same vitamin, and the two words are often used interchangeably. Folate is the form of the vitamin that occurs naturally in foods. Folic acid, the more stable form of the vitamin, is the form used in vitamin supplements and fortified foods. Folate supports enzymes that are necessary for building cells and genetic material, and the metabolism of amino acids. It is most commonly recognized as the nutrient that helps prevent neural tube defects (spina bifida and anencephaly). Insufficient folate can also significantly increase risk for heart disease as is linked to elevated levels of homocysteine (see page 37 for more information).

Measuring folate activity. When the new dietary recommended intakes (DRI) for folate, were set, a new unit of measure was introduced called the *dietary folate equivalent* (DFE). With this measure, the differences in availability of folate and folic acid are taken into consideration.

Current intakes. Average intakes for folate have been reported to be approximately 250 micrograms a day; however, this figure underestimates today's intakes because since this report, breads, pastas, rice, and ready-to-eat cereals have been fortified with folic acid, leading to considerably higher intakes. Vegetarians consume about 25-50 per cent more folate from whole foods, although total intakes may be comparable to that of nonvegetarians who use greater amounts of fortified foods.

Recommended intakes. The new RDA for folate is 400 micrograms of DFE. This is approximately twice the earlier recommendation. During pregnancy, the RDA is 600 micrograms of DFE. The upper limit (UL) for folate is 1,000 micrograms of DFE for adults. The reason for this relatively low UL is that excess folate intake may mask a vitamin B12 deficiency (for more information, see page 226).

Folate sources. The name folate comes from the word foliage, thus it is not surprising that green leafy vegetables are among the richest sources. Other important sources of folate include citrus fruits, fruit juices, legumes, and vegetables other than leafy greens. Foods fortified with folic acid (such as breakfast cereals) are also important contributors (Table 6.2 provides the folate content of various vegetables and fruits).

TABLE 6.2: *Nutrient Density of Selected Foods*

Food Serving Size	Vitamin A (RAE)	Vitamin C (mg)	Vitamin K (mcg)	Folate (mcg)	Potassium (mg)	Magnesium (mg)
Vegetables						
Asparagus, cooked, 125 mL (H cup)	24	10	80	131	144	9
Beets, cooked, 125 mL, (H cup)	1.7	3	1.2	68	259	20
Broccoli, cooked, 125 mL, (H cup)	54	58	113	39	228	19
Carrots, cooked, 125 mL (H cup)	958	2	10	11	177	10
Cauliflower, cooked, 125 mL (H cup)	1	27	20	27	88	6
Green beans, cooked, 125 mL (H cup)	21	6	11	21	187	16
Kale, raw, 250 mL (1 cup)	298	80	547	19	300	23
Mushrooms, raw, 250 mL (1 cup)	0	2	0	8	259	7
Peas, cooked, 125 mL (H cup)	24	12	4	50	217	31
Sweet potato, cooked, 125 mL (H cup)	1,091	25	1	23	348	20
Potato (white), cooked, 125 mL (H cup)	0	10	1	8	296	17
Romaine lettuce, raw, 250 mL (1 cup)	72	14	58	76	162	4
Spinach, raw, 250 mL (1 cup)	369	9	360	131	419	78
Winter squash, cooked, 125 mL (H cup)	132	10	1	28	448	8
Fruits						
Apple, 1 medium	4	8	2	4	159	7
Avocado, 1 medium	62	16	125	7	1,204	78
Banana, 1 medium	5	11	0	22	467	34
Blueberries, 125 mL (H cup)	3	9	6	4	65	4
Cantaloupe, 125 mL (H cup)	126	33	0	13	241	9
Grapes, 1 25 mL (H cup)	3	9	4	3	148	5
Kiwi, 1 medium	8	89	23	35	302	27
Orange, 1 medium	269	70	0	39	237	13
Peach, 1 medium	26	6	2	3	193	7
Pear, 1 medium	2	7	6	12	208	10
Strawberries, sliced, 125 mL (H cup)	23	47	1	15	138	9
Watermelon, 1 wedge	51	27	0	6	332	31

Source: USDA nutrient database: <http://www.nal.usda.gov/fnic/foodcomp/index.html>

Key Minerals in Vegetables and Fruits

Vegetables and fruits are key sources of potassium and magnesium, and can be important contributors to the intakes of most other minerals essential to human health, including calcium, iron, zinc, chromium, and copper.

Potassium

Potassium is an electrolyte—a charged particle capable of conducting electricity. It acts with sodium to keep the right amounts of fluid inside and outside of cells and to pass nerve impulses along to the brain. It is also necessary for muscle contraction, including every beat of the heart.

There is no specific RDA for potassium, although it is generally recommended that adults get at least 2,000 micrograms a day. Some experts suggest 3,500 micrograms may be preferable.

When we think of potassium-rich foods, the first thing that often comes to mind is bananas. While bananas do contain plenty of potassium, it's surprising that their fame is not shared with other fruits and vegetables as there are many other rich sources. Although animal products do contribute some potassium to the diet, they are not big contributors for most people. Vegetarians have no problem meeting potassium needs!

Magnesium

Magnesium plays key roles in both the structure and the function of the human body. It is necessary for strong bones and teeth (50-60 per cent of the magnesium in the body is in the bones), and helps to convert food to usable energy. Magnesium is also necessary for building numerous enzymes and our genetic material DNA and RNA. We also need it to transport potassium and calcium across cell membranes. This is one busy mineral, so we need to insure a plentiful supply.

The RDA for magnesium is 310 (nineteen to thirty years) and 320 milligrams (above thirty years) a day for women, and 400 (nineteen to thirty years) and 420 milligrams (above thirty years) for men. The primary sources of magnesium are green vegetables because the centre of the chlorophyll molecule contains magnesium. Other vegetables, fruits, legumes, whole grains, nuts, and seeds are also good sources. Most of the magnesium in the diet comes from plant foods, although animal products do contribute lesser amounts. The best way to insure magnesium needs are met is to eat plenty of whole plant foods, including at least five servings of vegetables and fruits each day. Vegetarians tend to have excellent magnesium intakes, unless they rely to heavily on refined grains.

Other Beneficial Components: Phytochemicals

For many years, experts presumed that vegetables and fruits were healthful because of all the vitamins, minerals, and fibre they contained. Of course they were right, but only partly so. During the past few decades scientists have discovered a whole new category of protective compounds loaded into each and every vegetable and fruit. Collectively these compounds are called phytochemicals ("phyto" meaning "plant"). Phytochemicals regulate growth, defend against attacks by insects or fungi, and provide flavour, colour, texture, and odour to plants. While vegetables and fruits are our most efficient phytochemical factories, other plant foods such as grains and legumes also contribute significantly to our total intakes. When we eat plants, these powerful little protectors go to work on our behalf.

The beneficial effects of phytochemicals are quite remarkable. Many phytochemicals are strong antioxidants, helping to quench destructive free radicals. Others have potent anti-cancer activity, blocking cell division, and helping to rid our bodies of carcinogens. Phytochemicals work to protect us against heart disease, reducing cholesterol production, blood pressure, blood clot formation, and damage to blood vessel walls. Phytoestrogens or "plant estrogens" block the destructive action of the potent form of estrogen (either by competing with estrogen for receptor sites, or by reducing the production of the potent form while increasing the production of the less potent form), thus possibly reducing the risk of osteoporosis and certain types of hormone-dependent cancers. Some phytochemicals have powerful anti-inflammatory activity; others have immune-enhancing, antiviral, antibacterial, anti-fungal, anti-yeast, and anti-motion sickness activity.

Choosing a wide variety of a glorious, rainbow-hued assortment of whole plant foods is your secret to a phytochemical-rich diet.

Phytochemical Superstars of the Vegetable and Plant Kingdom

Among the most outstanding are dark greens (kale, collards, and spinach), cruciferous vegetables (broccoli, broccoli sprouts), garlic, tomatoes, blueberries, and citrus fruits. Let's take a closer look at what makes these foods so protective:

Blueberries. In a study by the United States Department of Agriculture's Center for Aging at Tufts University, the oxygen radical absorbance capacity (ORAC) (ability to quench free radicals) of over forty vegetables and fruits was measured. Of all the foods, blueberries came out number one, ahead of the most revered dark green leafy vegetables. Indeed, blueberries had five times the ORAC of most other fruits and vegetables. The primary active component in blueberries is a powerful antioxidant called anthocyanin, which is responsible for their deep blue colour. (Other anthocyanin-rich foods are plums, deep purple grapes, and other berries.) Blueberries contain several other phenolic compounds, including flavonols and phenolic acids. In addition to their antioxidant activity, blueberries have been found to protect against urinary tract infections, improve "tired eyes," and possibly reduce the effects of aging.

Citrus fruits. Oranges, grapefruits, lemons, and limes contain vitamin C, folic acid, and a wonderful array of phytochemicals. A single orange contains over 170 different types of phytochemicals (with thousands of copies of each), including sixty flavonoids, forty limonoids, and twenty carotenoids. Flavonoids and carotenoids are strong antioxidants with significant anti-cancer, anticardiovascular disease activity, while limonoids help reduce our production of cholesterol and detoxify our systems.

Garlic. A king of the allium family, garlic is loaded with sulphur-containing compounds that give a characteristic aroma. These unique compounds help to lower blood pressure, reduce the stickiness of blood cells, dilate blood vessels, and destroy cancer cells. They also stimulate the immune system and act against bacterial, fungal, and yeast infections. It is little wonder that 2,400 years ago, Hippocrates used garlic to treat infections and pneumonia.

Kale. Competing against nineteen other leading veggies, kale came out on top in its phytochemical activity. Kale is rich in carotenoids such as lutein and zeaxanthin (antioxidants that protect the eyes), indoles, sulphoraphane (anticarcinogens that help rid the body of carcinogens), and quercetins (anti-inflammatory agents). Other dark greens such as spinach, collards, broccoli, and chard were also strong contenders.

Tomatoes. The superstar status of tomatoes is largely based on their exceptional content of lycopene, the carotenoid that gives their red colour. Some (but not all) red vegetables and fruits contain lycopene. Red and pink grapefruit, watermelon, and guava are coloured, in part, by lycopene, while red peppers and strawberries are not. Lycopene has strong antioxidant properties, and several studies have suggested that it may protect against prostate cancer and slow the growth of prostate tumours. As well, there is some compelling evidence that lycopene is a powerful protector against the development of heart disease. Cooking improves the absorption of lycopene, so eating tomatoes that are cooked (as in stewed tomatoes, tomato sauce, and tomato paste) provides us with considerably more lycopene than raw tomatoes.

Phytochemicals from Pills

Some people think that they can get all the phytochemicals they need by popping a pill containing a variety of concentrated phytochemicals. However, several studies have suggested that this practice could backfire. In some (but not all) cases, isolating individual phytochemicals has actually increased risk of disease. It seems as though phytochemicals work synergistically with one another, and the collaborative action of two or more chemicals may be needed to produce the beneficial effect. At this time, we just do not know enough about the complicated interactions of these dietary components to be confident about turning them into pills. Besides, whole vegetables and fruits come packaged with fibre, vitamins, minerals, plant sterols, and other protective components, and they are infinitely more pleasurable to consume!

Vegetables and Fruits Fight Disease

The evidence that vegetables and fruits protect against disease is highly impressive, and continually gaining ground. Those who eat the highest amounts of these foods seem to enjoy the greatest protection against cancer, heart disease, stroke, type 2 diabetes, obesity, osteoporosis, and gallbladder disease. Some of the more impressive findings follow:

Cancer. According the World Cancer Research Fund and the American Institute for Cancer Research, if we eat five servings or more of a variety of vegetables and fruits, we cut our risk of cancer by at least 20 per cent.

Heart disease. Data from the Nurses' Health Study and the Health Professionals' Follow-up Study (over 120,000 people in total) found that those who ate the most vegetables and fruit reduced their risk of coronary heart disease by 20 per cent compared to those with the lowest intakes. For every serving of vegetables or fruits included in the daily diet, the risk of coronary heart disease was reduced by approximately 4 per cent. Green leafy vegetables and vitamin C-rich fruits and vegetables appear to offer the greatest protection.

Stroke. Data from the Nurses Health Study and the Health Professionals Follow-up Study (over 120,000 people in total) suggests that people who eat the most vegetables and fruits reduce their risk of stroke by 31 per cent compared to those eating the least.

Type 2 diabetes. A large 1999 study showed that those eating the greatest amounts of vegetables were least likely to develop type 2 diabetes. Eating fruit also reduced risk, but to a lesser extent.

Recommended and Actual Consumption

Health Canada, in Canada's Food Guide to Healthy Eating suggests that we eat five to ten servings of vegetables and fruits each day. In the rainbow graphic, vegetables and fruits make up the second largest arc of the rainbow. The Vegetarian Food Guide is consistent with Canada's Food Guide to Healthy Eating, and also recommends five to ten servings of vegetables and fruits each day (see Chapter 9 for details on the vegetarian guide, including serving sizes). This recommendation is consistent with that of numerous other health organizations and governments. In Canada, the United States, and Australia, plus some countries in Europe, Asia, and Africa, a campaign called "five-a-day for better health" encourages consumers to eat at least five servings a day of fruits and vegetables. Many experts believe that increasing the minimum to seven servings or more could bring further benefits. Most suggest at least three servings of vegetables and two servings of fruits.

Approximately one-third of Canadians eat the minimum of five servings of vegetables and fruits each day. This includes 40 per cent of women and 22 per cent of men, and is somewhat more than the one in four Americans who meet these intakes (27 per cent of women and 19 per cent of men). A U.S. study found the most frequently consumed vegetables and fruits to be: iceberg lettuce, tomatoes, French fries, bananas, and orange juice. Intakes of dark green and cruciferous vegetables were quite dismal at 0.2 servings per day. Not surprisingly, vegetarians eat more vegetables and fruits than nonvegetarians. This is demonstrated in the menus on pages 88-94. Both the nonvegetarian menu (Menu #1) and the lacto-ovo vegetarian menu (Menu #2) provide five and a half servings of vegetables and fruits. The lacto-ovo vegetarian menu with more legumes (Menu #3) contains eight servings of vegetables, while the vegan menu has ten servings. Consuming seven to ten servings of vegetables and fruits a day is very typical for many vegetarians and vegans.

Getting the Goods: Guidelines for Increasing Vegetable and Fruit Intake

Think about your intake of vegetables and fruits. Do you eat the minimum five servings of vegetables and fruits per day? How about seven or more servings a day? Do you choose dark leafy greens, citrus fruits, berries, and other deeply coloured produce daily? If you know that your intake of vegetables and fruits could stand some improvement, consider why this might be the case. One common reason that people give for failing to eat their veggies is that they take too much time to prepare. Some people are unfamiliar with many of the choices in the produce department, and preparing them may seem an overwhelming task. Many complain that vegetables and fruits just don't satisfy them like a bowl of cereal, a sandwich, or a bag of chips, especially at snack time. Others say that fruits and vegetables are boring, tasteless, or expensive. Whatever challenges limit your intake, the following tips will help you sail past them, giving vegetables and fruits the celebrated position they deserve on your plate.

Make It Easy

- **Prepare vegetables ahead of time.** Wash, cut up, and store in an airtight plastic container or bag for handy snacking.

- **Cut up a huge salad that can last for up to five days and store it in a tight sealing Tupperware-type container.** This half hour of washing and chopping can be a pleasant event once or twice a week, done in the company of family members or a favourite radio program.

- **Keep a large marinated vegetable salad and a fruit salad in the refrigerator.** This will make it very easy for everyone in the family to have instant access to fresh vegetables and fruits.

- **Take advantage of the salad bars and deli of natural food stores and grocery stores.** They offer ready-to-eat raw vegetables and fruit, as well as prepared salads made with fruits and vegetables.

- **Look for precut and cleaned fruits and vegetables.** Many grocery stores now carry prewashed, bagged salad greens, and vegetable pieces such as baby carrots, celery sticks, and broccoli and cauliflower florets. Some also offer packaged precut fruits, such as melons and pineapple.

- **Keep canned and frozen fruit and vegetables on hand.** Stock up on frozen, canned, and bottled juices, and dried fruits and vegetables.

Get to Know Your Vegetables and Fruits

- **Buy an unfamiliar vegetable or fruit at least once a month.**
  Search out information about the new produce. Find out about
  where the product originates, historical uses, and its nutritional
  value. Check for suggested methods of preparation and good
  accompaniments. Share this new information with your family.

- **Ask your local produce manager, or the owner of your
  favourite ethnic store, how to prepare or use a specific item
  that interests you.**

- **Take a cooking class that focuses on vegetables and fruits.
  Ethnic classes are a great option.**

- **Buy a few good vegetarian cookbooks.** Purchase (or borrow
  from the library) a book that has pictures of the various plant
  foods and a description of how to use them. An Internet search
  will also prove fruitful!

- **Subscribe to an organic delivery service.** You can arrange for
  a set list or a wide variety of vegetables and fruits, along with suggestions for using many of them.

- **Order a menu item that includes a vegetable or fruit that
  you have never tried.**

Give Them Substance

- **Serve cut-up vegetables with a hearty dip such as hummus
  or another bean dip.**

- **Make a big batch of vegetable soup with beans and barley.**
  Keep handy for a quick lunch or satisfying snack. Freeze individual portions.

- **Top salad with nuts, seeds, beans, and/or marinated tofu for
  a filling meal.**

- **Fill pita bread with a mix of lettuce, sprouts, grated carrots,
  and peanut sauce.**

- **Make vegetable and bean stews using a variety of different
  vegetables such as winter squash, greens, sweet potatoes,
  and corn.**

- **Be creative with stir-fries. Add cashews, tofu, or gluten.**

- **Add grated carrots or zucchini to muffins, cookies, and other baked goods.**

- **Use fruits in smoothies with tofu or soymilk.** You can easily get three or four fruit servings in a single smoothie.

- **Make a big fruit salad and top it with granola and yogourt.**

- **Use fruits as the key ingredient in desserts, such as fruit crumble, cakes, and muffins.**

Think Economy

- **While vegetables and fruits may seem expensive, they are a nutritional bargain.** Compare the cost 100 per cent fruit juice with soda pop. While there is little difference in cost, there is a huge difference in nutrition.

- **Buy straight from the farmer whenever you can. Frequent farmers' markets.** Co-ops, organic delivery services, and produce stands offer excellent options. If you live near farming country, take advantage of it. Many farmers sell directly to the consumer, and some even allow you to pick produce, which can be great fun for family members of all ages.

- **Keep an eye out for bargains.** Every week there are great sales on produce. Stock up when you can.

- **Buy in season.** The prices are always more reasonable.

- **Can or freeze produce when you get it in volume.**

- **Clip money-saving coupons for your favourite canned and frozen fruits and vegetables and juices.**

- **Buy store brands over name brands, which can cost much more.**

Make Them Tasty

- **Always buy the freshest produce available.** Quality makes a tremendous difference where taste is concerned.

- **Do not overcook.** When vegetables are overcooked, they get mushy and lose flavour, texture, and colour. Instead, cook vegetables until they are tender crisp (except for tubers and some root vegetables, which need longer cooking).

- **Try eating more of your vegetables raw.** Grate or dice into salads or slice and serve as finger foods with meals.

- **Make healthy dips and sauces for vegetables.** Vegetarian cookbooks will give you some wonderful, novel ideas on how to do this. See the Angelic Tofu Sandwich Filling (or Dip) on page 396, and the book *Cooking Vegetarian* by V. Melina and J. Forest (Wiley Press, 1998).

- **If you aren't so fond of eating vegetables and fruits, try juicing them.** Invest in a juicer and a couple of good juicing books.

Keeping Your Produce Safe

Although not commonly associated with food poisoning, raw fruits and vegetables can harbour some not-so-friendly bacteria. About 5 per cent of food poisoning is caused by contamination in these foods. The source, is generally animal manure, or contamination during food preparation. To avoid food poisoning from vegetables and fruits:

- **Rinse all produce well with clean drinking water before eating (even if you don't eat the rind or skin).** Use a small, clean vegetable brush to remove dirt from cracks in the food. Do not use detergent or bleach when washing fruits and vegetables. Most produce washes are safe and effective, but costly.

- **Refrigerate whole and cut-up raw fruits, vegetables, and salads to keep bacteria from multiplying.**

- **Keep a separate cutting board for produce.** Boards used for cheese, eggs, and, of course, any other animal products should not be used for produce.

- **Wash your hands with warm water and soap for at least twenty seconds before and after handling food.**

Should I Buy Organic Produce?

The debate about conventional versus organic produce rages on. Proponents of conventional growing, including the controlled use of pesticides, argue that pesticides help protect crops from insects, diseases, weeds, and mould, increasing crop yield. This, they say, makes vegetables and fruits more affordable for the average consumer. Government authorities tell us that the amounts of pesticides on our vegetables and fruits are well within safe limits, and that they pose little threat to human health. They remind us that all major studies examining diet and pesticide residues have concluded that the benefits of eating produce far outweigh any risk.

On the other side of the fence stand the proponents of organic farming. They contend that organic produce tastes better, is lower in toxic pesticides, and is more nutritious. Organic food supporters stress that organic farming can help return our land and water to a healthy natural state, which, in turn, protects our health and that of all other living things. They add that most organic farms are small, family-owned businesses, and by buying organic, we help save family farms. In addition, we protect farm workers who would otherwise be exposed to high levels of pesticides. Among the strongest arguments put forward by organic enthusiasts is that organic foods are not genetically engineered. Genetic engineering isolates and transfers genes from one species into a foreign species. Once this technology is released into the environment, it cannot be recalled. Proponents of organic farming methods declare that while genetic engineering promises great things from a nutrition standpoint, thus far it has failed to deliver. Instead it has harmed non-target (beneficial) insects and soil micro-organisms, led to resistance in weeds and insect pests, and spread into wild environments, breeding with wild relatives.

In May 2002, the first detailed scientific analysis comparing the pesticide residues of conventionally and organically grown vegetables and fruits was published in the *Food Additives and Contaminants Journal*. This study showed that organic foods contain about a third as many pesticide residues as conventionally grown foods.

So what's the verdict? While eating conventionally grown vegetables and fruits is a positive first step for health, there are solid reasons to opt for organic beyond and including health benefits.

A complete set of references is available online at:
http://www.nutrispeak.com/bvreferences.htm

fat feuds

who's winning?

Few health messages have been as strongly pushed or as zealously embraced as the message that fat is bad. Some experts urge consumers to eat only very low-fat foods, and to avoid whole foods naturally high in fat such as nuts and seeds. Not surprisingly, a backlash has occurred. Naysayers have brought forth two distinct arguments. The first is that fat is not the villain; carbohydrates are. This theory is wildly popular among consumers of diet books who relish the thought of dining on steak, bacon, eggs, and cheese. The second is that it is not high intakes of fat that contribute to our health problems, but bad fats in particular. Proponents of this theory contend that high-fat diets such as Mediterranean-style diets, rich in healthy plant fats such as olive oil and avocados, are among the healthiest diets of all. To make matters even more complicated for vegetarians, heart health organizations urge people to eat a couple of servings of fatty fish each week, in an effort to increase intakes of omega-3 fatty acids. It is enough to make your head spin.

Fat nutrition is tricky because there are so many different types of fat, all with distinct effects on health. Many people assume that the switch to a vegetarian diet guarantees an improvement in fat intake. While it is true that most vegetarians eat less total fat, less of the potentially damaging saturated fat and cholesterol, and more unsaturated fats, becoming vegetarian is no guarantee of an improved fat intake. After all, there are plenty of junky snack foods that do not contain a single speck of meat. In addition, when we switch to a vegetarian diet, the concerns tend to shift away from getting too much of the "bad fats" to getting enough of very specific types of "good fats."

This chapter sorts through volumes of literature on fat, helping to clarify what we know and what is mere speculation. It lays outs the significant issues for vegetarians, and provides solid practical guidelines on making choices that support optimal health. Our examination of the issues will focus on four key questions:

1. What is more important, the amount or the type of fat?

2. Can a vegetarian diet provide sufficient essential fats?

3. How much fat is optimal?

4. What are the best sources of fat in the diet?

What Is More Important, the Amount or the Type of Fat?

There is no question that both the quantity and quality of fat can have a significant effect on our health. However, it is becoming increasingly clear that the *type* of fat has a greater impact than the *amount* of fat we eat. This does not mean that total fat intake is not important—it is. It means that eating a relatively high-fat diet can have minimal impact on our risk of disease if the fat comes from the right kinds of foods and we are not overeating. On the other hand, disease risk increases considerably when the fat comes from the wrong kinds of foods, even when total fat intake is moderate.

What Are Fats?

In scientific jargon, fats are known as lipids. Lipids are a family of compounds that do not dissolve in water. They include fats and oils (made up of fatty acids), sterols (such as cholesterol), and phospholipids (such as lecithin). As you can see, while fats are only one type of lipid, the words *fat* and *lipid* are commonly used interchangeably.

Fatty acids do not generally roam free in the body; most of them travel in threesomes as part of larger molecules called *triglycerides*. Most of the fatty acids that we need for survival can be produced in the body, but there are two that we cannot make and must obtain from food. These are called *essential fatty acids*.

The main feature that distinguishes fats from oils is that fats are hard at room temperature, while oils are liquid. Fats are generally found in animal products such as meat, poultry, and dairy, while oils are commonly derived from plant seeds like olive, canola, corn, and sunflower.

Fatty acids are saturated, monounsaturated, or polyunsaturated. Fats and oils all contain varying amounts of fatty acids from each of these three categories. For example, corn oil contains about 58 per cent polyunsaturated fat, 29 per cent monounsaturated fat, and 13 per cent saturated fat. Thus, it is referred to as polyunsaturated oil because most of the fat it contains is polyunsaturated. The breakdown of fatty acids in a variety of fats and oils is shown in Table 7.3 (page 209).

What are the Most Damaging Types of Fat?

Fats that have been shown to have negative effects on health, when eaten in excess, are saturated fats, trans-fatty acids, and cholesterol. Here's what you need to know about each of these types of fat:

Saturated Fat

Saturated fats have been pegged as "bad fats" for good reason. Excess intakes of saturated fats increase our risk for several diseases, including heart disease, several cancers, gallstones, kidney disease, and possibly type 2 diabetes.

Saturated fat is hard at room temperature. The harder the fat, the more highly saturated it is. The primary sources of saturated fat are:

- **Animal fat:** Beef and pork fat are about 40-45 per cent saturated, chicken and turkey fat about 30-33 per cent, and fish fat 20-30 per cent.

- **Dairy fat:** Dairy fat is about 65 per cent saturated.

- **Tropical "oils":** Coconut fat is about 91 per cent saturated, palm kernel oil about 87 per cent, and palm oil about 51 per cent.

By contrast, plant fats are about 6-25 per cent saturated, with most in the 10-20 per cent range.

How much saturated fat do we eat? Most North Americans eat too much saturated fat. Average intakes are about 20-30 grams of saturated fat a day, or 10-12 per cent of total calories for Canadian men and women. Vegetarian diets are naturally lower in saturated fat than nonvegetarian diets. Lacto-ovo vegetarian intakes average between 8-12 per cent of calories from saturated fat. Vegans eat even less, averaging 4-7 per cent of calories from saturated fat. In the menus provided in Chapter 3 (pages 88-94), saturated fat contributes the following proportions of total calories: Menu #1: Nonvegetarian, 14.9 per cent of calories; Menu #2: Lacto-ovo Vegetarian, 11.6 per cent of calories; Menu #3: Lacto-ovo Vegetarian with More legumes, 2.1 per cent of calories, and Menu #4: Vegan, 3.7 per cent of calories.

Are there specific recommendations for saturated fat intake? Most governments and health authorities recommend that saturated fat should not exceed 10 per cent of calories. The Dietary Reference Intakes for Energy, Carbohydrates, Fibre, Fat, Protein, and Amino Acids (Macronutrients) (2002) (DRI Macronutrients 2002) does not suggest an upper limit (UL) for saturated fat because "any incremental increase in saturated fatty acid intake increases CHD risk" (CHD = coronary heart disease). However the Joint WHO/FAO Expert Consultation on Diet, Nutrition, and the Prevention of Chronic Diseases (2002) (WHO/FAO Diet and Diseases 2002) suggests intakes of less than 7 per cent of calories. What does this mean in grams? It depends on your energy needs. For those consuming 2,000 calories a day, 7 per cent of calories amounts to a maximum saturated fat intake of 16 grams. A fast-food meal that includes one double cheeseburger, a milkshake, and a large order of fries provides about 31 grams of saturated fat. Vegetarians who eat a lot of full-fat dairy products could find themselves over the top almost as quickly. Sixty grams (2 ounces) of cheddar cheese contains 12 grams of saturated fat, while 250 millilitres (1 cup) of whole milk

has over 5 grams. On the other hand, a person could eat ten servings of fruits and vegetables, eight servings of whole grains, two
serving of beans, a serving of tofu, 60 grams (2 ounces) of nuts *and*
60 grams (2 ounces) of seeds, and still come in at under 10 grams of
saturated fat.

Should vegetarians avoid tropical oils? Is coconut an unhealthy
food? What about foods with coconut, palm kernel, or palm oil
added? While tropical oils are unquestionably high in saturated
fat, moderate amounts *can* have a place in healthy vegetarian diets.
Some experts believe that saturated fats from tropical oils are less
damaging than saturated fats from animal sources because they
are not packaged with cholesterol. In whole foods such as fresh
coconut, the oil also comes with protective fibre and phytochemicals. Studies suggest that when moderate amounts of coconut or
tropical oils are consumed as part of a high-fibre, low-, or no-
cholesterol, plant-based diet, their use does not increase heart
attack risk. By contrast, adding tropical fats to a standard North
American diet already containing excessive saturated fat and cholesterol may simply be adding fuel to the fire. The bottom line for
those eating a high-fibre plant-based diet, small amounts of tropical oils, coconut milk, or, better still, fresh coconut can be enjoyed
in moderation.

Trans-fatty Acids

Do you recall when the newly discovered connection between saturated fat and heart disease was splashed across the front pages of
newspapers and magazines? Consumers responded by demanding
that lard and tropical oils be removed from their favourite products.
Manufacturers provided just the thing to allay all their fears—vegetable fat. Liquid vegetable oil was processed to look and taste like
animal fat. Margarine was designed to replace butter, and shortening to replace lard.

Manufacturers were delighted because the replacements were
economical and stable. (They could sit on a shelf for a long time
without going rancid.) Consumers were pleased because they
believed that these spreads were healthier choices.

The process that turns vegetable "oils" into solid fats is called *hydrogenation*. This process changes the configuration of some of the healthy unsaturated fats to trans-fatty acids. Technically, trans-fatty acids are still unsaturated fats, but unlike the more common form of unsaturated fats ("cis" form), which are flexible and curved in shape, trans-fatty acids are straighter, more rigid molecules. These molecules behave much like saturated fat—only worse.

For many years trans-fatty acids were considered a relatively minor player in health and disease. There are two reasons for this. First, we eat far less trans-fatty acids than saturated fat (2-4 per cent of calories come from trans-fatty acids compared to 10-12 per cent of calories from saturated fat). Second, studies have shown that trans-fatty acids increase total cholesterol levels only 80 per cent as much as saturated fat. This figure is deceiving to say the least. While the impact on total cholesterol is not quite as high as it is with saturated fat, the overall damage to heart health is greater. Trans-fatty acids not only raise total cholesterol, they lower HDL cholesterol (good cholesterol). They also raise damaging Lp(a) (a particularly harmful form of LDL cholesterol or bad cholesterol), and potentially increase triglycerides. Gram for gram, the adverse effect of trans-fatty acids is estimated to be at least double that of saturated fatty acids.

What foods are highest in trans-fatty acids? Close to 90 per cent of the trans-fatty acids in foods come from hydrogenated or partially hydrogenated oils. These fats are used extensively in processed foods such as crackers, granola bars, chips and other snack foods, pies, cakes, pastries, cookies, and other baked goods, margarine, and shortening. Hydrogenated oils are also widely used in the fast-food industry, and in restaurants for deep-frying foods (see Table 7.1 for amounts of trans-fatty acids in common foods).

The remaining 10 per cent of trans-fatty acids come from animal foods, including meat and dairy products. Trans-fatty acids are formed naturally from bacterial fermentation within the intestinal tracts of ruminant animals.

How much trans-fatty acids do people eat? It is estimated that North American trans-fatty acid intakes average about 2-4 per cent of calories. Vegetarians generally consume fewer trans-fatty acids than nonvegetarians, although differences are negated with higher intakes of processed foods. Vegans generally have the lowest intakes of trans-fatty acids, with estimates averaging from 0-2 per cent of calories. In the menus provided in Chapter 3 (pages 88-94), trans-fatty acids contribute the following proportion of calories: Menu #1: Nonvegetarian, 1.4 per cent of calories; Menu #2: Lacto-ovo Vegetarian, 1.9 per cent of calories; Menu #3: Lacto-ovo Vegetarian with More Legumes, 0.7 per cent of calories, and Menu #4: Vegan, 0.2 per cent of calories. It is important to note that the use of processed and deep-fried foods is low in the first two menus, and negligible in the second two menus.

How much should we limit trans-fatty acids? The DRI Macronutrients (2002) does not suggest an upper limit for trans-fatty acids because "any incremental increase in trans-fatty acid intake increases CHD risk" (CHD = coronary heart disease). However, the WHO/FAO Diet and Diseases (2002) suggests that intakes of trans-fatty acids should be less than 1 per cent of calories. For someone eating 2,000 calories a day, that amounts to no more than 2.2 grams of trans-fatty acids.

In practical terms this means limiting, or completely avoiding, foods containing hydrogenated or partially hydrogenated fats, especially when they are major ingredients in a product. Fried foods should also be minimized.

TABLE 7.1: *Trans-Fatty Acid Content of Selected Foods*

Food	Total Fat (g)	Trans-fatty acids (g)
Microwave popcorn, 100 g (3.5 oz)	25	7.5
French fries, large	23.7	5
Cookies, chocolate chip, 4	12	5
Doughnut, honey-glazed, 1	15	3.8
Shortening, 15 mL (1 tbsp)	14	3.7
Cake, yellow commercial with frosting, 1 piece	12.8	3.2
Margarine, hard, 15 mL (1 tbsp)	12	3.1
Crackers, snack, 8	7	2.6
Margarine, soft, 15 mL (1 tbsp)	12	1.4
Potato chips, 60 g (2 oz)	19.6	1.1

Source: The USDA Nutrient Database.

Cholesterol

Have you ever wondered how much cholesterol a bowl of nuts or a whole avocado has? The answer is zero: not a single gram. Animals, not plants, make cholesterol. Thus, all animal products contain cholesterol, while all plant foods are cholesterol-free.

Cholesterol is an essential part of every human cell. The body makes about 800-1,000 milligrams of cholesterol each day, so we don't need any additional cholesterol from food. Too much cholesterol can cause blood cholesterol levels to rise, increasing the risk of blood clots, heart attack, and stroke. It may also increase the risk for certain types of cancer. For this reason, most governments and health authorities, including the WHO, recommend that we limit total dietary cholesterol to less than 300 milligrams a day. The DRI Macronutrients (2002) does not suggest an upper limit for cholesterol because "any incremental increase in cholesterol intake increases CHD risk" (CHD = coronary heart disease).

How much cholesterol do people eat? Average cholesterol intakes in the general population range from about 200-400 milligrams a day. In the menus provided in Chapter 3 (pages 88-94), cholesterol intakes are as follows: Menu #1: Nonvegetarian, 315 milligrams; Menu #2: Lacto-ovo Vegetarian, 86 milligrams; Menu #3: Lacto-Ovo Vegetarian with More Legumes, 11 milligrams; and Menu #4: Vegan, 0 milligrams. None of these menus contained eggs, which would have increased the cholesterol content significantly (a single egg contains over 200 milligrams of cholesterol).

The most concentrated sources of cholesterol are organ meats and eggs. Contrary to what many people believe, there is little difference in the cholesterol content of meat, poultry, or fish. Dairy products are moderate cholesterol sources.

What Are the "Healthy Fats"?

Fats that have been found to cause little or no adverse health effects, or to be protective to human health, are plant sterols, monounsaturated fats and polyunsaturated fats.

Plant Sterols

While animals make cholesterol, plants make their own family of sterols called *phytosterols*. These naturally occurring plant compounds are similar in structure to cholesterol, but they do not behave the same way as cholesterol in the body. We absorb far less plant sterols, which also help to block cholesterol absorption from the gut. All whole plant foods contain small amounts of these compounds. New margarines on the market, which have added sterols and stanols, contain higher amounts. Vegetarian diets are naturally higher in plant sterols than nonvegetarian diets.

Monounsaturated Fat

Monounsaturated fat has been shown to have neutral or slightly beneficial effects on health, with minimal effects on blood cholesterol levels. There is some evidence that monounsaturated fat may slightly reduce blood pressure and enhance blood flow.

Oils rich in monounsaturated fat are generally liquid at room temperature, but become cloudy and thick when refrigerated, as with olive oil. The richest dietary sources of monounsaturated fat are olives, olive oil, canola oil, avocados, most nuts (except for walnuts and butternuts), high-oleic sunflower oil, and high-oleic safflower oil ("Oleic" is the main type of monounsaturated fat). Sunflower and safflower oils are usually mainly omega-6 oils, but the high-oleic varieties are bred to have a high monounsaturated fat content.). Oleic is the main type of monounsaturated fat (see Figure 7.3 for the monounsaturated fat in various fats and oils).

Polyunsaturated Fat

Within this group of polyunsaturated fats are the fatty acids that cannot be made by the body and must be obtained in our diets. These are called *essential fatty acids*. These fats are needed for the formation of healthy cell membranes, and they help cells keep their shape and flexibility, and allow substances to flow in and out. They are critical to the development and functioning of the brain and nervous system, and are involved in the production of hormone-like substances called *eicosanoids*, which regulate many organ systems.

There are two distinct families of polyunsaturated fats, each with unique properties. They are known as the omega-6 family and the omega-3 family, and both are vital to health. Within each family there is one *essential fatty acid*. In the omega-6 family this is *linoleic acid* (LA). In the omega-3 family it is *alpha-linolenic acid* (ALA). There are several other very important fats in each family, called *highly unsaturated fatty acids* (HUFA). These fatty acids are critical to health; however, because they can be made in the body from the essential fatty acids, they are not "essential" in our diets.

Highly Unsaturated Fatty Acids (HUFA)

Highly unsaturated fatty acids (HUFA) are even more active in the body than essential fatty acids, and have powerful impacts on health. In the omega-6 family, the most important HUFA are *arachidonic acid* (AA), and *gamma-linolenic acid* (GLA). In the omega-3 family, the most important HUFA are *eicosapentaenoic acid* (EPA) and *docosahexaenic acid* (DHA). All of these HUFA, except for DHA, serve as raw materials for making eicosanoids. The eicosanoids formed from AA are very potent, increasing blood pressure, inflammation, cell proliferation, and many markers of heart disease. Those formed from EPA and GLA protect against these responses. While we need the eicosanoids formed from AA, when we produce too much, our risk of chronic disease increases.

DHA cannot form eicosanoids, but is an important part of the grey matter of the brain, the retina of the eye, and specific cell membranes. Low levels of DHA have been associated with several neurological and behavioural disorders such as depression, schizophrenia, Alzheimer's disease, and attention deficit hyperactivity disorder (ADHD). In addition, low levels of DHA can negatively affect brain and eye development in infants. Thus, while these long-chain fatty acids are not "essential" in our diets, we must get enough, either by making them from essential fatty acids or by getting them directly from foods.

Sources of Essential Fatty Acids

The primary sources of the two essential fatty acids—LA and ALA—are plants on land and in the sea. The most common sources of the long-chain fatty acids—AA, EPA, and DHA—are animal foods (although DHA and EPA are also available from sea plants). Table 7.3 lists specific amounts of these fatty acids in a variety of foods.

Omega-6 Fatty Acids Sources

LA: seeds and seed oils (sunflower, safflower, hemp, grape, pumpkin, sesame, cottonseed); nuts and nut oils (walnuts, butternuts); grains and grain oils (corn, wheat germ); and soybeans and soybean oil.
GLA: primrose oil, borage oil, blackcurrent oil, hempseed oil, and spirulina.
AA: meat, poultry, and dairy products.

Omega-3 Fatty Acids Sources

ALA: seeds and seed oils (flax, chia, hemp, canola); nuts and nut oils (walnuts and butternuts); green leaves of plants (dark green leafy vegetables, broccoli); seaweeds, soybeans, and soybean oil.
EPA and **DHA:** fish (especially cold-water fish), eggs (especially those from chickens fed flax or microalgae), seaweed, and DHA-rich microalgae (not blue-green microalgae).

How Much Omega-6 and Omega-3 Fatty Acids Do We Need?

The WHO/FAO Diet and Diseases (2002) recommends 5-8 per cent of calories from omega-6 fatty acids, 1-2 per cent of calories from omega-3 fatty acids. This means that the recommended amount of omega-6 fatty acids relative to omega-3 fatty acids (or the ratio of omega-6 to omega-3) is 2.5:1 to 8:1. The WHO/FAO recommendations are meant for the general population, and assume some direct intake of EPA and DHA. For vegetarians and vegans who consume little, if any, direct sources of EPA and DHA, a ratio of 2:1 to 4:1 has been suggested (with an upper limit of 6:1). These lower ratios have been shown to allow for maximum conversion of ALA to EPA and DHA. Most vegetarian diets have higher ratios of omega-6:omega-3 in the range of 10:1 to 20:1. This means that we do not eat enough omega-3 fatty acids, and possibly that we eat too much omega-6 fatty acids. To achieve the recommended 2:1 to 6:1 ratio, vegetarians would need to follow the 5-8 per cent omega-6 fatty acid recommendation, and increase the omega-3 fatty acid recommendation to 1.5-2.5 per cent of calories. How much fat is this? If we eat about 2,000 calories a day, we need approximately 12-18 grams of omega-6 fatty acids and 3-6 grams of omega-6 fatty acids.

How Much Omega-6 and Omega-3 Fatty Acids Do We Eat?

Vegetarians eat more omega-6 fatty acids than nonvegetarians. Vegans consume an average 9-12 per cent (20-27 grams per 2,000 calories) of their fats as omega-6 fatty acids and lacto-ovo vegetarians about 6-10 per cent (13-22 grams per 2,000 calories). Omega-3 fatty acid intakes are similar for vegans, vegetarians, and nonvegetarians averaging 0.5-1 per cent of total calories (1-2 grams per 2,000 calories). As you can see, we get slightly higher amounts of omega-6 fatty acids than we should, and only about a third of the omega-3 fatty acids recommended.

Intakes of very long-chain omega-3 fatty acids (EPA and DHA) are remarkably different in vegetarians and nonvegetarians. Vegans consume little, if any EPA and DHA, while vegetarians consume minimal EPA (less than 5 micrograms a day) and varying amounts of DHA depending on egg consumption (average DHA from eggs in lacto-ovo vegetarians is approximately 33 milligrams a day). Nonvegetarian EPA and DHA intakes vary with the use of fish and eggs, with averages in the 100-150 milligrams a day range.

In the four menus provided in Chapter 3 (pages 88-94), intakes of omega-6 fatty acids fall within usual intakes listed above. However, Menus #3 and #4 are much higher in omega-3 fatty acids than average intakes because of the use of flaxseed oil, which in Menu #3 provides 87 per cent of omega-3 fatty acids, and in Menu #4 provides 74 per cent. For essential fatty acids in all four menus, see Table 7.2.

TABLE 7.2: *Essential Fatty Acid Intakes in Menus*

Menus	Omega-6 Fatty Acids		Omega-3 Fatty Acids	
	Total (g)	Per cent of Calories	Total (g)	Per cent of Calories
Menu #1: Nonvegetarian	10.2	5%	1.2	0.5%
Menu #2: Lacto-ovo vegetarian	21.5	10%	2.0	0.9%
Menu #3: Lacto-ovo vegetarian with More Legumes	14.6	6%	4.9	2%
Menu #4: Vegan	19.4	9%	7.0	3%

TABLE 7.3: *Fatty Acid Composition of Selected Foods*

Food/serving size	Total Fat % of total calories	Saturated Fat % of fatty acids	Mono. Fat % of fatty acids	Omega-6 % of fatty acids	Omega-3 % of fatty acids	LNA (g)	EPA (mg)	DHA (mg)
Oils, 15 mL (1 tbsp)								
Canola oil	100	7	61	21	11	1.3	0	0
Coconut oil	100	91	7	2	0	0	0	0
Corn oil	100	13	29	58	0	0	0	0
Cottonseed oil	100	26	22	52	0	0	0	0
Flaxseed oil	100	9	18	16	57	8.0	0	0
Grapeseed oil	100	6	17	77	0	0	0	0
Hempseed oil	100	8	16	57	19	2.7	0	0
Olive oil	100	15	75	9	1	0.8	0	0
Palm oil	100	51	39	10	0	0	0	0
Palm kernel oil	100	87	11	2	0	0	0	0
Peanut oil	100	19	48	33	0	0	0	0
Safflower oil	100	6	14	75	0	0	0	0
Safflower oil, high oleic	100	6	75	14	0	0	0	0
Sesame oil	100	14	42	44	0	0	0	0
Soybean oil	100	15	24	54	7	0.9	0	0
Sunflower oil	100	11	20	69	0	0	0	0
Sunflower oil, high oleic	100	10	86	4	0	0	0	0
Walnut oil	100	9	23	53	13	1.7	0	0
Nuts, Seeds, Soy, and Wheat Germ, 30 g (1 oz) (about 48 mL/3.2 tbsp)								
Almonds	80	10	24	66	0	0	0	0
Butternuts	84	2	19	63	16	2.5	0	0
Cashews	72	21	61	18	0	0	0	0
Flaxseed, whole, 30 mL (2 tbsp)	41	9	18	16	57	5.2	0	0

TABLE 7.3:   *continued*

Food/serving size	Total Fat % of total calories	Saturated Fat % of fatty acids	Mono. Fat % of fatty acids	Omega-6 % of fatty acids	Omega-3 % of fatty acids	LNA (g)	EPA (mg)	DHA (mg)
Flaxseed, ground, 30 mL (2 tbsp)	41	9	18	16	57	3.8	0	0
Hazelnuts	87	7	78	15	0	0	0	0
Macadamia nuts	95	17	81	2	0	0	0	0
Peanuts	76	15	52	33	0	0	0	0
Pecans	94	8	63	28	1	0.3	0	0
Pistachios	72	12	56	32	0	0	0	0
Pumpkin seeds	76	19	31	45-50	0-5	0-0.7	0	0
Soybeans, cooked, 250 mL (1 cup)	47	15	24	54	7	1.0	0	0
Tofu, firm 125 mL (H cup)	54	15	24	54	7	0.7	0	0
Walnuts	90	7	15	63	15	2.6	0	0
Wheat germ, 30 mL (2 tbsp)	24	19	15	58	8	0.1	0	0
Seaweeds, 100 g (3.5 oz) raw								
Irish moss	<1	33	14	7	46	.001	46	0
Kelp	12	58	23	17	2	.004	4	0
Spirulina	13.5	50	12	23	15	0.2	0	0
Wakame	13	32	14	8	46	0.001	186	0
Fruits and Vegetables								
Avocados, 1 medium	86	17	69	13	1	0.25	0	0
Greens, 250 mL (1 cup)	12-14	28	5	11	56	0.1	0	0
Olives, 10 large	84	14	77	8	0.1	0.02	0	0
Animal Products for Comparison								
Egg, 1 large	61	37	48	14	0.4	.02	5	51
Wild Atlantic salmon, 90 g (3 oz)	40	18	40	3	39	0.1	517	948
Cod, 90 g (3 oz)	7	31	22	1	46	0	54	111

Can Vegetarian Diets Provide Sufficient Essential Fatty Acids?

Yes, we can be confident that vegetarian diets can provide plenty of
both essential fatty acids: the omega-6 fatty acid (LA), and the
omega-3 fatty acid (ALA). Vegetarian diets are rich in LA; however, like nonvegetarian diets, they tend to be low in ALA. The primary sources of ALA are plants. Therefore, if vegetarians select
ample amounts of omega-3-rich plant foods, they can easily obtain

sufficient amounts of ALA. The challenge for vegetarians is to convert these fats in our bodies to the active long-chain omega-3 fatty acids, EPA and DHA. Several studies have shown that vegetarians generally have lower EPA and DHA in their body tissues compared to nonvegetarians. Vegans are reported to have the lowest EPA and DHA status, with levels only about half that of nonvegetarians. Breast milk DHA levels in vegan and lacto-ovo vegetarian women are also lower than in nonvegetarians. While this is somewhat of a concern, there is good evidence to show that vegetarians and vegans can achieve excellent essential fatty acids status at every stage of the lifecycle with the right food choices.

Vegetarian Guide to Getting Enough Omega-3 Fatty Acids

For most vegetarians, the key to getting enough omega-3 fatty acids, and producing optimal amounts of EPA and DHA, is to increase the intakes of ALA, and achieve the right balance between omega-6 and omega-3 fatty acids. There are three simple steps that will help us improve our omega-3 fatty acid status:

1. **Include good sources of alpha-linolenic acid (the plant omega-3 fatty acid) in the diet.** The very best sources are flaxseeds, flaxseed oil, hempseeds, hempseed oil, canola oil, walnuts, and green leafy vegetables. Aim for 3-6 grams per day for most adults. Flaxseeds are by far the richest source of ALA (57 per cent of the fat is ALA). Five millilitres (1 teaspoon) of flaxseed oil or 23 millilitres (1 H tablespoons) of ground flaxseed, plus your usual intake of vegetables, walnuts, and other foods, provides plenty of omega-3 fatty acids for most people. (See Table 7.4 for amounts of ALA in various plant foods.) One delicious way to use flaxseed oil is in salad dressing. (See recipe for Liquid Gold Dressing on page 406.)

TABLE 7.4: *Omega-3 Content (ALA) of Selected Foods*

Food	Omega-3 Fatty Acids (ALA) (g)
Flaxseed oil, 15 mL (1 tbsp)	8.0
Hempseed oil, 15 mL (1 tbsp)	2.7
Canola oil, 15 mL (1 tbsp)	1.6
Soybean oil, 15 mL (1 tbsp)	1.0
Walnuts, 30 g (1 oz)	2.7
Flaxseeds, 15 mL (1 tbsp)	2.6
Soybeans, cooked, 250 mL (1 cup)	1.1
Leafy greens, raw, 250 mL (1 cup)	0.1
Wheat germ, 30 mL (2 tbsp)	0.1

2. **Consider including a direct source of EPA and/or DHA in the diet.** There has been some concern that vegetarians and others who do not include fish in their diets (the primary sources of EPA and DHA for the general population) may not be able to make enough EPA and DHA from the ALA they consume. While there is considerable evidence to suggest that most healthy people can convert sufficiently if appropriate amounts of essential fatty acids are consumed, those with increased requirements (e.g., pregnant and lactating women or those with diseases associated with poor EFA status), or those at risk for poor conversion (e.g., people with diabetes and the elderly) may benefit from direct sources of EPA and DHA. While fish is the most concentrated source of EPA and DHA, fish do not produce these fatty acids: the plants and microalgae that fish consume make them. EPA is found in seaweed, with up to 30 per cent of the fat in some varieties being EPA (seaweed has little DHA). However, seaweed is so low in fat that you'd need to eat a lot of it to make a significant contribution to your intake. One hefty serving of 100 grams (3.5 ounces) of seaweed provides about 100 milligrams of EPA. DHA is also found in specific types of microalgae (not blue-green algae), some of which contain as much as 40 per cent DHA by dry weight. This type of microalgae is currently being cultivated, extracted, and sold as a DHA supplement with 100-300 milligrams of DHA per capsule (some are sold in veggie caps).

Eggs from chickens fed flax or DHA-rich microalgae are also reasonable DHA sources for lacto-ovo vegetarians, providing 60-150 milligrams of DHA per egg. For those wishing to supplement with DHA, 100-300 milligrams of DHA from microalgae is recommended (the higher end of the range being appropriate for pregnant and lactating women).

Why Not Just Eat Fish?

Fish is loaded with omega-3 fatty acids. High-fat, cold-water fish contains up to 1,600 milligrams of DHA and 1,000 milligrams of EPA per 100-gram (3.5-ounce serving). So why not just eat fish? There are plenty of sound reasons to forgo fish. For starters, fish is our most concentrated source of two types of contaminents: heavy metals such as lead, mercury, and cadmium, and industrial pollutants such as PCBs, DDT, and dioxin. Needless to say, these are compounds that need to be minimized in the diet. Fish is also a primary source of food-borne illness, poisoning hundreds, perhaps thousands of people in North America each day. There are also compelling ecological and ethical arguments for avoiding fish. Large commercial fishing operations are leaving the vast majority of our fish stocks in jeopardy. The Natural Resources Defense Council estimates that about 70 per cent of the world's fish populations are now fully fished, overexploited, depleted, or slowly recovering. From an ethical perspective, eating fish requires taking a life, or several lives. Indeed, commercial fishing operations generally have huge bycatches (fish and other sea life that are unintentionally caught). These creatures do not generally survive, and are simply tossed back into the water.

---

3. **Moderate the use of oils rich in omega-6 fatty acids and high-fat processed foods rich in these oils.** Eating too much omega-6 fatty acids relative to omega-3 fatty acids can reduce omega-3 conversion by up to 40-50 per cent. While increasing omega-3 fatty acids is an important first step in correcting the imbalance, vegetarians with especially high omega-6 intakes would be well advised to moderate their omega-6 intake. The best way of doing this, without compromising nutrient intake, is to reduce use of omega-6-rich/omega-3 poor oils and

processed foods containing large amounts of these oils. Sunflower, safflower, corn, grapeseed, soybean, and cottonseed oils contain the greatest amounts of omega-6 fatty acids, relative to omega-3 fatty acids. While hempseed and walnut oils are rich in omega-6 fatty acids, they are beautifully balanced with omega-3 fatty acids, so are good options (although they cannot be used for cooking). The best choices for cooking oils are those rich in monounsaturated fats such as olive, canola, and high oleic sunflower or safflower oils. Omega-6-rich whole foods such as sunflower seeds, pumpkin seeds, sesame tahini, tofu, and wheat germ are wonderful nutrition powerhouses, so intakes of these need not be reduced.

How Much Fat Should We Eat?

How do we decide what how much fat to eat? This fat feud of health authorities and diet book gurus continues despite the growing body of evidence that provides us with sensible answers.

The new Dietary Reference Intakes for Energy, Carbohydrates, Fibre, Fat, Protein, and Amino Acids (DRI Macronutrients 2002) does not set an RDA, AI, or UL for total fat (accept for during the first year of life), but they do suggest something called the acceptable macronutrient distribution range (AMDR). The AMDR for fat is 20-35 per cent of calories for everyone four years of age and older, and 30-40 per cent of calories for children aged one to three years. The Joint WHO/FAO Expert Consultation on Diet, Nutrition, and the Prevention of Chronic Diseases (2002) recommends a range for total fat of 15-30 per cent of calories. This is consistent with many governments and health organizations. The optimal amount of fat for each person depends on his or her unique constitution. People who have very efficient metabolisms (those needing fewer calories) generally require less fat than people with less efficient metabolisms (those needing a lot of calories). In addition, activity level, climate, and gastrointestinal function can affect caloric and fat needs. For example, a person who is very lean, constantly hungry, and who lives in a cold northern climate will likely find that a diet in the upper range of fat intake would be most helpful (around 30-35 per cent of calories). By contrast, a person who is overweight, sedentary, and who lives in a hot climate would very likely do better with a diet containing fewer fat calories (in the range of 15-20 per cent). For the average healthy adult, a diet providing 20-25 per cent of calories from fat appears most beneficial for long-term health (providing the fat is from good sources).

It is important to recognize that there can be disadvantages to diets that are either very low in fat (under 15 per cent of calories), or very high in fat (over 35 per cent of calories). Very low-fat diets may provide insufficient calories (especially for children) and very low intakes of omega-3 fatty acids. They also reduce the absorption of fat-soluble vitamins and protective phytochemicals. In some cases, people who become very fat phobic may choose nutritional wash-outs such as fat-free cookies or fat-free pretzels over nutritious, whole plant foods such as nuts, seeds, and soy products. The end result may be a diet deficient in vitamin E and several trace minerals.

Very high-fat diets can also spell trouble. Large amounts of fat can contribute to overeating and add unwanted pounds. This is because fat is two and a half times more concentrated in calories than carbohydrates or protein. In addition, if the fat comes mainly from concentrated fats and oils, it can be a challenge to meet our needs for nutrients and protective dietary constituents. Fats and oils contain almost no vitamins and minerals and lack fibre and phytochemicals. There is also some evidence that very high-fat intakes contribute to certain types of cancer.

What Are the Healthiest Fat Sources?

People often look at nuts much the way they do potato chips: as high-fat snack foods that clog our arteries. Conventional wisdom tells us that nuts and other high-fat plant foods such as seeds, avocados, and olives are unhealthy. That wisdom is based upon a myth—that all high-fat foods are bad for us. There is absolutely no evidence that eating moderate amounts of higher fat whole plant foods is in any way detrimental to health. In fact, the evidence is quite the opposite.

High Fat and Healthful

The highest quality of fat is naturally present in fresh nuts, seeds, soybeans, avocados, olives, and other plant foods. There is simply no contest between the fats found in these foods and the chemically altered fats found in margarine, shortening, and other hydrogenated vegetables oils, or the highly saturated fats found in animal products. Even vegetable oils that are regarded as very healthful pale in comparison to the whole foods from which they were extracted. Why? Plant foods carry with them valuable vitamins, minerals, phytochemicals, plant protein, plant sterols, essential fatty acids, and fibre. Consider what we know about the health benefits of nuts and seeds:

Nuts. The studies looking at the health effects of eating nuts annihilate the myth that "all fat is bad fat." During the last decade, studies have consistently confirmed the health benefits of these foods. In three large studies, those eating nuts most frequently had a 39-60 per cent reduction in risk of dying from heart disease compared with those eating nuts the most infrequently. Numerous smaller studies looking at the effects of individual nuts, including peanuts (not technically a tree nut, but a legume), have provided further evidence that nuts are extremely protective to health.

Another large study found that consuming 28g (1oz.) of nuts five or more times a week resulted in a 27 per cent lower risk of developing type 2 diabetes compared to those who rarely or never ate nuts.

What is it that makes nuts so healthy? Nuts are loaded with good fats (mainly monounsaturated fat) and are low in saturated fat and free of trans-fatty acids and cholesterol. They are great sources of phytochemicals and vitamin E, and good sources of plant protein and fibre. Nuts are rich sources of several trace minerals, such as selenium, copper, magnesium, chromium, zinc, and potassium. So next time you get the urge to throw a few cashews in your stir-fry, sprinkle almonds on your salad, or crack open some walnuts after dinner, just do it!

Seeds. Seeds are the life-giving part of a plant, allowing them to carry on their species. They are complete nutrition packages, designed to nourish new plants. The value of seeds in human nutrition is sorely underestimated. These concentrated foods are our most plentiful sources of essential fatty acids. Pumpkin seeds, sunflower seeds, poppy seeds, hemp seeds, and sesame seeds are all rich in the omega-6 fatty acid, linoleic acid (LA). Flaxseeds, chia seeds (grown in the deserts of Mexico) canola seeds, and hemp seeds (hemp contains plentiful amounts of both essential fatty acids) are all rich in the omega-3 fatty acid, alpha-linolenic acid (ALA). Seeds vary in their protein content, ranging from about 12 per cent of calories to over 30 per cent of calories. They are among our richest sources of vitamin E, and provide an impressive array of other vitamins, minerals, phytochemicals, and fibre.

Flaxseeds offer a significant advantage for vegetarians as they have the greatest omega-3 content of any food, averaging about 57 per cent ALA. Thus, flax can go a long way toward correcting the imbalance in essential fatty acids. Flax is very high in soluble fibre (the type of fibre that lowers cholesterol), and is one of the richest known sources of boron (a mineral important to bone health). Studies show that flaxseeds can help to reduce blood cholesterol levels, triglycerides, and blood pressure. It also improves blood sugar response in people with diabetes, and may improve immune/inflammatory disorders. Flaxseeds are the best food source of lignans, possibly protecting against cancer.

Do Flaxseeds and Flaxseed Oil Increase Risk of Prostate Cancer?

At least seven studies since 1993 have found a positive connection between blood levels of ALA (the type of omega-3 fatty acids found in plants and animals, excluding fish) and prostate cancer. As a result, prostate cancer experts often warn men to limit their use of ALA-rich foods. Flaxseed and flaxseed oil, with their exceptionally high ALA content, have been singled out as foods to be cautiously avoided, especially by those with prostate cancer, or by those who are at high risk for the disease. Many experts suggest that men should stick to fish as their primary source of omega-3 fatty acids. While it certainly makes sense to assume that flaxseed would be a problem if high ALA increases prostate cancer risk, there are a couple of important details about these studies that are seldom mentioned. To begin, flaxseed and flaxseed oil were not the source of the ALA in any of these studies. Indeed, several of the authors made it clear that the ALA was animal-derived. In addition, the actual differences in the ALA intakes of the study participants (from the highest to lowest intakes) were small. At least four other large studies have found that high ALA does not increase prostate cancer risk. In one study, there was no association, and in three studies, higher ALA was associated with reduced prostate cancer risk.

In 1991, a research team decided to look specifically at the effects of flaxseed use in men with prostate cancer. While this was a small, short-term pilot study with only twenty-five participants, the results were most encouraging. The participants were given a low-fat diet (20 per cent of calories from fat or less) and about 30 grams (45 millilitres/3 heaping tablespoons) of finely ground flaxseed per day for an average of thirty-four days. There was a trend toward a decrease in PSA levels in men with early-stage prostate cancer. Also, there was a reduction in tumour cell division and a greater rate of tumour cell death in the entire group. Larger studies will be needed before conclusions can be made about flaxseed, flaxseed oil, and prostate cancer. However, for practical purposes, it is probably wise for vegetarians with prostate cancer to stick with ground flaxseed rather than flaxseed oil as a primary source of omega-3 fatty acids until more research is completed.

Could We Get Sufficient Fat without Using Any Concentrated Fats and Oils?

Absolutely! Just as you can get all the carbohydrates that your body needs from whole foods, without any added refined starches or sugars, so you can get all of the fat that your body needs without using *any* concentrated fats and oils. However, we do need to include a wise selection of fresh whole plant foods that are naturally high in fat. Nuts, seeds and their butters, avocados, olives, and soybeans and their products are all excellent sources of good-quality fats.

Is It OK to Use Some Concentrated Fats and Oils?

While there is no question that the best-quality fat comes from whole plant foods, moderate amounts of concentrated fats and oils can fit into a healthy vegetarian diet. High-quality oils can make meals more enjoyable, add extra calories (without adding bulk), and help to improve the absorption of certain vitamins and protective phytochemicals.

Although refined oils offer important advantages over hydrogenated oils, they provide little nutritional value other than fat calories. It is best to select unrefined, mechanically pressed organic oils when they are available, as these oils contain higher amounts of phytochemicals and antioxidant nutrients. Extra-virgin olive oil is generally the only unrefined oil available on supermarket shelves. The high monounsaturated fat content makes it an excellent choice. Other high-quality fresh-pressed oils are available in natural food stores (those with high omega-3 content must be refrigerated). Among the best choices are flaxseed, hempseed, canola, walnut, almond, and hazelnut oil. Your primary cooking oil should be mainly monounsaturated—olive, canola, or high oleic sunflower or safflower oil. Non-organic canola oil is often produced from genetically engineered crops, so if you want to be sure to avoid these products, buy organic.

The most highly unsaturated oils (flaxseed, hempseed, and walnut oil) should not be used in cooking at all. They are best reserved for salad dressings or on foods at the table. Only stable oils, higher in saturated or monounsaturated fats, are appropriate for higher-temperature heating (e.g., olive, high-oleic sunflower or safflower or peanut oil) Lower-temperature cooking such as baking is less destructive to oils.

How Are High-Fat Plant Foods and Oils Best Stored?

High-fat plant foods can easily become rancid if not properly stored. This could well be nature's way of letting us know that a food has lost its freshness and is no longer wholesome. Foods and oils rich in essential fats, especially omega-3 fatty acids, are best stored in the refrigerator or freezer. Nuts and seeds that are naturally preserved by a hard shell or coat will keep for about a year in a cool, dry place. Once this protective covering has been removed or broken, they will keep for three to four months in the refrigerator and up to a year in the freezer. Walnuts, ground flaxseeds, hempseeds, and wheat germ may be best stored in the freezer as they are higher in the more unstable omega-3 fatty acids.

Fine-tuning the Fat: Six Simple Steps

1. **Aim for 15-35 per cent of calories from fat for everyone four years and older, and 30-40 per cent for children one to three years.** Those who are inactive, overweight, or who have chronic disease should aim for the lower end of this range, while children, athletes, and those who are lean and active should aim for the higher end of this range. How much fat is 15-35 per cent of calories? For a person eating 2,000 calories, it would allow for 38-75 millilitres (2.5-5 tablespoons) of fat, including fat naturally present in whole foods, and concentrated fats and oils. The following foods provide approximately 15 millilitres (1 tablespoon) of fat each:

   - 60 millilitres (G cup) nuts or seeds

   - 250 millilitres (1 cup) medium tofu or 125 millilitres (H cup) of firm tofu or tempeh

   - 500 millilitres (2 cups) regular soymilk

   - 175 millilitres (I cup) boiled soybeans

   - half an avocado

   - twenty olives

   - 125 millilitres (H cup) shredded coconut

2. **Minimize intake of trans-fatty acids.** Trans-fatty acids should make up less than 1 per cent of total calories. To accomplish this, all foods containing hydrogenated or partially hydrogenated fats should be restricted. This includes processed foods (e.g., cookies, crackers, pastries, pies, and snack foods), hydrogenated margarine, shortening, and most fried foods. Don't be fooled by a declaration of "all-vegetable oil" on the label. Be sure to read the list of ingredients!

3. **Limit foods rich in saturated fats.** Aim to keep saturated fat under 7 per cent of total calories for adults. To reduce saturated fat in a vegetarian diet, limit your use of butter, cheese, and other high-fat dairy foods, eggs, and tropical oils. If you use dairy products, replace high-fat items such as whole milk and sour cream with non-fat or low-fat items such as skim milk and non-fat yogourt, and replace butter with oil or non-hydrogenated margarine. Try scrambled tofu instead of scrambled eggs for breakfast, and substitute ground flaxseeds or commercial egg-replacer for eggs in baking.

4. **Moderate intake of omega-6 fatty acids.** Most vegetarians consume plenty of omega-6 fatty acids, and some consume excessive amounts. Aim for 5-8 per cent of calories from omega-6 fatty acids. The best way to do this is to avoid using omega-6-rich oils as your primary cooking oils (e.g., corn, safflower, sunflower, grapeseed, soy, and cottonseed oils). Instead, replace these oils with oils rich in monounsaturated fats (e.g., extra-virgin olive oil) and/or omega-3 fatty acids (e.g., flaxseed oil, organic canola oil). Do not reduce intake of highly nutritious, omega-6-rich whole foods such as sunflower seeds, pumpkin seeds, and sesame seeds.

5. **Select reliable sources of omega-3 fatty acids each day.** Aim for 1.5-2.5 per cent of total calories as omega-3 fatty acids. For most people, this amounts to 3-6 grams of omega-3 fatty acids per day. The best omega-3 sources for vegetarians are flaxseeds and flaxseed oil, hempseeds and hempseed oil, canola oil, walnuts, soybeans (and products made from soybeans), dark green leafy vegetables, and wheat germ. The following foods provide roughly 1 gram of alpha-linolenic acid:

   - 1.7 millilitres (N teaspoon) flaxseed oil

   - 17 millilitres (1 H teaspoons) ground flaxseeds

   - 2.5 litres (10 cups) dark greens

   - 17 millilitres (1 H teaspoons) canola oil

- 5 millilitres (1 teaspoon) hempseed oil

- 250 millilitres (1 cup) soybeans

- 170 grams (6 ounces) firm tofu

- 23 millilitres (1 H tablespoons) walnuts

Consider getting a direct source of long-chain omega-3 fatty acids in your diet. The best source for vegetarians is DHA from a special type of microalgae that is cultured and sold in veggie caps. When using these supplements, 100-300 milligrams of DHA per day is generally recommended (higher end of the range for pregnant and lactating women). For lacto-ovo vegetarians, omega-3-rich eggs are also an option.

6. **Rely on whole foods for the bulk of your fat.** The highest quality fat comes from fresh, whole foods, such as nuts, seeds, olives, avocados, and soybeans. Wherever possible, rely on these foods instead of concentrated fats and oils for most of your fat. Whole foods come carefully packaged by nature to protect them from damaging light, heat, and air. Whole plant foods provide phytochemicals, including antioxidants, plant sterols, vitamins, minerals, and are the very best sources of essential fatty acids. Remember that fats and oils are essential for good health, so make the effort to choose those of the highest quality.

A complete set of references is available online at:
http://www.nutrispeak.com/bvreferences.htm

fine-tuning the vegetarian diet

vitamin B12

Have you ever heard someone say that if we can't get all the nutrients we need from plants, then it proves we are designed to eat meat? In such arguments, vitamin B12 is often used as the case in point. People may then go on about the palaeolithic diet and the evolutionary process. Obviously, they say, if B12 is found only in animal products, nature is telling us something.

The truth is that our requirement for B12 has nothing to do with a need for meat, nor does it indicate that vegan diets are somehow inferior. Animals do not make vitamin B12; bacteria do. Whatever is contaminated with B12-producing bacteria can provide us with B12—plants or animals. In the past, people got vitamin B12 from dirt clinging to plants, from water, and from bacterial contamination in animals. In our modern, sanitary food environment, we wash any bits of dirt from vegetables before eating them, and chlorinate our water before drinking it. In meat, the B12 produced by bacteria is contained within the product itself. This does not make meat a superior food. So where can people who prefer not to eat animal products get their B12? They can get it from carefully grown B12-producing bacteria. These bacteria provide a convenient, reliable, and well-absorbed supply of vitamin B12 that is added to fortified foods and used to make supplements. Today we are fortunate to have the option of choosing a diet that not only supports human health, but promotes a healthy environment and a more compassionate world. The amount of vitamin B12 that we need each day is tiny—smaller even than the period at the end of this sentence. A number of false B12 beliefs exist; in some cases, these myths have led to major health problems.

- **Myth #1: Some people manage perfectly well without a source of vitamin B12.**

- **Myth #2: Vitamins from supplements are never as good as those from foods.**

- **Myth #3: Vegetables grown in B12-rich soil can meet our B12 needs.**

- **Myth #4: Reliable sources of vitamin B12 include fermented foods (such as miso, tempeh, tamari, sauerkraut, umeboshi plums), or raw foods and spirulina, algae, seaweeds, sourdough bread.**

To begin, let's consider the nature of vitamins.

What Is a Vitamin?

"Vitamin" is one of those words that people toss around without being entirely sure about what it means. Put down this book for a moment and ask the person nearest you what a vitamin is. Odds are that you'll hear something vague, like "one of those tiny little things that keep us healthy." We asked our neighbours and got back these immediate responses: "A vitamin is something you take so you don't feel guilty about having a diet consisting primarily of luncheon meats, potato chips, and beer" and "What we give our kids because their diets are so desperately limited" and "A vitamin is what you take to avoid eating all that green stuff. You need vitamins on a boat; otherwise you will get scurvy. I'm not sure what scurvy is, but it's bad."

So what is the correct definition of a vitamin? Vitamins are organic molecules that are vital to life. (In this case, organic doesn't mean "grown without pesticides"; it means "carbon-containing.") These compounds are essential in tiny amounts, and cannot be made by our bodies. Vitamins are not fuels, as carbohydrate, fat, and protein are; yet they act as necessary catalysts in many reactions, such as processes that support growth or allow us to convert food to usable energy.

Vitamin B12 was first isolated in 1948, and was the very last vitamin to be discovered. It is the largest and most complex of all vitamins, a beautifully symmetrical molecule, similar in many respects to hemoglobin. Whereas hemoglobin has an atom of iron in a central position, the mineral cobalt is at the centre in vitamin B12. This vitamin is complex not only in its molecular structure. As you'll see, the story of vitamin B12 is complicated in many ways. This chapter aims to make B12's story understandable.

Vitamin B12 in the Body

Vitamin B12 helps our red blood cells to mature normally. This vitamin is essential to the function of our brain, spinal cord, and nerves; it helps to maintain the protective myelin sheaths that surround nerve fibres. During our body's processing of protein, a molecule called homocysteine is created and the buildup of this molecule can be toxic, resulting in heart disease and other damage. As part of its role, vitamin B12 helps us clear away homocysteine.

Symptoms of Deficiency

If we don't get sufficient B12, either in our food or from supplements, we will eventually develop a vitamin B12 deficiency. In some people, the deficiency can take years to manifest, while in others symptoms can show up in a matter of months. Early signs of deficiency are often non-specific such as fatigue, weakness, and loss of menstruation. However, symptoms can escalate involving many body systems. If left for too long, the damage can be irreversible. The following list provides a whole range of possible symptoms, though not all appear in every case of vitamin B12 deficiency.

Effects related to blood. Among the very first symptoms of deficiency are fatigue and a lack of energy. (Of course, there can be plenty of reasons for fatigue apart from a lack of this vitamin.) Shortness of breath and palpitations (abnormal, rapid beating of the heart and shaking) can also occur. These symptoms occur because the lack of vitamin B12 prevents red blood cells from maturing and dividing properly. This lack affects the blood's ability to deliver oxygen, and is called macrocytic (large cell) anemia. With a microscope, lab technicians can view unusually large, oddly shaped red blood cells. Tests that detect this condition are listed on lab reports as MCV (mean cell volume, a measure of the size of individual red blood cells) and hematocrit (a count of the red cells in a certain volume of blood). As soon as our bodies get enough vitamin B12, this problem can be repaired and normal blood cells created.

The B-vitamin known as folate, or folic acid, can step in even when vitamin B12 is in short supply and help red blood cells form normally. Vegetarian diets are typically high in folic acid. (Folate is related to the word "foliage"; it is found in leafy greens, legumes, oranges, whole grains, and fortified flours.) However, folate *can't* help with the neurological symptoms of B12 deficiency described in the next section.

Effects related to the nervous system. Because of vitamin B12's importance in creating a fatty myelin sheath that protects nerves, spine, and brain, its lack can be very serious. Numbness and tingling occur, especially in the legs and feet. This is the first nervous system sign of a B12 deficiency. Eventually, balance and ability to walk are affected. Memory and ability to concentrate decrease; dizziness, disorientation, and mood changes occur, including delusions and paranoia. Bladder and bowel control may be lost. Vision may blur and optic nerves be damaged. Changes happen gradually. If severe, nerve damage can be irreversible.

Effects related to artery walls. In the section "Vitamin B12 in the Body" we mentioned the vitamin's role in helping us clear away potentially damaging homocysteine, which can cause plaque to form along the inner wall of arteries, increasing risk of heart attack. (For more on this, see Table 2.3 on page 31.)

Effects related to the gastrointestinal tract. The tongue can become sore and changes appear in its colour and on its surface. Appetite may be lost.

Effects in infants and children. Because babies have not built up stores of this vitamin, B12 deficiency will develop much more rapidly than in adults. Symptoms include loss of energy, appetite, and alertness, and can progress to coma and death. Because vitamin B12 plays a role in cell division, it is especially necessary during times of growth. Thus, an adequate intake of vitamin B12 is particularly important for pregnant and lactating women, and for infants and children. Breastfed infants can become severely deficient if the mother has low B12 intake, even if the mother has no deficiency symptoms. Thus, a regular source of the vitamin is crucial for pregnant and breast-feeding mothers, and for breastfed infants if the mother's diet is not supplemented.

All symptoms are reversible *if caught early enough*; otherwise damage can be permanent, particularly in children. Nerve damage from prolonged vitamin B12 deficiency can be severe and irreversible, yet it rarely occurs because deficiencies are generally diagnosed before this point. Such tragedies can easily be prevented by supplementation.

Causes of Vitamin B12 Deficiency

Vitamin B12 deficiency is most often the result of one of two factors:

1. Reduced absorption of B12

2. A lack of B12 in the diet

While in the general population, reduced absorption is the usual cause of B12 deficiency, in vegetarians, and especially vegans, low or negligible dietary B12 is commonly implicated.

Reduced Absorption

Absorption of vitamin B12 is a complex process in which the vitamin is passed along the gastrointestinal tract to spots along the small intestine where it can be absorbed. All the while, it must be shielded from bacteria and enzymes that would consume or destroy the vitamin. Substances in our saliva, pancreatic juices, and stomach secretions help perform this protective role. Three substances produced by the cells that line our stomachs are of particular interest. These are a digestive enzyme called pepsin, hydrochloric acid, and a protein substance called intrinsic factor.

Decreased production of pepsin and hydrochloric acid. In order for people to absorb the protein-bound form of vitamin B12 in animal products, the joint action of hydrochloric acid (HCl) and pepsin are required to split the vitamin apart from the protein that binds it. If cells lining the stomach decrease their production of pepsin and hydrochloric acid, we lose our ability to absorb the protein-bound form of vitamin B12. However, we can still absorb the form of the vitamin in fortified foods and supplements. Absorption is simpler when the vitamin B12 is not bound to protein in fortified foods or supplements.

As we age, our stomach lining gradually becomes less adept at producing HCl and pepsin. Most of the B12 deficiency in North America is due to decreased production of HCl and pepsin. Of those aged fifty years and over, up to one person in three has lost the ability to absorb the protein-bound B12 present in animal products.

Decreased production of intrinsic factor. The stomach lining also releases intrinsic factor, which acts as a B12 bodyguard, shepherding B12 along, protecting it from bacteria and enzymes that would otherwise consume or destroy the vitamin, until it reaches particular spots along the small intestine where the vitamin can be absorbed into the bloodstream. Without intrinsic factor, our body absorbs very little vitamin B12 and a condition known as pernicious anemia results, in which vitamin B12 must be given by injection. A physician may order a Schilling test to check for pernicious anemia.

B12 and seniors. Some senior citizens who are admitted to nursing homes with a diagnosis of confusion are, in fact, suffering from a loss of ability to absorb vitamin B12 for one reason or another. Where this is true, in many cases the condition can be reversed quickly by injections of the vitamin.

Those who lack pepsin and HCl can manage well thereafter with fortified foods and supplements, whereas those who lack intrinsic factor will continue to require monthly B12 injections.

Absorption, Recycling, Storage, and Interpersonal Differences

We secrete vitamin B12 into our intestines (through bile from the liver), and then reabsorb as much as 75 per cent of it. The recycling systems of some people are more efficient than those of others. Excess vitamin B12 can be stored in the liver and other tissues. Most people have a supply that will last three years or more; however, stores vary considerably. (Infants have very little.)

Myth: Some people manage perfectly well without a source of vitamin B12.

From one person to another, there are great differences in how efficiently we absorb vitamin B12, and how well we reabsorb what is secreted (in bile) into the intestine. These variations explain why deficiency symptoms may arise in less than a year in one person who has no dietary source of B12, especially one whose initial vitamin B12 stores are low. Yet another individual with no B12 intake will recycle his stores of the vitamin efficiently and problems may not become obvious for a decade or more. Genetic variations between individuals influence how early damage to the nervous system begins, how quickly homocysteine accumulates, and what degree of damage results. This much is certain: no one manages indefinitely without sufficient intake of this essential nutrient. The effects of deficiency on the nervous system and artery walls are not something we want to risk when potential problems are so easily prevented with fortified foods or a supplement! It may come as a surprise that in this instance, the form of the vitamin that is present in supplements and fortified foods turns out to be a form that is well suited to our use. In fact, as we age, this becomes the preferred form. This brings us to consider another of the myths listed at the beginning of this chapter:

Myth: Vitamins from supplements are never as good as those from foods.

The form of B12 in supplements and fortified foods is not bound to protein in the same way as that in animal products and is actually easier to absorb for people whose gastric acidity and pepsin production is beginning to decline.

Laboratory Testing for Vitamin B12 Status

Deficiency can be detected by blood tests, even at early stages. Certainly this should be done before serious problems develop and is strongly recommended for the following people:

- anyone with early symptoms of B12 deficiency, such as numbness and tingling in the fingers and toes;

- anyone who eats little or no animal products and has not had a regular, reliable source of this vitamin for many months (or several weeks, in the case of children);

- a woman in an early stage of pregnancy, who is concerned about past intake;

- a person over fifty years of age with doubts about his or her vitamin B12 status.

Since adults have stores of this vitamin that can last months or years, a simple and effective course of action for an adult without symptoms, who has simply gone for a few months without B12 intake, is just to start using fortified foods or supplements regularly! This will get B12 to a healthy level and keep it there.

Normal Levels

Several lab tests are used to detect vitamin B12 deficiency. The two most commonly used are:

Serum B12. Blood serum levels above 300 picomoles per litre (pmol/L) of vitamin B12, or 400 picograms per millilitre indicate that we have sufficient B12. With levels below 300 picomoles per litre, the amount of homocysteine in blood increases to a point at which it could have a detrimental effect on health. (Note that the serum B12 test is not valid for people who regularly use spirulina or seaweed as these contain analogs that fool the blood test.)

Methylmalonic acid. In the section "Vitamin B12 in the Body," we mentioned that as part of its role, vitamin B12 helps us clear away homocysteine. In B12 deficiency, a related compound, called methylmalonic acid (MMA), builds up. One sensitive test for vitamin B12 status is a measure of MMA in blood or urine. Levels should be less than 370 nanomoles per litre in blood or less than 4 micrograms per milligram creatinine in urine.

Recommended Intakes: Simple Solutions

Because the vitamin is effectively conserved, our required intake of vitamin B12 is miniscule. The actual amount to take depends on how frequently we consume a source, as we absorb a much higher percentage from a small amount than from a large dose. For example, when we consume 1 microgram of vitamin B12 in 125 millilitres (H cup) of fortified soymilk, we are likely to absorb about 50 per cent of the B12 present. Yet from a 2,000-microgram vitamin B12 supplement, we may absorb about 1 per cent. The recommendations that follow allow for a range of personal choices.

Recommended intake based on several small amounts over the course of a day. The recommended dietary allowance (RDA) for those above the age of thirteen years is 2.4 micrograms per day. Microgram may be written as mcg or as µg and means 1/1,000 of a milligram. The RDA assumes that our intake is spread over the course of a day, for example, by using fortified foods, eggs, or dairy products at various meals. When we take in about 1 microgram or less at a time, we absorb 50-60 per cent of the B12 present.

Recommended intake from a single daily supplement. If we have our total in a single supplement instead of spread over several meals, we should take 10 micrograms per day. Most multivitamins provide at least 10 mcg, so this is certainly an option for most people.

Recommended intake from a single weekly supplement. Some people prefer to take a larger dose supplement once a week. In this case we must take 2,000 mcg per week. High intakes do not seem to present problems; we absorb only a small percentage of the total.

Needs during stages of growth. As this vitamin is used for the creation of red blood cells and for building the fatty sheath that protects nerves, it is very important throughout times of growth. During pregnancy, a fetus depends on the mother's intake for vitamin B12, rather than on the mother's stores. Thus, daily intake is advised during pregnancy, either spread over several meals or in a daily supplement. For intakes of children and of pregnant and lactating women, see Table 15.1.

Needs for those above fifty years of age. The Institute of Medicine of the National Academy of Sciences recommends that for those above fifty years of age, most or all of the B12 should be supplied by fortified foods or a daily supplement, rather than animal products. (B12 from animal products is bound to protein and can be more difficult to absorb.) The form in most supplements and fortified foods is called *cyanocobalamin* and is not bound to protein.

Intakes and B12 Status in Nonvegetarians and Vegetarians

Nonvegetarians tend to have vitamin B12 intakes that meet or exceed recommended intakes, and deficiency is generally due to absorption problems, not a shortage in the diet. Past studies have shown intakes and vitamin B12 status of vegans and other vegetarians to be relatively low compared to nonvegetarians. Often lacto-ovo vegetarian intakes were within the normal range, as were intakes of vegans who used B12-fortified foods or supplements. Studies have demonstrated that the longer people remain on a diet without a source of vitamin B12, the lower their serum B12 drops, and eventually problems can develop.

A 1999 American study by Ella H. Haddad and her colleagues observed serum B12 and MMA in two groups: nonvegetarians and vegans. The latter had followed vegetarian diets for twelve years, and been vegan for four years. Serum B12 and MMA were found to be similar in the two groups. This is because B12 intakes were similar in the vegans and nonvegetarians. Nonvegetarian women averaged 5.7 micrograms of vitamin B12 from foods and supplements, while vegan women averaged 6.0 micrograms. Nonvegetarian men averaged 5.3 micrograms of vitamin B12 from foods and supplements, while vegan men averaged 5.0 micrograms. This demonstrates that when a reliable source of B12 is provided in vegan diets, vitamin B12 status is similar to nonvegetarians. Indeed, vegans using adequate amounts of fortified foods or B12 supplements are much less likely to suffer from B12 deficiency than the typical meat-eater. This is because the type of B12 that vegans consume is exclusively cyanocobalamin; they do not rely on protein-bound B12 that is not as well absorbed, especially as we grow older.

Our Sources of Vitamin B12

The actual sources of vitamin B12 are some very helpful micro-organisms capable of building the intricate vitamin B12 molecule. We humans cannot make the vitamin in our bodies, nor can animals. We rely on bacteria and several other micro-organisms for our entire supply. Some of these bacteria live in the lower intestines of animals and humans. Unfortunately, we can't absorb the vitamin B12 made by these bacteria because absorption takes place higher up in the intestine than where they live (and they don't swim upward).

B12 in Animal Products

For most North Americans, dietary vitamin B12 comes primarily from animal products, yet animal products are not the original source of this B12. The B12 in animal flesh, seafood, eggs, and dairy products comes from bacteria and other one-celled organisms.

B12 in the Cycle of Nature

We may think fondly of times when we humans were "closer to nature." In the natural cycle, intestinal waste from humans, grazing animals, and wild animals, and waste from beetles, worms, and little burrowing creatures puts vitamin B12 back into the soil. Bugs and little bits of dirt, along with B12, ended up on plant foods eaten by our ancestors. But, to be perfectly honest, there are downsides to being that "close to nature."

B12, earth, and modern hygiene. Today we choose to be more hygienic and to avoid the pathogens (disease-causing organisms) that can also be present in soil. When plant foods are washed, bacterial contamination and vitamin B12 are scrubbed off, along with the dirt. Humanity's progress in hygiene has certainly cut down on many micro-organisms that we don't want, along with infectious disease and related deaths—but it has reduced the B12, too.

Myth: Vegetables grown in B12-rich soil can meet our vitamin B12 needs.

B12 and agriculture. Certainly there is more vitamin B12 in cobalt-rich soils that contain organic waste and have plenty of little "critters" burrowing through the earth. But we scrub this dirt off the veggies that go into our salads. Even in those that are not rinsed, the amount of B12 would be quite variable, and generally negligible. Unfortified plant foods simply cannot be relied on as B12 sources.

Myth: Reliable sources of vitamin B12 include fermented foods (such as miso, tempeh, tamari, sauerkraut, sourdough bread, umeboshi plums) and also spirulina, algae, and seaweeds.

B12 and food production methods. Fermented foods such as tempeh and miso had the reputation of containing vitamin B12. This reputation was based on less hygienic, less tightly controlled production methods that were used in the past. In traditional methods, all sorts of bacteria could get into the fermenting food, including some that produce vitamin B12. Modern sanitary controls eliminate the B12-producing bacteria. These foods cannot be counted on as sources of the vitamin, nor can spirulina or algae. If there is any B12 on seaweed, the amount is unreliable and depends on the type of seaweed and on the waste and bacteria present in the water in which it grew. Don't count on seaweed for your vitamin B12.

B12 analogs. Sea vegetables (seaweeds), spirulina, and other types of algae may contain vitamin B12 analogs (also known as non-cobalamin corrinoids). These analogs are similar to true vitamin B12, but are not exactly the same. They are near-identical twins, with something missing. Analogs can occupy the same locations on cell surfaces that are used by true vitamin B12, and crowd out B12 molecules from their rightful receptor sites. In the process, they can prevent the vitamin from performing its necessary functions. A substance that contains substantial amounts of analogs won't help you meet your need for vitamin B12. In fact, it could even make the situation worse. Scientific reports have shown that seaweeds, spirulina, and other types of algae are ineffective in reversing cases of vitamin B12 deficiency.

To add confusion, some lab tests used to detect vitamin B12 in foods have been unable to distinguish true B12 from analogs.

Foods that are *not* reliable sources of vitamin B12. None of the following should be relied on as B12 sources: fermented foods (such as miso, tempeh, tamari, sauerkraut, umeboshi plums), seaweeds, spirulina, algae, raw plant foods, and unfortified plant foods.

> When a fortified food or supplement label lists "cobalamin" or "cyanocobalamin" on the ingredient list, you know you're getting the real thing!

Reliable Sources of Vitamin B12 for Vegetarians

Lost in Label Lingo?

Unless fortified, no plant food contains significant amounts of true vitamin B12 (cobalamin). Labels of fortified foods show them to contain B12; however, it can be very confusing to figure out how much of your day's ideal supply is in a serving. This is because the amount set as 100 per cent some years ago (and used ever since as the basis for food labels) is not the same as 100 per cent of the adult recommended intake (RDA) today. (It would be immensely expensive for manufacturers to redesign their food labels every time nutritional scientists decided to adjust the recommended intake for any one of dozens of nutrients.)

Whereas the RDA for adults is now 2.4 micrograms of vitamin B12, a standard used for Canadian labels, the RDI, is still 2 micrograms. Thus, a serving that contains 1.2 micrograms, or half of our recommended intake (RDA) for the day, is labelled as having 60 per cent of the RDI for vitamin B12.

TABLE 8.1   *For Food Labels: Standards and Amounts of Vitamin B12*

Standard	Amount of Vitamin B12 Set as 100%
Adult recommended dietary intake (RDA), Canadian and American	2.4 mcg
Recommended daily intakes (RDI), Canadian	2 mcg
Daily value (DV), American	6 mcg

To add further to the confusion, if we look at American food labels we can see amounts of B12 described in terms of the daily value (DV). Based on an outdated U.S. standard that was higher, 100 per cent of the DV for vitamin B12 is 6 micrograms. As a result, the product that supplies 1.2 micrograms is labelled as providing just 20 per cent of the DV.

Reliable food sources of B12 that are used by vegetarians are listed in Table 8.2. Yeasts other than the brand listed generally are not fortified.

TABLE 8.2   *Vitamin B12 in Foods*

Food	Amount of Vitamin B12 (mcg)	RDI	DV
Fortified Foods			
Cereals, ready-to-eat, fortified, 30 g (1 oz)	0.6-6.0	30-300%	10-100%
Nutritional yeast (Red Star Vegetarian Support Formula), mini-flakes, 15 mL (1 tbsp)	1.5	75%	25%
Soymilk or other non-dairy milks, fortified, 125 mL (H cup)	0.5-1.55	25-77%	10-26%
Veggie "meats," fortified, 42.5 g (1.5 oz)	0.6-1.2	30-60%	10-20%
Infant formula	See label		
Animal Products			
Cow's milk, 125 mL (H cup)	0.4	20%	7%
Cheddar cheese, 21 g (.75 oz)	0.1-0.2	5-10%	2-3%
Yogurt, 125 mL (H cup)	0.3-0.7	15-35%	5-12%
Egg, large, 1 (50 g/1.75 oz)	0.5	25%	8%

To determine the amount of true B12 in a particular substance, a letter can be written to the technical department of the company producing the substance, requesting a laboratory report to verify the presence of cobalamin (vitamin B12) and the absence of non-cobalamin corrinoids (vitamin B12 analogs).

What About B12 Supplements?

When it comes to vitamins and minerals, generally our best plan is to try to meet our recommended intakes from foods, especially plant foods, because they have all sorts of phytochemicals, fibre, and other nutrients.

Yet in the case of vitamin B12, the situation is a little different. Some vegetarians use plenty of eggs and dairy products, while others use very little or none of these. B12 from supplements and fortified foods is essential for those who consume little or no animal products, and is the preferred form for older people.

In fact, most vitamins are absorbed well from vitamin pills. Though we can't duplicate the many healthful components of plant foods in a pill, when diets fall short, making up the difference with supplements or fortified foods works very well. In the 2,000-calorie Menu #2, egg and dairy products contribute some B12, though less than recommended intakes. Adding one or more fortified foods could easily bring the total up to recommended levels.

Vitamin B12 in Menus

TABLE 8.3   *Vitamin B12 in 2,000-Calorie and 2,800-Calorie Menus*

Menu and Page	Calories	Vitamin B12 (mcg)	Calories	Vitamin B12 (mcg)
#1 Nonvegetarian, page 88	2,000	3-3.4	2,800	4-4.4
#2 Lacto-ovo Vegetarian, page 91	2,000	2.0	2,800	2.6
#3 Lacto-ovo Vegetarian with More Legumes, page 92	2,000	3.5	2,800	3.6
#4 Vegan, page 94	2,000	4.9	2,800	5.0

B12 Basic: What You Really Need to Know

For a vegan, a suitable intake that meets the RDA of 2.4 micrograms of vitamin B12 might include a serving of fortified breakfast cereal and, at another time in the day, 125 millilitres (H cup) of fortified soymilk or a serving of a fortified veggie "meat," each providing 1.5 micrograms (or 25 per cent of the DV). On another day, the intake might come from a multivitamin-mineral supplement.

- Low B12 intakes can cause serious health consequences, especially in babies.
- Aim for enough B12 to prevent deficiency and to reduce homocysteine.
- Do not mess with insufficient vitamin B12!

Reliable Vegan B12 Sources Include:

1. Foods fortified with B12 (e.g. non-dairy beverages, some veggie "meats," some ready-to-eat cereals, and some nutritional yeasts)
2. Vitamin supplements

How Much Vitamin B12 Do We Need?

1. **From fortified foods:** At least 3 micrograms a day when divided among two or more times in the day.
2. **From supplements:** At least 10 micrograms a day when taken daily; at least 2,000 micrograms when taken once a week.

A complete set of references is available online at:
http://www.nutrispeak.com/bvreferences.htm

designing the diet

the vegetarian food guide

In Chapters 3 through 8 you learned about all of the key nutrients of interest in vegetarian nutrition, and the food sources of these nutrients. Key myths about protein, iron, and zinc were challenged, and outstanding plant sources of these valuable nutrients were discovered. We learned about the amazing world of calcium and vitamin D, and the many little known calcium powerhouses of the plant kingdom. A fresh perspective on grains was presented, and the important contribution these little gems can make to our overall nutrient intakes. We discussed the most highly protective, nutrient-dense foods in our diet—vegetables and fruits. The world of fat was explored, and a strong case was built for including higher-fat whole foods in the daily diet in place of processed fats and animal fats. Finally, we investigated vitamin B12, a nutrient that vegetarians sometimes fall short on, even with a varied vegetarian diet. Now we will condense this information in a single-page, practical pictorial tool called the *Vegetarian Food Guide*. This guide will assist us in designing a vegetarian diet that is practically foolproof!

As you can imagine, it's no simple task to develop a tool that is suitable for people of many ages, activity levels, and food preferences. A single guide must support the nutritional health of a teenage marathon cyclist, his preschool sister, and his grandmother. A vegetarian guide applies to those who use eggs and dairy products, and those who don't. It must assist beginners to "get it right" and help long-term vegetarians to fine-tune their way of eating.

In fact, there are many variations on a basic vegetarian theme to keep us in excellent health. Some like a simple, basic menu, repeated day after day with a few changes. Others want gourmet meals and elegant presentation. Many people don't want to cook, and rely on restaurant meals and take-out delis. Others eat much of their food raw. For some, preparation must be quick and easy, while for others the top priority is economy.

The Vegetarian Food Guide covers all these possibilities. It emphasizes whole foods, yet allows for the use of some processed foods. It supports us in meeting recommended intakes for the full spectrum of essential nutrients. At the same time it helps us avoid the diseases of excess.

These practical pointers will help you plan an excellent diet using the Vegetarian Food Guide:

- ✔ **Eat a wide variety of foods from each group.** Variety helps to ensure sufficient nutrients, phytochemicals, and fibre. It also makes our meals a whole lot more interesting!

- ✔ **Be moderate in your intake of concentrated fats, oils, and added sugars, if used.** These are generally high in calories, but poor sources of nutrients. Fats and sugar can crowd out foods that offer valuable nutrients.

- ✔ **Aim for an hour of physical activity each day.** Exercise is central to energy balance and overall health.

- ✔ **Drink six to eight glasses of water and other fluids each day.** Water is essential to good health. Drinking pure water is a great way to provide needed fluids. However, using vegetable or fruit juices and herbal teas to provide fluids is an excellent option, too.

The Vegetarian Food Guide

| Grains | Vegetables & Fruits | Milks & Alternates | Beans & Alternates | Other Essentials |

The Vegetarian Food Guide: A Guide to Daily Food Choices

The ranges in servings allow for differences in body size, activity levels, and age. For example, smaller and less active people need fewer servings; larger, more active people need more.

Food Group Servings per day	What Counts as a Serving?	Important Comments
Grains *5-12* *servings*	1 slice of bread 30 g (1 oz) ready-to-eat cereal 125 mL (H cup) cooked grains, cereal, or pasta 30 mL (2 tbsp) wheat germ 30 g (1 oz) other grain products	***Choose mainly whole grains.*** • Include intact whole grains such as brown rice, quinoa, millet, barley, and kamut. • Enjoy whole grain breads and cereals. • Limit refined grains such as white flour products and white rice.
Vegetables and Fruits *5 servings* *or more*	125 mL (H cup) vegetables 250 mL (1 cup) salad 125 mL (H cup) vegetable or fruit juice 1 medium apple, banana, orange, 125 mL (H cup) fruit 60 mL (1/4 cup) dried fruit	***Eat a wide variety of colourful vegetables and fruits.*** • Include deep green leafy vegetables. • Select plenty of vitamin C-rich fruits and vegetables such as citrus fruits, tropical fruits, and peppers.
Milks and Alternates *6-8 servings*	125 mL (H cup) fortified soymilk 125 mL (H cup) cow's milk or yogourt 125 mL (H cup) calcium-fortified orange juice 60 mL (G cup) calcium-set tofu 250 mL (1 cup) cooked or 500 mL (2 cups) raw of high-calcium greens (kale, collards, Chinese greens, broccoli, okra) 250 mL (1 cup) high-calcium beans, (i.e., soy, white, navy, Great Northern, black turtle beans) 60 mL (G cup) almonds 45 mL (3 tbsp) almond butter 21 g (.75 oz) cheese 15 mL (1 tbsp) blackstrap molasses 60 mL (G cup) dry hijiki seaweed 5 figs	***Get to know your calcium sources!*** • Include calcium-rich foods with every meal. • Foods should provide about 15% of the RDI or DV per serving to be included in this group. • Include servings of calcium-rich foods through out the day. • For lower calorie choices, pick greens more often.

Food Group Servings per day	What Counts as a Serving?	Important Comments
Beans and Alternates 2-3 servings	250 mL (1 cup) cooked legumes (beans, lentils, split peas) 125 mL (H cup) tofu or tempeh 1 serving veggie "meat" (burger, wiener, slices) 45 mL (3 tbsp) nut or seed butter 60 mL (G cup) nuts and seeds 500 mL (2 cups) soymilk 2 eggs	***For maximum benefit, eat a wide range of these protein-rich foods.*** • Select beans and lentils often for extra fibre. • Include nuts and seeds for a boost of vitamin E and minerals. • Try "veggie meats" for more concentrated protein.
Other Essentials: Omega-3 fatty acids *1-2 servings*	**Omega-3 fatty acids** 5 mL (1 tsp) flaxseed oil, 22 mL (1-H tbsp) ground flaxseed, 15 mL (1 tbsp) hempseed oil, 60 mL (G cup) shelled hempseeds, 20 mL (4 tsp) canola oil, 45 mL (3 tbsp) walnuts. For supplementary veggie DHA, see page 247. **Vitamin B12 (cobalamin)**	***Pay attention to these important nutrients.*** • Add an excellent source of omega-3 fatty acids to your daily diet.
Vitamin B12 to meet recommended intakes	Fortified foods, supplements, eggs, or dairy products supplying 2.4 mcg (adults); 2.6-2.8 mcg (pregnancy and lactation); 0.9-1.8 mcg (children) **Vitamin D**	• Whether you use vitamin B12-fortified foods or a supplement, be sure that a reliable source of vitamin B12 is included in your diet.
Vitamin D to meet recommended intakes	Fortified food or supplements supplying 5 mcg /day vitamin D2; 10 mcg (51-70 years); 15 mcg (70+ years); or sunshine.	• If you don't get enough sunshine, use vitamin D2-fortified beverages or supplements.

Here are additional notes about the different groups on the guide.

Grains

The whole grains, breads, cereals, and pasta in this group are key contributors of energy (each serving typically provides about 80 calories), protein, B-vitamins, and minerals such as iron. Whole grains are preferred as they provide a wide assortment of vitamins and minerals, plus fibre. The suggested number of servings ranges from five to twelve servings per day. The minimum of five servings is suitable for those who have low energy needs, such as people who are inactive or small in stature, and those who are limiting their caloric intake. Does a total of five servings sound like a lot? It is less than you might imagine. For example, a cup of cooked cereal at breakfast (two servings), a sandwich with two slices of bread at lunch, and a half-cup of rice or pasta at supper add up to five servings. Athletes and teenage boys, who have high energy requirements, can eat twelve servings from this group (or more)!

Vegetables and Fruits

Vegetables provide a wealth of vitamins, minerals, fibre, and phytochemicals, yet a serving of vegetables is just about 25 calories, so we can eat plenty without worrying about our waistline. Fruits make a wonderful alternative to sweet high-calorie desserts, delivering, on average, just 60 calories per serving. Variety is mentioned here because every unique vegetable or fruit delivers its own special package of nutritional benefits, including some of the rainbow range of phytochemicals. Calcium-fortified juice, figs, and many leafy greens do double duty as calcium sources. Greens and orange juice are also rich in folate and greens in vitamin K.

We receive more than a third of our day's vitamin C in 125 millilitres (H cup) of these fruits: guava, citrus fruits and juices, kiwi, papaya, cantaloupe, strawberries, mangos, and these vegetables: red and orange bell peppers, broccoli, kale, and Brussels sprouts. Many other vegetables and fruits are rich in vitamin C, and larger servings provide enough vitamin C to greatly improve iron absorption.

Beans and Alternates

Beans, peas, lentils, and soyfoods stand out as protein powerhouses for vegetarians. At first you may think, "I could never eat two servings of beans in a day." In fact, this group is rich with possibilities that take you far beyond beans, satisfying every taste. Choices run the gamut from fat-free, protein-packed veggie "meats" (about 80 calories per 60 g/2 oz serving) to hearty foods that deliver about 200 calories per serving (beans, soymilk, tofu, nuts) or as high as 270 calories in a 45-millilitre (3-tablespoon) serving of nut and seed butters. Legumes provide iron, zinc, a range of B-vitamins, and both insoluble and soluble fibre. Some beans are good calcium sources, and calcium-set tofu and fortified soymilk are great ways to get this mineral. Soyfoods deliver isoflavones. When it comes to nuts, each of these has its own special features. For example, walnuts are high in omega-3 fatty acids; almonds and almond butter are sources of calcium; cashews contain zinc. Peanuts (which are actually legumes) are economical, higher in protein than tree nuts, and contain health-protective phytochemicals.

Remember that iron absorption is increased substantially when we eat a vitamin C-rich fruit or vegetable at the same time. This occurs, for example, when beans or lentils are served in the same meal with red pepper or other vitamin C-rich vegetables, or when tofu is combined with orange juice or strawberries in a shake.

Cow's Milk, Fortified Soymilk, and Alternates

Increasingly, food guides are recognizing the importance of calcium sources that go beyond cow's milk. *The Manual of Clinical Dietetics*, developed by Dietitians of Canada and the American Dietetic Association, lists all of the options shown here in its vegetarian section. China's Food Guide Pagoda (similar to the pyramid) recognizes beans and calcium-set tofu as good calcium sources. The American Food Guide Pyramid includes fortified soymilk as an option, listed as a footnote.

Each serving in this group contains approximately 150 milligrams of calcium. (We also get small amounts of calcium from foods other than those in this group.) An excellent way to meet goals of 1,000 milligrams of calcium for adults up to age fifty, or 1,200 milligrams over age fifty, is by consuming at least six to eight of these calcium-rich foods at meals and snacks throughout the day. The percentage we absorb is highest when our calcium is delivered in small doses.

On national food guides, the size of a serving of cow's milk is doubled (250 millilitres/1 cup) and there are half as many servings in this group (two to four), so total amounts work out to be the same, or slightly less than in this guide. In the Vegetarian Food

Guide, a serving of fortified soymilk or cow's milk is 125 millilitres (H cup). *Label readers, note that foods and beverages containing about 150 milligrams of calcium are listed as providing about 15 per cent of the RDI (Recommended Daily Intake or DV).*

Low-calorie choices. Selections from this group can suit those who want very low-fat, low-calorie sources of well-absorbed calcium. In this case choose the greens listed, (250 millilitres/1 cup of cooked greens provides only about 20-40 calories). With these you'll get plenty of vitamins at the same time. A 15-millilitre (1-tablespoon) serving of mineral-rich blackstrap molasses or 125 millilitres (H cup) of skim milk is in a similar range, with about 45 calories. Fortified juice or soymilk, and various types of low- or full-fat cow's milk or yogourt, or goat's milk, provide about 55-80 calories per 125 millilitres (H cup).

Moderate-calorie choices. Cheddar cheese contains about 85 calories in 21 grams (0.75 ounces); this is the option with the most saturated fat (4.5 grams). Calcium-set tofu and tempeh are more hearty choices with about 80-180 calories per 125-millilitre (H-cup) serving, depending on brand.

High-calorie choices. Servings in this group that provide more calories are five figs (weighing 95 grams/3.3 ounces) or 250 millilitres (1 cup) of beans, each providing about 240 calories. For very high-energy ways to get calcium, we can load our toast with almond butter (45 millilitres/3 tablespoons gives 290 calories). The high-calorie foods are particularly valuable during the growing years, for athletes, and for people who tend to be underweight.

As we have mentioned, many foods in this group double as servings from other food groups. For example, 125 millilitres (H cup) of calcium-fortified orange juice also counts as a fruit serving; 125 millilitres (H cup) of calcium-set tofu counts in the beans group; and 250 millilitres (1 cup) of cooked kale counts as two servings of vegetables. Note that soymilk, rice milk, and orange juice that are not fortified with calcium are *not* options from this group.

It's wise to choose a cross-section of these alternative ways to get our calcium. For ideas about how to include them over the course of a day, see pages 134-135.

Omega-3 Fatty Acids

We require two essential fats, the omega-6 and omega-3 fatty acids. Generally we have no difficulty at all in getting enough of the omega-6 fatty acids from an assortment of plant foods in the various food groups, and from vegetable oils. However, we must take particular care to include the omega-3 fatty acids, as these are less widely distributed in the food supply. Our most efficient way to get this is from ground flaxseed or flaxseed oil. Other good options are hempseed or hempseed oil, canola oil, walnuts, or a hearty serving of tofu.

We can get DHA, one of the long-chain omega-3 fatty acids, present in fish, from the same source that fish get theirs-microalgae. DHA from microalgae is cultured and sold in veggie caps containing 100-300 milligrams of DHA per cap.

Vitamin B12

Those eating little or no animal products need fortified foods that supply at least 2.4 micrograms of vitamin B12 (cobalamin) over the course of the day or a supplement that provides 10 micrograms per day.

Dairy products or eggs supply some B12 (see Table 8.2 on page 236 for amounts). However, over the age of fifty years, fortified foods or a supplement are advised for lacto-ovo vegetarians,vegans and nonvegetarians. A weekly B12 supplement of 2,000 micrograms is another option.

For recommended intakes of vitamins and minerals for children and during pregnancy and lactation, see pages 269 and 280.

Vitamin D

Be sure to get adequate vitamin D from daily sun exposure or through fortified foods or supplements. Cow's milk, fortified soymilk, and margarines are fortified with vitamin D. *Label readers, note that milk (soy or cow's) that is fortified with 2.5 micrograms of vitamin D is shown on the label as providing 50 per cent of the RDI.*

Assessing Your Diet

How do you figure out whether you're meeting your nutritional needs? You can check off your day's food intake using the Score Sheet on page 250. Photocopy the Score Sheet and use it to assess your diet for a few days. This will give you an idea of the strengths and weaknesses of your current way of eating. If you find that you're short in a certain group, choose foods that you like from that group and put them on your shopping list. You can extend your cooking repertoire with the recipes in Chapter 12; these emphasize highly nutritious ingredients. After scoring your diet for a while and making a few adjustments, you can relax and realize you're on the right track.

The Simple Life

Here's a sample pattern with cereal, a milk, and fruit for breakfast; hummus, pita, and veggies for lunch; tofu with rice, salad, and broccoli for supper; and a fruit smoothie as a snack. This simple menu is packed with 75 grams of protein, and plenty of vitamins, minerals, essential fats, and fibre. The whole day's pattern comes to just 1,680 calories, so most active people have some calories to play around with. This allows for additional foods, such as larger portions or favourite treats. It's no harder to plan a nutritionally adequate vegetarian (or vegan) diet than a nonvegetarian diet. If you are aiming for a beautifully balanced diet, with plenty of fibre and protective antioxidants, you are actually at an advantage with your vegetarian eating pattern.

Common Questions (and Answers)

Q. *If I follow the guide, should I take a supplement?*

A. If you score your diet according to the Score Sheet, and meet the minimum servings in the Vegetarian Food Guide each day, you're not likely to need a supplement. However, a multivitamin-mineral supplement can help you to "top up" nutrients that may be marginal on certain days, depending on your food intake. In addition, in some situations, supplements can be quite useful. Here are five examples.

TABLE 9.1 Vegetarian Food Guide Score Sheet

Columns list the number of servings from each group.

Food	Grains	Vegetables and Fruits	Beans and Alternates	Milks and Alternates	Omega-3 Fatty Acids	Vitamin B12	Vitamin D
Breakfast							
Cereal, cooked, 250 mL (1 cup)	2						
Fortified soymilk or cow's milk, 250 mL (1 cup)				2		3 mcg	2 5mcg
Fruit or juice, 125 mL (H cup)		1					
Lunch							
Whole wheat pita bread, 2	2						
Hummus, 250 mL (1 cup)			1	1			
Raw veggies, 125 mL (H cup)		1					
Supper							
Rice, 250 mL (1 cup)	2						
Calcium-set tofu, 125 mL (H cup)			1	1			
Steamed broccoli, 250 mL (1 cup)		2		1			
Salad, 250 mL (1 cup)		1					
Dressing with 10 mL (2 tsp) flaxseed oil					2		
Snack							
Shake with fortified soymilk or cow's milk and fruit		1		1			2.5 mcg
TOTAL	6	6	2	6	2	3 mcg	5 mcg

- If your vitamin B12 requirement is not met by fortified foods, eggs, or dairy products, then a supplement that contains vitamin B12 is essential.

- If the need for vitamin D is not met by sunlight, or fortified soy or cow's milk, or margarine, then a vitamin D supplement is necessary.

TABLE 9.2   *Vegetarian Food Guide Score Sheet*
Under "Food," list your day's intake. Then, in the appropriate column, check off
the number of servings from each group.

Food	Grains	Vegetables and Fruits	Beans and Alternates	Milks and Alternates	Omega-3 Fatty Acids	Vitamin B12	Vitamin D
TOTAL							

- When life becomes extra busy, meals can become less than regular, and nutrient intakes far from ideal. In such cases, occasional or regular supplements can be helpful.

- When calories are limited or portions are very small (for example, with a finicky child or someone with a poor appetite), giving a supplement can help meet vitamin and mineral needs.

- At times of growth (such as during pregnancy) it can be a challenge to meet recommended intakes shown on pages 436 and 439 of the Appendix, or to consume the suggested amounts of food. Supplements give us reassurance at times like this.

Q. *Do I need to drink water, or are other fluids okay?*

A. Water is ideal, and it's a good goal to drink six to eight glasses during the day. We can count herbal teas, juices, various milks, and the water in soups, too. Caffeinated beverages (tea and coffee) don't fully count in the way water does, as these beverages have a diuretic effect; that is, they encourage water losses through our kidneys.

Q. *Do fruit drinks count as a fruit serving?*

A. No! They'd count as servings of sugar, if we had a sugar group—but we don't! Whereas real fruit juice gives us an assortment of vitamins, minerals, and phytochemicals, beverages that are called "drinks" do not. Even if a fruit "drink" has added vitamin C and a small percentage of real juice, it's primarily sugar, water, plus a vitamin.

Q. *Where do oils and sugar fit in? Do I need to count them?*

A. Oils rich in omega-3s, such as flaxseed, canola, or walnut oils, are in a special category and make an important contribution. Most other oils and sugar are mainly providers of calories and don't contribute many essential nutrients. The best way to regard these other oils and sugar is to allow them some space in our diet after recommended serving for food groups have been met. If we still have room on our day's menu (without taking in excess calories), then these can be included. This is more likely to be the case for active people who have higher caloric requirements. Generally it's best to make fresh and dried fruits our favourite sweets, and whole foods such as avocados, olives, nuts, and seeds our first choice in fats.

Q. *How do I get iodine?*

A. The mineral iodine is present in plant foods in amounts that vary from one geographic area to another, depending on how much iodine is present in the soil. In the past, people in low-iodine regions of North America developed iodine deficiency. Symptoms included the overgrowth of the thyroid gland to form a goiter in the area of the throat, and the tragic outcome of deficiency during pregnancy in which the child would be born with cretinism. This problem still occurs in some parts of the world. In Canada, this deficiency was eradicated by requiring the addition of iodine to all table salt. By 1946 the use of iodized salt was recommended in Canada's Food Rules. The adult recommended intake for iodine (150 micrograms) is easily met by 2 millilitres (H teaspoon) of iodized salt. Sea salt is generally not iodized (although it may be—check label), and contains negligible amounts of natural iodine as this mineral is lost in the drying process. Salty seasonings such as tamari, soy sauce, Bragg Liquid Aminos, and miso do not provide iodine.

In the United States it is not mandatory for table salt to be iodized and about 50 per cent of the general population uses iodized salt. In addition to variable amounts in plant foods, bread can be a source of iodine because the mineral is present in some dough stabilizers. Sea vegetables and supplements such as kelp powder or kelp tablets can be very high in iodine, leading to intakes by some vegetarians that exceed the recommended upper limit, which is 1,100 micrograms.

A complete set of references is available online at:
http://www.nutrispeak.com/bvreferences.htm

vegetarian
for life

There are several stages of the life cycle that deserve special attention. These include the years of peak growth (pregnancy, lactation, infancy, childhood, and adolescence) and the senior years. Each stage of growth is characterized by physical changes that result in unique nutritional requirements. During pregnancy and lactation, infancy, childhood, and adolescence, our needs for many nutrients are greater (per kilogram/pound of body weight) than at any other time in our lives. As we approach our senior yeaars, our caloric requirements decline, while our needs for some nutrients actually increase. This means we must be especially diligent about our food choices to ensure that our nutrient needs are met.

Although the dietary goals of optimal health and well-being are maintained throughout the various stages of life, the food patterns that best support these goals naturally differ. During the adult years, a primary focus is the avoidance and sometimes treatment of chronic diseases, such as heart disease, cancer and type 2 diabetes. Diets relatively low in fat and high in fibre are generally the most suitable choice. In contrast, during the growing years greater emphasis must be placed on adequate growth and development, so sufficient concentrated sources of energy and nutrients are necessary. However, these years establish the basis for prevention of chronic disease in later life, so laying the foundation of life-long healthy eating patterns is also essential. By recognizing the fundamental differences in our nutritional needs, the positive health consequences of a vegetarian diet can be fully realized at every stage of life.

Regardless of whether we are near-vegetarian, lacto-ovo vegetarian, or vegan, a plant-centred diet can support excellent health. The guidelines offered in this chapter will help to ensure that the special needs of those in the growing years, and in the prime of life, are met in a simple and enjoyable manner. This chapter will take us through each of four important life stages:

1. Pregnancy and Lactation

2. Infancy (Birth to Two Years)

3. Childhood (Two to Twelve and Beyond)

4. Focus on Teens (Thirteen and Over)

5. The Prime of Life (Fifty Years Plus)

Part 1: Pregnancy and Lactation

The months of pregnancy are filled with excitement and anticipation. At no other time in our lives are we are more focused on taking good care of ourselves. This is because we have the awesome responsibility of a precious little soul depending on us for her or his growth and development. It is not uncommon during this time to question whether or not our plant-centred diets are adequate to support this little person who shares our food. Sometimes concerned friends, relatives, and even health professionals start drilling us with questions that further shake our resolve. Thankfully, with a little planning and good sense, we can get all the nutrients we need for both our babies and ourselves.

Both lacto-ovo vegetarian and vegan diets can meet all the nutrient and energy needs of pregnant women. Babies of vegetarian mothers have birth weights that are, on average, similar to those of infants born to nonvegetarians mothers and within a healthy range. Vegetarians enjoy some advantages when it comes to pregnancy and lactation, including a lower risk for obesity, hypertension, and pre-eclampsia. The recommended nutrient intakes during pregnancy and lactation are provided in the Appendix (page 435).

Nutrition Guidelines for Pregnancy and Lactation

1. Increase energy intake by approximately 100 calories a day during the first trimester of pregnancy, 300 calories a day during the last two trimesters, and 500 calories a day during lactation.

One of the key factors in healthy pregnancy outcomes is weight gain of the mother. Insufficient weight gain can cause the baby to be very small. Low birth weight babies (under 2.5 kilograms/5 H pounds) are at higher risk for illness and death than are babies of normal weight. How much weight should we gain? For most adult women beginning pregnancy with a healthy body weight, a gain of 11.5-16 kilograms (25-35 pounds) is recommended. Table 10.1 lists recommended weight gain during pregnancy for a variety of circumstances.

TABLE 10.1 *Recommended Weight Gain During Pregnancy and Lactation*

Weight Category	Weight Gain Recommended**
Normal Weight (BMI* 19-24.9)	11.5-16 kg (25-35 lbs)
Underweight (BMI < 20) Adolescent (< 2 years after 1st menstruation)	12.5-18 kg (28-40 lbs)
Overweight (BMI > 25)	7-11.5 kg (15-25 lbs)
Normal weight with twins (BMI 19-24.9)	16-20 kg (35-45 lbs)
Normal weight with triplets (BMI 19-24.9)	23 kg (50 lbs)
* BMI means body mass index. For a definition, see page 324. BMIs listed are prior to pregnancy ** African Americans and young adolescents should strive for weight gain at the upper end of the range, while short women should aim for gains at the lower end of the range.	

In order to produce the desired weight gain during pregnancy, about 100 extra calories a day are needed during the first trimester and about 300 extra calories a day in the last two trimesters, in addition to normal food intake. A total caloric intake of 2,500-2,700 calories a day is appropriate for most women. A glass of soymilk or a slice of whole grain bread will provide about 100 calories, while a bowl of cereal (with milk) or a muffin with a piece of fruit will provide about 300 calories.

During lactation, we need an additional 200 calories above pregnancy needs or about 500 additional calories each day. This is because it takes a lot of energy to produce enough milk for a baby. Total energy needs are approximately 2,700-2,900 for most women. Five hundred calories can be found in a sandwich and a glass of fortified soymilk or cow's milk. The 500-calorie recommendation assumes that we will be using about 300 calories a day from our body fat stores that have accumulated during pregnancy. For moms who do not have extra fat stores, the increase in calories needs to be in the 800-1000 calorie range. It is important not let caloric intake slip below 1,800 calories a day, as this can reduce milk production.

What If I Have "Morning Sickness"?

If you experience morning sickness (varying degrees of nausea), you are not alone. It affects 50-75 per cent of all pregnant women, especially during the first trimester. Morning sickness can reduce appetite, slow weight gain, and even cause weight loss. To help reduce nausea associated with morning sickness, it is best to eat several small meals a day, and avoid having an empty stomach. Bland, starchy, low-fat foods such as pasta, bread, cereal, rice, potatoes, and crackers are good choices. Ginger, a natural anti-nausea herb, can also be helpful. Sweets and fatty foods can make matters worse, while sour and salty foods are said to be beneficial. Drink plenty of water. Be sure to take prenatal supplements.

2. Eat a wide variety of nutritious foods, as outlined in the Vegetarian Food Guide.

During pregnancy nutrient needs shoot up, although calorie requirements increase by only a small amount. What this means is that there is less room for "junk food" that provides little nutritional value. Instead, we must load up on the many wholesome foods described in the Vegetarian Food Guide. Include a wide variety of foods from each food group to achieve the best balance of nutrients possible. Avoid skipping meals, as a good supply of vitamins and minerals are needed throughout the day. To make the food guide work during pregnancy and lactation, strive for the higher end of the recommended numbers of servings within each food group.

Recommended Number of Servings During Pregnancy and Lactation

Beans and alternates: 3-4 servings
Milks and alternates: 6-8 servings
Vegetables and fruits: 7-10 servings
Grains: 7-12 servings

Other Essentials
Omega-3 fatty acids: 2 servings
Vitamin B12: 2.6 mcg (pregnancy); 2.8 mcg (lactation)
Vitamin D: 5 mcg

A suggested meal plan, based on the Vegetarian Food Guide, with the additions recommended during pregnancy and lactation, is provided in Table 10.2 Sample Meal Plan for Pregnancy and Lactation. This menu supplies the RDA for all nutrients during pregnancy and lactation, except for vitamin D and iron during pregnancy (although intakes are very high). About half the vitamin D is supplied by fortified soymilk. The other half can be obtained through sunshine or supplements. The iron in the menus provided is very close to recommended intakes during pregnancy, and far in excess of recommended intakes for lactation (45 milligrams in menu for pregnancy and 50 milligrams in menu for lactation).

3. Include three to four servings of beans and alternates each day.

During pregnancy, needs for protein, iron, and zinc increase, while during lactation, protein and zinc requirements increase. These nutrients are important for the growth of the uterus, and expanding blood volume, as well as the infant's growth and development (review Chapter 3 for more information on these nutrients). The increases in recommended dietary allowances (RDA) for each of these nutrients is as follows:

Protein: The RDA for protein goes up by 25 grams a day throughout pregnancy and lactation. On average this means an increase from 46 grams of protein to 71 grams a day. More precisely, protein needs climb from 0.8 grams to 1.1 per kilogram of body weight. For vegetarians who eat primarily whole plant foods (little tofu, soymilk, and veggie meats), an additional 10 per cent is suggested to allow for reduced protein digestibility in whole plant foods. That would bring us up to 1.2 grams per kilogram of body weight or about 78 grams of protein a day.

Iron: The RDA for iron rises from 32.4 milligrams a day for non-pregnant vegetarians to 48.6 milligrams for pregnant vegetarians (This is 1.8 times greater than the nonvegetarian RDA of 18 milligrams a day for non-pregnant women and 27 milligrams a day for pregnant women). Getting 48.6 milligrams of iron from any diet is very difficult, so iron supplements are recommended for pregnant vegetarians, as they are for all pregnant women. There is currently little evidence to suggest that the risk for iron deficiency in pregnancy is any greater in vegetarians than it is in nonvegetarians. However, vegetarian iron stores are lower, so theoretically, risk may be increased. To help ensure sufficient iron intake, an iron supplement of 30 milligrams per day is recommended for all pregnant women, and 60-120 milligrams per day for those with a low haemoglobin or hematocrit.

Iron needs are not increased during lactation, and indeed the RDA drops below non-pregnant levels to 16.2 milligrams a day for lactating vegetarians (9 milligrams a day for nonvegetarians). This is because women do not generally menstruate during lactation.

Zinc: The RDA for zinc increases from 8 milligrams a day for non-pregnant women to 11 milligrams a day during pregnancy and 12 milligrams a day during lactation. Vegetarians may need as much as

50 per cent higher intakes of zinc if intakes of inhibitors such as phytate and calcium are high. Although zinc supplementation is not routinely recommended during pregnancy, it may be wise for pregnant vegans to select a prenatal supplement that includes approximately 15 milligrams of zinc. This supplement should also contain 2 milligrams of copper, as zinc can reduce copper absorption.

Meeting the RDAs for Protein, Iron, and Zinc

Increasing our intakes of beans and alternates to three to four servings a day will help ensure sufficient protein, iron, and zinc. While this may seem like a lot of beans, when you include a variety of alternates, it is quite manageable. The following food combinations are examples of just what three to four servings of beans and alternates can look like:

- 125 millilitres (H cup) tofu, 250 millilitres (1 cup) soymilk, and 250 millilitres (1 cup) kidney beans

- 45 millilitres (3 tablespoons) almond butter, two veggie burgers, and 250 millilitres (1 cup) pea soup

- 60 millilitres (G cup) cashews, 250 millilitres (1 cup) black beans, and 125 millilitres (H cup) tempeh

- two eggs, three slices veggie back bacon, 250 millilitres (1 cup) soy milk, and 60 millilitres (G cup) pumpkin seeds

4. Include six to eight servings of milks and alternates each day, and a reliable source of vitamin D.
The RDA for calcium remains at 1,000 milligrams a day during pregnancy and lactation. There is no increase in calcium requirements because calcium is more efficiently absorbed during this time. Getting sufficient calcium during pregnancy is important for proper formation of a baby's bones and teeth, as well as proper nerve, muscle, and blood functioning. It is also important for a woman's own bone health.

The following examples provide at least six servings from the milks and alternates group:

- 45 millilitres (3 tablespoons) almond butter, 15 millilitres (1 tablespoon) blackstrap molasses, 125 millilitres (H cup) tofu made with calcium, and 500 millilitres (2 cups) fortified non-dairy milk or cow's milk (eight servings)

- 250 millilitres (1 cup) calcium-fortified non-dairy milk or cow's milk, 250 millilitres (1 cup) yogourt, 250 millilitres (1 cup) Chinese greens, and 60 millilitres (G cup) almonds (six servings)

- 250 millilitres (1 cup) steamed kale, 250 millilitres (1 cup) baked beans, five figs, 250 millilitres (1 cup) fortified non-dairy soymilk or cow's milk, and 250 millilitres (1 cup) calcium-fortified orange juice (seven servings)

- 250 millilitres (1 cup) broccoli, 250 millilitres (1 cup) black turtle beans, 60 millilitres (G cup) hijiki seaweed, 21 grams (.75 ounce) cheese, and 250 millilitres (1 cup) calcium-fortified orange juice (six servings)

For those who consume less than the recommended number of servings from the calcium-rich group, a calcium supplement may be warranted. While there are modest amounts of calcium in most prenatal supplements (about 100-250 milligrams), this may not be sufficient to make up for a diet containing few calcium-rich foods. If a calcium supplement is needed, select one that provides about 500 milligrams of calcium daily. Absorption is improved when this amount is taken in two doses at different times. It is best to take calcium supplements between meals and separately from iron supplements, as calcium can interfere with the absorption of iron and zinc.

Vitamin D partners with calcium assisting in its absorption. While vitamin D needs do not increase during pregnancy and lactation, a reliable source is necessary for the bone health of both mother and infant. Most prenatal supplements contain sufficient vitamin D. We can also get our vitamin D from sunshine or from fortified foods (see Chapter 4 for more information on amounts of sunshine required and fortified foods available).

5. Eat seven to ten servings a day of colourful vegetables and fruits, including leafy greens.

During pregnancy and lactation, needs for several vitamins and minerals rise, including many that are concentrated in vegetables and fruits, such as vitamins A and C, and folate (see Table 10.3 Nutrient Recommendations for Pregnancy and Lactation for each nutrient).

Vitamin A: Our needs for vitamin A increase by just under 10 per cent during pregnancy, but by almost 50 per cent during lactation. The greater increases of lactation are because an average of about 400 micrograms RAE of vitamin A goes into breast milk each day. Thus, vegetarians must take special care to include vitamin A-rich foods in the diet during this time (see Chapter 6 for more information about vitamin A). Most of our vitamin A comes from brightly coloured orange and deep yellow vegetables and fruits, and green leafy vegetables. It is best to strive for at least three to four servings of vitamin A-rich vegetables and fruits each day.

Vitamin C: The RDA for vitamin C increases by 12 per cent during pregnancy and 38 per cent during breastfeeding. The higher amounts needed in lactation reflect the 40 milligrams of vitamin C that appears in breast milk each day. Additional vitamin C can be easily obtained by eating the recommended number of servings of vegetables and fruits. Especially rich vitamin C sources are citrus fruits, strawberries, tropical fruits, broccoli, Brussels sprouts, spinach, and peppers.

Folate: The RDA for folate increases to 600 micrograms of Dietary Folate Equivalent (DFE) a day during pregnancy, and 500 micrograms of DFE a day during lactation. Folate is of tremendous importance because it is estimated that the occurrence of neural tube defects, including spina bifida and anencephaly, can be reduced by at least 50 per cent by increasing folate intake before conception and during early pregnancy. Thus, all women who are capable of becoming pregnant are advised to consume at least 400 micrograms of folic acid a day, either from fortified foods or a supplement. (Folic acid is the form of the vitamin in supplements and fortified foods, while folate is the form of the vitamin in foods. The two terms are often used interchangeably. See Chapter 6 for more information.) Note that very high folate intakes can mask a vitamin B12 deficiency. Therefore, while getting sufficient folate is necessary, intake from supplements and fortified foods should be limited to not more than 1,000 micrograms a day (excluding folate from foods).

6. Include at least seven to twelve servings of grains each day.
Needs for a number of B vitamins rise about 20-30 per cent during pregnancy and lactation. Eating more whole grains will ensure that these additional needs are easily met. The most nutritionally dense grains are intact whole grains such as quinoa, amaranth, oat groats and rolled oats, kamut, spelt and wheat berries, rye, and brown rice. Use these more often. See pages 409-412 for cooking instructions and recipe ideas. Muffins, breads, and cereals made with whole grains are also good options. If you are experiencing severe morning sickness, you may prefer refined grains, at least part of the time. If you opt for refined pasta, bread, cereal, and other processed grains, select those that are enriched with B-vitamins.

7. Increase intake of omega-3 fatty acids to 2 per cent of total calories.
During pregnancy and lactation, needs for long-chain omega-3 fatty acids, particularly DHA, rise. DHA is critical to the development and function of many different organ systems, and for the structure of the brain and retina of the eye. The primary source of DHA for nonvegetarians is fish. Vegetarians get can their DHA from the same place fish do—microalgae. Today, we culture microalgae (so it is free of environmental contaminants), and sell it in veggie caps. However, this DHA source has only recently become available, so DHA in vegetarian, and particularly vegan, diets has traditionally been very low. Lacto-ovo vegetarians can get some DHA from eggs, especially the DHA-rich varieties. Vegetarians generally have reduced DHA status compared with nonvegetarians. Past studies show vegans to have approximately one-half the DHA of nonvegetarians in their body tissues and breast milk, while vegetarians have slightly higher levels. While we do not know what

optimal levels of DHA are, there is some indication that higher levels provide some benefit to infants. Vegetarians have two ways of improving their DHA status. First, we can maximize our conversion of alpha-linolenic acid (ALA, the form of omega-3 fatty acids in plants) into DHA by ensuring sufficient ALA in the diet (see Chapter 7, pages 210-214 for more information). Second, we can take a supplement of vegetarian, microalgae-based DHA providing 200-300 milligrams of DHA a day. Many experts advise the direct DHA source during pregnancy and lactation, as conversion of ALA to DHA is very limited (about 2-5 per cent).

How much ALA do we need? Increasing intake to at least 2 per cent of calories is recommended. For someone eating 2,400 calories a day, about 5 grams of ALA should be sufficient. We can get 5 grams of ALA from two servings from the omega-3 fatty acid group. Examples include:

- 10 millilitres (2 teaspoons) flaxseed oil

- 15 millilitres (1 tablespoon) hempseed oil and 45 millilitres (3 tablespoons) walnuts

- 22 millilitres (1 H tablespoons) ground flax and 20 millilitres (4 teaspoons) canola oil

8. Include a reliable source of vitamin B12 in the diet every day.
The importance of getting sufficient vitamin B12 in pregnancy and lactation cannot be overemphasized. A lack of this nutrient during pregnancy can result in extremely poor stores in newborn infants. If vitamin B12 continues to be insufficient during lactation, the baby may end up with severe vitamin B12 deficiency (weakness, loss of reflexes, failure to thrive, delayed development, muscle wasting, and irreversible brain damage). The key determinant of a baby's vitamin B12 status appears to be the mother's current intake, rather than her B12 stores, so it is especially important to include a reliable source of vitamin B12 each day. To add to the concern, recent research has demonstrated that high homocysteine levels caused by insufficient vitamin B12 during pregnancy may increase the risk for neural tube defects in infants.

All pregnant and lactating women should aim for 5-10 micro-grams of vitamin B12 a day from fortified foods or supplements (most prenatal vitamins contain this much). While the RDA is 2.6 micrograms a day during pregnancy and 2.8 micrograms a day during lactation, the higher intakes will help to keep homocys-teine from rising. The best dietary sources of vitamin B12 for veg-etarians are Red Star Vegetarian Support Formula nutritional yeast, vitamin B12-fortified non-dairy beverages, cereals, and meat substitutes (see Chapter 8 for more information on B12 sources). Seaweed, fermented soyfoods, and organic vegetables are *not* reli-able vitamin B12 sources. For lacto-ovo vegetarians, dairy prod-ucts and eggs are also reliable sources of this vitamin, though amounts are small.

9. Take a prenatal multivitamin-mineral supplement.
Prenatal vitamin and mineral supplements provide protection against nutrient shortages during pregnancy, so they are advised for all pregnant women. All women capable of becoming pregnant should consume 400 micrograms of folic acid each day from sup-plements, fortified foods, or both, in addition to consuming folate from other foods. Also, an iron supplement of 30 milligrams per day is recommended for all pregnant women. Those who do not eat suf-ficient calcium-rich foods would be wise to use a daily supplement of 500 milligrams of elemental calcium.

Remember that vitamin and mineral supplements do not pro-vide protein, carbohydrates, fats, fibre, or phytochemicals, and can-not compensate for a poor diet. Make a healthful, balanced food intake your top priority. Higher dose supplements are not advised unless medically indicated, as they provide no added benefit and can interfere with the absorption of other nutrients. Single-nutrient supplements can be toxic to the developing baby and are generally best avoided unless medically indicated. There are three notable exceptions to the caution on single-nutrient supplements: calcium, vitamin B12, and essential fatty acids (specifically DHA).

10. Avoid alcohol during pregnancy.
Pregnant women who drink alcohol increase the chances of their babies being born with fetal alcohol syndrome (FAS), the world's

leading cause of mental retardation. This devastating condition can also result in central nervous system disorders, growth deficiencies, and abnormal facial features. Although the risk to the infant increases with the amount of alcohol consumed, safe lower limits are not known. For this reason, alcohol should be completely avoided during pregnancy.

11. Keep caffeine consumption under 300 milligrams per day. There is limited evidence that excess caffeine may contribute to prematurity, low birth weight, and reduced head circumference in infants. Caffeine passes easily across the placental barrier and is very poorly metabolized by the unborn baby. Caffeine is found primarily in coffee, tea (black and Asian green teas), cola beverages, chocolate, and some medications. While a limit of 300 mg a day is generally accepted, some studies suggest that intakes as low as 150 mg a day could contribute to low birth weight and increase risk of spontaneous abortion. A 140 gram (5-ounce) cup of coffee contains about 85 mg; a 1-ounce of expresso has about 40 mg; a 5 ounce cup of tea about 30 mg, and a 12 ounce cola about 36 mg.

Caffeine-free, grain-based beverages made from ingredients such as roasted malt, barley, chicory, and carob may be useful substitutes. Decaffeinated coffee is also an option, but its effects are not known. Herbal teas such as rosehip, mint, lemon, and fruit teas are also a good alternative, although not all herbal teas are safe. Examples of herbal teas that are not recommended for pregnant or lactating women include comfrey, pennyroyal, lobelia, sassafras, barberry, devil's claw root, chamomile, dong quai, golden seal, lily of the valley, rue, uva ursi, yarrow, coltsfoot, hawthorne berries, juniper berries, mandrake root, mistletoe, wormwood, and Scotch broom.

12. Minimize your intake of environmental pollutants. Environmental contaminants such as DDT and PCBs are highly toxic compounds that are extremely difficult to excrete from our bodies. Sadly, one way women get rid of some of these contaminants is through breast milk, so it's necessary to minimize exposure as much as possible. Vegetarians are at a considerable advantage in

this regard as the most concentrated sources of environmental contaminants are fish and animal fat. Not surprisingly, vegetarians, and
especially vegans, have been found to have lower levels of pesticides
such as DDT and PCBs in their blood and in their breast milk. In
one large study, vegans had only 1-2 per cent of the amounts found
in nonvegetarians. These findings have been supported by at least
three other studies, with not a single study suggesting otherwise.

To further increase protection, limit pesticide-laden plant
foods. Some of the worst offenders are non-organic peanuts, raisins,
and cottonseed oil, and foreign produce. A simple solution is to purchase organically grown foods whenever possible. All produce
should be thoroughly washed before eating (even organic produce!).

Additional Considerations for Breastfeeding

There is no better food for the mind and body of the human infant
than the warm milk of his or her mother. It is exquisitely designed
to provide the perfect balance of nutrients and protective substances
for optimal growth and development. Plus, there are numerous
health benefits for mom: breastfeeding helps us relax, and to return
to pre-pregnancy weight and shape more quickly; it prevents menstruation (during full-time breastfeeding), helping to maintain iron
stores and energy; it saves money, and it reduces long-term risk of
breast, uterine an ovarian cancers. Breast-feeding a baby for a minimum of one year and preferably for two years or more is best. Fortunately, more and more mothers are returning to this practice.
Whereas in 1970 just one infant in five was breastfed, now two in
three babies receive this excellent start, and half of these continue
for six months or more.

Moms need extra fluids while breast-feeding. It's a good idea to
keep a big glass of water handy while nursing. Drink 2-3 litres (8-
12 cups) of liquids a day. While water is among the very best choices, pure fruit juices, fortified milks, grain beverages, and soups can
all make an excellent contribution to overall fluid intake. Caffeine
should be limited. Alcohol does not need to be as strictly avoided as

during pregnancy, although intake should be very moderate, if it is used at all.

Nutrient needs of breast-feeding mothers are similar to what they were during pregnancy. Lactating mothers often are advised to continue prenatal vitamin/mineral supplements for a couple of months after the baby is born, then switch to a regular adult multivitamin-mineral preparation that contains vitamin B12 and vitamin D.

Most foods can be eaten during breastfeeding, although some babies are sensitive to garlic, onion, hot spices, soda pop, MSG, licorice, and artificial sweeteners. While allergy to breast milk is virtually non-existent, a baby can have allergic responses to foods eaten by the mother (intact proteins can make their way into breast milk). Colic, eczema, chronic congestion, or gastrointestinal distress can all be signs of allergy, especially if there is a family history of food allergies. The foods most commonly associated with these kinds of reactions are cow's milk (causing an estimated 75-80 per cent of the cases), eggs, wheat, soy, citrus fruits, nuts, and chocolate.

For more detailed information about nutrition and breastfeeding, we highly recommend *Raising Vegetarian Children* by J. Stepaniak and V. Melina (McGraw-Hill, 2002).

TABLE 10.2   *Sample Menu Plan for Pregnancy and Lactation*

Food	Pregnancy (2,400 calories)	Lactation (2,600 calories)
Breakfast		
Whole grain breakfast cereal (recipe, pp. 388)	250 mL (1 cup)	250 mL (1 cup)
Fortified soymilk	250 mL (1 cup)	250 mL (1 cup)
Blueberries	125 mL (H cup)	125 mL (H cup)
Whole grain toast	1 slice	1 slice
Almond butter	22 mL (1 H tbsp)	22 mL (1 H tbsp)
Blackstrap molasses	15 mL (1 tbsp)	15 mL (1 tbsp)
Calcium-fortified orange juice	250 mL (1 cup)	250 mL (1 cup)
Lunch		
Black bean soup (recipe, page 394)	375 mL (1 H cups)	375 mL (1 H cups)
Rye crackers	6	6
Muenster cheese (recipe, page 398)	60 mL (G cup)	60 mL (G cup)
Raw veggies (carrots, peppers, cucumbers)	250 mL (1 cup)	250 mL (1 cup)
Nutty date cookies (recipe, page 429)	1	2
Dinner		
Hot tofu with Cool Greens (recipe, page 414)	170 g (6 oz) tofu	170 g (6 oz) tofu
Go-for-the-Green Salad (recipe, page 405)	750 mL (3 cups)	750 mL (3 cups)
Liquid Gold Salad Dressing (recipe, page 406)	30 mL (2 tbsp)	30 mL (2 tbsp)
Pumpkin seeds	30 mL (2 tbsp)	30 mL (2 tbsp)
Lemon Teasecake (recipe, page 425)	1/16th of cake	1/16th of cake
Snacks		
Fruit smoothie	250 mL (1 cup)	250 mL (1 cup)
Muscle Muffin	–	1
Servings from Each Food Group		
Grains	8	11
Vegetables and Fruits	10	10
Beans and Alternates	4	4
Milks and Alternates	8	8
Omega-3 Fatty Acids	2	2
Vitamin B12	Yes	Yes
Vitamin D	In part (from soymilk). Additional needed from sunshine or supplement.	

TABLE 10.3   *Nutrient Recommendations for Pregnancy and Lactation*

Nutrient	Non-pregnant (19-50 years)	RDA or AI* (AI in italics)		Per cent Increase over Non-pregnant Needs	
		Pregnant (19-50 years)	Lactating (19-50 years)	Pregnant (19-50 years)	Lactating (19-50 years)
Protein	46 g	71 g	71 g	35%	35%
+10%**	51 g	78 g	78 g		
Minerals					
Iron ***	32 mg	49 mg	16 mg	35%	0
Zinc	8 mg	11 mg	22 mg	27%	33%
Calcium	*1,000 mg*	*1,000 mg*	*1,000 mg*	0	0
Magnesium	310-320 mg	350-360	310-320	11-12%	0
Selenium	55 mcg	60 mcg	70 mcg	8%	11%
Vitamins					
Vitamin A	700 mcg	770 mcg	1,300 mcg	9%	46%
Thiamin	1.1 mg	1.4 mg	1.4 mg	21%	21%
Riboflavin	1.1 mg	1.4 mg	1.6 mg	22%	30%
Niacin	14 mg	18 mg	17 mg	22%	18%
Vitamin B6	1.3 mg	1.9 mg	2.0 mg	32%	35%
Vitamin B12	2.4 mcg	2.6 mcg	2.8 mcg	8%	14%
Folic Acid	400 mcg	600 mcg	500 mcg	33%	20%
Vitamin C	75 mg	85 mg	120 mg	12%	38%
Vitamin D	5 mcg	5 mcg	mcg	0	0
Vitamin E	15 mg	15 mg	19 mg	0	21%

* **RDA (Recommended Dietary Allowance):** Average daily intake levels sufficient to meet requirements of 97-98 per cent of healthy people. **AI (Adequate Intake):** A recommended daily intake used when RDA cannot be determined with confidence. Based on observations and research on a group (or groups) of healthy people. *Nutrients stated as AIs are in italics.*

** **Protein:** The additional 10 per cent is to be used for vegetarians who get most of their protein from unprocessed whole foods such as beans, vegetables, whole grains, nuts, and seeds (as opposed to those who use tofu, soymilk, and meat analogs on a regular basis).

*** **Iron:** RDAs given in this table are for vegetarians, and are 1.8 times higher than they are for nonvegetarians.

Part 2: Infancy (Birth to Two Years)

The first two years of life are filled with discovery. Adventurous infants delight in the colours, textures, and flavours that surround them. As parents or caregivers, we must seize the opportunity to build a foundation for health that includes a wide variety of wonderfully nourishing foods.

During the first year of life, our babies triple their birthweight, a rate of growth that will not be surpassed. Their requirements for most nutrients, per pound of body weight, are two to three times those of adults. When we consider the small stomach capacity of a baby and this tremendous rate of growth, we can understand their need for a steady supply of energy and nutrients.

Infants can be very well nourished on lacto-ovo vegetarian or vegan diets. Parents or caregivers need to become well acquainted with food patterns that work and those that don't. We must pay particular attention to the energy, protein, and vitamin B12 in the baby's diet. Iron, zinc, calcium, and vitamin D must also be considered. After solid foods are introduced, foods that are more concentrated in energy and nutrients, such as tofu and nut and seed butters, are especially valuable for the vegan infant. As vegetarian diets grow in popularity, new products appear on the market, helping to make our task a whole lot easier.

Poorly planned or overly restrictive diets can have serious consequences for the growth, development, and overall health of an infant. The following guidelines will help to ensure that our baby grows up to be a happy, thriving toddler.

Nutrition Guidelines for Vegetarian and Vegan Infants

1. Breastfeed for a minimum of six months, and preferably for a full two years.

Breast milk is the only food our babies need for the first four to six months of life. The Canadian Paediatric Society and Dietitians of Canada recommend exclusive breastfeeding for the first four to six months of life, while the World Health Organization and the American Academy of Pediatrics recommend breastfeeding as the sole source of nutrition for the first six months of life. After solids are introduced, breast milk continues to be a primary source of nutrition and fluids, and should be provided for at least the first year. Ideally, breastfeeding will go on until the baby weans herself or himself, generally between two to four years of age.

Breast milk is perfectly designed to meet the needs of the human infant, just as the milks of other mammals are designed to meet the needs of their young. It provides just the right amount of protein, essential fatty acids, vitamins, and minerals, and supplies special substances that protect babies from infection. The breast milk of lacto-ovo vegetarian and vegan women is similar in composition to that of nonvegetarians. Mother's milk adjusts naturally to meet an infant's changing needs. The more scientists learn about the unique composition of human milk, the more they realize that an equivalent can never be formulated in a lab.

2. If breastfeeding is not chosen, not possible, or if an infant is weaned before one year of age, iron-fortified, commercial infant formula is recommended.
Commercial infant formula is the only acceptable alternative to breast milk during the first year of life. The Canadian Paediatric Society advises using the iron-fortified variety from birth for all formula-fed babies until the introduction of high-iron solid foods. If breastfeeding stops prior to one year of age, or if a baby nurses fewer than three times a day, an iron-fortified commercial infant formula should be used as the replacement. Apart from breast milk and commercial infant formula, no other substitute can safely serve as the primary milk source before a baby's first birthday.

Cow's milk is not recommended during the first nine to twelve months of life in Canada, and before twelve months in the United States. There are several important reasons for delaying the introduction of cow's milk. First, in the first six months of life an infant's gastrointestinal system is often sensitive to cow's milk protein, resulting in blood loss in the stool. In addition, cow's milk contains higher amounts of protein, sodium, potassium, and chloride than the immature kidneys of an infant can handle. Early introduction of cow's milk can also increase the risk of nutritional deficiencies, especially iron deficiency. Finally, cow's milk contains insufficient essential fatty acids, zinc, and vitamins C and E.

Never use homemade infant formulas as they provide grossly inadequate nutrition. Reports of malnutrition in vegetarian infants have been traced to such beverages.

Are There Any Formulas Suitable for Vegan Babies?

Most commonly used commercial infant formulas are not vegan as they are based on cow's milk. Soy-based commercial infant formulas are safe and adequate, and are the only alternatives for vegan babies who are not breastfed. However, it is important to read the label as at least one soy formula uses beef fat in its formulation. All soy-based formulas in North America currently use vitamin D3 in their products (the animal form of vitamin D). In addition, soybeans used in some infant formulas are not organic, so they may be genetically modified.

Questions have been raised about the use of soy-based formulas for infants, due to their high isoflavone content. Babies fed soy formula do have higher blood levels of isoflavones, and it is not known whether this would have a positive or negative effect on long-term health. Thus far, studies have not shown any adverse effects. In addition, these formulas have been in use for several decades, with no apparent harm to infants.

---

3. Provide 625-750 millilitres (20-24 ounces) of breast milk, formula, or cow's milk, or a combination of breast milk, formula, and full-fat fortified soymilk per day for infants between the ages of twelve and twenty-four months.

Providing the appropriate milk during the second year of life helps ensure sufficient energy, high-quality protein, vitamins, and minerals to support normal growth and development. While breast milk continues to be the best option, if a baby has weaned or is nursing only part-time (less than three times a day), a substitute can be used. The following milks can be safely used as substitutes during the second year of life:

Lacto-ovo vegetarian infants (twelve to twenty-four months). After twelve months of age, lacto-ovo vegetarian babies can use whole cow's milk in addition to, or in place of, breast milk or commercial infant formula. Two per cent cow's milk is not generally recommended, although it is thought to be acceptable in cases where the infant is growing well and eating a wide variety of solid foods. Lower-fat cow's milk (1 per cent and skim milk) is not suitable for babies up to two years of age.

Vegan babies (twelve to twenty-four months). Vegan infants and those with dairy allergies (or where there is a preference for soy) can be given full-fat fortified soymilk after one year of age (check with your physician regularly to ensure the baby is the appropriate height and weight for age). As soymilk is a little lower in fat than whole milk, it is important to ensure that the diet includes ample sources of fat such as tofu, nut butters, and avocado. Breast milk and/or commercial infant formula should continue to be offered as a supplementary beverage until the baby is two years old, or even longer. The baby should also be eating a good variety of solid foods as outlined in the Getting Enough to Grow on Guidelines on page 282.

Healthy Babies Alert!

Unfortified soymilk, tofu milk, rice milk, nut milk, and grain milks should not be used as the primary milk source during the first two years of a baby's life. These milks will not provide the nutrients necessary for optimal growth and development of infants.

---

4. Provide a vitamin D supplement of 400 international units (10 micrograms) per day for all breast-fed babies, from birth until sufficient vitamin D is obtained from foods.

While somewhat controversial, a vitamin D supplement of 400 international units (10 micrograms) for all breast-fed infants is generally recommended. Theoretically, infants can make enough vitamin D from sufficient warm sunlight; however, this is not considered a reliable source of vitamin D during infancy and is certainly not possible during Canadian winters. Infants are usually protected from ultraviolet rays with clothing or sunscreen. Babies with dark skin require from two to six times as much sunlight to produce sufficient vitamin D.

Breast milk is generally a poor source of vitamin D. Nursing mothers who do not receive sufficient vitamin D from food sources or sunlight will have very low levels of this nutrient in their milk.

Mothers who receive sunlight and/or vitamin D-fortified foods
have higher amounts of vitamin D in their milk, but amounts can
be quite variable, and may not be sufficient to meet infant needs.
Insufficient vitamin D intake in infancy causes rickets, a bone disease in infants and children that results in softening and weakening
of the bone structure and possibly permanent bone deformities.
Bow legs, knock knees, and misshapen ribs and skull are common
symptoms of advanced rickets. For more on vitamin D, see page 138.

Formula-fed infants don't need a vitamin D supplement as
infant formula is fortified with this nutrient.

5. Ensure a sufficient source of iron throughout infancy. Breast-fed infants require a source of iron apart from breast milk by six months of age.

In healthy, full-term infants, iron stores are plentiful at birth. Stores
begin to decline at about four months of age and can become
depleted by six months or shortly thereafter. Preterm and low birth
weight babies are born with low iron stores, which can very quickly become depleted. Iron deficiency is the most common nutritional
deficiency among children aged six months to three years. Symptoms of iron deficiency in infants include pallor (pale skin colour),
fatigue, irritability, decreased appetite, slow development, and
reduced cognitive function (reduced ability to learn).

Breast milk contains small amounts of highly absorbable iron;
however, by about six months of age, additional iron is needed
(sooner in preterm and low birth weight babies). Solid foods can
reduce the absorption of iron in human milk, so it is very important
that a baby's first foods provide iron. The first food generally recommended is iron-fortified infant cereal. To improve the iron
absorption from infant cereals, a good source of vitamin C can be
served with the cereal (after these foods have been appropriately
introduced—see guideline #7). Iron-fortified cereals can continue
to provide iron up to two years of age and beyond. If iron-fortified
infant cereals are not used, an iron supplement containing 1 milligram of iron per kilogram of body weight (0.5 milligram per
pound) can be given when solid foods are introduced. (For additional information on iron and iron sources, see pages 96-107 in
Chapter 3.)

The use of iron-fortified formula is recommended from birth for infants who are not breast-fed. Parents are sometimes concerned that iron-fortified formula may cause constipation and stomach upset in their infant. However, studies have found no differences in gastrointestinal symptoms or stool consistency when regular and iron-fortified formulas are compared.

6. Make sure that sufficient vitamin B12 is provided either through breast milk, formula, or a supplement.

Breast-fed infants of lacto-ovo vegetarian and vegan women can get sufficient vitamin B12 if the mother's vitamin B12 intake is adequate. It is possible to obtain sufficient vitamin B12 from fortified foods and/or from dairy products and eggs. However, including a prenatal or multivitamin-mineral supplement containing at least 10 micrograms of vitamin B12 each day provides extra insurance that B12 levels will be sufficient to meet infant needs. Vegan mothers who do not take care to include reliable sources of this nutrient can have very low levels of vitamin B12 in their milk. It is essential for both mother and child to have reliable B12 sources (read more about this in Chapter 8). If mothers have any doubt about past intake, it is important to have their vitamin B12 status assessed by their physician and laboratory testing. If sufficient vitamin B12 intake is not assured in the mother, a supplement of at least 0.5 microgram a day (birth to twelve months) or 1.0 microgram a day (twelve to twenty-four months) should be given to the infant until his or her diet provides sufficient vitamin B12 from fortified foods.

Commercial infant formula is fortified with vitamin B12, so no additional vitamin B12 is needed for babies on formula.

7. Delay the introduction of solid foods until about six months of age.

Not so long ago, a baby's first bite of solid food was considered a developmental milestone. Parents and caregivers had babies eating solids as quickly as possible, often by one or two months of age. Babies usually ended up with more food dribbling down their faces than what went into their bellies; however, the bits that got inside sometimes triggered allergies. Today we understand that most infants are not developmentally ready for solid foods before about six months of age, although some infants may be ready as early as four or five months, particularly if they are growing very quickly. Babies let us know when they are ready in several ways. They seem constantly hungry, even after nursing eight to ten times a day or drinking 1.25 litres (40 ounces) of formula; they can sit up and give signs they are full, such as turning their head away; and they can move solids to the back of their mouth and swallow without spitting out most of the food. Solids should not be delayed too much after six months of age, as the additional foods are needed to meet nutrient and caloric needs. Six months of age also seems to be a good stage in a baby's development to start the adventure of new foods; waiting until later can result in a reluctance to try different tastes and textures.

Guidelines for introducing solid foods are provided in Table 10.5, and a sample menu is provide in Table 10.6. Finally, there is the Vegetarian Food Guide for Twelve to Twenty-four-Month Babies. The following tips will help to make this experience a pleasant one for both you and your baby:

- Embark on this exciting food adventure when the baby is rested, alert, and happy.

- There are no hard and fast rules regarding the order of introduction for solid foods after six months of age, although the sequence often recommended is infant cereals, vegetables, and fruits, then protein-rich foods. This sequence takes into consideration both the nutritional value of these first foods and the maturity of the infant's gastrointestinal system.

- Introduce new foods one at a time, with at least three to seven days between each new food. This allows us to observe for possible allergies. If there is a family history of allergy, it is best to avoid introducing the foods that are most problematic for family members until the baby is at least twelve months old. Egg whites, due to their very high potential for causing allergy, should be delayed until one year in all infants. About 95 per cent of all allergies in infants are to cow's milk, egg, peanuts and other nuts, soy, fish, and wheat.

- Introduce single ingredient foods (e.g., rice or barley cereal) before offering combination foods (e.g., mixed cereal).

- Various textured foods can gradually be introduced as the infant becomes ready to chew. This usually happens around seven to nine months of age. Textured foods should not be delayed beyond nine or ten months (unless the baby's development is delayed), as the infant may continue to reject textures for some time. Progress from pureed to mashed, then soft, minced, diced, and finger foods.

- Begin with small serving sizes: 5-15 millilitres (1-3 teaspoons) at a time. Gradually increase serving sizes. Babies will let us know when they are full. Never force-feed.

- Some infants are ready for mashed vegetables and fruits by six months, while others are not ready for these types of foods until they are eight months old.

- Babies should be encouraged to feed themselves, using their hands and easy-to-handle baby utensils. Babies are naturally messy eaters. Do not worry about it; they'll learn table manners soon enough.

- Teething foods are unnecessary. Instead, give the baby, a clean, cold, damp washcloth that has been refrigerated.

8. Ensure sufficient high quality protein.
Vegetarian infants can get plenty of high-quality protein; however, some care must be taken to ensure that sufficient sources are provided, especially in vegan infants. From six to twelve months, vegetarian babies need about 1.7-1.8 grams of protein per kilogram (about 0.8 gram per pound) of body weight. This is about 10-20 per cent more than what nonvegetarian babies require. The additional protein allows for the reduced digestibility of plant foods. Infants twelve to twenty-four months of age need about 1.2-1.3 grams protein per kilogram (0.5 gram per pound) of body weight. Excellent protein-rich choices include tofu, very well-cooked legumes, quinoa, and amaranth, and eggs, yogourt, and cottage cheese for lacto-ovo vegetarian babies. By following the guidelines provided in Table 10.6 for infants six to twelve months and the Vegetarian Food Guide for Twelve- to Twenty-four-Month Babies, protein needs are easily met.

9. Fat and energy should not be restricted during the first two years of life, unless medically indicated.
Breast milk, the ideal food for infants, derives approximately 54 per cent of its calories from fat. Two hundred-fifty millilitres (1 cup) of breast milk contains about 175 calories. This could well be nature's way of telling us that babies need food that is concentrated in both fat and energy. Plant foods can be low in fat and calories, and high in fibre. Thus, it is important, when planning vegetarian diets for infants, to ensure that diets provide sufficient calories and fat and that fibre is not excessive. As we introduce solid foods, these suggestions will help keep fat and energy intake at a safe and adequate level:

- *Include plenty of low-fibre, high-fat foods in the diet.* Tofu, smooth nut and seed butters and creams, mashed avocados, soy yogourt, puddings, and soups made with an appropriate milk, in addition to dairy products and eggs for lacto-ovo vegetarian babies, are excellent choices.

- *Avoid fat-reduced food products.* While many healthful foods are naturally low in fat, special fat-reduced products are not appropriate for babies. Low-fat or skim milk, low-fat cheese, and other fat-reduced foods are best avoided, as are foods containing fat substitutes.

- *Avoid excessive fibre.* Concentrated fibre products such as raw wheat bran, bran cereals, and bran muffins should not be used for vegetarian babies. Use mainly whole grain breads and cereals (for example, brown rice, millet, quinoa, and oatmeal bread), as they contribute important minerals to the diet. Lesser quantities of refined grain products such as bread, pasta, and cereal can help to keep total fibre intake in check.

- *Serve regular meals and snacks.* Infants have very small stomach capacities, and thus should be fed five to six times a day. Choose snacks carefully, making sure that they contribute to the infant's overall nutrient needs. (Younger infants are still receiving enough breast milk or formula between meals so that regular snacks are not as important.) A few energy-packed favourites include spreads (hummus, tofu spreads, or nut butters) on crackers; bread with cheese (soy or dairy); homemade, wholesome cookies, muffins, or squares; rice, cornmeal, quinoa, or other Whole Grain Puddings with fruit, and yogourt (soy or dairy).

10. Include a good source of omega-3 fatty acids in the diet.
The very best source of omega-3 fatty acids for infants is breast milk. To maximize the long-chain omega-3 fatty acid, DHA (the critical fat in infant brain development), the mother must consume reliable sources of omega-3 fatty acids (see Part 1 of this chapter). One of the most important advantages for breastfeeding vegetarian infants into the second year of life and beyond is that they continue to receive this valuable fat. After twelve months of age, vegetarian infants should begin to receive good sources of omega-3 fatty acids such as flaxseed oil. Aim for about 2 millilitres (H teaspoon) of flaxseed oil a day. Blend into infant cereal, blender drinks, puddings, cereal, soup, or mashed potatoes. Flaxseed oil should not be cooked, but mixed into a food after the food has been removed from direct heat.

11. Include dietary supplements, if needed.
Vegetarian and vegan infants have similar needs for nutritional supplements as nonvegetarian infants, with the possible exceptions of vitamin B12 and zinc. A complete list of supplements recommended for breastfed babies can be found in Table 10.4 (formula-fed infants require only vitamin K at birth). Multivitamin and mineral supplements are not absolutely necessary, although they can provide an excellent way to ensure that needs for vitamin D, vitamin B12, iron, and zinc are met. Take care to store all supplements away from children.

TABLE 10.4   *Supplements for Breast-fed Vegetarian Infants*

Nutrient	Recommendations
Vitamin K	A single dose at birth is given routinely in hospital.
Vitamin D	400 IU (10 mcg) daily from birth until sufficient amounts are provided by fortified foods.
Vitamin B12	0.5 mcg daily beginning at birth, unless the mother's diet contains adequate, reliable sources (fortified foods, supplements, dairy products, or eggs).
Iron	1 mg per kg daily (0.5 mg per lb) beginning when solid foods are introduced (can be provided in fortified foods).
Zinc	3 mg per day, if insufficient sources are provided in the diet.
Flouride	0.25 mg per day beginning at 6 months if water supply contains less than 0.3 ppm fluoride.

12. Avoid giving infants foods that may cause choking, food poisoning, or could be otherwise harmful.

There are several foods that can pose a risk of choking, food poisoning, or toxicity in infants. The following items should not be given to infants:

- *Foods that may cause choking.* Unsafe foods are those that do not easily dissolve in the mouth, and are of a size and shape that can block the airway. These include very hard foods, small and round items, and smooth or very sticky foods. Examples are veggie dogs (cut veggie dogs in half or quarters lengthwise to reduce risk), nuts, seeds, raw peas, raw carrots, and other hard raw vegetable or fruit pieces, popcorn, whole grapes (these can be cut in half or quartered), and hard candies. Peanut or other nut or seed butter should not be served on a spoon or a finger, nor should they be used on bread or crackers until one year of age. However, they may be used in prepared foods or thinned and used in a "cream" form. Infants should be seated and supervised while eating.

- *Foods associated with food-borne illness.* Babies have less resistance to harmful bacteria than older children or adults. Thus, high-risk foods such as unpasteurized milk, unpasteurized apple cider, raw eggs, or foods containing raw eggs should not be fed to infants. Honey, and possibly other liquid sugars such as corn syrup, may contain Clostridium botulinum spores, causing a rare but very dangerous form of food poisoning in infants under twelve months of age, so these sweeteners should also be avoided during the first year. Care must be taken when handling foods for infants. All fruits and vegetables should be thoroughly washed, and all prepared foods stored in the refrigerator. If using commercial infant foods in jars, the safety seal in the middle of the lid should pop up when the jar is opened. If it does not, the food should be discarded. Do not feed directly from the jar and then return an uneaten portion to the fridge, as bacteria from the baby's saliva can cause the remaining food to spoil quickly. The unused portion of food can be stored in the refrigerator for up to three days.

- *Excessive amounts of fruit juice.* Too much fruit juice can cause diarrhea in infants and toddlers. It can also displace the primary milk (breast milk or formula in the first year), reducing nutrient intake. When given, juice should be limited to not more than 125 milli-litres (H cup) a day for babies under twelve months, and 250 millilitres (8 ounces) a day for babies twelve to twenty-four months. Juice should be fed in a cup and not a bottle. Putting juice in a bottle encourages excessive intakes, and may lead to nursing bottle syndrome (a pattern of tooth decay in infants caused by prolonged exposure of the teeth to sweet beverages from a nursing bottle).

- *Inappropriate beverages.* Fruit drinks, fruit punches, soft drinks, sports drinks, coffee, tea, herbal tea, and hot chocolate should not be given to infants. These beverages contain too much sugar, caffeine, or other potentially damaging compounds to be given to babies.

- *Added sugar.* The addition of sugar and salt to infant foods is both unnecessary and potentially harmful. Adding sugar to infant foods dilutes the nutritional value of the food and may contribute to dental decay.

- *Fried foods and hydrogenated fat.* Fats used in fried foods are generally hydrogenated and heated to very high temperatures. These fats are not appropriate for infants. Shortening and hydrogenated margarines should not be given to infants.

- *Heavily pesticide-laden foods.* To reduce exposure to pesticides, opt for organic foods for your baby whenever possible.

TABLE 10.5   *General Guide to the Introduction of Solid Foods*

Age	Foods to Introduce	Amount to Serve/Comments
5-6 months	• Iron-fortified infant cereals	• 15-60 mL (1-4 tbsp) twice daily • Begin with single grain cereals (e.g., rice, barley, or oats), then mixed cereals. • Mix with breast milk, formula, or water (cereal should be thinned).
6 months	• Vegetables and fruits	• 30-45 mL (2-3 tbsp) vegetables twice daily; pureed or mashed • 30-45 mL (2-3 tbsp) fruits two to three times daily; pureed or mashed • Hard fruits cooked and pureed or mashed (skin removed); soft fruit peeled and well mashed. • Avoid fruit desserts with added sugar and starch.
7-8 months	• Protein-rich foods	• 15-45 mL (1-3 tbsp) twice daily • Good choices are mashed tofu, beans, peas, and egg yolk (for lacto-ovo vegetarian babies). • Press beans through a sieve to remove skins.
	• Unsweetened fruit juice	• 30-125 mL (1-4oz) daily • 15-45 mL (1-3 tbsp) twice daily • Offer in a cup rather than a bottle • Juice is not a necessary addition to the diet • May be diluted 1:1 with water, if desired.

TABLE 10.5 *continued*

Age	Foods to Introduce	Amount to Serve/Comments
8-10 months	• Finger foods	• 30-75 mL (2-5 tbsp) fruit and vegetable pieces (cooked if hard), H slice toast, G bagel, crackers, unsweetened cereal pieces
	• Grains and grain products	• 30-45 mL (2-3 tbsp) once or twice a day • Offer well-cooked whole grains: rice, quinoa, millet, barley, or others, and pasta.
	• Dairy products (for lacto-ovo vegetarian babies)	• 30-45 mL (2-3 tbsp) cottage cheese, 15 g (0.5 oz) of cheese, 60 mL (G cup) yogourt
10-12 months	• Mixed dishes	• 125-250 mL (H -1 cup) • Mixed dishes such as stews, pasta dishes, casseroles, and loaves are good choices.
	• Meat analogs	• 60-125 mL (G-H cup) one or more times daily • Example of meat analogs or veggie meats are soy or gluten-based slices, veggie patties, tofu wieners, veggie nuggets, etc.
	• Whole eggs at 12 months (ovo-vegetarian babies)	• 1 egg (best prepared by boiling or poaching rather than frying).

• Solids should be given 5 to 6 times per day (3 meals and 2 or 3 snacks) and total amounts should be about 175-250 mL (I-1 cup) per meal.

Table 10.6 *Sample Meal Plans: Six- to Twelve-Month Infants*

Time of Day	6-9 Months	9-12 months
Breast milk or iron-fortified formula	• Nursing 3-5 times a day *or* • 750 mL-1 L (24-32 oz) formula daily	• Nursing 2-4 times a day *or* • 750 mL-1 L (24-32 oz) formula daily
Morning (on waking)	• Breast milk or formula	• Breast milk or formula
Breakfast	• Breast milk or formula • 30-60 mL (2-4 tbsp) iron-fortified infant cereal • 30-45 mL (2-3 tbsp) fruit	• Breast milk or formula • 60-90 mL (4-6 tbsp) iron-fortified infant cereal • 30-45 mL (2-3 tbsp) fruit
Mid-morning	• Breast milk or formula	• Toast, crackers, or dry unsweetened cereal, tofu cubes, cheese cubes, soy or dairy yogourt
Lunch	• Breast milk or formula • 30-45 mL (2-3 tbsp) vegetables • 30-45 mL (2-3 tbsp) fruit • 15-45 mL (1-3 tbsp) beans, peas,or lentils, tofu, or tempeh	• Breast milk, or formula • 45-75 mL (3-5 tbsp) vegetables • 45-60 mL (3-4 tbsp) fruit • 30-60 mL (3-4 tbsp) beans, peas, or lentils, tofu, or tempeh
Afternoon	• Breast milk or formula	• Breast milk or formula • Soft vegetables or fruit in small pieces • Crackers or dry unsweetened cereal
Supper	• Breast milk or formula • 30-60 mL (2-4 tbsp) iron-fortified infant cereal • 30-45 mL (2-3 tbsp) vegetables • 30-45 mL (2-3 tbsp) fruit	• Breast milk or formula • 45-75 mL (3-5 tbsp) vegetables • 45-60 mL (3-4 tbsp) fruit • 30-60 mL (2-4 tbsp) beans, peas, or lentils, tofu, or tempeh • 30-60 mL (2-4 tbsp) grains or pasta (optional)
Evening	• Breast milk or formula	• Breast milk or formula • Finger foods

Vegetarian Food Guide for
Twelve- to Twenty-four-Month Babies
Include a wide variety of foods.

Milks: Breast milk, commercial infant formula, cow's milk, full-fat fortified soymilk
Total 625-750 mL (20-24 oz)
About three 175-250 mL (6-8 oz) servings of breast milk, commercial infant formula, cow's milk, or full-fat fortified soymilk (breast milk or formula should supplement fortified soymilk).

Breads and Cereals: 4-6 toddler-size servings
1 toddler-size serving = H slice bread
60 mL (G cup) cooked grain or pasta
125 mL (H cup) ready-to-eat cereal
60 mL (G cup) cooked cereal

Vegetables: 2-3 toddler-size servings
1 toddler-size serving = 125 mL (H cup) salad or other raw vegetable pieces
60 mL (G cup) cooked vegetables
80 mL (N cup) vegetable juice

Fruits: 2-3 toddler-size servings.
1 toddler-size serving = H to 1 fresh fruit
60 mL (G cup) cooked fruit
60 mL (G cup) fruit juice (limit juice to about
250 mL/1cup per day)

Beans and Alternates: 2-3 toddler-size servings.
1 toddler-size serving = 125 mL (H cup) cooked beans, peas, or lentils
60 g (2 oz) tofu
15-30 g (0.5-1 oz) veggie "meat"
22 mL (1 H tbsp) nut or seed butter
1 egg

Other Essentials:

Vitamin B12: 1.0 mcg in fortified foods or supplement

Vitamin D: 400 IU (10 mcg) vitamin D from fortified foods or supplements

Omega-3 Fatty Acids: 2 mL (H tsp) flaxseed oil or other omega-3 source

Part 3: Childhood (Two to Twelve and Beyond)

The years of childhood provide an opportunity to introduce a world of interesting and enjoyable foods to impressionable little ones. In receiving a wide variety of wholesome vegetarian foods, children reap the benefits twice over. First, as children they'll be less likely than their nonvegetarian peers to become obese. Second, as adults they'll be at reduced risk for several chronic degenerative diseases (including heart disease, type 2 diabetes, and cancer) compared with the general population. Scientists are discovering that diets during childhood and adolescence can set the stage for later health problems—or help prevent these conditions. There's a third advantage, a bonus for adults. As we make efforts to ensure that our children's diets are balanced and packed with nutritious foods, our diets as caregivers and role models inevitably improve!

In past decades, a common criticism of vegetarian and vegan diets was that they might place children at risk for nutritional deficiencies. The reality is that such insufficiencies are related to poorly designed diets, and not to whether the meals are vegetarian or nonvegetarian. Studies have clearly established that well-planned vegetarian and vegan diets can support normal growth and development in children.

In planning a child's diet, it helps to consider how his or her needs differ from those of an adult. Small children have limited stomach capacities along with high nutrient requirements. A diet consisting mostly of fruits and vegetables, big bowls of salad, and whole grains can be too low in calories and certain minerals and too high in fibre to meet a child's needs. Their menus must include an emphasis on more concentrated sources of calories and minerals such as soyfoods, nut butters, and plenty of meal and snack ideas mentioned in this chapter.

Children who are raised from birth as vegetarians generally accept a wide variety of healthful foods without any problem, especially when the adults around model these attitudes. If a family becomes vegetarian or shifts from a heavily meat-centred, highly processed diet to a vegetarian, whole foods diet a number of years after a child is born, there may be a little resistance, as would be expected with other major changes. Do not despair. There are ways we can ease the transition and make life easier for everyone.

- Include children in food preparation. They love to help stir, knead, roll, decorate, and do just about anything else in the kitchen that they're ready for. For those with small appetites, try Sneaky Dad's Power Punch Smoothie, page 393, or create your own version.

- Involve little ones in food selection. (Of course this process may prove more successful at a farmers' market, in the garden, and after you've purchased the groceries and brought them home, rather than in the middle of the sugar-laden cereal aisle!)

- Consider children's preferences when planning menus and include something that they enjoy at each meal.

- Serve vegetarian versions of traditional favourites: pizza, spaghetti, lasagne, tacos, chili, burgers, hot dogs, stews, and stir-fries.

- Stock the cupboards and refrigerator with a variety of foods that are both wholesome and appealing for children.

- Include "fun foods." It can be tough to be vegetarian among friends who love cheeseburgers and shakes, so allow your version of treats. When our veggie burger or dog celebration includes some of these fixin's—ketchup, barbecue sauce, mustard, mayo, pickle relish, chili sauce, lettuce, sprouts, sliced tomato, dill pickles, onion, and avocado slices—everyone has a great time assembling his or her own creation. Try the shakes on pages 390 and 392.

- Keep offering new foods, even if they are rejected. A child who turns up her nose at something one day could adopt it as her favourite meal a month later—it really does happen!

- Respect a child's right to dislike a few foods. Children can't be expected to love everything, nor is it necessary for good nutrition.

- Let a child decide when he or she has had enough to eat.

- Make mealtime a pleasant time. Set a pretty table, light a candle, and encourage positive family interaction.

As parents, we are responsible for providing our children with safe and adequate food. Our children are responsible for how much they eat from the items we provide. The whole thing can seem a little overwhelming at times, especially when children go through periods of food refusal or strange eating behaviours. Be assured that if we provide a variety of nourishing foods in a pleasant atmosphere, food intake balances out over time and a child will manage to get enough to eat.

Nutrition Guidelines for Vegetarian Children and Teens

1. **Include a variety of foods from all food groups in the Vegetarian Food Guide.** Children learn to enjoy the foods they grow up with. If they are served whole grains, a wide variety of vegetables and fruits, legumes, tofu, and other healthful foods as described in the Vegetarian Food Guide for Preschool Children (Two to Four Years) on page 291, and after that, the Vegetarian Food Guide (pages 241-242), they are likely to accept and enjoy these foods throughout their lives. When we offer a variety of foods from each food group, a child becomes familiar with different tastes and textures. When children are small, they will need the number of servings at the lower end of the range and portions may be somewhat smaller than those listed on the guide. Toward adolescence, amounts and numbers of serving sizes increase dramatically. Every child has his or her unique pattern of growth, appetite, and preferences.

2. **Include sufficient servings of Milks and Alternates each day: at least four servings for preschoolers (two to four years), six servings for young, school-age children (five to eight years), and eight servings for children aged nine years or older and adolescents.** Sufficient calcium can be obtained from appropriate milks or alternates. However, using milks as the primary calcium source, particularly in preschoolers and young children, is the easiest and most efficient way of meeting calcium needs. Appropriate milks for preschoolers

include breast milk, formula, fortified soymilk, and cow's or goat's milk. These are valuable sources of calcium, vitamin D, riboflavin, protein, and other nutrients. Although it is uncommon in our culture to continue breastfeeding beyond two years of age, human milk can continue to provide immune protection and a valuable complement of nutrients for preschoolers. From a nutritional perspective, the longer we continue to provide our preschoolers with human milk and its unique balance of high-quality protein, vitamins, minerals, and long-chain omega-3 fatty acids, the better. Although the idea might not occur to us, commercial iron-fortified infant formula could also save the day for a child who isn't eating well. Formula, or expressed breast milk, can be mixed into cereals, puddings, and other dishes. Every little bit helps! Two to four years of age is a time of nutritional vulnerability when children's diets are in transition, and nutritional needs are high because of growth and activity.

By five years of age, children can progress to using the Vegetarian Food Guide (pages 241-242). From ages five to eight, children require at least six servings from the Milks and Alternates group. While needs can be met by using a variety of calcium-rich foods, providing four servings as milks (500 mL/2 cups of fortified soymilk or cow's milk) helps tremendously in meeting the recommended number of servings from this group. At age nine, recommended intakes for calcium increase dramatically from 800 milligrams to 1,300 milligrams. The density of bones and our defence against osteoporosis in later life depends, at least in part, on getting enough calcium and vitamin D during childhood and the teen years when calcium needs are greatest. To meet these high needs, preteens and teens need about eight servings of Milks and Alternates each day.

Fortified soymilk is an acceptable choice whereas unfortified soymilk does not contain the necessary calcium and vitamin D, and is not included as a choice in this group. Soymilk contains 6-8 grams of protein per 250 millilitres (1 cup), whereas the same amount of rice milk has only 0.5 grams of protein though they can be used by those with soy allergies, along with other high protein plant foods. Rice milks, other grain milks, potato milks, nut milks, and unfortified milks are not recommended for use as primary milks for children as they do not provide sufficient nutrients.

For lacto-ovo vegetarian children, 2 per cent or 1 per cent cow's milk may be used, depending on the needs of the individual child. If a child is overweight, lower-fat milk may be appropriate.

Milks tend to be our mainstay when it comes to meeting children's calcium needs. Yet there are plenty of other ways to get calcium into kids, too. Be sure to buy the type of tofu that is made with calcium. Tofu can be used for a quick breakfast scramble, an Angelic Tofu Sandwich Filling, or a quick tofu stir-fry (see the recipe section). Add cubes of tofu to soups, stews, spaghetti sauces, and casseroles. Introduce broccoli, kale, collards, and Chinese greens early on and make them a part of the normal fare. Use the calcium-fortified variety of orange juice. If dairy products are used, include cottage cheese, other cheeses, yogourt, and puddings. Almond butter is a delicious spread; though expensive, it's a fine treat. Blackstrap molasses, as a sweetener for baking, adds calcium and other minerals.

Cheese, yogourt, and the alternatives listed above give the necessary calcium, but they do not contain vitamin D, so it is important that a reliable source be provided (sunshine, fortified foods, or a supplement).

3. **Provide at least two servings of Beans and Alternates each to ensure sufficient protein, iron, and zinc.**
   Protein sources and needs. Though we also get protein from grains and vegetables, beans and the alternates in this group tend to be the most concentrated sources. When a child is getting enough calories from a variety of nutritious foods as outlined in the Vegetarian Food Guide for Preschool Children (page 291), and the Vegetarian Food Guide (pages 241-242), protein needs are assured.

Vegetarian Food Guide for
Preschool Children (Two to Four Years)
Include a wide variety of foods.

Milks and Alternates: 4-6 servings
1 serving = 125 mL (H cup) human milk, cow's milk, full-fat fortified soymilk
60 mL (G cup) calcium-set tofu
125 mL (H cup) calcium-fortified juice
45 mL (3 tbsp) almond butter
250 mL (1 cup) cooked calcium-rich greens (kale, collards, Chinese greens, broccoli)
15 mL (1 tbsp) blackstrap molasses
5 figs

Breads and Cereals: 4-6 toddler-size servings
1 toddler-size serving = H slice bread
60 mL (G cup) cooked grain or pasta
125 mL (H cup) ready-to-eat cereal
60 mL (G cup) cooked cereal

Vegetables: 2-3 toddler-size servings
1 toddler-size serving = 125 mL (H cup) salad or other raw vegetable pieces
60 mL (G cup) cooked vegetables
80 mL (N cup) vegetable juice

Fruits: 2-3 toddler-size servings.
1 toddler-size serving = H to 1 fresh fruit
60 mL (G cup) cooked fruit
60 mL (G cup) fruit juice (limit to about 250 mL/1cup per day)

Beans and Alternates: 2-3 toddler-size servings.
1 toddler-size serving = 60 mL (G cup) cooked beans, peas, or lentils
60 g (2 oz) tofu
15-30 g (.50-1 oz) veggie "meat"
22 mL (1 H tbsp) nut or seed butter
1 egg

Other Essentials:

Vitamin B12: 1.0 mcg in fortified foods or supplement
Vitamin D: 200 IU (5 mcg) vitamin D from fortified foods or supplements
Omega-3 Fatty Acids: 2 mL (H tsp) flaxseed oil or other omega-3 source to provide 1.5 omega-3 fatty acids)

Table 10.7 shows amounts of protein recommended for children and teens of different ages. Due to slight differences in digestibility of plant foods and animal products, slightly more protein is advised for vegans than for nonvegans. For vegan children, the higher end of the range given is if the diet is mostly based on whole foods, rather than some processed foods and soyfoods. Yet typical intakes tend to be well above the recommended levels for children on either dietary pattern. If a child's weight is somewhat different, you can adjust the recommended protein intake proportionally.

TABLE 10.7   *Recommended Protein Intake per Day for Non-vegan and Vegan Children and Teens at Different Ages*

Age (years)	Weight	Recommended Protein for Non-vegans (g)	Recommended Protein for Vegans (g)
2-3	13 kg/29 lbs	16	18-21
4-6	20 kg/44 lbs	24	26-28
7-10	28 kg/62 lbs	28	31-34
11-14, male	45 kg/99 lbs	45	50-54
11-14, female	46 kg/101 lbs	46	51-55
15-18, male	66 kg/146 lbs	59	66-73
15-18, female	55 kg/121 lbs	44	50-55

Legumes and soyfoods. Legumes are so nutritious that they are valuable for everyone; this is particularly true for children who do not consume animal products. Become familiar with different legumes: black beans, red lentils, pinto beans, adzuki beans, mung beans, and lima beans. Experiment with every kind of tofu you can lay your hands on, in menu items from appetizers to dessert. Try other soyfoods such as tempeh, miso, soy burgers, veggie "meats," and textured soy protein. Soymilk contains 6-8 grams of protein per 250 millilitres (1 cup).

Eggs and dairy. Cow's milk provides 8 grams of protein per 250 millilitres (1 cup) and a large egg 6 grams of protein. Lacto-ovo vegetarians note that one large egg contains 213 milligrams of cholesterol, and 250 millilitres (1 cup) of whole milk or yogourt or 30 grams (1 ounce) of cheddar cheese each provide 30 milligrams of cholesterol. The American Academy of Pediatrics suggests that cholesterol be limited to not more than 300 milligrams per day. Plant foods contain no cholesterol.

Seeds, nuts, and peanuts. Seeds have only 3-5 grams of protein per 60 millilitres (G cup), and nuts are lower still, yet they do provide a little. Peanuts, which are actually legumes, contain much more—9 grams of protein in 60 millilitres (G cup), and 8 grams of protein in 30 millilitres (2 tablespoons) of peanut butter. You'll find nut butters in many of the recipes in this book, especially the children's favourite, African Stew on page 419.

See amounts of protein in various foods in Table 3.9 Iron, Zinc, and Protein in Foods, and in the menus on pages 88, 91, 92, 94. You'll find that protein intake over the course of a day can mount up fairly quickly.

Iron. Iron deficiency is the most widely recognized nutritional deficiency in North American children. Here are three main reasons for iron deficiency in vegetarian children.

i. **Insufficient dietary iron.** Beans, split peas, lentils, soyfoods, and peanut butter are highly important iron sources. See Table 3.9 Iron, Zinc, and Protein in Foods for amounts. There are iron sources in other food groups, such as prunes and dark green veggies. A good source of vitamin C, eaten at the same time, can greatly increase iron absorption (see vitamin C-rich fruits listed on the next page). Iron-fortified infant cereal works, too, and not just for infants; it can be added to other hot cereals, pancakes, and baked goods. Use cast iron cookware when possible. It adds iron to foods cooked in it, especially acidic foods such as tomato sauce.

ii. **Too much of the inhibitors of iron absorption, phytates, and oxalates.** Phytates are present in wheat bran, and oxalates in spinach, Swiss chard, and beet greens. (Though the latter three foods contain iron, we absorb very little of it.)

iii. **Too much dairy.** Lacto- vegetarian children may not get enough iron if dairy products are used as the main source of protein. Dairy foods are not only poor sources of iron, they inhibit its absorption. It is not uncommon for a child to consume cheese, yogourt, ice cream, or other dairy foods at almost every meal and with snacks, in addition to drinking three or four glasses of milk during the day. When dairy products are the central focus of the diet, it can be difficult to make room for iron-rich legumes, tofu, and greens.

For children's recommended intakes of iron, zinc, and other nutrients, see page 280. For amounts of these nutrients in foods, see Table 3.9 on page 100.

Zinc. Although we seldom hear of problems relating to zinc deficiency, many children (and adults) have difficulty in meeting the recommended intakes. Shortages can cause a lack of appetite, delays in growth and development, and slow wound healing. For sufficient zinc, serve legumes, tofu, and seed and nut butters on a regular basis. Fortified soymilk contains plenty of zinc as it is added in Canada. Among veggie "meats," many of the Yves products are fortified with zinc; these can be handy for lunchboxes. Nuts and seeds are concentrated sources of calories and minerals such as zinc; some families keep a little bowl of them on a kitchen counter for passersby to nibble on.

Apart from the Beans and Alternates food group, whole grains are good zinc sources; they provide two or three times as much zinc as refined breads and cereals. Wheat germ contains zinc, too.

4. **Include five or more servings of Grains in the diet each day, at least half of which should be whole grains.** Carbohydrates, meaning the complex carbohydrates in whole grains, are ideal sources of calories. Experiment with millet, quinoa, spelt, barley, amaranth, kamut and brown, red or wild rice, on

their own or in combinations. Whole Grain Pudding can be both breakfast cereal and soothing dessert or snack, sweetened with dried fruit (see recipes page 387 and 389). Instead of the same type of sliced bread day after day, provide a variety: rye, pumpernickel, pita bread, chapatis, bagels, multigrain rolls, and oatmeal scones. Of course, making one's own bread is a tremendous adventure, especially punching down the dough! Whole grain flours and wheat germ can be used in baking cookies, muffins, squares, or other goodies for a nutritious treat.

Pasta comes in assorted shapes (from letters to big tubes) and made from assorted grains, including whole grains. It's all right to use some refined grains, especially for little ones whose small stomachs can be quickly filled up if the diet is very high in fibre. Aim to keep refined grains to not more than half the total grain servings used.

5. **Include at least three servings of Vegetables and two servings of Fruits each day.** This goes for young and old alike. Even if we did not learn to enjoy vegetables when we were children, here's a chance to start. We can visit an ethnic store and discover entirely new Asian vegetables or other foods. If we ask for tips on how to prepare unfamiliar vegetables, we'll get great ideas. With children, it's so easy to make these experiences into real adventures! We can sample avocados, eggplant, zucchini, different types of tomatoes, peppers and squashes, or broccoflower (a cross between broccoli and cauliflower). Discuss which part of the plant this is, or make a guessing game (to see more about this, see page 176.) Children often love to sample unusual fruits such as mangos, Chinese pears, and pomegranates. Vegetables and fruits provide an abundance of vitamins, minerals, and phytochemicals. For love of vegetables, we can:

    • Encourage an interest in vegetables by growing some in a garden or even in containers on your balcony. If that isn't possible, bring children on an excursion to a farm and let them see how these foods grow.

- Older children and teens can prepare all sorts of salads, stir-fries, and other dishes with what they harvest.

- Grow sprouts. Youngsters enjoy rinsing them and watching them change day by day (page 407).

- Get children accustomed to dark greens early on. Broccoli is often a favourite. Use a variety of dark greens in salads, stir-fries, casseroles, and spaghetti sauces.

- Show enthusiasm when bringing home an unusual plant food.

- Preserve the nutritional value and bright colour of vegetables by cooking them in a minimum of water, steaming, or stir-frying them. Children often prefer their vegetables raw or tender-crisp rather than mushy, so don't overcook!

- Serve two or more different vegetables with dinner. Include one that your child or teen already likes.

- Make these healthy foods fun. Children love vegetables and dip. They make a great snack, even before dinner. Fancy shapes and patterns are most inviting for little ones. Vegetable pieces can be arranged into wonderful pictures on a plate. (Faces are a favourite.)

  For love of fruit, we can:

- Go for variety! There are so many flavourful fruits from which to choose that it's not hard to find a dozen or two that appeal to even the fussiest eater.

- Serve vitamin C-rich fruit often. Whole fruits such as oranges, grapefruits, kiwi, cantaloupe, and strawberries are our best choices. Fruit juices can be used, but only in moderation; that is, not more than about 250 millilitres (1 cup) per day. Juice can cause chronic diarrhea in small children and displace other foods in the diet when used in excess. Do not use fruit "drinks" in place of juice, even if they do have vitamin C added and a dribble of real juice. They don't contribute much more than vitamin C; the rest is sugar, flavour, and colour.

- Make fruit fun. Kids love fruit kabobs, fruit salads, and fruit platters (arrange the fruit in a flower shape).

- Offer dried fruits for a change. Dried fruits are convenient, portable, and nutritious. Try something different like dried peaches, pears, apples, or your own homemade fruit leather. Unfortunately, dried fruits aren't so great for the teeth; remember to brush afterward.

- For a real treat, occasionally squeeze your own fruit juice.

- If you have dessert (which is certainly not a necessity), make fruits your main theme. Fresh fruit salads or platters, blueberry crepes, or fruit crisp make wonderful endings to a special meal. Try Berry Delicious Ice Cream (page 433).

6. **Include a source of omega-3 fatty acids in the diet.** Omega-3 fatty acids are very important to normal growth and development and sources should be included in a child's diet each day; aim for about 2-3 grams of omega-3 fatty acids each day. The most concentrated source is flaxseeds or flaxseed oil. Five millilitres (1 teaspoon) of flaxseed oil provides about 2.7 grams of omega-3 fatty acids. Other good sources include hempseeds and hempseed oil, organic canola oil, walnuts, and green leafy vegetables. Soy products and wheat germ also provide some omega-3 fatty acids; however, they are also very high in omega-6 fatty acids. For lacto-ovo children, omega-3-rich eggs provide a good source of DHA, one of the important long-chain omega-3 fatty acids. Of course, for preschool children, human milk is an excellent source of the long-chain omega-3 fatty acids, EPA and DHA. For more information about omega-3 fatty acids, see Chapter 7.

7. **Include a reliable source of vitamin B12 in the diet every day.** Unfortified plant foods cannot meet our needs for vitamin B12. It is essential that vegetarian, including vegan, children receive reliable sources of this nutrient. The RDA for vitamin B12 is 0.9 micrograms for children ages one to three years, 1.2 micrograms for four to eight year olds, 1.8 micrograms for nine to thirteen year olds, and 2.4 micrograms for everyone

above fourteen years of age. Lacto-ovo vegetarian children can obtain vitamin B12 from dairy products and eggs, fortified foods, or supplements. Vegan children can obtain vitamin B12 from supplements or fortified foods including soymilk, meat analogs, Vegetarian Support Formula nutritional yeast, and cereals (see Table 8.2 on page 236). Be sure to read food labels.

9. **Provide concentrated sources of calories as part of the daily fare.** Vegetarian and vegan diets can be very high in bulk, making it difficult for small children to meet their needs for energy. In the few cases where this is an ongoing problem, protein is used as energy, rather than for building body tissues, and growth can be compromised. This situation is most often seen when foods rich in fat and protein are restricted.

   The solution is simple. Small children need nutritious, energy-packed foods throughout the day. By following some or all of these suggestions, we will help to ensure that a child gets enough fat and calories:

   • Provide three meals a day, plus regular snacks in-between. For many children it is difficult to pack in enough food at a meal to tide them over for five or six hours until the next meal.

   • Don't restrict fat excessively. Allow liberal use of tofu and other soy products, avocados and nuts, seeds and their butters. Whole nuts and seeds can be included after four years of age, but not before that, due to the danger of choking. Include some fats and oils in baking and cooking. Milk, yogourt, cheese, and eggs provide concentrated fat and energy for lacto-ovo vegetarian children.

   • Don't overdo raw foods as they can be so bulky for small stomachs. Use some cooked vegetables and fruits and their juices.

   • Well-cooked whole grains are fine, but avoid the use of high-fibre foods such as wheat bran and fibre supplements. Choose whole grain breads and cereals, but do not add extra fibre to foods. It's all right to include some refined grains such as pasta, crackers, and couscous, but don't overdo it because their mineral content is inferior.

- Offer an assortment of protein-rich foods that are also low in fibre. Great choices include tofu, nut butters and creams (which are nuts and seed butters thinned with milks), soy cheese and yogourt, plus dairy products and eggs for lacto-ovo vegetarians.

Meal Memo

Rather than massive meals, most children need small, frequent servings such as three meals with snacks between. Appetite can fluctuate considerably in this age group, and there are certainly going to be times when your child will eat more or less than what is suggested in the guide. Having a quiet time before meals can help to improve appetite.

We might impress our neighbours by being gourmet cooks, but our children, those sometimes masters-of-simplicity, tend to like a carrot that still resembles a carrot, a cracker, and a simple chunk of cheese or tofu (marinated or plain).

Children should be seated while eating, rather than running around. Supervise small children in case they choke on something. (See the list of potential problem foods for infants on page 280)

If we don't make foods into bribes or rewards, we can avoid plenty of problems, including possible obesity, and we don't place an unrealistic value on certain foods.

Breakfast

Children do better at school when they've eaten breakfast. But there are a lot of ways to deliver that breakfast, such as a glass of fortified soymilk or orange juice and a couple of muffins grabbed on the way out the door; a Quick Chocolate Shake or Fruit Smoothie; scrambled tofu with toast; or leftovers from last night's supper. (See Recipe section, page 379.) Muesli can be made the night before.

Lunch

Although people have been known to get by on seven years' worth of peanut butter sandwiches, we'd probably be a little more content with the selections provided in the Ten Tempting Ways to Fill a Sandwich, page 402. Be creative with children's lunch boxes. Be sure to include something from each food group:

Beans and Alternates. Marinated tofu, bean or pea soup, hummus, veggie slices, and veggie burgers.

Milks and Alternates. Fortified soymilk or cow's milk, yogourt, figs, and almonds or almond butter.

Vegetables and Fruits. Vegetables and dip, salad, whole or cut-up fruits, and dried fruits.

Grains. Whole grain rolls, pita bread, multigrain bagels, rice cakes, muffins, and other nutritious baked items.

An entire book on the topic is Judy Brown's *The Natural Lunchbox: Vegetarian Meals for School, Work, and Home* (The Book Publishing Company, Summertown, Tennessee, 1996).

Supper

See Seven Super-Simple Suppers, with recipes on pages 414-423. These were developed with families in mind. Also, *Raising Vegetarian Children* by J. Stepaniak and V. Melina (McGraw-Hill, 2002) contains a wealth of child- and teen-friendly recipes.

Snacks

"Snack" does not automatically mean junk food. Snacks often contribute one-third of our children's calories; they should also contribute one-third of other nutrients. Provide youngsters with appealing and wholesome snacks. Offer nutritious squares, muffins, loaves, cookies, crackers and cheese (soy or dairy), nut butters, yogourt (soy or dairy), plus trail mixes for older children. Set out a plate of sliced raw veggies, or wedges of cut-up fruit for TV time and for potential nibblers who wander by the kitchen.

Let's Have a Little Action

Childhood is an important time to establish habits of exercise. Our joy in play is natural. Often the trick is how to retain it while living in apartments, trailers, and when parents don't want all that joyful noise around. Make a commitment to get active—join a ski club, swimming club, or sports facility. Encourage children to pick at least one sport, and sign them up. Often we adults need more of this too, and all of our lives are improved by cycling together, by Sunday hikes, and by taking part in activities at the local community centre.

The Question of Supplements

Children can be wellnourished without supplements, (as long as a balance of foods as described in the Vegetarian Food Guide is provided). For vegan children, vitamin B12-fortified foods must be included; otherwise, a supplement of vitamin B12 is necessary. A regular children's multivitamin-mineral supplement generally contains enough vitamin B12—read the label. Five hundred millilitres (2 cups) of fortified milks (soy or cow's) provide enough vitamin D. This or a vitamin D supplement is needed except during the warmest half of the year if there is regular, brief exposure to sunlight. If insufficient servings from the milk and milk alternates group are consumed, then a supplement of approximately 200-500 milligrams of calcium per day can help "top up" the diet; choose a formulation that includes vitamin D.

If a supplement is used, it is best to select one that contains a variety of vitamins and minerals including vitamin B12, vitamin D, zinc, and iron in amounts that approximate the recommended intakes (see Appendix on page 435). Many children's supplements contain no minerals except iron. Read the label. Avoid single-nutrient supplements other than calcium, unless medically indicated.

Part 4: Focus on Teens (Thirteen and Over)

Many teens today are independently making the decision to eliminate meat from their menu. Their motivation often comes from concerns about the environment or animal rights rather than from a

desire to improve the nutritional quality of their diet. This doesn't
mean that food is not of prime importance. It just means that the
criteria for food selection may be a little different than it is for the
average health-conscious vegetarian adult. The two main criteria for
food selection by teens generally are:

1. How fast can it be ready?

2. Does it taste good?

The most acceptable answers to these questions are: "It is
ready," and "It tastes great." In other words we're talking instant,
delicious food. Our society is fairly well set up for instant and delicious, but not so well for vegetarian (although this is beginning to
change).

Many teens who grow up on standard North American fare
simply stop eating meat when they become vegetarian. Instead of a
hamburger and fries for lunch, they opt for a double order of fries.
When chicken, potatoes, and corn arrive on the dinner table, they
eat just the potatoes and corn. There are a few problems with this
kind of approach. First, parents tend to be less than supportive
because they see their teenager eating very poorly. Second, the poor
nutrition can take its toll on the teen, eventually causing him or her
to feel run down and develop nutritional deficiencies.

An immediate solution that will often satisfy parents and teens
alike is to venture into the world of veggie "meats." The possibilities are endless: slices, burgers, wieners, Veggie Ground Round, and
even little nuggets. Some teens learn to make hummus, and even
enjoy the process. Tofu is a great food for teens; it's convenient and
loaded with nutrients. Parents generally become a little less resist-
ant to the whole vegetarian idea if they know that their teen is getting some concentrated sources of protein, iron, and zinc. In many
cases, the parents begin to extend their range of meals, and some
even become vegetarians themselves. The result could well be a
healthier family.

There are also teens who have been raised on a vegetarian diet.
This group generally does very well. Some studies show that these
vegetarian teens are well nourished, have less tendency to obesity,
and eat less junk, less fat, and more fibre, fruit, and vegetables than
their meat-eating peers. A large study by John Sabate, looking at

Seventh-day Adventist teens, showed that these vegetarians actually outgrew their omnivorous peers by an average of 2.5 centimetres (1inch).

The nutritional needs of a vegetarian teen are similar to those of any other teen. Many physical changes are taking place, and the demands for nutrients are high. There are several things that a parent can do to help a vegetarian teen be well nourished:

- Keep a variety of super-fast and wholesome foods handy. Stock up on fresh fruits, trail mixes, nutritious baked goods, and soy or dairy yogourt and cheese, as well as whole grain breads and cereals.

- Encourage teens to contribute to meals by helping with meal planning and preparation. Teens can be expected to prepare whole meals, heat, and serve a partially prepared meal, make a salad, or create a nutritious dessert. This will give them a head start for managing on their own. The recipes in this book are a great place to start.

- Offer vegetarian versions of popular dinner favourites: baked beans, bean tortillas, pizza with vegetarian sausage or pepperoni, burgers and dogs, burritos, lasagne, chili, spaghetti, sloppy Joes, cabbage rolls, and tamale pie. Red lentils, beans, or vegetarian "ground round" work well as meat replacements.

- Remember that your teenager is responsible for his or her own food choices. Your job is to stock the pantry with a wide variety of healthy foods.

- Encourage involvement in groups and activities that will increase their knowledge of vegetarianism and the vegetarian way of eating.

The Vegetarian Resource Group provides many resources and sponsors an annual essay contest for students nineteen and under with $50 savings bonds awarded in three categories. Details can be found at www.vrg.org. You'll also find recipes and interesting articles. Also, keep up-to date by visiting the Web site www.vegetarianteen.com/.

An organization founded and run by teens and young adults is YES! (Youth for Environmental Sanity) www.yesworld.org. This group promotes vegetarianism and educates teens about the environment with their popular YES! tour, which travels to schools in the United States, Canada, and Mexico. Contact YES! at (877) 293-7226 or email camps@yesworld.org.

The Nutrition Guidelines for Vegetarian Children and Teens (page 288) gave many practical tips on nutrition for teens. Yet teens seem to manage even under conditions that are less than ideal. Don't get too concerned if things don't go precisely according to plan. Here are a few additional pointers (written by two moms who have been there.)

> A good sense of humour will get us through most problems in life (unfortunately, mostly in retrospect.)

The Instant Eater

Teenagers are notorious for skipping meals, especially breakfast and lunch. This can lead to bouts of hunger that are too often filled with potato chips and chocolate bars. We can also be fairly certain that teens will vanish for hours and then, in the company of friends, they will descend on the kitchen like a horde of locusts (or a single very hungry one).

One way to deal with this is by having nourishing "fast foods" on hand. Snacks that are also nutritious can salvage an otherwise marginal diet. Food can be ready at a moment's notice. Instant meals, especially breakfast and lunch, can be ready to grab and go.

The high quality and tremendous variety of convenient "natural" foods on the market today may surprise you—some are truly healthful! If you haven't explored your local natural food stores, you are in for a real treat. For economy, you can buy in bulk and make your own baked items and veggie burgers. Any food that fits into the food guide is a good choice. Here are some suggestions for making the most of the choices in each food group:

Beans and Alternates

- Serve hummus as the dip with raw veggies.

- Have spaghetti sauces on hand, in jars and cans. Add Veggie Ground Round. Try Chunky Red Lentil Tomato Sauce (page 416) and store some in the freezer.

- Legumes (peas, beans and lentils) are indispensable! Simply open a can, drain well, and add them to a home "salad bar." Marinated bean salads can be always at the ready.

- Mash pinto or kidney beans to make taco fillings.

- Tofu picks up the flavour of any seasonings or sauces that are used, so try it with family favourites like barbecue or sweet and sour sauce. Tofu is one of the most versatile foods imaginable and good on kebobs, in sandwiches, and nibbled as snacks.

- Stir-fry meals can be made with almonds, cashews, tofu, tempeh, or firm beans such as garbanzos in place of the meat. (See recipe, page 420.)

- Vegetarian patties, sausages, loaves, and deli slices are available in supermarkets, health food stores, ethnic stores, and food co-ops. Many are delicious; all are fast and easy to prepare. Some brands, such as many of the Yves products, are fortified with vitamin B12 and zinc.

- Stock several containers of fruit-flavoured soy yogourt.

Milks and Alternates

- Keep a covered jug of calcium-fortified fruit juice ready-mixed and in the refrigerator at all times.

- Use fortified soymilk, or cow's milk for lacto-vegetarians.

- Include dried figs in trail mixes.

- Buy almonds in bulk and keep them in the freezer.

- Use almond butter instead of peanut butter on sandwiches.

- Add broccoli florets to plates of veggie sticks.

- Enjoy tofu (made with calcium) in a variety of ways: scrambled, baked, barbequed, and stir-fried.

Vegetables and Fruits

- Put out a tray of raw vegetables and a dip for everyone to munch on. Even teens who turn their noses up at cooked vegetables seem quite happy to polish off a platter of raw veggies and dip.

- Grow a garden. Teens love to plant, watch things grow, and enjoy the fruits (and vegetables) of their labour.

- Arrange a colourful big bowl of fresh fruits and set it on the table, ripe for the picking.

- Keep plenty of dried fruit or fruit leather, or a bag of apple chips on hand, as instant snacks (remember to brush teeth afterwards).

- Grate vegetables into patties, loaves, and salads.

- Cut up a variety of fruits and offer at snack time.

Grains

- Keep a variety of whole grains products on hand for instant snacking. Whole grain breads, bagels, cereals, muffins, and rice cakes all work well.

- Keep the freezer stocked with scrumptious homemade or commercial baked goods.

- Make a variety of different whole grains—quinoa, millet, amaranth, kamut, barley, and oat groats. Use in soups, salads, pilafs, and desserts.

- From time to time, have Whole Grain Pudding available as a creamy dessert.

The Supplement Question

A teenager's need for nutritional supplements depends entirely on eating habits and individual needs. Supplements are not necessary if the Vegetarian Food Guide is being followed, including foods that are fortified with vitamin B12 and vitamin D. However, supplements can be useful in a number of situations. A good choice is a regular (rather than high-potency or stress type) adult multivitamin-mineral supplement that provides close to recommended levels of a wide range of nutrients, including iron, zinc, and magnesium (see Appendix).

Iron can be a problem for both vegetarian and non-vegetarian teens, especially for girls. Those who are watching calories, are very active in sports, or have replaced the meat in their diet mainly with cheese and eggs may also have a tough time getting enough iron. A multivitamin-mineral supplement with iron and zinc may be appropriate in these cases.

A calcium supplement will be necessary if an average of eight servings from the Milks and Alternates group is not consumed: remember, we're aiming for 1,300 milligrams of calcium per day, and this is a challenge on any diet! If exposure to sunlight or consumption of vitamin D-fortified foods is low, a vitamin D supplement of 10 mcg is also recommended.

Part 5: The Prime of Life (Fifty Years Plus)

As we reach fifty and then seventy years of age and older, our requirements for certain nutrients change. Oddly, these changes veer off in two opposite directions at once. In order to maintain the same body weight, we require *fewer* calories. Simultaneously, we need *more* of two vitamins (D and B6) and one mineral (calcium). At the same time, our recommended intakes for twelve vitamins, ten minerals, and protein stay the same.

What does this mean in terms of our food choices? Simply, it means that we need to get "more bang for our buck." Returning to the idea of nutrient density that was covered in Chapter 6, if we're going to get these amounts of vitamins D and B6, calcium, protein, and other vitamins and minerals while eating fewer calories, then every 100 calories in our diets must deliver a little *more* protein, vitamins, and minerals.

Changes with Age

Calories, Muscle Mass, and Activity

There are two main reasons that most of us need fewer calories as we get older:

First, with age, we lose muscle mass. Our caloric requirement depends in part on our metabolic rate, which in turn depends on our total amount of lean body mass or muscle tissue. Muscle mass tends to shrink as we age. When a person's muscle mass at age twenty-five and age sixty-five are compared, men typically have lost 11.8 kilograms (26 pounds) of muscle tissue and women may have lost 5 kilograms (11 pounds) of muscle tissue over four decades. Thereafter, 1 or 1.5 kilograms (2 or 3 pounds) of muscle tissue is lost each decade. This gradually reduces our caloric requirement.

Second, with age, activity levels decrease. Unfortunately, most of us exercise less as we become older. We have found so many ways to make life easy for ourselves that in wealthy nations, it is customary to think of sedentary behaviour as the norm. Health problems such as adult onset diabetes are viewed as almost inevitable aspects of becoming older. Yet these are actually linked to inactivity and increased fat in the abdominal region, rather than to age.

The amount of muscle we carry on our frame affects our rate of metabolism, insulin sensitivity, need for calories, appetite, breathing, and ability to move; ultimately it affects our independence. Losing pound after pound of muscle is not an advantage!

As we become older, perhaps some stresses from earlier stages of life—raising children, getting ahead in the world—have lessened. We may consider that we'd like to enjoy years of vibrant good health, and have fun with our loved ones. According to the *Manual of Clinical Dietetics*, "The older adult who maintains a high activity level can preserve muscle mass and requires a higher energy intake to maintain body weight." In other words, by exercising, we can keep our muscle mass, plus we get to eat more, without getting fat!

Physical activity has an *immense* impact on our health and quality of life as we age. It helps us keep our muscles and remain strong. It is crucial to retention of bone mass. The function of our heart, oxygen delivery system, and lungs are improved. Our bodies remain more flexible. Exercise is an important factor in mental health and well being. It results in our feeling better about ourselves, and improves the quality of our social interactions. Our sleep and our sex life improve. We are better able to maintain a healthy body weight. In ways that can be measured, exercise improves the effective function of our immune systems. It cuts our risk of chronic diseases: colon cancer, heart disease, diabetes, arthritis, and hypertension.

"If the effects of exercise could be bottled, it would be the most widely prescribed medication."

—*Linn Goldberg, M.D.*

Would it be best if we take up marathon running? No, that's neither necessary nor ideal. There is general agreement among experts that our target for the day should be at least an hour of exercise. Which activities are best? It matters far less what activities we choose than that we do something. To keep motivated, we need to seek out forms of exercise that we really enjoy and look forward to. Gardening, cycling, swimming, or doing yoga are all great options. Join a fitness program on land or in a pool. Dance, hike, or cross-country ski. Put on music and whirl around the living room; the family dog may be pleased to join in and perhaps the person next door would, too. Stroll through inspiring places: a park, a beach, or a quiet road. Share a brisk power walk with a friend. Play table tennis, fly a kite, or toss a Frisbee with grandchildren or neighbours. Some combination from this list is likely best, as this way we can work out every part of our bodies.

Protein

Whether we're twenty, fifty, or seventy years of age, our recommended protein intake is the same as that described for adults on page 65—about 1 gram of protein per kilogram of body weight.

We need more protein if we're dealing with illness, infection, or recovery from surgery; in these situations our requirement may be around 1.25 gram of protein per kilogram of body weight. Either level—1 gram or 1.25 grams of protein per kilogram of body weight—easily can be met on a vegetarian diet if protein-rich plant foods, such as legumes or soyfoods, are eaten daily. Table 3.10 and the menus on pages 80, 91, 92, 94 give an idea of the amounts of protein in various foods.

Though our protein needs stay the same per kilogram of body weight, we actually need more protein relative to the amount of calories we eat. That means our diets need to be more protein-dense (more protein per 100 calories of food). This is because with shrinking muscle mass, our caloric requirements decrease, but protein needs stay the same. We must make sure that good sources of protein are included in our daily diet, and take care not to squander too many calories on junk foods. Physical changes that occur with age often attract people toward plant protein and away from meats. Poor dentition and swallowing difficulties, combined with cost factors, often mean that meat is less appealing. The softer textures of tofu and split pea or lentil soups can be ideal. Concern about chronic disease (both prevention and treatment) also draws people toward plant foods.

Sometimes questions are raised about beans causing stomach upset and gas. The solutions are to introduce these foods gradually. Start with the smaller beans, lentils, and split peas, as well as tofu, and take the time to chew foods well.

When soaking and cooking beans, discard the soaking water as it contains oligosaccharides that result in intestinal gas. Then make sure beans are well cooked. There is a tremendous "up" side to switching from meat to beans. Meat is a fibre-free food. When we eat mainly meat and processed foods, and we are inactive, constipation can become a real concern. The problem seems to escalate with age. The switch to a vegetarian diet rich in beans, peas, and lentils can help to resolve this problem permanently. Exercise and drinking water help too.

For a quick protein boost, a shake (recipe, page 390) is a pleasant way to get 7 grams of protein. A serving of Scrambled Tofu (page 389) can provide half one's protein for the day. We should not discount the contribution of cooked cereal: 250 millilitres (1 cup) of oatmeal with 175 millilitres (3/4 cup) of soymilk provides 11 grams of protein, which may be one-quarter of the day's requirement. We'll get the same amount from an English muffin with 30 millilitres (2 tbsp) of almond butter (and more if we use peanut butter). Browse through the recipes in this book, including the nutritional analysis, to see many ways to reach our recommended grams of protein per kilogram of body weight.

Vitamin B6

When we reach the age of fifty-one years, our recommended intakes for a vitamin B6 increases dramatically by 30 per cent to 1.7 milligrams for men and 1.5 milligrams for women from 1.3 milligrams per day for both sexes before age fifty-one. Typical Canadian intakes are 1.8 milligrams for men and 1.3 milligrams for women. Since these are averages, it seems that half the women in the general population may fall below recommended intakes. Yet the recommended intakes include a large safety margin and deficiency symptoms are not common.

Vitamin B6, also known as pyridoxine, plays a role in the metabolism of more than 100 amino acids. Along with two other B vitamins, B12 and folate, it helps us get rid of potentially toxic homocysteine (described in more detail on page 37 in Chapter 2). Vitamin B6 helps us build the blood protein, heme.

Symptoms of deficiency are depression, anemia, and increased homocysteine levels accompanied by increased risk of heart disease. Vitamin B6 is present in many vegetarian foods. A few examples are shown in Table 10.8. We can reach the level of 1.7 milligrams with a banana, a baked potato, a cup of lentils, plus a handful of nuts or seeds.

TABLE 10.8 *Vitamin B6 in Foods*

Food and Serving Size	Vitamin B6 (mg)
Fruits	
Banana, 1 medium	0.7
Cantaloupe or honeydew melon, G	0.2
Figs, dried, 5	0.2
Prunes, 7	0.2
Apple, medium, 1	0.1
Vegetables	
Kale, raw, 250 mL (1 cup)	0.2
Potato, baked, 1 medium with skin	0.4
Sweet potato, baked and peeled, 1	0.3
Broccoli, collards, raw, 250 mL (1 cup)	0.1
Carrot, medium, 1	0.1
Squash, cooked, 125 mL (H cup)	0.1
Beans and Alternates	
Lentils, soybeans, cooked, 250 mL (1 cup)	0.4
Navy, pinto beans, 250 mL (1 cup)	0.3
Adzuki, garbanzo, kidney beans, cooked 250 mL (1 cup)	0.2
Yves Veggie Ground Round, 60 g (2 oz)	0.3
Tempeh, 125 mL (H cup)	0.2
Tofu, 125 mL (H cup)	0.1
Nuts and Seeds	
Flaxseed, 30 mL (2 tbsp)	0.2
Hazelnuts, 60 mL (G cup)	0.2
Sunflower seeds, 60 mL (G cup)	0.3
Peanut butter, 45 mL (3 tbsp)	0.2
Grains	
Barley, cooked, 125 mL (H cup)	0.1
Ready-to-eat-cereal, unfortified, 1 serving	0.2
Ready-to-eat-cereal, fortified, 1 serving (see label)	0.5
Wheat germ, 30 mL (2 tbsp)	0.2
Dairy Products and Eggs	
Cow's milk, 2%, 125 mL (H cup)	0.05
Egg, 1	0.05

Calcium

As we grow older, we become less efficient at absorbing calcium. For example, from age forty to sixty, this efficiency may drop as much as 25 per cent. At age fifty, our recommended intake of calcium increases to 1,200 milligrams per day (from 1,000 milligrams for adults below age fifty). To reach these levels, we need eight servings from the Milks and Alternates group, each providing about 15 per cent of the DV for calcium. For more on the Milks and Alternates group, see page 245 in Chapter 9 and for more on calcium, see Chapter 4. For many people, these intakes are most easily achieved, at least on some days by adding a few hundred milligrams in supplement form to the amount derived from food to reach the total.

Vitamin D

This vitamin, which can be derived from the effects of sunlight on our skin, or from fortified foods, is essential for our absorption of calcium. In Canada, we are rather short of sunlight during winter months, and the average serum vitamin D levels of adults hover around the low end of the normal range. This means, of course, that some people's levels are below the ideal range. To make matters worse, as we age, our skin becomes much less efficient at doing its part in building vitamin D, even when sunlight does manage to reach our hands and face. Thus at age fifty, recommended intakes for vitamin D double to 10 micrograms per day, and there is a further increase to 15 micrograms for those over seventy years old.

Fortified soymilk, rice milk, and cow's milk each provide 2.5 micrograms of vitamin D per day, so people aged fifty to seventy can get their quota from 1 litre (4 cups) of any of these fortified beverages. For more on vitamin D sources, see page 145. Over the age of seventy, it is difficult to achieve recommended intakes from fortified foods alone, so supplementation with 15 micrograms per day is advised.

Certain medications such as laxatives, steroids for arthritis, and anticonvulsants can interfere with vitamin D and increase requirements.

To get sufficient vitamin D from sunlight in spring, summer, and fall, we can expose our face, hands, and forearms to twenty minutes of sun (mid-morning to mid-afternoon); people with darker skin may require more. Of course, avoid excess sun exposure.

Vitamin B12

Changes in our gastrointestinal tract as we age, that affect our absorption of vitamin B12, were well described in Chapter 8. As many as one in three adults over the age of fifty may have difficulty absorbing vitamin B12 from animal products, so vitamin B12-fortified foods or supplements are advised for all people in this age group (not just vegetarians). The amount we need in our diets is not increased over that of younger people, it's just that we need to make sure we take in B12 in a form that we can absorb. (For a small proportion of people, monthly injection is necessary.) For examples of B12-fortified foods, see Table 8.2 on page 236.

Omega-3 Fatty Acids

As we grow older, our ability to convert the plant form of omega-3 fatty acids (ALA) to long-chain omega-3 fatty acids (EPA and DHA) diminishes. Thus, we must be especially diligent to insure adequate intake of ALA. For most people, an intake of 3-6 grams a day is sufficient. Some people, such as those with chronic diseases such as diabetes, arthritis, or neurological disorders, may wish to consider taking direct sources of the long-chain omega-3 fatty acids and GLA. (See Chapter 7 for more information on omega-3 fatty acid sources.)

Other Important Aspects of Diet for Seniors

Antioxidants. Vitamins A and C (from fruits and vegetables), and vitamin E and the mineral selenium (both found in nuts, seeds, and whole grains) are powerful protectors against free radical damage. Antioxidants are linked to a reduced risk of cataracts, macular degeneration, heart disease, various forms of cancer, and even wrinkles. Antioxidants seem to protect our brain function from deterioration, too. Vegetarian diets tend to be high in these antioxidants. We do the cells throughout our bodies a favour by following the Vegetarian Food Guide on pages 241-242.

If we develop dental problems, there can be a tendency to cut back on intake of fresh produce; however soft fruits, cooked vegetables, and fresh-squeezed vegetable or fruit juices can take the place of foods that are more difficult to chew while the problems are resolved. The three shakes and smoothies on pages 390-394, or your own variations, will also help at times like this. Consider buying a good juicer—it will be well worth the investment.

Water and Other Fluids. Though we don't need more fluids as we get older, we do need the usual 1.5-2 litres (6-8 cups) each day. With age, one's sensitivity to thirst may decrease, yet it's important to drink water even when one is not particularly thirsty. Fear of incontinence can also lead to decreased fluid intake. Dehydration can result in constipation and other health problems, so it's important to drink water, juice, soymilk, grain beverages, and herbal teas. All of these count toward our day's quota.

Words of Wisdom on Health and Fitness

Gratitude

There is always a lot to be thankful for if we take time to look for it. For example, we can thank the mercy of nature that wrinkles don't hurt!

Bowel Health

We know we've hit middle age when we choose our cereal on the basis of fibre rather than the free toy. We know we're over the hill when our wild oats have turned to prunes and all bran.

Exercise

Use caution when you start a walking program. My grandmother began walking five miles a day when she was sixty. Now she's ninety-seven years old and we have no idea where on earth she is!

Community Support

All this nutritional advice may be very fine, but often it's not the lack of knowledge about vitamins or protein that is a problem, but a matter of lifestyle and social support. For instance, it's not so much fun creating nourishing meals when one sits alone at the table day after day. Whereas ads might show a happy pair of seniors cycling off into the sunset or enjoying a candlelit dinner on the balcony, for many of us, our partner is gone, and other family members live far away.

Since there are so many of us in the same situation, it's worthwhile doing some exploring. Soon problems of that sort will be a distant memory.

Solutions to Isolation

Reach out. You have no idea how happy you will make someone if you do the unexpected and invite him or her over to share a meal, and perhaps to prepare it together. Your guest might even help pick a recipe from those at the end of this book and join you in shopping for ingredients.

Join a vegetarian association. More and more communities have a lively vegetarian association, and membership spans the spectrum from newborns to those arriving by wheelchair or in their nineties. If you don't find such a group, ask around for one or more people with whom you can start a monthly potluck (even for two). This is how the existing groups got started!

Explore cohousing or similar living solutions. One of the authors of this book lives in a cohousing community, which is the modern form of village that originated in Denmark several decades ago. Dozens of these wonderful groups have formed across North America and they offer the joint advantages of privacy and community. See www.cohousing.ca or call 604-878-3311 (Western Canada) or 416-738-0850 (Eastern Canada) or 877-980-2700.

Assistance in Provision of Food, and More

Grocery delivery. Arrange to have fresh organic produce delivered to your door each week (see page 361). Many supermarkets, including some natural foods stores, offer delivery services.

Meal delivery. If you are housebound or have difficulty getting around or preparing meals, programs such as Meals-on-Wheels may be just the answer. Though not all programs cater to vegetarians, supply depends on the local demand, so do inquire. Your local caterer may not be aware that a four-week set of vegetarian menus has been developed for use by the National Meals on Wheels Foundation. These are online at
http://www.vrg.org/fsupdate/fsu974/fsu974menu.htm

Care facilities and vegetarian food. If you or a loved one are in search of a suitable care home with expertise in vegetarian food preparation, check on those run by the Seventh-day Adventists as these are more capable of providing nutritious, delicious, and varied meals than many care homes. See telephone listings; a local Seventh-day Adventist church can help you. In other facilities, you may be pleasantly surprised to find that kitchen staff are willing and able to accommodate a vegetarian senior, especially if you discuss with them suitable and acceptable entrées (marinated tofu, soy burgers, and thick bean, pea, or lentil soups).

Seniors online. For helpful information on everything from heartburn to quick, inexpensive meals, visit the Vegetarian Resource Group's Web site at www.vrg.org and do a search for "seniors."

Potential Advantages of Vegetarian Diets in the Senior Years

Populations of vegetarians living in affluent countries appear to enjoy unusually good health, characterized by low rates of cancer, cardiovascular disease, and total mortality. These important observations have fuelled much research and have raised 3 general questions about vegetarians in relation to nonvegetarians:

- Are these observations the result of better nondietary lifestyle factors, such as lower prevalences of smoking and higher levels of physical activity?

- Are they the result of lower intakes of harmful dietary components, in particular meat? and

- Are they the result of higher intakes of beneficial dietary components that tend to replace meat in the diet?

Current evidence suggests that the answer to all 3 questions is "Yes."

—Walter C. Willett,
Department of Nutrition,
Harvard School of Public Health, Boston

**A complete set of references is available online at:
http://www.nutrispeak.com/bvreferences.htm**

chapter 11

vegetarian victory over weight

North Americans are obsessed with food: we have more food products and more fast-food outlets than anywhere on the planet. We are equally preoccupied with matters of weight and shape: women strive to be model thin, men to be muscular. Yet somehow, amid all the diet foods, weight-loss centres, protein powders, and gyms, we keep getting fatter. Overconsumption leading to overweight and obesity is now an epidemic and the fastest-growing form of malnutrition in the world. Over 55 per cent of Americans are overweight, and Canadians are close behind. The proportion of American adults over twenty-five who are overweight soared from 25 per cent in 1950 to 61 per cent in 2002. Since 1980, obesity rates have doubled in adults and tripled in children. All of this has devastating consequences for health.

Vegetarians are at a distinct advantage where body weight is concerned. We are leaner and have remarkably lower rates of obesity than the general population. While a vegetarian diet cannot guarantee a leaner body weight, it can make the struggle a little less ominous. This chapter will explore issues of body weight and shape, and provide practical tips for achieving a healthy weight for life.

Society's Double-edged Sword

At twenty years old, 162 centimetres (5 feet, 4 inches) and 71 kilograms (156 pounds), Jennifer felt fat. She had struggled with her weight since she was a little girl. Efforts to lose weight had been successful only in the short term. It seemed that for every pound that she lost, she would gain two. One night, a college friend asked her to a screening of a documentary film called The Witness,* which moved her so deeply, she decided to become a vegetarian. While she was worried about what she would eat, and how her family would respond, she felt an underlying excitement. Perhaps it was more than a coincidence that she had been invited to this movie. Maybe the payoff for being kinder to animals would be a thinner body. After all, every vegetarian she could think of was a bean pole.

Jennifer's family always centred their activities around food: big family dinners; homemade pies, cakes, and cookies; and wonderful cele-bratory meals. When Jennifer announced that she was giving up meat forever, her family was appalled, feeling that she was turning her back on family traditions.

For Jennifer the biggest challenge was replacing the meat. She had never eaten beans, apart from the odd can of baked beans while camping, and she had not even tasted tofu. It seemed to her that eggs and cheese were the quickest, easiest, and tastiest substitutes. Her parents tried to compen-sate for what they perceived as deprivation by providing Jennifer with more of her favourite dishes, such as pizza, scalloped potatoes, and hot fudge sundaes. Jennifer had a hard time resisting, as they were so much more than just food; they were tokens of love and family unity. To top it all off, her younger brother constantly hassled her about her new food choices, which triggered her to eat more. To Jennifer's dismay, her vegetarianism was not producing any weight loss.

(*The Witness is an award-winning documentary by Tribe of Heart about a construction worker who opens his heart to animals and spreads his message of compassion through the streets of New York City. For more information see: www.tribeofheart.org/index.htm)

The Vegetarian Advantage

There is no doubt about it, vegetarians are thinner than nonvege-tarians. These differences cannot be explained by some miraculous side effect of sprouts. Experts suspect that the vegetarian advantage can be attributed largely to differences in fat and fibre.

Vegetarians eat less fat, and particularly less saturated fat. Some studies suggest that relative to saturated fat, polyunsaturated fat increases metabolic rates. Vegetarians also eat two to three times more fibre than nonvegetarians. Fibre adds bulk to the diet, without adding calories. It also helps speed food through the digestive system, slightly decreasing our absorption of calories. In addition, fibre reduces hunger and gives us a feeling of fullness. Vegetarians also tend to lead healthier lifestyles, with higher activity levels.

However, becoming vegetarian does not guarantee freedom from being overweight, as Jennifer can attest to. While eliminating cheeseburgers, fried chicken, and barbequed ribs can certainly help, we must remember that French fries, potato chips, and coconut cream pie are all classified as vegetarian foods.

So, while being vegetarian offers clear benefits for weight control, there are a significant number of overweight vegetarians who struggle every bit as much as nonvegetarians to lose weight. The reasons for their weight struggles are not a whole lot different from anyone else's.

Causes of Overweight

Popular opinion would suggest that the primary cause of obesity is a lack of willpower: overweight people are "couch potatoes" who eat too much. If only it were that simple. While it is true that too much food and too little exercise are often technically the cause of being overweight, this is rarely the whole story. For many people, overweight has as much to do with self-preservation and social pressures as it does with overeating and underactivity. Our current popular opinion serves only to pour salt on the wound. The main causes of overweight fall into one of three groups of factors: physical, environmental, and emotional.

Physical Factors

Jennifer is overweight, just like her mom, her aunt, and her grandmother. She inherited her father's eyes, and her mother's and her grandmother's metabolism. These genes would be a real advantage to Jennifer in the face of famine, but in the midst of abundance, they seem like more of a curse. Very low-calorie diets can make matters worse by slowing metabolism and sending our body into conservation mode. If we diet enough, our body becomes even more efficient, allowing us to survive on fewer calories. Less commonly, obesity is caused by medications or rare endocrine disorders such as hypothyroidism (underactive thyroid reduces metabolic rate).

Environmental Factors

Like most of us, Jennifer puts a lot of emphasis on social interactions involving food. Whether it is enjoying a family gathering or a night at the movies with friends, food is a fundamental part of the experience. Our society has created an ideal environment for overconsumption. We no longer need to do physical work to get food. We simply open a refrigerator or freezer and pop a ready-made snack or meal into the microwave. When we are out and about, food beckons us at every turn. Jennifer can't seem to resist stopping for fries or pizza at the mall, or running into the corner store for a chocolate bar. We are surrounded by an abundance of food and, not surprisingly, it shows.

The icing on the cake is that this easy access to food comes hand-in-hand with reduced physical activity. We catch a bus to school or drive to work. Much of the day involves sitting at a desk. In our spare time, we watch television, play video games, or surf the Net. Every convenience possible has been developed to reduce energy expenditure—remote controls, bread machines, electric can openers, elevators, electric mixers, dishwashers, and the list goes on.

Emotional Factors

Following a confrontation with her brother, Jennifer often turns to the refrigerator, even when she isn't hungry. Like Jennifer, many people eat to satisfy an emotional hunger rather than a true physical hunger. This is often referred to as "emotional eating" and is well recognized as a major contributor to overweight. Others use food as a means of constructing walls around themselves that protect them against intimacy or pain. Food never judges, never condemns, and always seems to comfort. These apparent advantages are deceiving as they come at an enormous cost to both physical and emotional well-being.

To add a little fuel to the fire, society comes along with a clear message to eat, drink, and be merry—just don't let it go to our hips. If we do happen to accumulate a little excess, we'd better prepare for battle, or learn to live with the social consequences.

The Cost

The price we pay for the abundance we now enjoy is hard to quantify. Obesity causes a five-fold rise in our risk of type 2 diabetes. Being overweight increases blood pressure, cholesterol levels, triglycerides, and angina, markedly increasing our chances of sudden heart attack or stroke. It is also linked to several types of cancers, including breast, uterine, cervical, ovarian, gallbladder, and colon cancers in women, and rectal, prostate, and colon cancers in men. Excess body weight contributes to our risk of osteoarthritis, sleep apnea (pauses in breathing during sleep), gout (painful swelling in the joints), gallbladder disease, and gallstones.

These health consequences are contributing more to America's rising health care and drug costs than smoking and alcohol abuse. Even more stunning, being obese effectively ages us twenty years in terms of health risk. That puts an obese thirty-year-old in the same risk group as a normal-weight fifty-year-old for developing serious medical problems such as cancer, heart disease, and diabetes.

Determining Healthy Body Weight

Humans come in a wide variety of shapes and sizes. There is no one "ideal" weight for a person of a particular height because our healthiest weight depends on our bone structure, muscle mass, and general body build. Thus, weight charts are of limited value. So how do we know if we are overweight or obese? The best way is to determine how much of our body weight is fat. A body fat level greater than 17 per cent in men and 27 per cent in women indicates being overweight, while a body fat level of greater than 25 per cent in men and 31 per cent in women indicates obesity.

Unfortunately, getting accurate body fat measurements can be a challenge. The more widely used method of determining body fatness is called *body mass index (BMI)*. Our BMI can be calculated using a simple equation, or a chart (see Table 11.1). BMI is recommended for people ages twenty to sixty-five years, but has not been considered valid for some people. For example, it does not factor in muscle mass, so very muscular people will have a high BMI, but low body fat (thus, they appear "overweight" according to BMI, but are actually very lean). In addition, very short people (less than 1.5 metres/5 feet tall) may have higher BMI than would be expected relative to their size. BMI is not useful for pregnant women or those over the age of sixty-five. To find your BMI, plot your height and weight on Table 11.1.

What's Jennifer's BMI? Recall that Jennifer is 162 centimetres (5 feet, 4 inches) tall, and 71 kilograms (156 pounds). Thus, her BMI is 27—right in the middle of the overweight range. She is about 6.5 kilograms (14 pounds) over being classified at a "healthy weight for most people," and 8.6 kilograms (19 pounds) short of being classified as "obese."

TABLE 11.1   *Body Mass Index (BMI)*

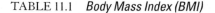

Understanding Your BMI

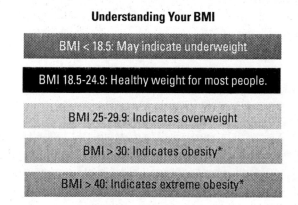

BMI < 18.5: May indicate underweight

BMI 18.5-24.9: Healthy weight for most people.

BMI 25-29.9: Indicates overweight

BMI > 30: Indicates obesity*

BMI > 40: Indicates extreme obesity*

TABLE 11.1 *continued*

	Height in Inches																
WT/lbs	**60**	**61**	**62**	**63**	**64**	**65**	**66**	**67**	**68**	**69**	**70**	**71**	**72**	**73**	**74**	**75**	**76**
100	20	19	18	18	17	17	16	16	15	15	14	14	14	13	13	12	12
105	21	20	19	19	18	17	17	16	16	16	15	15	14	14	13	13	13
110	21	21	20	19	19	18	18	17	17	16	16	15	15	15	14	14	13
115	22	22	21	20	20	19	19	18	17	17	17	16	16	15	15	14	14
120	23	23	22	21	21	20	19	19	18	18	17	17	16	16	15	15	15
125	24	24	23	22	21	21	20	20	19	18	18	17	17	16	16	16	15
130	25	25	24	23	22	22	21	20	20	19	19	18	18	17	17	16	16
135	26	26	25	24	23	22	22	21	21	20	19	19	18	18	17	17	16
140	27	26	26	25	24	23	23	22	21	21	20	20	19	18	18	17	17
145	28	27	27	26	25	24	23	23	22	21	21	20	20	19	19	18	18
150	29	28	27	27	26	25	24	23	23	22	22	21	20	20	19	19	18
155	30	29	28	27	27	26	25	24	24	23	22	22	21	20	20	19	19
160	31	30	29	28	27	27	26	25	24	24	23	22	22	21	21	20	19
165	32	31	30	29	28	27	27	26	25	24	24	23	22	22	21	21	20
170	33	32	31	30	29	28	27	27	26	25	24	24	23	22	22	21	21
175	34	33	32	31	30	29	28	27	27	26	25	24	24	23	22	22	21
180	35	34	33	32	31	30	29	28	27	27	26	25	24	24	23	22	22
185	36	35	34	33	32	31	30	29	28	27	27	26	25	24	24	23	23
190	37	36	35	34	33	32	31	30	29	28	27	26	26	25	24	24	23
195	38	37	36	35	34	33	32	31	30	29	28	28	27	26	25	24	24
200	39	38	37	35	34	33	32	31	30	29	28	27	26	26	25	25	24
205	40	39	37	36	35	34	33	32	31	30	29	29	28	27	26	26	25
210	41	40	38	37	36	35	34	33	32	31	30	29	28	28	27	26	26
215	42	41	39	38	37	36	35	34	33	32	31	30	29	28	28	27	26
220	43	42	40	39	38	37	36	35	34	33	32	31	30	29	28	27	27
225	44	43	41	40	39	37	36	35	34	33	32	31	31	30	29	28	27
230	45	43	42	41	39	38	37	36	35	34	33	32	31	30	30	29	28
235	46	44	43	42	40	39	38	37	36	35	34	33	32	31	31	29	29
240	47	45	44	43	41	40	39	38	36	35	34	33	33	31	31	30	29
245	48	46	45	43	42	41	40	39	37	36	35	34	33	32	32	30	30
250	49	47	46	44	43	42	40	39	38	37	36	35	34	33	32	31	30

The Battle of the Bulge

Most people who are overweight at some point become engaged in the usually futile "battle of the bulge." There are thousands of diets, herbal formulas, metabolic stimulants, appetite suppressants, fat blockers, weight loss patches, and other diet aids. The excess fat can be suctioned out or cut off and, if all else fails, our stomachs can be stapled, effectively shrinking them down to tiny pouches. Unfortunately, none of these weapons have proven overly effective, and some even backfire.

Jennifer knows the frustration of diet failure only too well. She has been on one diet after another since the age of twelve. She has tried low-calorie diets, low-carbohydrate diets, the cabbage soup diet, and meal replacement diets. They all worked beautifully—for about a month. Each and every one managed to keep calories down sufficiently to produce weight loss. Then as old patterns were slowly resumed, the weight would creep back, stopping only after an extra 2.26 kilograms (5 pounds) was packed on. She would feel like a complete and utter failure. What Jennifer didn't realize was that her odds of permanent weight loss through dieting were about 5 per cent—some 95 per cent of all weight-loss methods fail. The obvious question is, why? The answer: weight-loss diets end. Not too many people are willing to live on protein powders for the rest of their lives or consume ten grapefruits a day.

The fatal flaw of the weight-loss industry is that it is focused on the pursuit of thinness at all costs. Thus, it peddles promises of speedy success with miracle cures for obesity. Of course, if a miracle cure for obesity actually existed, the problem would quickly disappear. Yet, somehow the numbers of overweight people continue to escalate.

What's the answer? It is simple—we must shift our focus from thinness to health.

Healthy Mind, Healthy Body

Shifting our focus from thinness to health can be a scary prospect. Most dieters have their sights set on shedding pounds, not on good health. In fact good health may appear to have little connection with our goal. Yet trying to achieve thinness by methods that don't support our health and well being is like trying to build a house on sand. When we focus solely on thinness, weight loss efforts usually fail because changes are generally short-lived.

When health is an integral part of our focus, we make gradual changes that tend to be permanent. This shift in mind-set does not mean we will have to simply accept being overweight. Far from it: when we make choices for health, weight loss naturally occurs in those who are overweight. We eat fewer low fibre foods such as sweet baked goods and deep-fried foods, and more vegetables and fruits. We watch less television and go biking, hiking and swimming more often. We spend less time being stressed, and more time practicing stress management techniques. Our goal of weight loss will be achieved, but that's not all. We will look great and feel great. Our muscle tone will improve, our endurance will escalate, and we'll be more content.

If we go back and look and Jennifer's situation, we can see that a few important changes are required for her to reach her health goals. First, she can dump the dieter's mentality, and concentrate on eating more healthful foods and becoming more physically active. She might enlist family support by inviting her family to go hiking or biking. She can encourage her family to focus more on healthful eating by preparing wonderfully delicious and nutritious foods for them to share. The following guidelines will support Jennifer, and all of us, in creating a lifestyle that fully supports health and healing.

Prescription for Lifelong Healthy Weight

A healthy lifestyle requires a balance of body, mind, and spirit, and each must be nourished in a way that is mindful of everyone and everything around us. The prescription for lifelong healthy weight involves making health-oriented behaviour changes in three key areas:

- healthful eating,

- active lifestyle,

- and positive self- and body image.

Healthful Eating

1. Cultivate a healthy relationship with food. Learn to respond to natural hunger signals, and avoid the temptation of eating when not hungry, or depriving oneself when famished. Take pleasure in eating a wide variety of nourishing foods, while enjoying the occasional indulgence. Make meals a special time—set the table, light a candle, and play some quiet music, perhaps. Encourage the participation of everyone in your home, and keep the atmosphere cheerful.

2. Build good food habits. We are all creatures of habit. We tend to stick with the same routine day after day, whether it is healthful or not. Examine habits, and replace those that undermine health with better choices. It doesn't need to happen overnight—one small step at a time will do. For example, switch from 2 per cent milk to 1 per cent, then to skim milk. Finally, consider forgoing the dairy for any of a number of delicious fortified beverages like soymilk, rice milk, or oat milk. If backsliding occurs, don't be consumed with guilt. Instead, work on ways to make new healthy habits even more enjoyable. Begin the quest by taking these simple steps:

- *Eat regular meals.* Skipping meals can reduce performance and leave us so hungry that we are more apt to gorge at the next meal.

- *Keep portion sizes moderate.* The more food on our plate, the more we end up eating. Overeating causes weight gain, and often a sore stomach as well.

- *Eat slowly.* This not only enables us to better appreciate our food, it can help control the amount we eat and improve digestion.

- *Eat sitting down, with a proper place setting.* Always put food in a dish and sit down to eat. This makes us more conscious of exactly how much we are taking in.

- *Avoid eating while cooking.* Sometimes we eat as much while preparing a meal as we do when the meal is served. If need be, suck on a mint or chew a piece of gum or a fresh herb.

- *If television is a trigger to overeat, fight it.* Limit TV to a few hours a week. If watching a show or movie, keep hands busy with a craft or ironing, or do stretching exercises. A platter of raw veggies is your best snack option.

• *Get hooked on healthy foods when eating out.* If tempted, go for fresh fruit, fresh-squeezed juices, an oriental stir-fry, some popcorn (hold the butter), or a frozen yogourt. Steer clear of deep-fried foods.

3. Make healthful food choices. As we shift to a vegetarian diet, whole plant foods should move from the periphery to centre stage. A variety of vegetables, legumes, whole grains, fruits, and small amounts of nuts, seeds, and fruit should form the foundation of the diet. Processed foods should be limited, especially those with added fats and sugars. Concentrated sweets, such as chocolate bars, cakes, pies, and candy, are high in calories, but low in nutrients. These should not be a regular feature of our diet.

Fat is our most concentrated source of energy. Every 15 milli-litres (1 tablespoon) of fat has 100 calories (two and a half times more than the same weight of protein or carbohydrate), so go light-ly on the fats and oils used in cooking and at the table. Make the fat you do use count nutritionally. Rather than butter on toast, try almond butter. Instead of using sour cream for a dip, pick hummus. Replace chips with trail mix. (While nuts are high in fat, they pro-vide valuable nutrients.)

A healthful diet is one that is low in saturated fat and choles-terol, rich in fibre, phytochemicals, vitamins, and minerals, and pro-vides ample protein and essential fatty acids. By following the Vegetarian Food Guide on pages 241-242, we will be off to an amazing start in building such a diet. The following tips will help make great choices a breeze in each food group.

• *Grains: Five to twelve servings a day*
Use mainly intact whole grains such as brown rice, oat groats, barley, quinoa, milletand kamut berries. Grains are inexpensive, can often be bought in the bulk food section of your market, and are easy to prepare. If using breads and cereals, select those made from whole grains; high-fibre foods increase feelings of fullness. Beware of highly processed items: snack crackers, com-mercial granolas, cookies, muffins, cheese breads, garlic breads, croissants, and sweet baked goods. Many derive more than 40

per cent of their calories from fat. Make your own low-fat, high-fibre muffins, pancakes, and other baked goods.

- *Vegetables and Fruits: Five to ten servings a day*
  Vegetables and fruits are our biggest bargains nutritionally and should be a feature at every meal. Most are very low in fat and loaded with nutrients. Select cooking methods that don't use added fat—steam, bake, or boil. Avoid deep frying, and use little or no fat in stir-fries. Leafy greens are especially important; include at least one or two servings a day. Go easy on the dried fruits—they are a fairly concentrated source of calories, as are avocados. Eat whole fruit instead of just drinking the juice.

- *Milk and Milk Alternates: Six to eight servings a day*
  The lowest calorie choices in this group are greens such as broccoli, kale, collards, and Chinese greens. Eat them more often. Fortified soymilk or rice milks are also good options. If using dairy products, select the low-fat or skim varieties of milk, low-fat (1 per cent milk fat or less) yogourt, and low-fat cottage cheese (1 per cent). Cheese is high in fat (even many of the "low-fat" cheeses derive over 50 per cent of their calories from fat), and should be used sparingly, if at all.

- *Beans and Bean Alternates: Two to four servings a day*
  Apart from soy, most legumes are very low in fat and are ideal sources of protein and calories for the weight-conscious vegetarian. They are rich in protein and complex carbohydrates, and give us great staying power between meals. Experiment with all kinds of legumes. Sprout lentils (see page 408), stew beans, add chickpeas to salads, black beans to soups and white beans to casseroles, or just eat beans as a side dish. Many veggie "meats," such as veggie burgers and deli slices, are very low in fat and are also excellent choices. Tofu is higher in fat, so keep portions moderate. Nuts and seeds are very high in fat, providing about 175-225 calories per 60-millilitre (1/4-cup) serving (16-20 grams of fat) so enjoy them in small quantities.

4. Select beverages with care. It is amazing how many calories can sneak into the diet in the form of fluids. A 375-millilitre (12-ounce) serving of lemonade, fruit punch, or soda pop can contain up to 150 calories. A typical milkshake chalks up 350 calories, as does a mere 250 millilitres (8 ounces) of non-alcoholic eggnog. Alcoholic beverages can also send calories soaring. Three hundred seventy-five millilitres (12 ounces) of beer provides 110-170 calories, distilled spirits about 110 calories per 38 millilitres (1.5 ounces), liqueurs 150-190 calories per 38 millilitres H(1.5 ounces), and wine about 80 calories per 125 millilitres (4 ounces). While black coffee or tea is calorie-free, what we add to these beverages is another story. A tall 375-millilitre (12-ounce) café mocha with whole milk and whipped cream might be considered a piece of chocolate cake in a cup with close to 350 calories. Most of these beverages are filled with "empty calories"—calories with little nutritional value. Drinking four or five calorie-rich beverages a day could easily mean an extra 500-1,000 calories.

So what do we drink? Pure water is among our very best bets for fluids. Herbal teas are a tasty alternative. Vegetable and wheat grass juices offer the very best nutrition for minimal calories. Fruit juices, fruit smoothies, and soy, rice, or other grain milks are other excellent choices, although they are higher in calories.

Active Lifestyle

1. Make exercise a priority. Physical activity tends not to happen unless it becomes a real priority in our lives. It needs to be looked upon as a necessity, like brushing our teeth or going to the bathroom. Our bodies need activity if we are to achieve our health goals. Exercise offers huge advantages when it comes to weight loss. It increases stamina, energy output, and metabolism. Our goal is an hour of exercise each day, though we may begin slowly with half an hour of exercise every second day. We are most likely to stick with an activity if it is something that we enjoy. It doesn't have to be a gruelling workout to provide benefit. Even a brisk walk or low-impact aerobics will do the trick. Visit a friend over a stroll in the park or a game of squash, instead of over coffee and a doughnut.

2. Make the most of daily activities. Choose the more physical options in daily activities. Take the stairs instead of the elevator, walk or bicycle instead of driving whenever possible, and use manual tools instead of electric ones (i.e., use a manual beater instead of an electric one). Not only will this improve personal health, it will make an important contribution to the environment.

3. Be adventurous. Take up hiking, biking, canoeing, skating, skiing, rollerblading, tennis, golf, or some other challenging sport. Recruit a friend to join you so that you can encourage each other to continue.

4. Don't be a "couch potato." Be aware of how much time is devoted to television, videos, and computer games. Time spent on these pursuits leaves less time for energetic activities, such as playing tennis or going for a bike ride. Gradually replace sedentary activities with more active ones.

Positive Self- and Body Image

1. Recognize that each of us is far more than the sum of our parts. Appreciate the value in each and every person, regardless of body size and shape. Be critical of messages that focus on unrealistic thinness or huge muscles. Take the time to pay someone a compliment that has nothing to do with his or her physical beauty, weight, or shape. Enjoy the uniqueness of each person.

2. Be grateful for the body and all it does for you. Take a moment to appreciate the unfailing efforts of your body from head to toe. Instead of begrudging a protruding stomach, focus on how huggable it makes you. Rather than moaning about chubby legs, think about the great job your legs do in getting you around.

3. Don't rely on weight scales. Weigh scales can make us crazy. Weight naturally fluctuates up to 2.30 kilograms (5 pounds) in one day. In addition, muscle weighs more than fat, so with increased exercise, weight may not fluctuate at all, even though fat is lost and muscle gained. Our clothes will fit better, but the scales won't tell us that. For women, weight can also vary according to menstrual cycle. So, we can spare ourselves the misery and the self-condemnation associated with ritual weigh-ins. Instead focus on well-being, energy, and performance.

4. Enjoy life in spite of body weight. Don't let shape or size serve as an excuse to avoid living life to its fullest. Go swimming, buy a new outfit, or visit an old friend. If we wait until we are content with our body weight, life could just pass us by.

5. Take care of the inner being. Great health is the product of both a healthy mind and a healthy body. Making major changes in lifestyle can have a profound effect on our social, family, and business interactions. While this can be a very positive experience, it can also bring up uncomfortable issues. Through it all, take time for pampering and self-care. Treat yourself to a massage, join a yoga class, or enjoy a concert. We deserve to be treated with love and respect ... first and foremost from ourselves.

How Is Jennifer Doing?

Jennifer has a new attitude. She gave up on weight-loss diets and her big goal of being skinny. Great health is her new-found passion. Instead of rich desserts, she prepares fruit salads, fruit "ice cream," and grain-based puddings for herself and her family. She uses a variety of new vegetables, as well as legumes, whole grains, and tofu, instead of cheese and eggs for dinner. Jennifer even joined a gym with her mom. Not only do they both feel more energetic, their relationship is closer too. Jennifer's brother doesn't bug her about being vegetarian anymore, as she responds with such light-heartedness that it doesn't seem worth it anymore. Jennifer feels like she's gained a new kind of freedom. Weight loss is just a bonus.

Underweight and Eating Disorders

There are two challenges of weight and shape that are said to affect vegetarians at somewhat greater rates than nonvegetarians: underweight and eating disorders (specifically anorexia nervosa and bulimia nervosa). Vegetarians, and especially vegans, are underweight slightly more often than nonvegetarians. Being underweight is not a problem that attracts a lot of sympathy in our society. However, gaining a pound can be every bit as difficult for a person who is underweight as losing a pound is for a person who is overweight. Being underweight can be particularly frustrating, as there are far fewer support systems in place.

As many as 50 per cent of people suffering from anorexia nervosa or bulimia nervosa are vegetarian. That leads many people to believe that vegetarians must be at high risk for these disorders, and vegetarian diets may actually contribute to these disorders. While this may seem like a logical conclusion, we must realize that most vegetarians with eating disorders developed the eating disorder before they became vegetarian. Their goal in making the switch to a vegetarian diet was simple: to legitimize the removal of fatty foods such as pork chops, burgers, ice cream, and cheese from their diet. The truth is that vegetarians are not at greater risk for eating disorders. It is simply that many people with eating disorders shun animal products along with all the fat they contribute. For more information on both underweight and eating disorders, read *Becoming Vegan* by B. Davis. and V. Melina (The Book Publishing Co., 2000).

A complete set of references is available online at:
http://www.nutrispeak.com/bvreferences.htm

vegetarian diplomacy

Imagine this. You finally decide to give up meat forever. You had been toying with the idea for some time, but couldn't seem to take the final plunge. Then you attend a lecture that inspires you to take the next step. You feel terrific, as if a burden has been lifted from your shoulders. You race home to tell your wife and kids. You walk into the house and say, "Honey, I have something important to tell you." Your wife looks worried. You blurt it out, "I've decided to become a vegetarian." Her look of concern dissolves as she throws her arms into the air and shouts for joy. "Oh Dan," she says, "this is better than winning the lottery!" She dashes out the back door, beckoning the children to come inside. "Emily, Michael, come quickly! Dad has something to tell you." The children race inside and you break the news to them. They begin jumping up and down wildly and the four of you join hands and dance around in a circle. Then your wife says, "I think you should call your mom and dad right away." You rush into the kitchen, dial the number, and get both your parents on the line before you break the big news to them. Your mother is so overcome with emotion that she can hardly get the words out. "Dan, I have never been more proud of you than I

am at this moment." Your father chimes in, "This calls for a celebration—how about this weekend?" On Monday, when you walk
into the office, everyone begins cheering. There is a card on your
desk that reads, "Congratulations, Dan! Your example of compassion is an inspiration to us all. Your colleagues want to treat you to
lunch at the Veggie Garden." The only negative thought that enters
your mind, is "Why didn't I make this decision years ago?"

A more likely story.... You race home to tell your wife and kids.
You walk into the house and say, "Honey, I have something important to tell you." She looks worried. You blurt it out, "I've decided
to become a vegetarian." "I beg your pardon?" she says. "By vegetarian, do you mean that you don't want to eat red meat anymore?"
"Well, not exactly," you reply. "I don't want to eat any meat, poultry, or fish any more." "That's crazy! Are we supposed to cook separate meals every night?" "Oh no," you reply. "Eating vegetarian will
be good for all of us, and I am happy to do the cooking. If you and
the kids want meat, you can cook it on the side." "Oh right, fried
chicken will be just lovely with lentil stew," she says with a note of
sarcasm in her voice. "I'll cook normal food," you say. "What about
all of our family favourites and our holiday meals? These are our traditions, Dan," your wife adds. "Don't worry honey, we'll come up
with new family favourites, and even better family traditions," you
offer. "Thanks, but no thanks," she replies and walks away.

That weekend you make the trek out to your parents' place.
Before you take a step in the door, your wife announces, "You aren't
going to believe this, but your son has become a vegetarian." Your
parents both exclaim in unison, "You're kidding!" Your dad adds, "I
hope you don't try to turn your kids into vegetarians. You'll stunt
their growth." Your mom chimes in, "I hope you won't be fanatic
about it, and at least eat turkey on special occasions." When you
arrive at work on Monday, the whole staff seems to know about
your new diet. "Hey Dan!" your buddy Ben shouts, "How's about
you and me go for some nice big juicy steaks for lunch?" You want
to fade into the woodwork, but instead you just say, "Very funny,"
and sit quietly at your desk. Gosh, you think to yourself, people can
be such jerks. Yet, somehow, instead of giving up, you strengthen
your resolve.

Becoming Vegetarian in a Nonvegetarian World

Perhaps someday the first scenario will become commonplace, but we'd be wise advised not to hold our breath.

Becoming vegetarian in a nonvegetarian world can be both frustrating and empowering at the same time. It is frustrating because we have discovered a profound truth, one that could effectively reduce disease, environmental destruction, and animal suffering. Yet the more we try to share this amazing revelation, the more people resist hearing it. It is empowering because we must draw on our inner strength to stand firm in what we believe, not caving in to social pressures. Thankfully, as each year passes and the number of vegetarians rise, that task becomes a little less intimidating.

Our personal transition, and our impact on others, depend largely on two things. The first is our awareness of the underlying issues that inspired our change. The second is our example—our choices, and our responses to those around us who may oppose or resist our change.

Change presents a unique paradox. It threatens our security, yet it is the one thing we can always count on. Sometimes it is embraced, and other times it is resisted. Much depends on our motivation. When we are inspired by love and compassion, change is more likely to be welcomed and long lasting. When change stems from fear, or from a desire to impress or please others, it is often resented and quickly abandoned. Sometimes we fight change because it seems too overwhelming. When people can't face certain realities, a typical response is to pretend they don't exist and continue with comfortable, old patterns. If we want change to be smooth and enriching, we must be clear about our motivation. When we are solidly rooted in knowledge and truth, our choices become easier, even in the face of ominous obstacles.

Some people are able to make huge changes overnight; however, most adjust more easily when the changes are gradual. For those who are more inclined to make a more gradual shift towards becoming vegetarian or vegan, the following suggested steps may be helpful. They are entirely flexible, and should be adjusted to suit our individual needs.

Becoming Vegetarian ... Step by Step

1. **Awareness.** Our first step in the change process is awareness about our motivation for becoming vegetarian. What factors attract and inspire us? Which hold us back? How will this new way of eating affect our health, family, friends, and colleagues at work? Consider the long-term goals associated with this choice. How would these things be affected if we kept eating meat? While our primary motive may be health, or the environment, or concern for animals, as our knowledge increases, these reasons become intertwined. Think about it. While these may seem like separate issues, they are not. They are deeply connected. For example, if our first motivation is our own health, we soon learn that human health suffers when our environment is poisoned. Factory farming, and production and transportation of animal fodder are among the greatest contributors to environmental destruction, and to the pain, suffering and death of billions of animals every year. Life cannot be compartmentalized. If we make a choice based on love of life, as our awareness grows, our circle of compassion naturally expands. Books, magazines, newsletters, newspapers, Web sites, lectures, conferences, discussion groups, and courses can enrich and sustain us. (For a few examples, see page 378.)

2. **Connections.** Talk with family and friends about the changes we are making. In the process, help them to understand the reasons behind these choices. Be open, honest, and, most of all, be compassionate. Share carefully selected reading materials, videos, and Web sites. Invite friends and family to lectures. Honour the perspectives of others and their right to see things differently. Even if we are fortunate enough to have loved ones join us in our journey, their rate of change may be different from our own.

3. **Choices.** Decide what we are prepared to do at this moment, and what will have to wait. Establishing new routines and traditions will help those around us feel safe and connected to us. Typical steps we might take to accomplish our goals are listed below. There is no set amount of time required for each

step; this depends on our unique situation. The sequence can be personalized according to our priorities, ethical perspective, and social commitments. These steps can be switched around and adjusted until the plan feels right. We may take an extended pause or stop at some point along the way.

To eliminate meat, fish, and poultry, we can:

- Begin by cutting back on animal flesh foods by 50 per cent. Perhaps reduce red meat to once a week, chicken to twice a week, and fish to twice a week.

- Drop red meat completely. Eliminate beef, pork, and lamb.

- Drop poultry, including chicken, turkey, Cornish hens, duck, and geese.

- Drop fish. Some people prefer to keep fish until the end, eliminating it after eggs and dairy foods are cut. Others find it easier to drop fish first because dairy products are used so extensively.

To improve overall nutrition, we can:

- Reduce the "junk foods" in our diet. Eat less fast food, processed snack foods, sodas, and other nutritionally depleted products. Replace refined grains with whole grains. Select lower-fat dairy products and eat smaller portions of animal products.

- Incorporate more plant foods: vegetables, fruits, legumes, whole grains, nuts, and seeds into the diet. Try new "veggie meats"; explore some types of tofu and tempeh. Experiment with vegetarian recipes.

To replace eggs and dairy products, we can:

- Incorporate dairy and egg substitutes: fortified soymilk, rice milk, or other non-dairy milks, non-dairy cheeses, ice cream, yogourt, margarine, and nut and seed butters. Tofu works well as an egg substitute. In addition, there are a number of commercial and homemade egg substitutes for baking (see pages 374-375).

- Eliminate all visible dairy and eggs. Begin reading labels and purchasing products that are egg- and dairy-free.

To replace other consumer products, we can:

- Begin to seek out non-food items that are not tested on animals or made with animal ingredients. Consider clothing, household items such as furniture, cleaning supplies, and personal care products.

With careful steps, we build a foundation that can weather the toughest storms. There's no need to waste time and energy feeling guilty about what we have not yet done. Instead, we can delight in what we have accomplished, even if we take only small steps. We can continue to challenge ourselves and find inspiration.

Understanding the Resistance, Objection, and Hostility

One of life's great truths: *"Today's mighty oak is just yesterday's nut that held its ground."* When secure in our own position, we are better able to respond appropriately to others. However, it is imperative that we understand why people condemn, ridicule, or otherwise oppose a change that so obviously promotes kindness, compassion, and life itself. Is it because people are heartless and cruel? Far from it. The vast majority of people are caring, considerate, and inherently good. So why do they respond as they do? It can be boiled down to two factors: personal habit and cultural tradition.

Habits are hard to break. They are easy, familiar, and comfortable. It is immensely painful for people to adopt a set of beliefs that do not fit their actions. (For example, if they consider meat-eating bad, they may view themselves as "bad" people.) In seeing this, we observe the complex framework that must be dismantled for change to occur.

Tradition has, for centuries, been used to justify numerous atrocities, For example, it was once considered foolish to think of Black people as human beings, so they were enslaved and treated as little more than personal possessions. Today, we know the truth, and we look back on this practice with immeasurable shame and guilt.

Now those who assert that all living creatures deserve freedom from torture and suffering are often viewed as extremists. Dr. Albert Schweitzer offers some thought on this position:

> ... the time is coming when people will be amazed that the human race existed so long before it recognized that thoughtless injury to life is incompatible with real ethics. Ethics is in its unqualified form extended responsibility with regard to everything that has life.

Bearing this in mind, we can understand the power of our opposition. We have unlimited ability to alter personal habits, but to shift cultural norms is a far greater challenge. We can push the envelope in a number of ways: by writing letters, articles, or books; by protesting or even practising civil disobedience. The most powerful tool of all is our own personal example. Arguing with others about why they choose not to be vegetarian may only stimulate them to come up with more and better counter-responses. However, it is important for us to be aware of reasons commonly given, and to be clear within ourselves about how these justifications fall short.

Most Common Reasons People Give for Rejecting the Vegetarian Option

Reason: Nutrition. Many people believe meat to be necessary for good health. They know it provides high-quality protein and iron, and assume that without meat we will fall short in these nutrients. Some consider vegetarian diets to be all right for some people, but not for them. They are convinced that meat makes them more energetic, stronger, or otherwise healthier. Many believe that they must eat meat because of their blood type.

Reality. Humans do not need meat for good health, no matter what their blood type or ethnic origin. Humans are designed to be primarily plant-eaters, like other primates. However, we are able to adapt to nonvegetarian and vegetarian diets, as evidenced by cultures around the world. Numerous studies have demonstrated that not only are vegetarian diets safe and adequate, they offer significant health advantages. Compared to the general population, vegetarians suffer about half the rates of chronic disease. Studies have demonstrated these health advantages regardless of blood type. If someone feels less well on a vegetarian diet, perhaps their diet needs some nutritional adjustments. Often we find the root cause is that people have no idea how to transform a cup of lentils or a block of tofu into a delicious meal.

Reason: Social situation. Even those who are open to issues of animal suffering generally draw the line at "food animals." Many feel that being vegetarian just wouldn't fit into their lifestyle. ("What would the guys think?") Eating meat plays a significant role in our family traditions, workplace interactions, and social lives. Being vegetarian is a major inconvenience. Eating meat is easier.

Reality. We must acknowledge these feelings and the reality that some people are simply not comfortable with being vegetarian. This does not mean that they do not care about animals—most people do. However, the acceptance of the slaughter of food animals is so deeply ingrained in our society that it has become part of the status quo. This is the result of intensive education that begins at home, and continues in our schools and medical facilities. It is perpetuated by nutrition education literature from governments and food industries, and condoned by most major religious institutions in the Western world. In other words, our society encourages and supports the use of animals for food. We cannot blame any one individual for falling into line. Some people are comfortable standing alone in their beliefs; others have a strong desire to share beliefs and actions with their peers and are changing more slowly along with our broader culture. Those who are affected by people around them will certainly be influenced by our example.

Reason: Food chain champions. Many people believe that we must preserve our rightful place at the top of the food chain. They say we are naturally hunters; it's just the way things are.

Reality. While humans are at the top of the food chain, we are also at the top of the morality and intellect chain, or so we claim. Being at the top of the food chain does not override our responsibility as humans to make moral and ethical choices. We have no justification for causing needless pain and suffering to other thinking, feeling beings. Though it is easier to justify if our survival depended on it, most people have no need to kill for food. We enjoy an abundant food supply that includes sufficient plant-based alternatives and have no need for animal flesh.

Reason: Food animals' purpose. Some people believe that animals raised for food exist for the specific purpose of becoming our dinner. If we did not eat them, they would not exist. Thus, they should be grateful for the lives they have.

Reality. If we buy into that logic, the same would apply to whatever animals we choose to raise for food—chimpanzees, elephants, or any other animal. Most animals raised for food live in factory farming conditions where they never see the light of day. Many are so tightly confined that they never experience normal social interactions. Many are driven insane. Would any of us choose such a miserable existence?

Reason: Taste. Some people argue for meat-eating on the basis of taste. They say that they couldn't ever imagine giving up barbequed steak, fried chicken, broiled salmon, or whatever their favourites happen to be.

Reality. The flavour of meat can be appealing; we can't argue that. However, taste should not be the only consideration when it comes to food selection. Apparently, horses, dogs, or cats taste pretty good too, but North Americans generally don't eat them. In fact, we may look upon people who do as being somewhat uncivilized. Why is it wrong to kill a cat for food, but not wrong to kill a pig? Pigs are significantly more intelligent than cats, and bear many genetic similarities to humans. The only thing that seems to justify this choice is tradition. As humans, we need to take responsibility for what we consume, even when we do not grow, catch, or kill it ourselves. Fortunately, we have numerous delicious vegetarian options to choose from today. We do not need to rely on animals for tasty food.

Reason: Care about people. Some criticize those who work toward ending the suffering of animals. They ask "How can we justify spending time and money saving animals when so many humans are starving to death, being abused, or being terrorized?"

Reality. Being vegetarian, and especially being an advocate for animals, in no way lessens our concern about the suffering of other people. Reverence for life does not exclude human life. Those who have reverence for life are pushing an agenda of peace, kindness, and compassion for all living beings. If everyone adopted this mentality, abuse and terrorism would cease. Meat-eating by affluent populations adds to global hunger problems, as much land in developing countries is devoted to livestock production or to raising animal fodder, rather than to growing food staples for local people. Becoming vegetarian allows for much more efficient use of global resources.

Mastering the Fine Art of Diplomacy

> "If you have men who will exclude any of god's creatures from the shelter of compassion and pity, you will have men who will deal likewise with their fellow men."
>
> —*St. Francis of Assisi*

Diplomacy is the fine art of honouring our own ethical principles and social consciousness without judging, condemning, or otherwise injuring another person. While there will always be situations that trigger less-than-diplomatic responses, such responses generally do little to support our position. It is important to distinguish between being diplomatic and being spineless. Being diplomatic in no way precludes standing firm for what we believe, or openly opposing a particular position. It simply means that we do so in a way that does not harm others. True diplomacy is lost if our own values and ethics are not honoured. Few of us are born diplomats. Rather, diplomacy is a skill that must be developed and nurtured. The following guidelines are meant to assist in this task.

Guidelines to Getting Along

Be kind, compassionate, and empathetic. Our quest for a kinder, more compassionate world must begin with ourselves. Kindness can be as simple as a smile, lending a hand to someone in need, or lifting someone up with our words. Compassion recognizes that each person is of value, and it strives to improve emotional and physical well-being. It requires a keen sensitivity to each individual and his or her unique situation. Compassion depends on our ability to empathize or to see ourselves in someone else's shoes, without losing our sense of self. Extending our kindness and compassion to all living beings sends a powerful message about ethics.

Respect each person's right to her or his own values and choices. While we will never all agree on issues of ethics, politics, religion, or anything else of consequence, it is important that we respect one another's perspectives. This does not imply that we must applaud everyone's choices and actions, but that we honour the worth and dignity of each human being. Showing respect for those with little social status, those we dislike or with whom we disagree, is a true reflection of character. We must treat others the way we would want to be treated. We can begin by listening with our hearts. This involves being attentive, not constantly challenging everything that is said, having appropriate eye contact, and possibly reflecting thoughts and feelings back to the person we are talking with. If we disagree, we can say so without judging or belittling the other person. Putting people down does nothing but hurt them, make them resentful, push them away, and strengthen their opposition. Recognize that most people try in their own way to make this world a better place. They may donate to charity, volunteer, lead healthy activities for children, or advocate for the less fortunate.

Make choices that are consistent with personal beliefs and values. Our example is the most powerful tool at our disposal. When our actions and behaviour are consistent with our words—when we "walk the talk"—we demonstrate integrity and earn the trust of others. We can communicate volumes without saying a word. We can inspire others to select more healthful plant-based foods by striving for excellent health through wise food choices and by regular physical activity. We can encourage people to show greater compassion for animals by treating all animals with love and kindness, and not supporting animal abuse in any way. We can demonstrate our commitment to the environment by reducing our use of all material things, buying second hand, recycling, and purchasing environmentally friendly products. We can promote non-violence by choosing to avoid entertainment that supports cruelty—whether it is a circus with animals, a dog race, or violent films. Mahatma Gandhi once said, "Be the change you want the world to be." Few words have conveyed more meaningful advice.

Do not apologize for your choices. As we respect the choices and beliefs of others, so must we value our own. We all have a right to our own values, and if others are to take our position seriously, we must stand clear and strong. In our society, where meat is front and centre of many social interactions, vegetarians can feel a little intimidated. Draw courage and fortitude from those who have set an example in far less tolerant times—people such as Leonardo da Vinci, Albert Schweitzer, George Bernard Shaw, and Ben Franklin. Rather than retreating from social interactions, become more socially involved, and use every appropriate opportunity to get others thinking about the traditions that have so crippled our consciousness.

Share information. When we become vegetarian, it is often a major revelation that has motivated our shift. The information we have acquired is so profound that we want to shout it from the rooftops. While doing this may make people sit up and take notice, it is unlikely to provoke dietary changes. Fortunately, there are much better ways to get our points across. If we are to succeed in influencing family, friends, and colleagues, we need to be sensitive and positive in our message, rather than pushy or critical. We can begin by sharing things in subtle ways. For example, we can bring extra servings of visually appealing and delicious vegetarian foods to work, with copies of the recipes. We can invite friends or colleagues for a wonderful homemade vegetarian meal, or treat them to lunch at a great vegetarian restaurant. When we think it is an appropriate time to be more obvious in our efforts, we can share interesting books, magazines, and videos, or invite them to a lecture, conference, or vegetarian cooking class.

Lighten up and laugh more. As vegetarians, we are faced with many grim realities about life and the state of the world. We recognize the atrocities committed against billions of animals every year. Understandably, this can make us angry and even cynical. Yet if we go through life with a sour and serious view of just about everything, our attitude will only serve as a barrier to creating a kinder, more compassionate world. If our quest is to succeed, we need to lighten up and laugh more. Laughter is the quickest way to shorten the distance between two people. It is necessary to good mental health. It lifts our spirits, eases stress, and brings joy to those around us. Set time aside for laughter—rent a funny movie, see a comedy performance, or get together for fun games with friends. Relax, let loose, and do not feel guilty. Laughter will likely add as many years to our lives as our vegetarian diets.

Diplomacy in Action

Whenever we go against the status quo, repercussions can be expected. They may come in the form of criticism, taunting, or teasing; they may involve threats to our relationships or to our work; or they may cause inconvenience or embarrassment. The sticky situations we face as vegetarians can lead to discomfort, sadness, frustration, and anger. In some cases, we feel ill equipped to handle the challenge. After such an event is over, we may dream up dozens of better responses. How we manage difficult situations can make all the difference in the outcome and our influence on other people. Now that we have covered all the bases regarding what diplomacy is all about, let's consider how we can put our knowledge into action. In the following section, we will explore a variety of sensitive situations. We can put ourselves in the place of each person described and think about how we would respond. In each case, a diplomatic solution is provided.

1. Mixed Relationship

Situation. When you and your partner married twelve years ago, you were both meat-eaters. Over the past two years, you have gradually transitioned to a near-vegan diet. While your partner has not objected to this choice for you personally, there is no indication that a switch to a vegetarian diet is anywhere in the horizon for him or her. Your dietary choice has caused several serious disagreements

where children and holidays are concerned. Your partner is adamant
that the children be given a balanced diet that includes animal products such as milk, poultry, and fish. You feel strongly that the children should be gradually weaned off these products, especially flesh
foods. While you are not opposed to allowing them to make their
own choices when outside of the home, you would prefer that they
not eat meat in the house. Currently, your children, ages ten and
seven, eat meat at home at least two or three times a week, and
order meat at restaurants most of the time. Your partner is absolutely firm that holidays include a turkey. You believe that holidays
should be about love and compassion, and should not include such
barbaric traditions. How far should you push the issue of no meat
in your home?

Diplomatic solution. Ideally, families share beliefs and values.
However, one partner can change his or her core beliefs and values, and grow in a direction that is quite separate from the spouse
and children. When this happens it can create a lot of tension and
threaten the family's foundation. In this case, you are hoping that
your spouse and the children will abide by your wishes and agree
to give up meat at home. While for a near-vegan, life is more comfortable without meat around, asking other family members to
make this sort of sacrifice goes against one of the basic principles
of diplomacy—respecting each person's right to her or his own
beliefs and values. You must remember that the vegetarian ethics
you have adopted are yours, not your family's. Just as you have a
right to your values, so other family members have equal rights to
theirs. Remember that your family's eating habits were formed
over many years, with your willing participation. Attempting to
suddenly change deeply ingrained habits will result only in frustration and resentment. If the family is to remain intact, you must
simply agree to disagree on these issues. Accept where your spouse
and children are at, and do not attempt to force your beliefs on
them. In practical terms, this means that it is unreasonable to
expect them not to eat meat in your home, unless they are very
willing to do so, because it is their home too. However, it is fair to
expect that your spouse and children take over the purchase,

preparation, and cleanup of these products. You may need separate pots and pans, and two main dishes (stuffed squash and turkey) on holiday tables. That said, it does not mean that you should give up trying to influence loved ones. It is very important that everyone clearly understands why you are making the choices you do. If your family is open to hearing more, you can share magazines, books, and videos. You can bring them to lectures and vegetarian festivals. If they appear very closed to hearing any of this, be patient. Make wonderful vegetarian feasts and get them turned on to vegetarian food. Show appreciation when they shift even a little. Focus on the things you all thoroughly enjoy, and set an example of compassion, kindness, and love.

2. Teenager Becomes Vegetarian

Situation. You have always loved animals, and were inwardly attracted to the vegetarian message while growing up. However, you kept silent about it as meat was always the highlight of family meals, outings, and celebrations. You recall that when you were little, if you were full, your parents would predictably tell you to finish your meat. With increasing independence as a fifteen-year-old teenager, you have drifted to being more and more vegetarian. When your English teacher assigned a project that involved presenting two sides of a debate, you decided to tackle the topic of food animals. You borrowed three books from the city library, and started reading. You didn't get even ten pages into the first book when you vowed never to touch a piece of meat again. As you expected, your parents were not exactly thrilled with the news. They expressed concern about your health, especially your protein intake. The hardest part for you was that they seemed wounded by your words. You recognize that they feel betrayed; you have rejected important family values. They suggest that perhaps you could be vegetarian at breakfast and lunch, and when you aren't home, but continue to eat regular dinners with the family. How can you make Mom and Dad understand that you do not want to eat meat anymore?

Diplomatic solution. You are concerned about how your parents feel, and do not want to hurt them. In this attitude, you are demonstrating the first component of diplomacy—kindness and compassion. This concern will help all of you through this challenging transition. Be careful not to fall into a pattern where you become critical or judgmental of their choices. It may be tempting to respond by saying something like, "You just don't get it. I don't want to eat dead animals anymore. It is disgusting and you can't make me do it—ever!" However, this sort of response will serve only to upset your parents more and make them feel attacked. It would be far more effective to establish your position without being critical or condescending. Begin on a positive note, making it more about you than about them. Tell your parents how much you appreciate them, and the many wonderful traditions with which you have been raised. Then gently explain that you do not want to eat any meat at all. Let them know about the many delicious and nutritious veggie "meats" on the market and suggest that you would be happy to eat these foods when meat is served. Think of ways you can help to make your vegetarian diet less of a burden to your family. Offer to help with meals, and possibly even to prepare a family meal each week. You could seek out a variety of ethnic dishes that you think they would enjoy. Your parents may love having a night of no cooking and the opportunity to try some new dishes. Reassure your parents that you love the holiday meals, and that adjusting for a vegetarian alternative can be very easy. While the main dish is turkey for most people, you can stuff a squash, make a more elaborate tofu-filled creation, buy "tofurkey," or have some delicious marinated tofu. Almost all of the trimmings can be shared. Let your parents know that your health is important to you, and that you will take care to ensure that all your nutrition needs are met, including getting enough protein. Show them this book, and encourage them to read the chapter on protein. Share information with them when you feel they are ready to hear it. Give them time to adjust. Help in any way you can to make your "being different" less of a hassle for the other people in your family. With the right attitude and commitment, your family will soon not only accept, but also respect your decision to be a vegetarian.

3. Holiday Hassles

Situation. Every year you take turns with your sister and parents in hosting the Thanksgiving feast. This will be your first year as a vegetarian host. You dad has let you know in no uncertain terms that he expects turkey for dinner. Your sister reminds you that it's only once a year, and that turkey is the primary part of the feast. You don't want to cook a turkey, nor do you want to end up in a huge fight with your family. What should you do?

Diplomatic solution. First, you must decide whether or not you are comfortable having turkey in your home. If it is just the cooking of the turkey that is unacceptable to you, there are a couple of options. You could ask your mom or sister to bring the turkey, or you could opt to purchase one prepared by a caterer. Make your part of the feast extra-special. Prepare a gorgeous main dish and go all out with the trimmings. Create wonderful new traditions for your immediate family, and in time you can help your extended family to see that holiday meals can be every bit as fabulous without any meat at all. If you are not willing to have turkey in your home, you will have to graciously ask your parents or sister to host the feast. You can offer to prepare all the trimmings and dessert, and/or offer to host another part of the holiday such as brunch or an after-skating party in your home.

4. Dealing with Rude or Hurtful Comments

Situation: You're part of a small social group. The members of the group all know each other fairly well, and almost everyone knows that you are a vegetarian. One evening, a close friend makes a light-hearted comment about your food choices, and another group member suddenly clues into the fact that you're a vegetarian. This person had no idea about your food choices, appears quite shocked, and blurts out a less than tactful response. "You're a vegetarian? I can't believe it. I hope you're not an animal rights activist too. All they are good for is putting the farmers out of work." The whole group falls silent. What should you say?

Diplomatic response. In this kind of situation it is very tempting to completely ignore the person, or to respond with something equally hurtful. It is just human nature to become defensive when we are attacked. However, being equally nasty will only further convince this person that you are some sort of extremist. You can choose to offer a quick lighthearted response, but is hard to think of one that does not ooze with sarcasm. Your best option is to respond in a manner that demonstrates confidence, conviction, and respect for others. Say something along these lines: "In answer to your questions, yes, I am a vegetarian, and I do believe in animal rights. My becoming vegetarian was originally brought on by heart disease. I believe that my vegetarian diet saved my life. As I learned more, I discovered that vegetarian diets help preserve the environment and reduce animal suffering. I see my vegetarian diet as being similar to your work at the gospel mission—something I can do to make this world a better place." By responding in this manner, you are demonstrating a high level of maturity and sensitivity. Instead of a barricade, you build a bridge.

5. Dealing with Bullying or Teasing at School

Situation. Your eight-year-old son, Jeremy, comes home from school and runs straight to his room. When you go up to speak with him, you discover that the relentless teasing by the two class bullies is beginning to escalate. At first, it was just little things like poking fun at his lunch. Today, the bullies starting mocking him in the schoolyard and pushing him around. One boy noticed a big spider crawling by and said, "Oh look, at the nice big spider." Then he slowly raised his foot above it and, just as Jeremy screamed "Nooooo!" he stepped on it. Jeremy, unable to control his emotions, burst into tears. Then the two boys began laughing hysterically. He was devastated. How can you best help your child to respond effectively to this kind of bullying?

Diplomatic solution. Being bullied can do serious damage to a child's self-esteem. Thus, when children are bullied, they often do everything in their power to hide it. It is a very good sign that your son is willing to share this experience with you. Do whatever you can to keep those lines of communication open. Reassure your child that you will always be there to support, assist, and encourage him, no matter what the situation.

Explain to Jeremy that many bullies are insecure, and often live in a household with bigger bullies. Sometimes bullies are just seeking attention, or trying to make themselves seem more important. While this in no way excuses their behaviour, it may help your child understand why people behave in such cruel ways. Provide Jeremy with practical advice on how to avoid being bullied, and to respond effectively when it occurs. Let him know that avoiding encounters with bullies does not mean he is a coward; it means he is being smart. He needs to take precautions not to be alone with these guys. He can steer clear of the places they are likely to be, and/or enlist the support of friends or older siblings. If Jeremy does find himself alone with them, he should leave immediately. If they have already made a rude remark, he should very loudly tell them to stop and then walk away. Teach him not to submit to bullying; bullies love to see people cry, so try to ignore them. If vegetarian lunches seem to be a big source of teasing at school, consider making lunches that do not attract so much attention. Sandwiches using veggie meats, raw vegetables and dip, homemade treats, and fresh fruit all work well. It is important that Jeremy understands that for the sake of his safety, school authorities need to be aware of the bullying. At no point do the bullies need to know where the information came from. The teacher can say it was observed by a supervisor or by other children. One of children's greatest fears is that bullies will beat them up in retaliation. Explain to your son that everyone at the school will make sure this doesn't happen. If the opportunity arises, and the situation feels safe, he can speak to the bullies individually about how what they are doing makes him feel. This is generally best done in the presence of a teacher or school counsellor. Finally, praise your child for his kindness and compassion toward other people and all creatures. Let him know that these are among the greatest qualities a person can have.

6. Being a Gracious Dinner Guest

Situation. You and your partner have been part of a bowling league for two months, and really hit it off with another couple. After a great game, they suggest that you should get together outside of the bowling alley, and invite you to dinner. These friends have no idea that you are vegetarians. How should you best handle the invitation?

Diplomatic solution. While you may be tempted to suggest a non-food-related activity instead, food is so central to socializing that if your friendship is to develop, it is important that you are comfortable eating together. The cardinal rule in such situations is to disclose your dietary requirements right away. Never show up for a dinner invitation assuming that you'll just eat the vegetables and bread. This is extremely inconsiderate, as the host has prepared the feast in your honour, with a primary objective of pleasing you, the special guests. In addition, meat is usually the focus of the meal. Often when having company, expensive cuts of meat, seafood, and other such extravagances are purchased. In fact, meat, poultry, or seafood could well be a part of every dish. When you tell your friends that you are vegetarian, their response will give a big clue as to how to proceed. If they say, "Oh my goodness, do you eat fish?" you know that preparing a vegetarian meal will be quite a stretch for them. You may want to suggest that they come to your place, or that you go to a restaurant and go back to their place for dessert. If their response is, "No problem," you can relax. However, it is still important to be specific about what you don't eat. Offer to help prepare or bring part of the meal. See page 373 in the next chapter for vegetarian dinner options that are familiar to most nonvegetarians.

7. Dealing with Hurtful Comments

Situation. You have been involved in the church youth league for two years, and want to invite your five co-volunteers to dinner. While they are well aware that you are vegetarian, most of them view a vegetarian diet as boring and have said so. Some have even made remarks that suggest they actually pity you. You decide that the best way to educate these people would be to surprise them with a wonderful vegetarian feast. When you invite them, one person immediately asks, "Could we make this a potluck? I'd be happy to bring some of my famous chicken Kiev." Everyone quickly chimes in, agreeing that a potluck sounds like a great idea. How should you respond? What sort of menu should you select?

Diplomatic solution. This is one occasion that calls for a light-hearted response. Recognize that everyone is a little nervous about having a vegetarian meal. They are likely imagining little more than a plate full of vegetables. You need to do two things here. First, allay their fears. Second, let them know in no uncertain terms that this is not a potluck, and they are not welcome to bring food to your party. You might say something like this: "Absolutely not! This is my treat. Have some faith; I won't let you go hungry. In fact, if you aren't stuffed by the time dinner's over, I'll order pizza!"

Now for the menu. Avoid ingredients with strong flavours that may be an acquired taste, such as cilantro, strong curries, or seaweed. Make plenty of food, with lots of variety. You may wish to choose an ethnic theme, as many have familiar vegetarian entrées. If you know everyone loves a certain type of ethnic restaurant, such as Greek or Chinese, you may want to stick with one of those cuisines. Alternatively, you can offer vegetarian versions of traditional favourites. A menu with plenty of choice could look something like this (or you may prefer a simplified version):

Start with a sparkling strawberry/kiwi punch or other beverage, and a nice appetizer such as Hazelnut Pâté (page 399) with crackers. Begin the main meal with a flavourful soup such as Zucchini Chedda Soup (page 395) and fresh bread. For the entrée, serve a vegetarian version of a traditional favourite. Go-for-the-Greens Salad with Liquid Gold Dressing (pages 406 and 407) and fresh pasta (select two varieties of gourmet filled pastas available at most supermarkets) would be an excellent choice. With the pasta offer two sauces, Chunky Red Lentil Tomato Sauce (page 416) and perhaps a simple white wine sauce. If you are especially ambitious, you may want to prepare some stuffed portabella mushrooms on the side. Top off the meal with Lemon Teasecake (page 425) or German Chocolate Cake (page 427). Bon appetit!

8. Pressure from Other Vegetarians

Situation. It has taken about a year for you to make the complete switch to a vegetarian diet, and the experience has been among the greatest challenges of your life. You got rid of most of your cookbooks. You gave up foods that you adored, such as barbequed steak, fast-food cheeseburgers, and pepperoni pizza. You even gave up

favourites that you always considered healthy, such as roast chick-
en breast and baked fish. No longer will you order those thick
salmon sandwiches at the local lunch hotspot. No longer do you dig
in when your office buddies order a bucket of chicken. Sometimes
it is tough, but you persevere. You spend hours trying to figure out
what to feed dinner guests, and have been chided by your family for
not eating "normal" food, especially at Thanksgiving. Yet despite all
the hardships you endured, you feel overwhelmingly positive about
the experience. You have shown more willpower in a year than in
the rest of your life put together. You started making more friends
in the local vegetarian community, and many of them are more vegetarian than you. Some have been vegetarian for many years, like
Kevin, Laura, and Stacey. Kevin doesn't use a single drop of dairy
or eggs and even reads the labels to avoid the tiniest speck of casein.
He also buys everything organic and drinks wheat grass juice. Laura
and Stacey are completely vegan. They go so far as to avoid any animal products in their clothing, makeup, and cleaning supplies. Just
the thought of it all makes your head spin. Still, it is so nice to be
around people who understand the whole concept of being vegetarian. It builds your confidence and determination to forge ahead.
One day your new vegetarian friends are over to watch a movie. You
dash off to the kitchen to find a few snacks and come out with a
bowl of mixed nuts, some chips, and chip dip—ordinary chip dip.
You know some of them won't eat it, but that's OK because it's
optional. Kevin says, "Gee whiz, you still eat chip dip?" Laura adds,
"Don't you realize that the veal industry is just a by-product of the
dairy industry? Buying dairy products is no different than buying
beef." Suddenly you feel as though you don't belong, that you will
never belong. You're too vegetarian for your family, and not vegetarian enough for your new friends. What could you say to help
your friends understand your position?

Diplomatic solution. You have two reasonable options. You could
respond in a very lighthearted way. Simply say something like, "I
am just a baby vegetarian, so have patience." Alternatively, you could
use the opportunity to let your friends know how much you need
their support, rather their disapproval. Say something like this: "I
don't want to spoil the fun, but can I just share something with you?

I love hanging out with all of you because I feel connected to you at a very different level than I do with my nonvegetarian friends. You guys have been doing this for a long time, and I get so much strength and inspiration from you that it helps me to keep moving forward. But when you criticize me, it makes me feel like no matter how hard I try, I'll never catch up, and I'll never be good enough." It is important when you share these feelings that you begin by saying something positive.

As we progress on our personal journey, it is easy to start comparing how well we are doing, relative to other vegetarians. This is a potentially destructive waste of energy. As we get caught up in playing a game of mirror, mirror on the wall, we lose sight of what really matters. No two people are at exactly the same stage in their journey, and that is the way it is meant to be. Each of us brings unique experiences and different strengths to the picture, all helping to work toward the ultimate goal of compassion and reverence for life. When we point a finger and judge another person, we sabotage our connection with that person, effectively putting up a barricade along his or her path. No one likes to be degraded, ridiculed, or otherwise abused. Instead, we need to be supported, encouraged, and commended, especially by one another.

9. You're Vegetarian, But Your Fiancé Is Not

Situation. You and your fiancé have been engaged for almost a year. The wedding is to take place in just over four months. About six months ago, you made the decision to become a vegetarian. Discussions about the issue have ended in tears on more than one occasion. Your fiancé loves meat, and just does not understand the whole vegetarian thing. You've shared literature and videos, but to no avail. When you discuss the wedding meal, you usually end up in a heated argument. Just yesterday you brought up the subject of children, and the fact that you intend to raise them as vegetarians. Your partner just about lost it. The notion of raising children as vegetarians seemed to hit a nerve. Over the past few weeks you have started to wonder how this marriage will ever work if you can't come to an agreement on these vital issues. Should you break off the engagement?

Diplomatic solution. While no one can tell you what is right for you in such a situation, you are very wise to be questioning the relationship at this point. If you are an ethically committed vegetarian, and your fiancé is a staunch meat-eater, your core values are at odds. Shared values are extremely important to lasting relationships, especially when children come into the picture. Chances are that if your becoming vegetarian is the result of concern about animals, you will continue to move toward a more vegan lifestyle. Thus, if you are feeling uneasy now, the gap between you may continue to widen, especially if your fiancé is well informed about the issues, but continues to oppose your vegetarian stance. Remember that food is a central part of our social world, especially when it comes to our partners. While it is nice to believe that love can overcome anything, the reality is that love is simply not enough. You and your partner need professional couple counselling as soon as possible. While your marriage could be successful, it will take considerable work to get it off on the right foot. It is extremely important that your partner completely understands your decision, from a deeply personal perspective. It is equally important that you understand why your fiancé is opposed to your vegetarian diet, or raising children as vegetarians. Listen without interrupting and without passing judgment. Once your perspectives have been laid out and fully understood, you will need to construct guidelines for your relationship that are acceptable to both of you. Consider everything from grocery shopping, cooking and eating out, to how you will raise your children. While you may never completely agree on these issues, you will need to come to a reasonable compromise. If you remain in a gridlock, you will need to seriously consider going your separate ways.

10. Going Out for Lunch

Situation. You started a new job only two weeks ago. No one is aware you are a vegetarian. All is going very smoothly until the day everyone decides to go out to lunch to celebrate Barb's promotion. One of your colleagues says, "I know the perfect spot—a wonderful little steakhouse. They specialize in filet mignon and lobster." You were hoping to suggest an Asian restaurant that offers a whole section of vegetarian options, but everyone is so excited about the steak and lobster that you decide it would be best not to mention it. You reach the restaurant without having voiced your concerns. You feel increasingly uneasy as you scan the menu and notice that there are only about ten items, none of which are vegetarian. Even the salads contain meat or seafood. There are only two soups—clam chowder and French onion, which is likely made with beef broth. What should you do?

Diplomatic response. You could fake the stomach flu or discreetly eat around the meat, but what would this accomplish? Think about your motivation for hiding the fact that you are a vegetarian. Being vegetarian is something to be proud of, not something that you need to hide or apologize for. Instead, scrutinize the menu and see what items are vegetarian. Stir-fries and salads can easily be prepared without added meat. At the very least, there will be baked potatoes and a variety of vegetables. When the waiter arrives, say, without any hint of apology, "I'm vegetarian. I don't eat meat, poultry, or fish. Could you suggest something?" Nine times out of ten, the chef can create a lovely option that isn't listed on the menu. If the waiter is at a loss, suggest something yourself, based on ingredients you see on the menu.

In hindsight, your best bet would have been to let your colleagues know that you are vegetarian when the steakhouse was mentioned. You could have simply asked if anyone knows if there is a vegetarian option. Chances are the steakhouse idea would have been abandoned and everyone would have tried to think of an alternative that would work well for everyone. Another plan that generally works well is to call the restaurant ahead of time and discuss your options.

For additional information and suggestions on challenging social situations, see these excellent Web sites:

1. Grassroots Veganism with Joanne Stepaniak includes an "Ask Joanne" question and answer section: www.vegsource.com/joanne/qa/qafeud.htm

2. John Robbins Website includes an "Ask John" question and answer section: www.foodrevolution.org/askjohn/

A complete set of references is available online at:
http://www.nutrispeak.com/bvreferences.htm

from market to meals

What does "change" mean to you? A dictionary says "change" means "to exchange for or replace; to lay aside, abandon, or leave for another; to switch; to transform." A comedian says "Change is inevitable, except from a vending machine." Change can be viewed as an essential part of life. It may be viewed as a loss. When it comes to changing food habits that we've had since infancy, the prospect can be daunting.

Certain questions might make us uneasy about switching to a vegetarian way of eating. Will we be more limited in the range of foods available? Must we shop only at special stores? Will it cost a lot more? Must we dine at restaurants where none of our friends will want to go? Does vegetarian cooking require a lot of time, expertise, and fancy equipment?

While it is understandable that questions like these race through our minds, it is reassuring to discover that this particular change can be an extraordinary adventure to a delightful destination. And, for those who aren't quite ready for much of an adventure, the process can be very gradual, unfolding just enough to pique our curiosity. As with any change, we can ease the transition by preparing ourselves well. This chapter will serve as a valuable companion in this journey.

Where to Shop

Perhaps you are ready to bound out the front door, armed with cloth shopping bags and determined to fill them with wholesome foods that will transform meals into vegetarian masterpieces. Yet where should this expedition begin?

Shopping for vegetarian food can be a bit intimidating if we're not sure what to buy or where to buy it. Perhaps the items we seek are not to be found in the same, well-known supermarket aisles. Shelves are lined with a vast array of products, many claiming to be nutritional powerhouses—yet are they? If one's normal practice is to rush into the store, grab our familiar favourites and check out as fast as possible, the transformation that has taken place in some sections of the marketplace in recent years may come as a surprise.

Our exploration of new foods is an adventure waiting to happen. Acquaintance with new fruits, vegetables, and whole grains brings marvellous taste sensations. The preparation of delicious new recipes (including those in the next chapter) can be a great deal of fun. This can be the foundation of many pleasant evenings shared with one or more friends or family members. Those of us who aren't so keen on cooking will be thrilled with the instant gratification of a veggie burger that rivals our favourite beef burger, veggie back bacon that tastes like the real thing, and is low in fat, and a divine, dairy-free frozen strawberry dessert. These, and many other tasty and convenient items, await us in supermarket coolers and freezers. With time, we may find that the quality of breakfast, lunch, and supper surpasses what we'd ever thought possible.

There are many interesting places to discover fresh, wholesome foods. We are likely to come across new options that are very close to home: some amazing little store that we never knew existed or an organic farmer who delivers produce right to the door. Here are a few of the more popular choices.

Supermarkets

The large chains have come a *long way* in the past five years and many have expanded their organic produce departments, bulk food areas, ethnic options, and natural food sections, including fresh, frozen, and dried vegetarian convenience foods. It may come as a surprised to find that most of the items we need are available in nearby supermarkets. Although most mainstream supermarkets do not carry as many vegetarian or organic product lines as natural food stores, some have already responded to consumer demand. It helps to let local store managers know of specific products we'd like them to order. They are interested in staying in touch with current and potential customers and are often happy to accommodate us. The more demand they have, the more they will stock.

Natural Food Stores

Large natural food stores are becoming more popular and easy to locate. Though some "health food" stores seem to stock nothing but supplements, many specialize in vegetarian and organic foods. These carry many types of beans, less common whole grains, and products made with whole grain flours such as quinoa, spelt, and kamut. On the shelves and in coolers and freezers we'll find "convenience" foods that are free of hydrogenated vegetable oils, food colours, artificial flavours, preservatives, and other additives. These stores tend to offer bulk foods at moderate cost, organic produce, hearty baked goods, tofu, soymilks, refrigerated nuts with a good turnover (so they're fresh), soy and dairy yoghurts and cheeses, nut butters, and wholesome snacks such as fat-free tortilla chips and fruit bars. A good natural food store can be a real ally in creating fast, delicious vegetarian meals.

Farmers' Markets

If there are farms nearby, there is likely to be a farmers' market, perhaps even one that sells organic produce. Farmers' markets tend to undercut supermarkets prices by 30 per cent or more on many items. Most or all of the produce is locally grown, goods are fresh, and the variety is superb, including great greens like collards and kale. Some farmers may sell directly to consumers or have "U-pick" options. Some offer shares in their farm, making payment in produce according to the number of shares owned; the result can be a nourishing and mutually beneficial connection between family and food supply. If all this is new, FarmFolk CityFolk Society maintains a Web site with many links at www.ffcf.bc.ca.

Organic Delivery Services

Many communities now offer organic delivery services that provide customers with healthy, high-quality, organically grown fruits and vegetables in a fun and exceptionally convenient way. These services deliver a box of fresh, often locally grown (when possible) produce right to our doorsteps. Many such services allow us to custom order (select the items we want each week), and some offer additional items such as organic breads, oils, salad dressings, and apple cider. Buying from such a service not only supports a small local business, but it supports many organic farmers in your area and elsewhere.

Ethnic Shops

Most cities have fascinating ethnic sections that are steeped in the exotic flavours and aromas of foreign travel. We enrich our lives with a Saturday trip to one of these parts of town. We can take a friend and our shopping lists, and include lunch at a local restaurant where we're sure to find more than one delicious vegetarian option. Larger cities have districts that reflect many different cultures; on a limited budget, we can almost travel the world!

When we discover a good ethnic store, it's like finding a little treasure chest. Asian stores carry a wonderful selection of tofu, fresh greens, seaweeds (more respectfully known as sea vegetables), seitan (gluten), edamame, and Asian sauces. Some of these cost a fraction of what we would pay at a natural food store or supermarket. Greek stores supply the best tahini in town, as well as a good assortment of chickpeas, lima and white beans, olives, olive oil, Mediterranean herbs, and pita bread. East Indian stores carry a variety of flours, many types of beans, grains, and spice mixes; their curry pastes are great for spicing up vegetable or lentil dishes. Ethnic stores also stock delicious vegetarian convenience foods.

Co-ops

Food co-ops are grocery stores that are owned and often operated by members. This reduces overhead costs, thus food prices are kept fairly reasonable. Members generally enjoy special discounts. Food co-ops are usually health-oriented and offer a wide selection of vegetarian and organic options.

Buying Clubs

A buying club generally includes at least three or four people or families, as most wholesalers require minimum orders of several hundred dollars. We can find the name of a big, local natural food wholesaler in the phone book or by asking staff at a health food store. Our discount may be almost as much as the discount given to stores. Foods are ordered by the case, half case, 10-kilogram (22-pound) sack (for grains, beans, and flour), or in large containers (for tahini and tamari). Although we'll need to organize some extra storage space and plan our shopping a little differently, the whole process can actually simplify life, as shopping may be done less frequently. The work of placing orders, picking up the food, and distributing items can be shared among club members. A weigh scale will be an immense help in dividing the goods. The cost savings are generally so impressive; we're hooked in no time.

Bakeries

Discovering a wonderful bakery reawakens our senses in a most delightful way. Although many supermarkets and natural food stores have amazing in-house bakeries, those little specialty shops tucked away in the corners of our communities offer some spectacular products. Some specialize in whole grain products, use organic ingredients, or provide options that are free of dairy and eggs. Many ethnic bakeries sell hearty rye and wheat breads, bagels, and tortillas.

If we want to have a hint of bakery aroma wafting through our homes, a bread maker can make it easy. We'll have fresh bread and complete control over the ingredients, which is ideal for those with food allergies. In addition, we can prepare dough in the bread maker, and use it to make buns, pizza, cinnamon rolls, and many other treats.

What to Buy

After we've considered where to shop, we can decide which items we'll need to stock our pantry. Our shopping list will include certain basics for everyday cooking. We might write down breakfast, lunch, and supper ideas for several days or a week. The list on the next page can be photocopied and will help to plan shopping sprees.

If we were concerned that being vegetarian might limit our options, we soon discover that a whole new world of food choices has opened up. There are so many grains, beans, types of produce, and convenience foods that we can introduce new items every week and never get bored.

Basic Shopping List

Grain Products

- [ ] Barley
- [ ] Brown rice
- [ ] Bulger
- [ ] Flours (whole wheat, unbleached, gluten, other)
- [ ] Millet
- [ ] Mixed cereals
- [ ] Oatmeal
- [ ] Other grains
- [ ] Pasta
- [ ] Popcorn
- [ ] Quinoa
- [ ] Ready-to-eat cereal
- [ ] Wheat germ
- [ ] Whole grain bread, buns, bagels
- [ ] Whole grain crackers

Vegetables and Fruits

- [ ] Fresh greens (kale, collards, Chinese/Napa cabbage, broccoli)
- [ ] Seasonal vegetables
- [ ] Seasonal fruits
- [ ] Frozen fruit
- [ ] Frozen vegetables
- [ ] Garlic and onions
- [ ] Canned water-packed fruits
- [ ] Dried fruits (apricots, cranberries, currants, dates, figs, prunes, raisins, others)
- [ ] Fruit and vegetable juices (fresh, frozen, bottled, canned, or in tetra packs)
- [ ] Tomato or pasta sauces, canned tomatoes

Beans and Lentils and Products

- [ ] Canned legumes (garbanzos, pinto beans, kidney beans, baked beans)
- [ ] Dried legumes (navy beans, garbanzos, pinto beans, kidney beans, lentils, split peas)
- [ ] Instant dried legume dishes (hummus, soups, casseroles, refried beans)
- [ ] Meat analogues, vegetarian patties, soy wieners, veggie slices, sausages
- [ ] Prepared bean dishes such as soups and chili
- [ ] Seitan
- [ ] Soy nuts
- [ ] Tofu, tempeh

Nuts, Seeds, and Butters

- [ ] Nut butters
- [ ] Nuts (raw cashews, almonds, walnuts, pecans, filberts, peanuts)
- [ ] Seed butters (tahini, sunflower)
- [ ] Seeds (flax, pumpkin, sesame, sunflower)

Soy and Grain Beverages and Related Products

- [ ] Fortified soy or grain milks
- [ ] Soy cheese
- [ ] Soy ice cream or other frozen desserts
- [ ] Soy yogurt

Dairy Products and Eggs (for lacto-ovo vegetarians)

- [ ] Cheese
- [ ] Cow's milk
- [ ] Eggs
- [ ] Yogourt

Sweeteners

- [ ] Barley malt, rice syrup, maple syrup, agave syrup
- [ ] Blackstrap molasses
- [ ] Dried cane sugars
- [ ] Jams and conserves

Beverages

- [ ] Cereal grain beverages
- [ ] Leaf and herbal teas
- [ ] Organic coffee

Fats and Oils

- [ ] Extra-virgin olive oil
- [ ] Flaxseed oil
- [ ] Mayonnaise or mayonnaise-like spread
- [ ] Non-hydrogenated margarine
- [ ] Nut oils (hazelnut, walnut)
- [ ] Organic canola oil, high oleic sunflower or safflower oils
- [ ] Toasted sesame oil
- [ ] Vegetable or lecithin spray

Seasonings, Condiments, and Other

- [ ] Bottled sauces (teriyaki, barbeque, sweet and sour, other)
- [ ] Bragg Liquid Aminos
- [ ] Cooking wine
- [ ] Ketchup, mustard, and relish
- [ ] Lemon juice
- [ ] Miso
- [ ] Patak's or other curry paste
- [ ] Pickles
- [ ] Tamari or soy sauce
- [ ] Seaweed (hijiki, wakame, nori, agar)
- [ ] Vegetable broth powder or cubes, or chicken-style seasoning
- [ ] Vegetarian support formula nutritional yeast (Red Star brand)
- [ ] Vinegar (rice, wine, balsamic or apple cider vinegar)

Herbs and Spices

- [ ] Chili powder or hot chili peppers
- [ ] Cinnamon, allspice, nutmeg, cumin, curry
- [ ] Dried herbs (oregano, sage, savory, thyme, rosemary, marjoram)
- [ ] Fresh ginger
- [ ] Fresh herbs (parsley, cilantro, basil)
- [ ] Mixed seasonings (e.g., Spike)
- [ ] Mustard (Dijon type), jar or powder
- [ ] Salt and pepper

Food Storage Tips

When we arrive home with loads of wonderfully nourishing vegetarian food, we'll need to know how to care for it. In storing food, there are three primary objectives:

1. to keep food fresh and appealing

2. to prevent spoilage, mould, rancidity, or infestations of bugs

3. to retain nutrients

Appropriate food storage is especially important when our diet is based on unrefined foods. These foods grow people well; they also grow bugs well! In contrast, items with little nutritional value, such as white sugar, white flour, refined corn oil, and soda pop will keep in the pantry for years as they are of little interest to pests.

Grains: Whole Versus Processed

In their original form, nature gives grains protective packaging. Intact wheat berries (the whole grains) keep for a couple of years in a tightly covered container that is stored in a cool, dry place. However, if we grind the wheat berries into flour, the fats in the germ are exposed to air and can become rancid and storage time is reduced to a couple of months. Whole grain flour, in a sealed bag or container that excludes moisture, lasts for three or four months in the freezer and many bread makers keep it there. It should be warmed to room temperature before baking. Some people prefer to grind fresh flour on a regular basis for their Sunday pancakes! Wheat germ, which contains much of the natural oils in the grain, goes rancid much more quickly than wheat bran, which contains little fat.

Nuts, Seeds, and Their Butters

Whole nuts in the shell are far better keepers than shelled nuts. Nature has thoughtfully designed their hard outer packaging so that they keep for a whole year until the next nut harvest. Once removed from the shell, nuts and seeds should be stored in the refrigerator (where they last for four months) or freezer (in an airtight container, where they will last for a year). Walnuts are unusually vulnerable to rancidity due to their high content of omega-3's; they are best kept in the freezer, or at least refrigerated. Other shelled nuts and seeds can be stored unrefrigerated, in containers with lids, for up to two months. Chopped nuts (in which more fat is exposed to air) and nuts and seeds that have been roasted (in which fat is pushed to the surface) have even shorter shelf lives under these various storage conditions. Nut and seed butters must always be refrigerated after opening the jar.

Fruits and Vegetables

Fresh fruits and vegetables are perishable, and are generally best stored in the refrigerator. Certain vegetables (onions, potatoes, and squash) will keep well in a cool, dry place for several weeks. Most fruits and tomatoes can be stored at room temperature for up to a week; however, those that are already ripe may be stored in the refrigerator (which slows further ripening). During certain times of the year local produce is so plentiful that we want to preserve it to enjoy until the next harvest. One solution may be to spend a little time in the kitchen preparing the vegetables and fruits for freezing, canning, drying, or turning into jams, pickles, chutney, salsa, etc. to be enjoyed year-round.

Dry Storage of Foods on Pantry Shelves

When we expand our range of grains and beans, we may end up with so many items stuffed into cupboards that it's a challenge to locate ingredients for a given recipe. A little organization will make food preparation a lot less stressful. If we keep grains, beans, and flours in plastic bags from the store, eventually little critters will find their way into the bags. A simple way to avoid problems is to store foods in mason jars or other jars with lids. Buy about two or three dozen wide-mouth canning jars, label them, and arrange the filled jars on an open shelf or in the pantry. Bulkier items such as flour can be kept in larger jars, canisters, or plastic buckets with tight-fitting lids. Spices can be stored in small, tightly closed containers, preferably away from the warm stove area.

Refrigerator Storage

Fresh foods are best stored in the refrigerator as they quickly per-
ish at room temperature. The refrigerator tends to dry things out,
so make sure foods are covered. Lettuce and other greens keep
especially well in plastic containers with tight-fitting lids. Some
people wash leaves, wrap them in a slightly damp clean tea towel,
and place the wrapped greens in a plastic bag. Buy only as much
fresh produce as can be used in a week. (Potatoes, squash, onions
and garlic do not require refrigerator storage.)

TABLE 13.1   *Food Storage*

Food Group	Store in a Cool, Dry Place	Store in the Refrigerator	Store in the Freezer
Grains	Whole grains, dry pasta, crackers, dry cereals	Whole grain flours, fresh pasta	Wheat germ; breads rolls, muffins (for longer storage)
Vegetables and Fruits	Onions, garlic, potatoes, squash, dried fruits, unripe fruits, bananas	Vegetables, fruits, opened containers of juices	Frozen vegetables, fruits and juices
Beans and Alternates	Dry beans, split peas, lentils, textured soy protein	Tofu, nuts, seeds and their butters, ground flaxseed (or in freezer), eggs	Frozen patties, loaves, tempeh, cooked legumes (for longer storage)
Milks and Milk Products	Fortified soymilk in tetra packs, milk powder (non-dairy or dairy)	Fortified soymilk and cow's milk, soy or dairy yogourt and cheese	Non-dairy and dairy ice creams
Other foods, seasonings, and condiments	Molasses, honey, olive oil, sesame oil, spices, dried herbs	Fresh herbs and ginger, opened jars of cold-pressed oils condiments, sauces, maple syrup	Fresh herbs (freeze in a plastic bag, crumble for instant use)

Freezer Storage

A freezer can be a great asset. It allows us to store precooked beans, to buy or harvest large batches of fruits and vegetables in season and preserve them, and to stock up on perishable bulk foods such as whole grain flours, wheat germ, seeds, and nuts. We can make dozens of healthy muffins and have them ready to grab-and-go. (This is an excellent strategy when there are hungry teens in the house.) We can cook huge batches of lentil or bean soups and freeze individual or family-sized portions.

Foods That May Be Kept in Several Places

Tempeh, a soyfood commonly used in Indonesia, is often found in the freezer section of grocery stores. It may be kept in the refrigerator for several days or in the freezer for longer-term storage.

Dry baker's yeast, if stored in its unopened package (brick or jar), may be kept at room temperature in a dry place until its expiration date. Once the jar or brick is opened, it must be kept airtight and refrigerated. Nutritional yeast can safely be stored in a cool, dry place, however, to preserve B-vitamins, it may help to store larger quantities in the freezer, keeping out only as much as would be used up in about a month.

Kitchen Equipment

These tools allow us to perform with ease and speed, and are well worth the investment:

1. **Three good-quality knives.** The items that will most increase our enjoyment and efficiency in the kitchen are a 20-centimetre (8-inch) chef knife that stays sharp and feels good in the hand, a small paring knife, and a high-quality bread knife with a serrated edge.

2. **Cutting board.** Though wooden boards are aesthetically pleasing and provide excellent performance, plastic boards are more easily cleaned. The minimum size is 20 × 30.5 centimetres (8 × 12 inches); for greater chopping pleasure, a 33 × 51-centimetre (13 × 20-inch) board is a treat.

3. **Mixing bowls.** We need at least three glass or stainless steel bowls of varying sizes. A 40-centimetre (16-inch) diameter stainless steel bowl is great for mixing a salad that can last five days. The salad can then be stored in one or more large Tupperware-type, tightly sealed containers. Narrow and deep bowls are especially handy for mixing baked goods.

4. **Non-stick skillet and oil spray.** The winning combo is a non-stick skillet and a refillable oil sprayer. Skillets should have good conducting ability and disperse heat evenly.

5. **Two pots.** As a minimum, get a larger pot for soup or pasta and a smaller pot for cooked cereal, sauces, or steamed vegetables. Exact sizes depend on the number of persons served.

6. **Stainless steel basket steamer.** This inexpensive gadget fits into almost any size pot and is used to steam vegetables or veggie wieners.

7. **Blender.** Blenders are extremely useful for pureeing dressings, soups, shakes, and smoothies.

8. **Colander or strainer.** These drain liquid from cooked pasta, potatoes, and legumes.

9. **Hand-held tools.** The essentials for most cooks are: measuring cups and spoons, wooden spoon, food grater, can opener, vegetable peeler, pancake flipper, rubber spatula, spring-loaded tongs, and perhaps a whisk.

10. **Food processor.** While not essential, a food processor is useful for making hummus and thicker spreads (which would burn out the engine of some blenders), and saves time in chopping.

11. **Juicer.** This can be a fancy machine or a simple stainless steel hand juicer. Look for one with two parts—the top part where the fruit is held, and the bottom part that holds the juice.

Making the Transition to a Vegetarian Diet

What's for Dinner?

Most people have eight or nine favourite supper meals they return to again and again. Does switching to vegetarian foods seem a challenge? You may find that you're part way there, with three vegetarian meals that you enjoy. Here is a three-step plan that makes the transition simple.

1. Think of Three Vegetarian Meals You Already Like

For cooking at home. How about spaghetti with tomato sauce, vegetarian chili, and bean burritos?

At restaurants and for take-out meals. Popular favourites are vegetarian pizza, veggie burgers, and veggie dogs, Italian pasta dishes, Chinese stir-fries, East Indian curries and samosas, Middle Eastern falafels and tabouli salad, and Mexican bean burritos or tortillas.

2. Choose Three Recipes That You Can Modify, or Ask for a Switch in a Restaurant Meal

For cooking at home. Split pea soup is just as good without a ham bone. A taco, tortilla, or enchilada is great when made with refried beans or veggie ground round instead of beef. Fajitas can be made with plain or seasoned firm tofu instead of chicken. There's a scrumptious version of Shepherd's Pie on page 421.

At restaurants and for take-out meals. Chinese food can be prepared with tofu or cashews. Japanese nori rolls can be made with tofu. Some nonvegetarian restaurants have extensive all-you-can-eat salad bars that provide abundant, very reasonably priced meals. These hearty salads are good with a baked potato, too.

3. Over the Next Month or Two, Try Out Three New Recipes or Restaurants.

For cooking at home. Look through the Seven Super-Simple Suppers on pages 414-423. Have fun as you experiment with delightful new flavours and healthful ingredients.

At restaurants and for take-out meals. If you glance through the phone book, keep your eyes open as you drive around the neighbourhood, and ask a few friends; you're bound to make some very appealing discoveries.

Whether you're a cook or restaurant diner, when you've found your three hits in each category, you've done it! You have nine delicious, tasty vegetarian choices.

Does Vegetarian Eating Require a Lot of Time and Cooking Expertise?

For those of use who enjoy cooking, making delicious meals from scratch is a pleasure, but this is not the only route to marvellous meals. Convenience items such as soyfoods, veggie burgers, dogs, slices, and "ground round," frozen vegetarian meals, and packaged dinners are among fast-growing categories in the grocery trade. Canned beans and soups are handy to keep on the shelf for everyday use, for emergencies, or for camping trips. All of these enable us to have healthy meals ready to serve in minutes.

Recipes from Breakfast to Dessert

In the next chapter, we take you from breakfast through supper, and then on to outstanding desserts, with some of the tried and true recipes we love best. If you'd like to switch some of your former favourite recipes into more "plant-based" versions, here are substitutions you can make.

TABLE 13.2   *Instead of Meat, Egg, or Dairy: Substitution Basics*

Instead of Meat, Fish, or Poultry and Products	
250 mL (1 cup) meat or chicken stock	• 250 mL (1 cup) liquid vegetable stock from vegetable stock cubes or powder (see package directions for amounts); Bragg Liquid Aminos, tamari, or miso mixed with water (to taste)
1 serving meat, chicken, fish	• Equal weight or volume of veggie "meats," plain or marinated tofu, tempeh, beans, gluten (seitan), gluten-based "meats" from Asian restaurants • Equal volume of portobello mushrooms

TABLE 13.2 *continued*

250 mL (1 cup) ground beef	• Equal weight or volume of vegetarian ground round (such as Yves) • 110 mL (Hcup less 1 tbsp) dry textured soy protein, covered with boiling stock or water, stirred and soaked for ten minutes
15 mL (1 tbsp) gelatin	• 15 mL (1 tbsp) agar flakes (thickens 250 mL/1 cup liquid) • 2 mL (H tsp) agar powder (thickens 250 mL/1 cup liquid) • 15 mL (1 tbsp) veggie gel such as Emes Kosher-Jel, cara-geenan, or locust bean gum (thickens 500 mL/2cups liquid)

Instead of Egg
Note that sometimes just leaving out an egg from a muffin or pancake recipe makes very little difference.

1 egg	• 15 mL (1 tbsp) ground flaxseed mixed with 45 mL (3 tbsp) water • 30-60 mL (2-4 tbsp) soft tofu • 60 mL (1G cup) mashed, very ripe banana • 5 mL (1 tsp) starch-based egg substitutes (or see package directions) such as EnerG Foods "Egg Replacer" which is a powdered product that replaces eggs in baking. Available in natural food stores • 0.5 mL (J tsp) baking powder, added to dry ingredients, replaces leavening action of 1 egg or egg white in baking

Instead of Dairy Products

250 mL (1 cup) cow's milk	• 250 mL (1 cup) fortified soymilk or rice milk
250 mL (1 cup) buttermilk	• 250 mL (1 cup) soymilk plus 10 mL (2 tsp) lemon juice or vinegar
250 mL (1 cup) yogourt	• 250 mL (1 cup) soy yogourt
30 g (1 oz) cheese	• 30 g (1 oz) soy cheese
250 mL (1 cup) cottage cheese (in recipes)	• 250 mL (1 cup) drained, mashed tofu (medium firm tofu works well)
250 mL (1 cup) ricotta cheese (as in lasagne)	• 250 mL (1 cup) drained, mashed tofu (firm works well)
250 mL (1 cup) ice cream	• 250 mL (1 cup) frozen soy or rice dessert, fruit sherbet, sorbet, or Berry Delicious Ice Dream (recipe, page 433)
375 mL (1 H cup) whipping cream	• 340 g (12 oz) package firm silken tofu, 60 mL (G cup) maple syrup, 15 mL (1 tbsp) lemon juice, and 5 mL (1 tsp) vanilla blended
butter	• Use olive oil or non-hydrogenated margarine in cooking; almond butter or other nut butter as spread on toast; Liquid Gold Dressing as topping for baked potatoes (recipe, page 406)

Travel Tips

Top Tip

The Web sites that list vegetarian restaurants worldwide are travellers' best friends. Before going anywhere we can visit one of several. Our favourite is www.vegdining.com. We can click on the destination country or countries, print a comprehensive list of vegetarian restaurants, pack our bag, and know we'll be well nourished. Three other sites are www.vegeats.com/restaurants, www.happycow.net, and www.ivu.org/global.

For those who like to take along a book rather than surf the Internet, an excellent choice is the *Vegetarian Journal's Guide to Natural Food Restaurants in the U.S. and Canada*, available from the Vegetarian Resource Group at 410-366-8343 (or order online at www.vrg.org/catalog/order.htm).

Taking a Few Essentials

Containers of various sizes that have tight-fitting, spill-proof lids are travellers' other best friends. These can transport several handy items. One is a serving of a protein-rich food such as hummus, marinated tofu, chickpeas, or curried lentils. Another item to bring could be a little of a favourite salad dressing, or perhaps a serving of fortified soymilk. With these, the rest of a meal may come together fairly easily and be very tasty. Certain vegetarian items are easily available practically anywhere: airports, planes, trains, bus depots, and the homes of nonvegetarian friends. These items are oatmeal, cereals, rice, baked potatoes, salads, vegetables, fruit, and juices. If we just bring a hearty, protein-rich food, then we can end up with an acceptable meal. A favourite salad dressing will taste surprisingly good on bland white rice (as in certain airplane meals) or on a baked potato (salsa is good, too). The fortified soymilk is valuable for those who don't use dairy products as it's good on cereal and in tea or coffee. The Nalgene brand of spill-proof containers, available at outdoor equipment stores, make transporting foods and beverages a *lot* simpler!

It's often a good idea to bring along an assortment of nuts, seeds, and dried fruit. Treat yourself to a few of the more exotic ones, such as hazelnuts, cashews, figs, dried mango, cranberries, or cherries.

Air Tips

Airlines are accustomed to plenty of vegetarian meal requests and provide meals that are vegan, lacto-ovo vegetarian, Asian vegetarian, fruit plates, or raw foods. To be relatively certain of actually getting our choice of meal, it is a good idea to reconfirm the request a day or two ahead of the flight. However, the "meal" may be little more that a bagel and a banana, so it is always wise to bring a little something extra, such as a bag of nuts and dried fruits, soy yogurt, or a veggie "meat" sandwich, just in case.

Support and Inspiration

Support Organizations

In communities across Canada and the United States, vegetarian associations arrange potlucks, cooking classes, speaker presentations, and turkey-free Thanksgiving dinners to inspire and nourish others who wish to shift their diets in a healthful, earth-friendly direction.

Festivals

Vegetarian festivals provide very pleasant interludes, not to mention outstanding food. A great way to see the world is to plan to attend the World Vegetarian Congress, held in a different country every two years (see www.ivu.org). The Toronto Vegetarian Association hosts an immense and very popular event every September (see www.veg.ca). Summerfest, in a beautiful Pennsylvania setting, provides a 5-day getaway with well-organized workshops, great speakers, and excellent meals (see www.navs-online.org). EarthSave groups in Vancouver, Seattle, Louisville, and several cities in California sponsor an annual Taste of Health (a healthy food festival). See www.earthsave.org.

Compassionate Living

Inventive and thoroughly livable solutions have been found for people who wish to live more lightly on the planet and make vegetarian choices. Here are two Web sites that can help tremendously in making sensible choices. We can search these and their many links for anything from cooking schools, to summer camps, to non-leather shoes, to socially responsible investing.

KEY WEB SITES

These will open the door to a world of

vegetarian-friendly resources:

www.ivu.org   *International Vegetarian Union*

www.vrg.org   *Vegetarian Resource Group*

A complete set of references is available online at:
http://www.nutrispeak.com/bvreferences.htm

recipes

simple treasures

"This is a new era in food preparation, and we are all responsible for making healthier food taste really wonderful for those we love."
—*Graham Kerr, Chef, author and TV legend*

Many people, beckoned by the numerous compelling reasons to go vegetarian, face one giant stumbling block—they love their food. They can't even begin to imagine life without barbequed steaks, fried chicken, baked salmon, and Thanksgiving turkey. When they think of vegetarian fare, a pile of beans and brown rice springs to mind. Alas, it seems like far too great a sacrifice. This chapter will shatter the myths that vegetarian food is somehow gastronomically inferior to nonvegetarian food. Here we will tantalize your taste buds, and introduce you to a world of diverse, delicious, and nourishing plant-based meals and snacks. Some of the recipes are extremely easy to prepare, a few are more complex and gourmet. Ingredients used are widely available, from Victoria to St. John's. In addition to our own creations (both of us love cooking and taste-testing), we have invited guest chefs to contribute several very special recipes, which results in a wonderful variety in cooking styles. We feature a delectable German Chocolate Cake and its accompanying Coconut Squash Icing as an example of chef Ron Pickarski's genius with food. Ron Pickarski and his team of expert chefs achieved Gold Medal status in the Culinary Olympics in Germany, with an entirely plant-based spread, competing against nonvegetarian gourmet foods. Chocolate lovers should definitely try this cake! There's a Lemon Teasecake from Seattle's famous Café Ambrosia. We've shown you what to do with whole grains, kale, and flaxseed oil, so that your family will enjoy these highly nutritious ingredients. We include some sure-fire winners for family gatherings, potlucks, parties, and for a week of supper menus. There are shakes that are welcomed by seniors and by the hungry hordes after school. Athletes will appreciate Hot Tofu with Cool Greens, and Muscle Muffins. The whole family will love African Stew and a vegetarian version of Shepherd's Pie.

Nutritional Analysis of Recipes

In addition to great taste, all of our recipes have been designed with nutrition in mind. Thus, below each recipe, you'll find a nutritional analysis. For example, below the recipe for Timesaving Tacos (page 418) you'll see:

> *Per taco:* calories: 149, protein: 4 g, fat: 7 g, carbohydrate: 20 g, dietary fiber: 5 g, calcium: 54 mg, iron: 1.6 mg, magnesium: 28 mg, sodium: 302 mg, zinc: 2.7 mg, folate: 63 mcg, riboflavin: 0.1 mg, vitamin B12: 0 mcg, vitamin C: 14 mg, vitamin E: 1.8 mg, omega-3 fatty acids: 0.2 g.%
> *Calories from:* protein 13%, fat 32%, carbohydrate 55%

The analysis does not include optional ingredients. Where two or more choices are given for an ingredient, the analysis is based on the first choice. Where there is a range in amount, the lower amount is used for analysis.

Below the grams of protein, carbohydrate, fat, and fibre in each serving, we show the percentage of calories that come from protein, fat, and carbohydrate. Note that 35 per cent or less *calories from fat* is very different from 35 per cent or less of the food's *weight* coming from fat. For example, the name "2 per cent cow's milk" indicates that two per cent of the weight of this milk comes from fat; (89 per cent comes from water). Yet 35 per cent of the calories in this milk come from fat (along with 29 per cent of calories from protein and

36 per cent from carbohydrate, primarily sugar. For comparison, the pattern suggested for everyone over 3 years of age to maintain good health and prevent chronic disease is 15-35 per cent of our calories from fat, 10-20 per cent from protein, and 50-70 per cent from carbohydrate.

Some of the foods you eat—salad dressings, a salad that contains nuts, a favourite entrée, or dessert—will provide more than 35 per cent calories from fat. These higher fat items will be balanced by many plant foods—grains, vegetables, fruits, lentils, and many beans—that provide 15 per cent or less of their calories from fat. All of these contain healthful plant oils and little or no saturated fat. Building your diet around these foods helps you keep a healthy balance. Here are recipes "to feed the body and nourish the soul."

Breakfast Favourites:
Cashew French Toast
Banana Walnut Pancakes
Jiffy Fruit Sauce
Marvellous Morning Muesli
Basic Whole Grain Cereal
Your Very Own Whole Grain Cereal
Scrambled Tofu

Shakes and Smoothies for Breakfast or Snacks
Quick Chocolate Shake
Fruit Smoothie
Sneaky Dad's Power-Punch Smoothie

Soups, Spreads and Sandwiches
Black Bean Soup
Zucchini Chedda Soup
Angelic Tofu Sandwich Filling
Muenster Cheeze
Hazelnut Pâté
Veggie Clubhouse Spreads and Sandwiches for Every Taste

Greens and Dressing
World's Greatest Greens
Go-for-the-Green Salad
Liquid Gold Dressing
Simple Sprouting

Cooking the Basics
Great Grains
Legume Lore

Seven Super-Simple Suppers
Hot Tofu With Cool Greens
Chunky Red Lentil Tomato Sauce
Time saving Tacos
African Stew
Cashew and Vegetable Stir-fry
Shepherd's Pie
Easiest-Ever Curried Lentils

Delectable Desserts and Goodies
Muscle Muffins
Lemon TeaseCake
German Chocolate Cake
Coconut Squash Cake Icing
Super-Simple Chocolate Icing
Nutty Date Cookies
Chocolate Mint Nut Bars
Berry Delicious Ice Cream

Breakfast Favourites

Cashew French Toast

If you can't imagine French toast without eggs, you are in for a pleasant surprise. This version is easy and delicious. If you are slicing your bread, cut thick slices.

H cup	"raw" cashew pieces	125 mL
1 cup	fortified soymilk	250 mL
H tsp	vanilla	2 mL
1 Tbsp	maple syrup	15 mL
2 tsp	high oleic sunflower or safflower oil	10 mL
6	slices of whole grain bread	6

In a blender, grind cashews to the consistency of a powder. Add soymilk, vanilla, and maple syrup, and puree. Pour mixture into a shallow bowl or casserole dish. Heat a heavy skillet on medium heat. (A good non-stick skillet is best; however, any heavy skillet will do. See page 372 for more information on skillets.) If using a non-stick skillet, lightly oil or spray the pan. Preheat pan on medium heat. If using a cast iron or other heavy skillet, generously oil the pan. Dip the bread in the cashew mixture, then place two or three pieces on the skillet (depending on skillet size). Do not overlap the French toast; instead leave a little space between pieces. Cook until nicely browned, then flip the French toast and cook on the other side. Serve hot with Jiffy Fruit Sauce (page 385), maple syrup, or chopped fresh fruit. Makes 6 slices.

Per slice (without oil): calories 169, protein 6 g, fat 7 g, carbohydrate 23 g, dietary fibre 2 g, calcium 77 mg, iron 2 mg, magnesium 64 mg, sodium 173 mg, zinc 1.4 mg, folate 32 mcg, riboflavin 0.1 mg, vitamin B12 0.5 mcg, vitamin C 0 mg, vitamin E 1.1 mg, omega-3 fatty acids 0 g
% calories from: protein 13%, fat 36%, carbohydrate 51%

Banana-Walnut Pancakes

These pancakes are reminiscent of Sunday breakfast at Grandma's house. They are perfect for company or a special occasion. For oil, we recommend the use of organic canola, high oleic sunflower or safflower oil, or melted, non-hydrogenated margarine. If children or teens make this recipe, use 60 mL (G cup) of batter for each pancake so they will be even easier to turn over.

2 cups	fortified soymilk, rice milk, or cow's milk	500 mL
1 tbsp	ground flaxseed	15 mL
1 H cups	whole wheat flour	375 mL
2 tbsp	wheat germ	30 mL
1 tbsp	natural sugar or other sweetener	15 mL
2 tsp	baking powder	10 mL
H tsp	salt	2 mL
N cup	walnuts, chopped	85 mL
1	banana, thinly sliced	1
2 tbsp	oil	30 mL

In a large bowl, combine the milk and ground flaxseed. In medium bowl, place flour, wheat germ, sweetener, baking powder, and salt and mix well. Add the flour mixture to the wet ingredients and stir just until mixed. Fold in the walnuts and banana. Preheat a heavy skillet (preferably non-stick) over medium heat. The pan should be very hot before putting in the batter. Lightly coat non-stick pan with cooking spray or a few drops of oil. If using a regular skillet, you will need to add 5-10 mL (1-2 tsp) additional oil, and a little more between each batch. Pour about 125 mL (H cup) batter on heated pan for each pancake. When well browned on one side and bubbles appear across the surface of the pancake, turn it over and cook the second side until golden brown. Serve hot with Jiffy Fruit Sauce below, maple syrup, or chopped fresh fruit. Makes 7 18-cm (6-in) pancakes (875 mL/3 H cups batter).

Per pancake: calories 230, protein 7 g, fat 9 g, carbohydrate 33 g, dietary fibre 5 g, calcium 104 mg, iron 2 mg, magnesium 65 mg, sodium 274 mg, zinc 1.4 mg, folate 19 mcg, riboflavin 0.1 mg, vitamin B12 0.8 mcg, vitamin C 2 mg, vitamin E 4 mg, omega-3 fatty acids 0.7 g.
% calories from: protein 12%, fat 34%, carbohydrate 54%

Jiffy Fruit Sauce

Fruit sauces are a refreshing change from sugary syrups. This simple combination contains no added sugar and requires no cooking. Raisins provide additional sweetness. You may wish to experiment and invent your own blend using favourite fruits or use 15-30 mL (1-2 tbsp) of orange juice concentrate in place of the orange.

1	medium banana, peeled	1
1	medium orange, peeled, seeds removed	1
1-2 tbsp	raisins (optional)	15-30 mL
1 H cups	fresh or frozen blueberries or raspberries, or peeled, sliced kiwi fruit	375 mL

Place banana, orange, raisins (if using), and 185 mL (I cup) of the berries or sliced fruit in blender and puree until smooth. Pour into a medium bowl. Stir in the remaining half of the berries or sliced fruit. Serve with French toast, pancakes, or waffles. Makes 500 mL (2 cups).

Per 60 mL (1G cup): calories 31, protein 0.4 g, fat 0.2 g, carbohydrate 8 g, dietary fibre 1 g, calcium 9 mg, iron 0.1 mg, magnesium 7 mg, sodium 1 mg, zinc 0.1 mg, folate 9 mcg, riboflavin 0 mg, vitamin B12 0 mcg, vitamin C 12 mg, vitamin E 0.4 mg, omega-3 fatty acids 0 g
% calories from: protein 5%, fat 4%, carbohydrate 91%

Marvellous Morning Muesli

This recipe provides an ideal balance between protein, fat, and carbohydrate and is ideal for a nourishing breakfast that can be prepared the night before. A hungry person who eats the whole batch will start the day with 21 g of protein. Leftovers make a delicious evening snack. You may like to try some of the other grain flakes that are available, such as wheat, barley, kamut, or rice flakes, or a combination.

I cup	rolled oats or other grain flake	185 mL
2 tbsp	raisins, currants, or dried cranberries	30 mL
2 tbsp	chopped walnuts, almonds, or other nuts	30 mL
		1 mL
G tsp	cinnamon	
1 cup	fortified soy or rice milk, cow's milk, or fruit juice	250 mL
1	apple, grated or finely chopped	1

In a medium bowl, combine flakes, raisins, nuts, cinnamon, milk, and apple. Cover and refrigerate overnight. Alternatively, the apple may be stirred in just before serving. Serve with or without added milk or juice. Makes 500 mL (2 cups).

Per 250 mL (1 cup): calories 333, protein 10 g, fat 9 g, carbohydrate 56 g, dietary fibre 6 g, calcium 192 mg, iron 2.9 mg, magnesium 99 mg, sodium 73 mg, zinc 1.6 mg, folate 77 mcg, riboflavin 0.1 mg, vitamin B12 1.5 mcg, vitamin C 28 mg, vitamin E 3.2 mg, omega-3 fatty acids 0.7 g
% calories from: protein 12%, fat 24%, carbohydrate 64%

Basic Whole Grain Cereal

This is a great way to begin the adventure of using whole grains. It is satisfying and delicious for breakfast. Leftovers make a nourishing, soothing snack any time, and can be refrigerated and used as warm cereal or cold pudding for several days. Begin with this basic recipe, using 190 mL (O cup) each of barley, brown rice, and wheat berries to give a total of 500 mL (2 cups) grain. Then experiment with combinations (see box on page 388). Next, invest in a crockpot and start creating Your Very Own Whole Grain Cereal (recipe, page 382).

1 cup	uncooked grain	250 mL
4 cups	water	1 L
H tsp	salt (or to taste)	2 mL
H cup	dried fruit	125 mL
H cup	fortified soymilk, rice milk, or cow's milk	125 mL

Place grains, water, and salt in a heavy pot or the top of double boiler and bring to a boil.

If using double boiler, place above boiling water and allow to simmer for 2-3 hours. If pan is directly over heat, lower heat and simmer for 2-3 hours, checking occasionally that it does not boil dry. If necessary, add a little water.

Add dried fruit and milk and cook for another H hour. Serve with fresh fruit, Jiffy Fruit Sauce (page 385), and your choice of milk. Makes 1.25 L (5 cups).

Per 250 mL (1 cup): calories 201, protein 6 g, fat 2 g, carbohydrate 42 g, dietary fibre 4 g, calcium 52 mg, iron 1.7 mg, magnesium 34 mg, sodium 256 mg, zinc 1.2 mg, folate 12 mcg, riboflavin 0.1 mg, vitamin B12 0.3 mcg, vitamin C 1 mg, vitamin E 1 mg, omega-3 fatty acids 0.1 g
% calories from: protein 11%, fat 8%, carbohydrate 81%

Analysis was done using oat groats, kamut berries, millet (all whole grains), and raisins.

A New World of Whole Grains

Create combinations that are uniquely yours. Equal proportions of barley, kamut berries, and oat groats make a delightful mixture. Use any combination to total 500 mL (2 cups) of grain; the mixture might include wheat groats, millet, or brown rice. To boost the protein and mineral content, include quinoa or amaranth. For dried fruit, experiment with raisins, cranberries, or chopped apricots, prunes, figs, or dates. Add some, or all, of the optional ingredients listed in the recipe. When it comes to nuts and seeds, choose among chopped almonds, walnuts, cashews, hazelnuts, whole or ground flaxseeds, and sesame, pumpkin, or sunflower seeds.

Your Very Own Whole Grain Cereal

A crock-pot is ideal for cooking whole grains because you can sleep through the night, while your cereal simmers gently, to be ready when you awake. This slow method allows even more of the natural sweetness to develop and increases mineral availability. Refrigerate leftovers for next day's breakfast, or to have later in the day as a creamy pudding. Leftovers will thicken and need additional liquid, and can be served warm or cold. See the box above for new ideas.

2 cups	uncooked grain	500 mL
8 cups	water	2 L
1 tsp	salt (or to taste)	5 mL
1 cup	dried fruit	250 mL
1 cup	fortified soymilk, rice milk, or cow's milk	250 mL

Optional Ingredients

H cup	nuts and seeds	125 mL
H cup	coconut	125 mL
2 tsp	vanilla	10 mL
2 tbsp	maple syrup	30 mL
1 tsp	cinnamon	5 mL

Using a sieve, rinse grains well. Place grains, water, and salt in a large slow cooker (crock-pot) and cook on low heat for about 8 hours or overnight, until most of the water has been absorbed.

Then add dried fruit, milk, and any optional ingredients, and cook for another H hour or more. If the mixture is too thick, add more water, soymilk, or other milk. Serve hot or cold for breakfast with fresh fruit or Jiffy Fruit Sauce (page 385) and your choice of milk. Makes 2.5 L (10 cups).

For nutritional analysis, see previous recipe.

Chef's Tip: *How to Press Excess Water from Firm and Medium Tofu*

For recipes such as Scrambled Tofu and Angelic Tofu Salad Filling (page 396), if tofu is used without first pressing out excess water, the liquid may seep onto the serving plate. To remove excess liquid, drain tofu and place the block on a plate or shallow bowl. Cover the tofu with a plate or small cutting board, and on that carefully set a weight, such as a large can of tomato sauce or a 1-L (32-oz) Tetra pack of soymilk. Press tofu for 15-20 minutes. At this time, about 125 mL (H cup) of liquid will have pooled on the bottom plate; this fluid can be discarded. Pat block of tofu dry with a clean towel, place in a bowl, mash with a fork, and proceed with recipe.

Scrambled Tofu

This dish can be the foundation of a hearty breakfast, and is a favourite with vegetarian teens and athletes. Its texture makes it appealing for seniors, too. Nutritional yeast and turmeric give this dish a yellow colour similar to scrambled eggs. In nutritional yeast, this colour is given by the bright yellow vitamin, riboflavin. Turmeric contains a golden substance called curcumin that inhibits cancer and is an effective anti-inflammatory agent. For bone-building, choose tofu that includes calcium on the ingredient list (amounts vary from brand to brand).

1 lb	firm tofu, drained and mashed	450 g
1 cup	sliced mushrooms	250 mL
2 tbsp	chopped green onion (It must be chopped before measuring)	30 mL
2 tbsp	chopped green onion	30 mL
1-2	garlic cloves, minced	1-2

2 tsp	olive oil	10 mL
2 tbsp	nutritional yeast flakes	30 mL
G tsp	turmeric (optional)	1 mL
G tsp	salt, or to taste	1 mL
	pepper, to taste	
2 tbsp	chopped fresh parsley	30 mL

Drain tofu well and mash with a fork (see Chef's Tip, page 389). In a heavy pan or cast iron frying pan over medium heat, sauté mushrooms, onion, and garlic in oil until soft. To mashed tofu, add yeast, turmeric (if using), salt, and pepper, and then parsley. Mix well with a fork, and then add to vegetables in pan. Stir and cook for 2-3 minutes until warmed through. Serve immediately with toast. Makes 3 servings (375 mL/1 H cups).

Per 125 mL (H cup): calories 286, protein 28 g, fat 17 g, carbohydrate 12 g, dietary fibre 6 g, calcium 1,045 mg, iron 17 mg, magnesium 102 mg, sodium 221 mg, zinc 4 mg, folate 171 mcg, riboflavin 5 mg, vitamin B12 4 mcg, vitamin C 5 mg, vitamin E 0.5 mg, omega-3 fatty acids 0.9 g
% calories from: protein 37%, fat 48%, carbohydrate 15%

Analysis done using Red Star Vegetarian Support Formula nutritional yeast, which is the source of vitamin B12, and calcium-set tofu.

Flavour Boost Variation

For added flavour, add 15-30 mL (1-2 tbsp) of tamari or Bragg Liquid Soy and up to 5 mL (1 tsp) of your favourite mixed seasoning (e.g. Spike or Italian seasoning).

Shakes and Smoothies for Breakfast or Snacks

Quick Chocolate Shake

This shake is an excellent source of calcium, vitamins B12, and D, as well as instant energy. For a shake that provides 31 g of protein, try the variation below, using 60 mL (G cup) soy protein isolate.

| 1 | banana, fresh or frozen (see Chef's Tip), peeled and broken into chunks | 1 |

2 tsp	cocoa powder	10 mL
I cup	fortified soy or rice milk	185 mL
	or cow's milk*	

In blender, place banana, cocoa, and milk. Process until smooth. Makes 310 mL (1 G cups).

Per recipe: calories 175, protein 7 g, fat 3 g, carbohydrate 35 g, dietary fibre 4 g, calcium 222 mg, iron 0.9 mg, magnesium 52 mg, sodium 107 mg, zinc 1.8 mg, folate 24 mcg, riboflavin 0.4 mg, vitamin B12 2.3 mcg, vitamin C 11 mg, vitamin E 0.5 mg, omega-3 fatty acids 0.1 g
% calories from: protein 14%, fat 15%, carbohydrate 71%

*Nutritional analysis done using vanilla soymilk that is fortified with vitamins B12, D, riboflavin, zinc, and calcium.

Protein Boost Variation

For an extra 10 g of protein, blend in 30 mL (2 tbsp) soy protein powder plus an additional 10 mL (2 tsp) cocoa powder. This shake tastes best when served cold.

CHEF'S TIP: *Use Frozen Bananas for Thick, Cold shakes, smoothies, and Ice Cream!*

- Select ripe bananas for freezing as they are much sweeter and have less starchy aftertaste.
- To prepare bananas for freezing, peel, leave whole or break into chunks, place in plastic bags or containers, and freeze.
- A squeeze of fresh lemon juice sprinkled on the bananas will keep them from turning brown.
- Frozen bananas last several weeks, depending on their ripeness and on freezer temperature.

Fruit Smoothie

For delicious combinations, try apple juice with blueberries, raspberries, or mango. Made with apple juice and blueberries, this smoothie provides 2 mg of vitamin E and plenty of phytochemicals. With orange juice and strawberries, it's rich in vitamin C. Using 60 mL (G cup) protein powder, as in Variation #2, you'll get 14 g of protein per 250 mL (1 cup) of smoothie. For increased thickness, use frozen fruit. If using room temperature fruits, those who prefer a colder drink can add a few ice cubes before blending.

1	banana, fresh or frozen (see Chef's Tip, page 391), peeled and broken into chunks	1
1 cup	berries or sliced fruit	250 mL
1 cup	fruit juice	250 mL

Place fruit and juice in a blender and process until smooth. Makes 500 mL (2 cups).

Per 250 mL (1 cup): calories 135, protein 2 g, fat 0.7 g, carbohydrate 33 g, dietary fibre 4 g, calcium 26 mg, iron 0.6 mg, magnesium 38 mg, sodium 3 mg, zinc 0.3 mg, folate 80 mcg, riboflavin 0.1 mg, vitamin B12 0 mcg, vitamin C 101 mg, vitamin E 0.8 mg, omega-3 fatty acids 0.1 g
% calories from: protein 5%, fat 4%, carbohydrate 91%

Nutritional analysis done using orange juice and strawberries.

Smoothie Booster Variations

1. **Vitamin C boost (132 mg of vitamin C).** This is the Pink Cadillac of smoothies, and is especially refreshing. Use fresh-squeezed orange juice as your base (three oranges will make about 250 mL/1 cup juice). Replace banana with 250 mL (1 cup) mango slices, and use strawberries as your berries.

2. **Protein boost.** Blend in 30 mL (2 tbsp) soy protein powder (isolated soy protein) and/or replace juice with soymilk.

3. **Omega-3 boost.** Add 5 mL (1 tsp) flaxseed oil.

4. **Energetic B boost.** Add 10 mL (2 tsp) nutritional yeast.

Sneaky Dad's Power-Punch Smoothie

This recipe was developed by Louisville lawyer John Borders as a nutrient-dense breakfast or snack for his three children, one of whom, in particular, is a persistent picky eater. He guarantees this recipe will reduce stress for concerned parents who worry that their children have eaten little else all day. If you like, any needed supplements may be added to it. Set your young helper alongside you on a stool near the blender, and begin!

1 cup	calcium-fortified orange juice	250 mL
1 cup	fortified vanilla soymilk	250 mL
1 H	bananas, peeled and frozen (see Chef's Tips, page 391)	1 H
1 cup	frozen strawberries	250 mL
1-2 tbsp	ground flaxseed (or 1-2 tsp/ 5-10 mL flaxseed oil)	15-30 mL
1 tbsp	nut butter (such as cashew or almond butter)	15 mL
G	avocado, peeled (optional)	G

In blender bowl, place juice, soymilk, banana, strawberries, flaxseed, nut butter, and avocado (if using). Blend until smooth and creamy, with no lumps. Serve with a straw. Makes 2 servings (875 mL/3 H cups).

Per half recipe: calories 300, protein 8 g, carbohydrate 54 g, fat 8 g, dietary fibre 6 g, calcium 326 mg, iron 2.5 mg, magnesium 74 mg, sodium 80 mg, zinc 3.0 mg, folate 55 mcg, riboflavin 0.2 mg, vitamin B12 1.5 mcg, vitamin C 78 mg, vitamin E 3.2 mg, omega-3 fatty acids 0.7 g
% calories from: protein 10%, fat 22%, carbohydrate 68%

Nutritional Note

For a child weighing about 14 kilograms (30 pounds), a serving of this smoothie provides about 25 per cent of the day's recommended intake for calories, iron, vitamin A, vitamin D, niacin, and omega-3 fatty acids; 33 per cent of the protein, zinc, manganese, thiamin, riboflavin, folate, and fibre; 50 per cent of the calcium, phosphorus, and vitamin E; and all the copper, magnesium, and vitamins B6, B12, and C.

Soups, Spreads, and Sandwiches

Black Bean Soup

Black beans are a staple in Mexico, and Central and South America, and form the basis of wonderful salads, stews, and soups. Vegetable stock can be made from stock cubes or powder or purchased ready-made. Water can be used instead of stock, though your soup will be less flavourful. If you use a little less liquid, this recipe makes a fine stew. Lime juice, added just before serving, gives a bright note, in this recipe from _Cooking Vegetarian_ by V. Melina and chef J. Forest (John Wiley & Sons, 1998).

1 cup	diced carrot	250 mL
1 cup	diced celery	250 mL
H	onion, diced	H
1	garlic clove, minced	1
1 tbsp	olive oil	15 mL
3 cups	cooked or canned black turtle beans or black beans	750 mL
4 cups	vegetable stock	1 L
G cup	tomato paste	60 mL
1 H tsp	ground cumin	7 mL
1 tsp	dried oregano	5 mL
1 tsp	dried thyme	5 mL
2 tsp	lime juice	10 mL
	salt and pepper to taste	

In large pot, sauté carrot, celery, onion, and garlic in oil over medium heat for 5 minutes. Stir in beans, stock, tomato paste, cumin, oregano, and thyme. Cover and simmer for 20 minutes or until vegetables are cooked. Just before serving, stir in lime juice. Add salt and pepper and adjust the seasoning. Makes 4 servings (1.5 L/6 cups).

Per 125 mL (1 H cup) serving: calories 256, protein 13 g, fat 4 g, carbohydrate 44 g, dietary fibre 10 g, calcium 131 mg, iron 6 mg, magnesium 90 mg, sodium 217 mg, zinc 1.4 mg, folate 140 mcg, riboflavin 0.2 mg, vitamin B12 0 mcg, vitamin C 14 mg, vitamin E 2 mg, omega-3 fatty acids 0.1 g
% calories from: protein 19%, fat 15%, carbohydrate 66%

Zucchini Chedda Soup

This marvellous soup, created by Joanne Stepaniak, is adapted from *Dairy-free and Delicious* by B. Davis, J. Stepaniak, and B. Clark Grogan (The Book Publishing Company, 2001). It features a rich, tempting broth with lots of delicate zucchini. Cheese lovers adore it!

3	medium zucchini, diced	3
1	medium onion, diced	1
4 cups	water	1 L
H cup	pimento pieces, drained or chopped red pepper	125 mL
1/4 cup	tahini	60 mL
1/4 cup	quick cooking rolled oats	60 mL
3 tbsp	nutritional yeast flakes	45 mL
G cup	"raw" cashew pieces (see Chef's Tip, page 384)	60 mL
2 tbsp	tamari	30 mL
4 tsp	fresh-squeezed lemon juice	20 mL
H tbsp	dried oregano leaves	7 mL
1 tsp	salt	5 mL
2	small garlic cloves, chopped	2
J tsp	allspice	0.5 mL
J tsp	dill seed	0.5 mL
	freshly ground black pepper, to taste	

In a large pot, place the zucchini, onion, and water and bring to a boil. Lower the heat and simmer for 20-25 minutes, or until the vegetables are very tender. Using a large measuring cup, take out about 375 mL (1 H cups) of the broth, including some of the zucchini and onion, and place in a blender. Add the pimento, tahini, oats, nutritional yeast, cashews, tamari, lemon juice, oregano, salt, garlic, allspice, dill, and pepper. Process until very smooth. Pour the blended ingredients back into the soup pot with the diced zucchini, onion, and water. Heat soup gently, stirring often, until slightly thickened and warmed through, about 10 minutes. Do not boil. Makes 1.75 L (7 cups).

Per 250 mL (1 cup): calories 127, protein 6 g, fat 7 g, carbohydrate 12 g, dietary fibre 3 g, calcium 54 mg, iron 2.2 mg, magnesium 49 mg, sodium 634 mg, zinc 1.5 mg, folate 74 mcg, riboflavin 1.8 mg, vitamin B12 1.3 mcg, vitamin C 22 mg, vitamin E 1 mg, omega-3 fatty acids 0 g
% calories from: protein 16%, fat 49%, carbohydrate 35%

Analysis done using Red Star Vegetarian Support Formula nutritional yeast, a source of vitamin B12.

Angelic Tofu Sandwich Filling

How about making a switch from devilled egg sandwiches, to "angelic" tofu sandwiches? The flavour similarity is remarkable. Make a batch for lunchbox sandwiches. (Leftovers can be refrigerated to fill sandwiches the next day.) Serve filling on a lettuce leaf, with raw veggies, and a crusty roll. Try it as a spread on crackers or serve it as a dip. Use it to fill half a pita pocket bread, along with chopped tomatoes and lettuce or sprouts. If using the water-packed Chinese-style tofu, you will need to press out water (see Chef's Tip: How to Press Excess Water from Firm Tofu on page 389).

1 lb	medium-firm or firm tofu, drained	454 g
2-3 tbsp	Nayonnaise or other mayonnaise	30-45 mL
2 tsp	tamari, Bragg Liquid Soy, or soya sauce	10 ml
1 tbsp	nutritional yeast flakes	15 ml
G cup	onion, finely chopped	60 ml

H cup	celery, finely chopped	125 ml
	salt and pepper to taste	

Optional Ingredients

2 tsp	mustard, any kind	10 mL
2 tbsp	parsley, finely chopped	30 mL
6	olives, diced	6
N cup	pickles, sweet or dill, diced	85 mL
3 tbsp	toasted sunflower seeds	45 mL

Place the drained tofu in bowl and mash with a fork or potato masher. Stir in Nayonnaise or mayonnaise, using just enough to make the tofu stick together (generally about 30 mL/2 tbsp for moister varieties of tofu and 45 mL/3 tbsp for drier types). Add tamari, nutritional yeast, onion, celery, salt, pepper, and any of the optional ingredients you are using. Makes filling for about 6 sandwiches (625 mL/2 H cups).

Per 125 mL (H cup): calories 152, protein 16 g, fat 9 g, carbohydrate 6 g, dietary fibre 3 g, calcium 627 mg, iron 10 mg, magnesium 58 mg, sodium 183 mg, zinc 1.7 mg, folate 51 mcg, riboflavin 0.9 mg, vitamin B12 0.6 mcg, vitamin C 2 mg, vitamin E 0.1 mg, omega-3 fatty acids 0.5 g
% calories from: protein 38%, fat 48%, carbohydrate 14%

Analysis done using calcium-set firm tofu and with Red Star Vegetarian Support Formula nutritional yeast, a source of vitamin B12.

CHEF'S TIP: *Agar*

Agar, also known as agar-agar, is derived from a type of red seaweed. It is an excellent replacement for gelatin (which comes from bones and hooves of cattle and horses). Agar is sold at health food stores in the form of dried white flakes, and very inexpensively at Asian stores in the form of powder or bars.

Agar must be thoroughly dissolved in liquid for it to gel. As its gel-forming abilities are powerful, take care to use the amount and type specified in recipes. (Even then, there can be some variation from one brand to another.) We discovered this by trial and error when we created recipe failures that could double as hockey pucks!

15 mL (1 tbsp) agar flakes will thicken 250 mL (1 cup) liquid
4 mL (I tsp) agar powder will thicken 250 mL (1 cup) liquid

As with gelatin, increased amounts of agar are required with more acidic liquids.

Muenster Cheeze

This recipe, from *The Uncheese Book* by Joanne Stepaniak (The Book Publishing Co.) is reminiscent of the German original. It has a mild-to-mellow flavour, with a nice nip from the jalapeno pepper. For a blander version, eliminate jalapeno pepper. The dome-shaped "cheese" can be cut into wedges or slices. Paprika provides the appearance of the red outer coating, surrounding the creamy interior.

N cup	agar flakes	85 mL
	or	
2 tsp	agar powder	10 mL
1 H cups	water	375 mL
H cup	"raw" cashew pieces	125 mL
H cup	firm silken tofu	125 mL
G cup	nutritional yeast flakes	60 mL
G cup	fresh lemon juice	60 mL
2 tbsp	tahini (optional)	30 mL
1 H tsp	onion granules	7 mL
1 tsp	salt	5 mL
H tsp	mustard powder	2 mL
G tsp	garlic granules	1 mL
G tsp	ground caraway seed (optional)	1 mL
H-G cup	canned jalapeno pepper, chopped	125-185 mL
H tsp	paprika	2 mL

In a small saucepan, stir agar into water and bring to a boil. Reduce the heat and simmer for 5 minutes, stirring often. Place in a blender along with cashews, tofu, nutritional yeast, lemon juice, tahini (if using), onion granules, salt, mustard, garlic, and caraway (if using). Process until completely smooth. It should be very thick. Stir in chopped jalapeno pepper after blending, just before pouring into the moulds. Lightly oil two nicely shaped round bowls, each able to hold 375 mL (1 H cups). Pour in the cashew mixture and allow it to cool. Cover and chill for several hours or overnight. To serve, turn out of the mould onto a serving plate. Sprinkle with paprika from a spice shaker. Leftovers may be stored, covered, in the refrigerator for several days. Makes 625 mL (2 H cups).

Per G cup (60 mL): calories 62, protein 3 g, fat 4 g, carbohydrate 5 g, dietary fibre 1 g, calcium 13 mg, iron 0.7 mg, magnesium 26 mg, sodium 283 mg, zinc 1 mg, folate 46 mcg, riboflavin 1.6 mg, vitamin B12 1.2 mcg, vitamin C 5 mg, vitamin E 0.8 mg, omega-3 fatty acids 0 g
% calories from: protein 20%, fat 51%, carbohydrate 29%

Analysis done using calcium-set firm tofu and with Red Star Vegetarian Support Formula nutritional yeast, a source of vitamin B12.

CHEF'S TIP: *Roasting Nuts*

Roasting nuts is a wonderful way to bring out their flavour. It's essential to watch the timing and check them frequently; nuts and seeds can burn easily, since they contain so little water.

Oven method. Place nuts on baking sheet or pan and place in oven preheated to 175°C (350°F), and roast for about 5 minutes.

Stove-top method. Place nuts on pan and cook over medium heat for about 5 minutes, stirring occasionally.

Microwave method. Place nuts in microwave-safe pan or plate and roast on medium-low heat for 3-4 minutes or on medium-high heat for 1-2 minutes.

Hazelnut Pâté

This spread, from our original edition of *Becoming Vegetarian* won the "Best Appetizer of the Show" award at North America's largest natural foods show, Natural Products Expo West, held annually in Anaheim, California. It is an innovative way to take advantage of the full flavour of hazelnuts and mushrooms. Serve it on crackers or sliced French bread, or use it as a sandwich filling. For festive occasions, form into a ball on a plate, decorate with parsley, chives, or basil leaves and flowers, or chopped hazelnuts, and surround by crackers.

H cup	onion, sliced	125 mL
1 tsp	olive oil	5 mL
1 cup	mushrooms, sliced	250 mL
2	garlic cloves, chopped	2
1 cup	roasted hazelnuts	250 mL
	(see Chef's Tip on page 399)	
G cup	fresh parsley	60 mL
1 tbsp	tamari or soy sauce	15 mL
2 tsp	nutritional yeast	10 mL
G tsp	salt, or to taste	1 mL
pinch	pepper	pinch
	lemon juice or water	

In preheated pan, sauté onion in oil over medium heat for about 5 minutes or until beginning to brown. Add mushrooms and garlic and cook for about 3 minutes until soft. In food processor, grind hazelnuts until they form a fine powder. Add sautéed mixture and puree together until very smooth, occasionally scraping down the sides. Add parsley, tamari, salt, and pepper and blend well. Add a small amount of lemon juice or water to thin the mixture, if desired. Makes 500 mL (2 cups).

Per 30-mL (2-tbsp) serving: calories 61, protein 2 g, fat 5 g, carbohydrate 2 g, dietary fibre 1 g, calcium 13 mg, iron 0.6 mg, magnesium 16 mg, sodium 64 mg, zinc 0.3 mg, folate 16 mcg, riboflavin 0.2 mg, vitamin B12 0.1 mcg, vitamin C 2 mg, vitamin E 1 mg, omega-3 fatty acids 0 g
% calories from: protein 10%, fat 75%, carbohydrate 15%

Analysis done using Red Star Vegetarian Support Formula nutritional yeast, a source of vitamin B12.

Variations

Add 60 mL (G cup) cooked kale or carrot, or 15 mL (1 tbsp) black olives, to the food processor at the same time as the sautéed mixture.

Veggie Clubhouse Sandwich

For this sandwich, we have suggested the Yves products, as they are fortified with zinc, iron, and vitamin B12. With the wide variety of veggie "meats" available near the produce section in supermarket coolers, sandwich making becomes super simple. Try vegetarian alternatives for old favourites such as the clubhouse or BLT (bacon-lettuce-tomato). This "triple decker," for those with hearty appetites, is packed with protein, B vitamins, and minerals. It is an appealing combination of colours, textures, and flavours. The Veggie Bacon can be sautéed to bring out the flavour, though this step may be omitted, as the slices are precooked.

3	slices whole wheat bread	3
2 tbsp	Vegenaise or mayonnaise	30 mL
3	slices Yves Veggie Turkey	3
1 or 2	lettuce leaves	1 or 2
3	slices Yves Canadian Veggie Bacon	3 (45 g)
H tsp	olive oil (optional)	2 mL
4	slices tomato	4
pinch	salt	pinch
pinch	black pepper	pinch

Toast bread and spread Vegenaise on one side of each slice. Place veggie turkey slices and lettuce on bottom piece of toast; cover with second slice of toast. If you wish to cook the veggie bacon, sauté it in oil in a pan over medium heat for 30 seconds on each side. (Do not overcook, as low-fat veggie meats will become too dry.) Place veggie bacon and tomato on second slice of toast. Sprinkle salt and pepper on tomato and top with remaining piece of toast. Cut diagonally into 4 pieces and serve. Makes 1 sandwich.

Per sandwich: calories 457, protein 38 g, fat 12 g, carbohydrate 52 g, dietary fibre 7 g, calcium 140 mg, iron 6 mg, magnesium 82 mg, sodium 1,129 mg, zinc 2 mg, folate 59 mcg, riboflavin 0.2 mg, vitamin B12 3 mcg, vitamin C 23 mg, vitamin E 2 mg, omega-3 fatty acids 0.1 g
% calories from: protein 33%, fat 23%, carbohydrate 44%

Sandwiches and Spreads for Every Taste

Beyond the basic peanut butter sandwich, what can vegetarians take in their lunchbox or arrange on a pretty sandwich plate? When you begin to search, you'll be delighted by what you discover. The options are never-ending. Here are just a few favourites!

TABLE 14.1   *Ten Tempting Ways to Fill a Sandwich*

Bread or Roll	Spread or Filling	Veggies	Other Spreads
Baguette or bagel	Hazelnut pâté (recipe, page 399) or store-bought sunflower seed pâté	Cucumber slices, onion, sprouts	
Sourdough roll	Veggie burger (hot or cold)	Lettuce, tomato, onion	Vegenaise or mayonnaise, mustard, ketchup, relish.
Russian rye bread	Veggie salami or deli slices	Pickles or sauerkraut, onions, lettuce	Vegenaise or mayonnaise, Dijon mustard
Rice paper wrap	Marinated or flavoured tofu strips (from supermarket or homemade) with or without rice	Shredded carrots, cucumber strips, lettuce, sprouts, sunflower seeds, chopped peanuts	Peanut sauce or plum sauce
Whole wheat sub	Veggie ham, turkey, and soy cheese slices	Onions, shredded lettuce, cucumber tomatoes, sprouts	Vegenaise, mayonnaise or mustard
Crusty roll	Veggie pizza pepperoni (small) slices	Shredded lettuce, black or green olives, tomatoes, onions, sliced green or red pepper	Vegenaise or mayonnaise
Multigrain bread	Angelic Tofu Sandwich Filling (recipe, page 396)	Lettuce, sprouts, tomato slices	Non-hydrogenated margarine

TABLE 14.1 *continued*

Bread or Roll	Spread or Filling	Veggies	Other Spreads
Toasted whole wheat bread	Canadian veggie bacon and soy cheese slices	Tomato and onion slices	Olive oil brushed on outside of bread, sandwich cooked on skillet until browned on both sides.
Dried tomato or spinach flour tortilla	Refried beans	Roasted cashews and peanuts, sunflower sprouts, avocado slices, shredded , carrots, green onions	Salsa
Pita bread	Hummus (homemade or from deli)	Diced tomato, onions, sprouts, olives, shredded romaine lettuce	

This is just a beginning. There are plenty of flavourful veggie "meats" that make excellent sandwich fillings. You can combine slices to make a hero sandwich, or spread a roll with guacamole. A book that gives great sandwich and spread recipes is *The Natural Lunchbox* by J. Brown (The Book Publishing Company, 1996).

Greens and Dressing

World's Greatest Greens

Greens such as kale and collards are great calcium sources, but we may be at a loss about how to prepare them in ways that we like. This recipe solves that problem in a most delightful way! It's so delicious that it's practically addictive. You may use just kale or collards, or a combination, or include 250 mL (1 cup) or so of sharper greens such as mustard greens or watercress. All these contain calcium that is well absorbed. Chinese greens are excellent choices, too.

12 cups	kale or collard greens	3 L/(900 g/2 lb)
1-2 tbsp	olive oil	30-45 mL
4	garlic cloves, minced	4
2 tsp	paprika	10 mL
2 tsp	cumin	10 mL
3 cups	parsley, cilantro, or a mixture, chopped	750 mL
H tsp	tamari, or to taste	2 mL
1	lemon, cut in wedges or	1
2 tsp	lemon juice	10 mL

Remove stems from kale or collards and chop in strips that are roughly 3 cm (1 in) wide. Place the greens in a steamer (for example, a steamer basket in large pot), cook until soft, and then drain well. In large preheated frying pan, combine oil, garlic, paprika, and cook over medium heat for about 1-2 minutes, without letting garlic get too brown. Add parsley, greens, and tamari; stir so that seasonings are well distributed. Serve with wedges of fresh lemon. (Alternatively, you may sprinkle with lemon juice before serving.) Makes 4 servings (750 mL/3 cups).

Per 175 mL (I cup) serving: calories 172, protein 9 g, fat 6 g, carbohydrate 28 g, dietary fibre 6 g, calcium 371 mg, iron 7 mg, magnesium 100 mg, sodium 156 mg, zinc 1.4 mg, folate 135 mcg, riboflavin 0.4 mg, vitamin B12 0 mcg, vitamin C 312 mg, vitamin E 2.5 mg, omega-3 fatty acids 0.5 g
% calories from: protein 18%, fat 25%, carbohydrate 57%

Nutritional Note

In addition to all the minerals, folate, riboflavin, vitamins C and E, and omega-3 fatty acids listed above, your 185 mL (I cup) serving provides 13,570 mcg of beta carotene, and 1,838 mcg of vitamin K. This is a delicious replacement for a vitamin-mineral supplement!

Go-for-the-Green Salad

This colourful salad is packed with health-supportive antioxidants and phytochemicals. A serving provides 100 mg calcium with almonds and seeds, 80 mg without. Be creative with your choices of additional vegetables—radishes, cucumbers, snow peas, cauliflower, broccoli, daikon, celery, alfalfa sprouts, sprouted lentils, and slices of avocado work very well.

8 cups	romaine or leaf lettuce, torn into bite-sized pieces	2 L
4 cups	kale, stem removed and thinly sliced	1 L
2 I cups	broccoli or sunflower sprouts (100 g container)	700 mL
1 cup	grated carrots or golden beets	250 mL
1 cup	cherry tomatoes	250 mL
H	each, sweet red and yellow pepper, sliced	H
G cup	pumpkin seeds (optional)	60 mL
G cup	almonds, raw or toasted (optional)	60 mL

In large salad bowl, place lettuce, kale, sprouts, carrot, tomatoes, and sweet pepper, along with seeds and almonds (if using). Toss with Liquid Gold Dressing or other favourite dressing. Makes 3.5 L (14 cups).

Per 500 mL (2 cup) serving: calories 48, protein 3 g, fat 0.6 g, carbohydrate 10 g, dietary fibre 3 g, calcium 86 mg, iron 2 mg, magnesium 27 mg, sodium 30 mg, zinc 0.5 mg, folate 113 mcg, riboflavin 0.2 mg, vitamin B12 0 mcg, vitamin C 100 mg, vitamin E 1.2 mg, omega-3 fatty acids 0.2 g
% calories from: protein 24%, fat 10%, carbohydrate 66%

Liquid Gold Dressing

Vesanto developed this dressing for use on salads, baked potatoes, rice, steamed broccoli, and other veggies. We gave it the name "Liquid Gold," and not just because of the colour! Thirty millilitres (2 tbsp) provides 5 g of omega-3 fatty acids (your day's supply, and then some) along with 40 per cent of your B12 for the day, when it's made with Red Star Vegetarian Support Formula nutritional yeast. This creamy dressing is packed with riboflavin and other B vitamins—plus, it's very tasty. If you add ground flaxseed, use the larger amount of water (125 mL/H cup); if not, use 85 mL (N cup) water. You'll find that when it's made with ground flaxseed, the dressing gradually thickens.

H cup	flaxseed oil	125 mL
N-H cup	water	85-125 mL
N cup	lemon juice	85 mL
2 tbsp	balsamic or raspberry vinegar	30 mL
G cup	tamari or Bragg Liquid Soy	60 mL
G cup	nutritional yeast flakes	60 mL/25 g
2 tsp	Dijon mustard	10 mL
1 tsp	ground cumin	5 mL
1 tbsp	ground flaxseed (optional)	15 mL

Place oil, water, lemon juice, vinegar, tamari, yeast, mustard, cumin, and flaxseed (if using) in blender and blend until smooth. Dressing can be kept in a jar with lid, refrigerated for two weeks. Makes 375 mL (1 H cups).

Per 30 mL (2 tbsp) serving: calories 96, protein 1 g, carbohydrate 2 g, fat 7 g, dietary fibre 0.4 g, calcium 4 mg, sodium 180 mg
% calories from: protein 7%, fat 85%, carbohydrate 8%

Variation: Green Goddess Dressing

Replace mustard and cumin with 250 mL (1 cup) fresh herbs (basil, oregano, and parsley work very well), and 3 cloves garlic, chopped. As this variation doesn't contain mustard, the oil and water layers are more likely to separate; (mustard helps hold emulsions together.)

Simple Sprouting

The process of sprouting greatly increases the availability to the body of zinc and other minerals in legumes, grains, nuts, and seeds. Sprouts, which are also loaded with vitamins and phytochemicals, add an interesting texture and flavour to salads, sandwiches, and stir-fries. They can be a valuable way to get fresh foods in challenging circumstances, for example, in northern winters, when little local produce is available, while sailing, or when one is far from produce markets. Campers and people living in remote areas (such as tree planters) can set up sprouting centres. Backpackers and cyclists have even been known to dangle mesh bags of sprouts from their packs! Sprout care is so simple that rinsing them and watching them grow may become a favourite occupation of young children.

Basic care of sprouts involves keeping them moist while providing drainage and air circulation. In the kitchen, place them on a countertop near a sink. Sprouts are healthiest when they are rinsed often and well drained. In warm weather, they mature more quickly and require frequent rinsing to keep them cool. Hot direct sunlight can "cook" them; shade is better. To "green" alfalfa sprouts and sunflower greens, a balance of sun and shade works well.

Home sprout growing can be set up with jars, sprout bags, trays, or an automatic sprout grower. With all of these, you follow more or less the same method. In Table 14.2, we summarize the basic steps for a few of the dried legumes or raw, unhulled, unsalted seeds that you might like to sprout, giving the amounts for a 1 litre (1 quart) jar. You may grow your sprouts in wide-neck mason jars (these come in 1 litre (1 quart) sizes and in 2 litre (H gallon/2 quart) sizes. Replace the lids that come with the mason jars with sprouting lids, available at many health food stores (these have little holes that allow for the necessary air circulation) or with mesh held on with an elastic band. After this basic introduction, if you become an avid sprouter, you may want to explore other options. If so, get *The Sprouting Book* by A. Wigmore (Avery Publishers, 1986) or *Sprout Garden: Indoor Grower's Guide to Gourmet Sprouts* by M. Braunstein (The Book Publishing Company, 1999).

TABLE 14.2   *Sprouting Summary*

In jar, cover lentils, beans, or seeds with about double the amount of water and soak for the time specified. Then drain, rinse, and set jar upside down on a bowl or tray and at a 45° angle (the angle allows air circulation). Rinse sprouts twice a day by filling jar with water and allowing it to overflow. Then drain and again set at 45° angle. At harvest, rinse (with alfalfa sprouts, rinse off seed hulls), drain, place in clean glass jar, with lid that allows air circulation, and refrigerate. Sprouts will last for four or five days.

Legume or Seed	Soaking Time (hours)	Amount Dry, for Litre/Quart Jar	Length at Harvest	Days Until Ready	Sprout Tips
Lentils	12	125 mL (H cup)	0.6-2 cm (G-to I in)	3-5	Try regular (green, brown, or grey) dry lentils and the smaller French dry lentils. Grow to either short or longer lengths.
Mung beans	12	60 mL (G cup)	4 cm (1 H in)	3-6	The long mung bean sprouts of Chinese cooking are grown away from light, and a small weight is placed above the sprouts so that they grow under pressure. This helps them become long. Here we give just the basic sprouting method.
Alfalfa Seeds	4-6	30 mL (2 tbsp)	2.5-4 cm (1-1 H in)	4-6	To develop chlorophyll and make the sprouts green, place in light 1-2 days before harvest.

TABLE 14.2 *continued*

To make sunflower greens (below), unsalted sunflower seeds that are still in their hull are first soaked for 12 hours, left to drain for another 12 hours, rinsed, and then scattered on top of 2.5 centimetres (1 inch) of topsoil on a tray. A temperature of 18-24°C (65-75°F) is best. The sprouting seeds are sprinkled with water daily for a week. To exclude light for the first two days , the tray can be covered with a few clean, damp sheets of paper, or placed in a dark cupboard. For days 3 through 7, the tray is moved to an area with indirect light.

Seed	Soaking Time (hours)	Amount Dry, for Litre/Quart Jar	Length at Harvest	Days Until Ready	Tips and Comments
Unhulled Sunflower seeds	12	175 mL (I cup)	13-20 cm (5-8 in)	7	delicious greens with scissors or sharp knife.

Cooking the Basics

Great Grains

A whole world of grains awaits you! You will be amazed at the variety and nutrition they add to your meals. Whole grains may be cooked in many ways: simmered on the stove-top, pressure-cooked, baked, or microwaved. (Below, we feature the standard stove-top method.) Whichever method you choose, be sure to use a pot or dish that is large enough to allow for the expansion of the grain. Millet, barley, and quinoa expand to four times their original size, while other grains usually expand two to three times.

Cooking Whole Grains in under 25 Minutes

Sometimes people don't use whole grains, thinking they take too long to cook. For most grains, the cooking time is 45 minutes to 1 hour. However, some small grains such as quinoa, millet, and whole wheat couscous can be prepared in 15-20 minutes. With larger grains such as pot barley, brown rice, oat groats, and whole grain berries (rye, wheat, spelt, or kamut), you can cut the usual cooking time in half by presoaking the grains for several hours or overnight in about twice the volume of water.

Standard Cooking Method for Grains

To cook grains in the standard stove-top manner, use the amount of water suggested in Table 14.3. (A little added salt is optional.) When you are ready to cook the soaked grains, cover and bring to a rapid boil. Stir, cover, and reduce heat to a simmer. Cook without lifting the lid for approximately the time specified in Table 14.3. Larger grains take longer than smaller ones. If you use a little less water, the cooking time will be slightly shorter and the texture of the cooked grain chewier. With millet, some people prefer to use 4 cups of water per cup of grain for a more creamy product whereas some prefer the distinct grains produced using 2 cups of water. If more water is used, grains are softer and stickier. Short grain rice tends to be stickier than medium or long grain rice.

General directions. Whole grains generally need to be washed before they are cooked. Place the grains in a pot, cover with about 2 inches of water, swirl it around, and pour off hulls and bits of debris that float to the surface. Repeat if necessary. Then pour off all water, using a sieve so you don't lose grains. In pot with lid, combine rinsed grains with the measured amount of water, bring to a boil, cover, reduce heat, and simmer for the recommended time. If you have hard water, cooking time will be longer.

For a fluffier product, cook the grain as shown in Table 14.3, then remove the pot from the heat and allow it to sit, covered, for 5-15 minutes. This works, for example, when using millet, quinoa, or bulgur wheat.

TABLE 14.3 *Water, Cooking Time and Yield for Whole Grains (without presoaking)*

Grain 250 mL (1 cup)	Water mL (cups)	Time* (minutes, after lowering heat)	Yield
Amaranth	500 mL (2 cups)	25	500 ml (2 cups)
Barley, pot or pearled	750 mL (3 cups)	45	875 mL (3 H cups)
Buckwheat groats, kasha	500 mL (2 cups)	15-20	560 mL (2 G cups)
Bulgur	500 mL (2 cups)	15	625 mL (2 H cups)
Cracked wheat	500 mL (2 cups)	30	625 mL (2 H cups)
Kamut	1 L (4 cups)	90	810 mL (3 G cups)
Millet	750 mL (3 cups)	25	1 L (4 cups)
Oat groats	750 mL-1 L (3-4 cups)	60	750 mL (3 cups)
Quinoa	500 mL (2 cups)	20	875 mL (3 H cups)
Rice, brown, any type	500 mL (2 cups)	45	875 mL (3 H cups)
Rice, wild	1 L (4 cups)	60	1.25 L (5 cups)
Rye	1 L (4 cups)	60	625 mL (2 H cups)
Wheat berries	1 L (4 cups)	90	750 mL (3 cups)
Wheat, bulgur	625 mL (2 H cups)	5-10	625 mL (2 H cups)
Wheat, cracked	500 mL (2 cups)	30	625 mL (2 H cups)

* It is important to note that cooking times for grains can vary considerably depending on how long the grains have been stored. Older grains will take longer to cook than grains that have been recently harvested.

CHEF'S TIPS *for Great Grains*

Bulgar. Can be prepared without cooking (unless it is the very coarse kind). Add boiling water and cover for 20-30 minutes.

Millet. For a wonderful nutty flavour, toast millet in a heavy frying pan over medium heat for 2-3 minutes before boiling. Millet is a sticky grain, thus is excellent for use in patties and loaves.

Quinoa. As quinoa is coated with a bitter resin, it needs to be well rinsed before cooking. Some brands are pre-rinsed.

Barley. One of the creamiest of all grains, barley makes a superb replacement for the rice in rice pudding recipes. Delicious!

Kamut or Wheat Berries. Water needs to be drained after cooking.

Perfect Pilaf

Pilafs are quick and easy to make and they allow freshly cooked or leftover grains to come alive with colour, flavour, and nutrition. For example, you may lightly sauté chopped onion and garlic in a little oil. Add seasonings (choose from list below or use your own ideas), and any combination of cashews, cubes of plain or marinated tofu, tempeh, sliced mushrooms or grated carrots, fresh or frozen peas, chopped sweet red peppers, or celery. Then stir in the cooked rice or other grain and heat for a few minutes, tossing, to warm through and mix the flavours. Grains that work especially well are wheat berries, brown rice, a combination of brown rice and wild rice, or combinations of barley, wheat berries, and quinoa. Adjust seasoning with salt, pepper, etc. Serve on a platter, garnished with chopped nuts, cherry tomatoes, or parsley.

Seasoning Ideas

With each of the following combinations, you may use any or all of the ingredients in that set.

Asian. Tamari, Bragg Liquid Soy or soy sauce; sesame seeds; grated ginger; seaweed powder.

Mediterranean. Chopped fresh parsley; diced sweet peppers; marjoram, oregano, basil.

East Indian. Curry powder, garam masala, or ground cumin; chopped cilantro, hot or sweet peppers; green onion; orange sections, cashews.

Legume Lore

Beans are such important providers of protein, iron, and zinc that it makes good sense to discover ways to use them that suit your lifestyle. A secret of many vegetarians is to stock the freezer with a variety of cooked beans to use in quick food preparation. These might include chickpeas for hummus or a stir-fry, kidney or pinto beans for a big batch of chili, black beans for soup, and several different beans (lima, pinto, and red) that can be made into a colourful stew or marinated bean salad. Whenever you cook beans (say, once a week), make extra. Then put some of the beans into freezer bags or plastic containers, freezing many portions that are sized to suit the number of people in your household. Lentil, pea, and bean soups also freeze well. Legumes can be divided into two groups, based on size. Each requires a different cooking method.

Group 1: Legumes That Do Not Require Presoaking

These are the smaller cooking legumes, about the size of a lentil. Presoaking is not required with the legumes in Group 1. However, if you have time to presoak them, it will speed up cooking time and increase mineral availability. Times listed can be variable. Freshly harvested legumes cook quickly; you can expect very old lentils and beans to take much longer. For each 250 millilitres (1 cup) of lentils or mung beans, add 750 millilitres (3 cups) of water. Thus, for 750 millilitres (3 cups) of lentils add 2.25 litres (9 cups) of water.

TABLE 14.4   *Cooking Time for Quick-Cooking Legumes (Group 1)*

Legumes	Cooking Time
Lentils, red	25-30 minutes
Lentils, brown or green	50-60 minutes
Mung beans	40-50 minutes
Split peas	40-50 minutes

Group 2: Legumes That Require Presoaking

This group includes all other beans, such as adzuki, kidney, lima, pinto, garbanzo, and black beans. These must be presoaked before cooking. Look through the beans to remove any small stones, and soak overnight for at least 6 hours in at least three times the volume of water. Discard the water and rinse the beans thoroughly. Cover the beans with about 7.5 centimetres (3 inches) fresh, unsalted water and boil hard for 1 minute. You may wish to add fennel seeds or kombu seaweed to reduce the gas produced during digestion. Cover and simmer for 1-2 hours. The cooked beans should be soft enough that you can mash these beans with your tongue against the roof of your mouth. Using very hard water (high in minerals) or beans that have been stored for several years can increase bean cooking time.

Don't add salt, tomatoes, or other highly acidic foods to dried beans until they are cooked to the point of being tender or they will not soften properly and will remain hard to digest. (Herbs are all right; they do not interfere with the softening process.) When cooked, you may add seasonings and continue to cook for 10 minutes more. The cooked beans are ready for eating as they are, or you can use them in recipes.

CHEF'S TIP *for Reducing Presoaking Time*

The long presoaking time of 6-10 hours can be shortened by bringing the beans to a boil, then removing from heat and soaking for 1 hour. Next, discard the liquid, rinse, cover with fresh water, and cook for the recommended time or until tender.

Cooking Beans in a Slow Cooker (Crockpot)

Many people prefer to cook beans all day or overnight in a slow cooker. For every 250 millilitres (1 cup) of presoaked beans, add 750 millilitres (3 cups) of fresh water. You may also add bay leaves, peppercorns, or your favourite herbs. Turn on the slow cooker in the morning, cover, and by dinner your beans will be perfect.

Seven Super-Simple Suppers

These all-time favourites bring you flavours from around the globe: North America, India, England, Mexico, China, Africa, and Italy

Hot Tofu with Cool Greens

This is one of Brenda and her husband Paul's very favourite meals. Served the warm, seasoned tofu on a bed of cool leafy greens (such as ready-to-eat organic salad mix, an assortment of greens with sprouts, or the Go-for-the Greens Salad on page 405). Dress the greens with Liquid Gold Dressing (recipe, page 416) or another favourite dressing before putting on the tofu. This meal is reminiscent of a California-style hot chicken salad. Choose extra-firm tofu that is set with calcium, and shred it with the large grate on a vegetable/cheese grater. Herbed tofu is especially delightful, if it is available. This recipe is very versatile—you might also add steamed asparagus, sautéed Portobello mushrooms, artichoke hearts, or black olives—let your imagination run wild!

2 tsp	olive oil	10 mL
12 oz	extra firm tofu, herbed or plain, grated	340 g
2 tbsp	Bragg Liquid Soy or tamari	30 mL
1 tbsp	nutritional yeast	15 mL
2	garlic cloves, minced	2
G tsp	each of dried oregano, basil, parsley, or other herbs (or 15-30 mL/1-2 tbsp fresh herbs) freshly ground black pepper, to taste	1 mL
G cup	almonds, raw or toasted	60 mL

In a large skillet, heat olive oil. Add tofu, Bragg Liquid Soy, nutritional yeast, garlic, herbs, and pepper. Sauté for about 5 minutes or until tofu is browned. Heap two 2 dinner plates with salad (approximately 1 litre/4 cups of salad each), and top each salad with half of the tofu mixture and half of the almonds. Serve immediately with your favourite salad dressing. Makes 2 hearty servings.

Per half recipe (without salad or dressing): calories 422, protein 34 g, carbohydrate 13 g, fat 29 g, dietary fibre 7 g, calcium 1230 mg*, iron 18 mg, magnesium 104 mg, sodium 677 mg, zinc 3.3 mg, folate 105 mcg, riboflavin 2.4 mg, vitamin B12 1.6 mcg, vitamin C 1.5 mg, vitamin E 4.5 mg, omega-3 fatty acids 1.0 g
% calories from: protein 30%, fat 58%, carbohydrate 12%

Analysis was done using Red Star Vegetarian Support Formula nutritional yeast, a contributor of Vitamin B12.

*Calcium content varies considerably between different brands of tofu; check labels.

Variations

1. Instead of grating tofu, cut it in strips about 5 cm (2 in) by 1.25 cm (H in). Cook as you would the grated tofu.

2. Use pumpkin seeds in place of almonds, or in addition to almonds; (use 30 mL/2 tbsp of each).

3. Be creative with the seasonings. Replace the Mediterranean-style seasonings with any herbs and spices of your choice.

Chunky Red Lentil Tomato Sauce

Red lentils are the fastest cooking of all legumes as they cook in 15-20 minutes. When vegetables are added, the lentils almost dissolve into the sauce. The flavour develops best by simmering for 1 hour or more, or all day in a crock-pot. If your family is just getting used to legumes, you might start with just 125 mL (H cup) of dry lentils; alternatively, you may use extra for added protein. "Chunky" refers to the vegetables; you can use those listed here or substitute others that you have on hand.

4 cups	water	1 L
1 cup	uncooked red lentils	250 mL
1	large onion, chopped	1
2-3	garlic cloves, minced	2-3
1	large carrot, sliced diagonally	1
1	stalk broccoli, stem peeled, chopped	1
1 cup	sliced mushrooms (fresh or canned)	250 mL
H cup	diced green pepper,	125 mL
1	small zucchini, sliced or grated	1
28 oz	canned stewed tomatoes, whole or diced	796 mL
28 oz	canned prepared tomato sauce	796 mL
2 tbsp	each, fresh basil and oregano (or 10 mL/2 tsp dried)	30 mL
2 tbsp	tamari or Bragg Liquid Soy	30 mL
2 tbsp	cooking wine (optional)	30 mL
2 tbsp	miso (optional)	30 mL

Stove-top method. Place water and lentils in a large pot, bring to a boil, then turn heat down, cover and simmer for about 20-25 minutes, until lentils are soft. Add a little water if necessary. Add onion, garlic, carrot, broccoli, mushrooms, green pepper, zucchini, tomatoes, tomato sauce, basil, oregano, tamari, and wine (if using). Bring to boil, then cover, turn heat down and simmer sauce for about 1 hour. If using miso, place it in a small bowl; add about 125 mL (H cup) of sauce and stir to make a smooth paste; then return the paste to the sauce and stir in before serving.

Crock-pot method. Place all ingredients in crock-pot. Cook on low for 6-8 hours, or on high for about 4 hours.

Serve with your favourite pasta or spaghetti squash. Makes about 2.75 L (11 cups).

Per 250 mL (1 cup): calories 125, protein 7 g, fat 0.3 g, carbohydrate 26 g, dietary fibre 6 g, calcium 61 mg, iron 2.3 mg, magnesium 51 mg, sodium 703 mg*, zinc 1.1 mg, folate 105 mcg, riboflavin 0.2 mg, vitamin B12 0 mcg, vitamin C 38 mg, vitamin E 1.6 mg, omega-3 fatty acids 0 g
% calories from: protein 22%, fat 2%, carbohydrate 76%

*Sodium is lower if amounts in canned tomatoes and tomato sauce are low.

Variations

1. For an extra-fast sauce, use precooked or canned lentils. Steam the carrots and broccoli for about 10 minutes. Sauté the onions, mushrooms, peppers, and garlic in 15 mL (1 tbsp) of olive oil for about 7 minutes, or until tender. In a large pot, add tomatoes, and tomato sauce, cooked vegetables, lentils, optional ingredients, and seasoning. Simmer for about 20 minutes.

2. Try other vegetables in this recipe; chopped cauliflower, asparagus pieces, sweet peppers, celery, spinach, or kale work well. Cooked leftover vegetables may be used too.

CHEF'S TIP: *Amount of Spaghetti Per Person*

It can be a challenge to figure out how much spaghetti to cook per person. One estimate that may be useful is to grasp an amount of dry 25-cm (10-in) spaghetti noodles the diameter of a 25-cent piece, and cook this much for each person. This is about 125 g (4 oz) of dry pasta, and makes a hearty serving of 500 mL (2 cups) per person when cooked.

Timesaving Tacos

For an instant meal, one of the fastest, yet nutritionally balanced combinations you can serve is the well-loved taco. Just warm the shells and beans, heat up the Veggie Ground Round (if using), chop the veggies, and set out the colourful fillings in pretty bowls. Let people assemble their own, to suit their individual preferences. If you prefer burritos, replace the taco shells with soft, flour tortillas.

12 oz	package Yves Veggie Ground Round Mexican (optional)	680 g
2 tsp	olive oil (optional)	10 mL
14 oz	canned refried beans	398 mL
1	ripe avocado, mashed or chopped	1
2 tsp	lemon juice	10 mL
10	hard corn taco shells, warmed in oven or microwave	10
2 cups	shredded lettuce	500 mL
2	large tomatoes, chopped	2
1	large carrot, grated	1
3	green onions, finely diced	3
1 cup	salsa or taco sauce	250 mL
H cup	pitted olives, sliced (optional)	125 mL
1 cup	grated soy or cheddar cheese (optional)	250 mL

If using Veggie Ground Round, sauté in olive oil on medium heat for 5 minutes, or until lightly browned. Meanwhile warm the refried beans in a small saucepan, vegetable steamer, or microwave. If too thick, stir in 15 mL (1 tbsp) of salsa or taco sauce. Mash avocado and stir in lemon juice. Place taco shells, beans, lettuce, tomato, carrot, green onion, avocado, lemon juice, and salsa, along with Veggie Ground Round, olives, and cheese (if using) in serving bowls on table, allowing for individual assembly. Makes 10 tacos; serves 3-5 people.

Per taco: calories 149, protein 4 g, fat 7 g, carbohydrate 20 g, dietary fibre 5 g, calcium 54 mg, iron 1.6 mg, magnesium 28 mg, sodium 302 mg, zinc 2.7 mg, folate 63 mcg, riboflavin 0.1 mg, vitamin B12 0 mcg, vitamin C 14 mg, vitamin E 1.8 mg, omega-3 fatty acids 0.2 g
% calories from: protein 13%, fat 32%, carbohydrate 55%

African Stew

Peanut butter makes a wonderful creamy sauce for this nutrition-packed stew that is likely to become a family favourite. Vegetable stock may be purchased ready-made or made from cubes or powder. Lemon juice, added at the end, adds a lively nuance to the flavour. Season with a dash of hot pepper sauce, fiery chipotle sauce, or Vietnamese chili sauce. Recipe from *Cooking Vegetarian* by V. Melina and J. Forest (Chronimed/Wiley, 1998.)

1	onion, chopped	1
4 cups	vegetable stock or water	1 L
2 cups	peeled, diced yams or sweet potatoes	500 mL
1 cup	canned chickpeas	250 mL
1 cup	brown rice	250 mL
G tsp	salt	1 mL
G cup	peanut butter	60 mL
2 cups	chopped collards or kale	500 mL
2 tbsp	lemon juice	10 mL
H tsp	pepper	2 mL
1 tbsp	tamari, Bragg Liquid soy, or soy sauce	15 mL
	chili sauce to taste	

In large pot over medium heat, sauté onion in 30 mL (2 tbsp) of the stock for 5 minutes, adding more stock if necessary. Add remaining stock, yams, chickpeas, rice, and salt; simmer for 45 minutes. In small bowl, blend peanut butter and 125 mL (H cup) of liquid from stew to make a smooth paste. Stir into stew along with collards and cook for 5 minutes. Stir in lemon juice, pepper, and tamari; add chili sauce to taste. Adjust seasoning. Makes about 4 servings (1.5 L/6 cups).

Per 250 mL (1 cup): calories 295, protein 9 g, fat 7 g, carbohydrate 51 g, dietary
fibre 7 g, calcium 62 mg, iron 2 mg, magnesium 92 mg, sodium 233 mg, zinc 1.6
mg, folate 97 mcg, riboflavin 0.1 mg, vitamin B12 0 mcg, vitamin C 17 mg, vitamin E 2.4 mg, omega-3 fatty acids 0.1 g
% calories from: protein 12%, fat 21%, carbohydrate 67%

Cashew and Vegetable Stir-fry

For this stir-fry, we have suggested an assortment of vegetables;
however, you can try others such as asparagus, cauliflower, Chinese
greens, daikon radish, mung bean sprouts, or mushrooms. To give
appealing textures in a stir-fry, the denser vegetables are added at
the beginning for longer cooking, and the more leafy vegetables at
the end. Use Chinese chili garlic sauce (available at Asian grocery
stores and many supermarkets) or a Thai chili sauce with garlic in
it; these can be hot, so if you prefer milder tastes, use much less, or
none at all. Serve over brown rice. Recipe can be doubled to serve
three or four people.

Sauce

2 tbsp	cashew butter or peanut butter	30 mL
1-2 tbsp	Chinese or other chili garlic sauce	15-30 mL
1 tbsp	tamari, Bragg Liquid Soy, or soy sauce	15 mL
1 tbsp	water	15 mL

Stir-fry

G c	cashew nuts	60 mL
1	large red, yellow or white onion, sliced	1
1-2 tsp	olive oil	5-10 mL
1	large carrot, sliced diagonally	1
1 cup	broccoli florets, chopped	250 mL
1	red pepper, diced	250 mL
1 cup	chopped bok choy or Chinese cabbage	250 mL
1 cup	snow pea pods	250 mL

In a small bowl, stir together cashew butter, chilli garlic sauce, tamari, and water to make a smooth paste. If you wish, toast cashew nuts lightly in small frying pan or oven for a few minutes. (See Chef's Tip: Roasting Nuts on page 399.) In preheated hot wok or pan, cook onion in oil over high heat for 3 minutes or until beginning to brown. Add carrot and cook for 1 minute; add broccoli and cook for another 30 seconds; then add red pepper, bok choy, and snow peas, cooking just long enough to heat through. Add sauce, stir to combine, sprinkle with cashews, and serve over rice. Makes 2 moderate servings. (2 cups each)

Per H *recipe, without rice:* calories 312, protein: 11 g, fat 19 g, carbohydrate 30 g, dietary fibre 8 g, calcium 157 mg, iron 4.8 mg, magnesium 134 mg, sodium 889 mg, zinc 2.5 mg, folate 122 mcg, riboflavin 0.3 mg, vitamin B12 0 mcg, vitamin C 147 mg, vitamin E 4 mg, omega-3 fatty acids 0.2 g
% calories from: protein 14%, fat 50%, carbohydrate 36%

Shepherd's Pie

This classic comfort food may stir fond memories from childhood, with the dark, rich, meaty-flavoured bottom layer, then a layer of bright yellow corn, and smooth topping of mashed potato. To give a pleasant texture, we used a combination of equal amounts of creamed and niblet corn. We suggested the use of white pepper because black pepper gives a speckled appearance to mashed potatoes; however, black pepper will do, too.

Pie Mixture

2 O cup	diced onion	690 mL
6	garlic cloves, minced	6
1 H cup	chopped celery	375 mL
1 tbsp	olive oil	15 mL
12 oz	Yves Veggie Ground Round (2 packages)	680 g (2 tbsp +)
2 tsp	vegetarian Worcestershire sauce (such as Wizard Brand)	40 mL
2 tbsp	tamari, Bragg Liquid Soy, or soy sauce	30 mL
1 tsp	salt (optional)	5 mL
H tbsp	tarragon	8 mL
1 tsp	thyme	5 mL

H tsp	black pepper	2 mL
14 oz	canned creamed corn	398 mL
14 oz	canned niblets corn, drained	398 mL
	or	
1 H cup	frozen corn kernels, thawed	375 mL

Potato Topping

8	large russet potatoes, peeled (1.8 kg/4 lbs)	8
3-4 tbsp	olive oil	45-60 mL
H cup	fortified soymilk	125 mL
H tsp	salt	2 mL
G tsp	white or black pepper	1 mL
G tsp	paprika	1 mL

Preheat oven to 180°C (350°F). Cut each potato into thirds and cook in boiling water until tender. Meanwhile, in skillet, sauté onion, garlic, and celery in oil over medium-high heat until soft. Turn off heat, add crumbled Veggie Ground Round, Worcestershire sauce, tamari, salt (if using), tarragon, thyme, pepper, and mix thoroughly. Transfer Veggie Ground Round mixture to sprayed or lightly oiled 23 × 33-cm (9 × 13-in) casserole dish. Spread mixture evenly. Mix creamed corn and corn kernels. Spread corn mixture over Veggie Ground Round mixture. Drain potatoes, add oil, soymilk, salt, and pepper and mash until fluffy. Evenly spread potato topping over corn. Sprinkle top with paprika and bake for 20 minutes or until heated through. Makes 8 servings (310 mL/1 G cups each).

Per 250 mL (1cup): calories 262, protein 6 g, fat 6 g, carbohydrate 48 g, dietary fibre 5 g, calcium 56 mg, iron 1.9 mg, magnesium 54 mg, sodium 627 mg, zinc 1.4 mg, folate 51 mcg, riboflavin 0.1 mg, vitamin B12 0.2 mcg, vitamin C 37 mg, vitamin E 1.2 mg, omega-3 fatty acids 0.1 g
% calories from: protein 9%, fat 20%, carbohydrate 71%

Easiest-Ever Curried Lentils

This recipe is a favourite with Vesanto because it's so simple. The hands-on preparation takes about 5 minutes; then it simply cooks for another 45 minutes. Salt is added near the end of the cooking time; if added earlier, it can prevent lentils from softening properly. The texture and nutrition are best with brown or green lentils, or with the small French lentils. However, the quick method in Variation #4 uses red lentils and is ready in 25 minutes. Patak's brand of curry paste is suggested because it has superb flavour; even the mild variety is plenty hot enough for most tastes. Serve this dish with rice and a salad. Leftovers keep, refrigerated, for four days; they also freeze well.

2	medium onions (or 1 large onion), chopped	2
4 tsp-3 tbsp	Patak's mild curry paste (or to taste)	20-45 mL
5 cups	water	1.25 L
2 cups	brown, green, or French lentils	500 mL
2 tbsp	tamari, Bragg Liquid Soy, or soy sauce *or*	30 mL
1 tsp	salt	5 mL

In large pot, place onion, and stir in curry paste, water, and lentils; mix and bring to a boil. Cover, reduce heat, and simmer for 45 minutes or until lentils are soft enough to mash on the roof of your mouth with your tongue. If desired, add more curry paste and tamari. Makes 4 servings (6 cups/1.5 L).

Per 250 mL (1 cup): calories 256, protein 19 g, fat 2 g, carbohydrate 42 g, dietary fibre 21 g, calcium 55 mg, iron 6 mg, magnesium 75 mg, sodium 350 mg, zinc 2.4 mg, folate 279 mcg, riboflavin 0.2 mg, vitamin B12 0 mcg, vitamin C 8 mg, vitamin E 0.5 mg, omega-3 fatty acids 0.2 g
% calories from: protein 29%, fat 8%, carbohydrate 63%

Variations

1. Add chopped raw cauliflower at the same time as adding lentils or, if you like it a little crunchy, after 25 minutes of cooking.

2. Stir in cooked vegetables, such as cauliflower, near the end of cooking time.

3. Add diced raw tomato to the final dish as a garnish.

4. For fastest cooking, use red lentils and simmer for 20 minutes.

5. For a soup-like consistency, use more water.

Delectable Desserts and Goodies

Muscle Muffins

These muffins are quite different from cake-type muffins; they're more hearty, satisfying, and nutritious. Made with soy protein, each muffin provides 8 g of protein, 3.5 mg of iron, and 143 mg of calcium. Store them in individual plastic bags in your freezer to grab for a mid-morning snack, hiking treat, or a boost after the gym.

1 cup	whole wheat flour	250 mL
1 cup	unbleached flour	250 mL
H cup	soy protein powder (optional)	125mL
1 tbsp	baking powder	15 mL
1 tsp	baking soda	5 mL
1 tsp	cinnamon	5 mL
2	frozen or fresh ripe bananas	2
I cup	fortified soymilk	185 mL
G cup	vegetable oil	60 mL
G cup	blackstrap molasses	60 mL
G cup	maple syrup	60 mL
2 tsp	apple cider vinegar	10 mL
1 cup	raisins or chopped dates	250 mL

Preheat oven to 180°C (350°F). Lightly oil or spray a 12-cup muffin tin. In a large bowl, place flours, protein powder (if using), baking powder, soda, and cinnamon and stir to combine. In a smaller bowl, mash bananas, then stir in soymilk, oil, molasses, syrup, and vinegar. (If you prefer, you can puree these together in a blender.) Add wet ingredients to dry ingredients, stir until just blended, and then stir in raisins. Fill muffin tins and bake for 30-35 minutes or until done. You can tell muffins are done when they pull away from the side of the tin and when the dent made by a finger pressed in the centre of a muffin pops up again to original shape. Makes 12 muffins.

Per muffin: calories 226, protein 8 g, fat 5 g, carbohydrate 39 g, dietary fibre 3 g, calcium 143 mg, iron 3.5 mg, magnesium 54 mg, sodium 216 mg, zinc 1.5 mg, folate 38 mcg, riboflavin 0.2 mg, vitamin B12 0.5 mcg, vitamin C 5 mg, vitamin E 1.3 mg, omega-3 fatty acids 0.4 g
% calories from: protein 14%, fat 20%, carbohydrate 67%

Variations

1. Add 125 mL (H cup) chopped walnuts or pecans.

2. Replace mashed bananas with 2 apples, cored and grated.

Lemon Teasecake

This is one of the scrumptious desserts at Seattle's gourmet vegetarian restaurant, Café Ambrosia, developed by executive chef Francis Janes. With a revolving international menu, Café Ambrosia is an absolute must-visit for those who wish to experience innovative, organic vegetarian fine dining (www.cafeambrosia.com). People with allergies will be delighted to find that both crust and filling in this dessert are free of eggs, dairy, wheat, and soy. Choose Meyer lemons when in season as they are sweeter and milder than the Eureka and Lisbon varieties common to most produce departments. Meyer lemons are available from November through March in specialty food stores. Cherry or other fruit preserves are fruit juice-sweetened jams.

Oatmeal Cinnamon Crust

1 cup	rolled oats	250 mL
H cup	brown rice flour	125 mL
H cup	ground walnuts	125 mL
1 tsp	cinnamon	5 mL
H tsp	sea salt	2 mL
1 tsp	vanilla extract	5 mL
3 tbsp	maple syrup	45 mL
G cup	canola oil	60 mL

Filling

H cup	dry millet	125 mL
2 H cups	water	625 mL
H cup	raw unsalted cashews	125 mL
N cup	fresh lemon juice	80 mL
N cup	maple syrup	80 mL
2 tsp	vanilla extract	10 mL
1 tsp	lemon extract	5 mL

Topping

8 oz	cherry or other fruit	250 mL
	preserves	
2	kiwi fruit, peeled and sliced	2
	thin into rounds, or other	
	sliced fruit or berries for	
	decoration	

Crust

Preheat oven to 180°C (350°F). In large bowl, combine oats, flour, walnuts, cinnamon, and salt and mix well. In smaller bowl or measuring cup, combine vanilla, maple syrup, and oil and stir well. Add liquid ingredients to dry ingredients and mix to incorporate liquid. Press firmly into 20-cm (8- or 9-in) springform pan. Bake for approximately 15 minutes or until lightly browned. Cool about 30 minutes before pouring on filling.

Filling

In medium saucepan with tight-fitting lid, bring millet and water to boil. Cover and simmer over low heat for about 30 minutes, until water is completely absorbed and millet is soft. While millet is cooking, place cashews, lemon juice, maple syrup, and extracts in blender. Process on high speed for 3 minutes or until perfectly smooth. If necessary, scrape down sides of blender with spatula and process for another minute. While cooked millet is still warm, add it to blender mixture. Process on high speed for another 3 minutes until creamy. Pour into cooled crust.

Cool filling and crust at room temperature for 1 hour. Place plastic wrap over surface to prevent excess cracking on surface. Place in refrigerator and chill for at least 4 hours before serving. Teasecake will keep for about three days, refrigerated.

Topping

Place fruit preserves in small saucepan and stir over medium-low heat until barely melted. Spread this topping evenly over filling that has chilled and set. When ready to serve, garnish with slices of kiwi fruit or any combination of sliced fruit and/or berries. Makes 10 servings.

Per 1/10 cake: calories 360, protein 5 g, carbohydrate 57 g, fat 14 g, dietary fibre 3 g, calcium 41 mg, iron 2.2 mg, magnesium 49 mg, sodium 131 mg, zinc 1.6 mg, folate 31 mcg, riboflavin 0.1 mg, vitamin B12 0 mcg, vitamin C 22 mg, vitamin E 2 mg, omega-3 fatty acids 1.1 g
% calories from: protein 6%, fat 33%, carbohydrate 61%

German Chocolate Cake

The recipes of chef Ron Pickarski are designed to support personal health and the health of the natural environment, while at the same time tantalizing the most sophisticated taste buds. They are truly amazing! You will find his books, *Eco-Cuisine* (Ten Speed Press, 1995) and *Friendly Foods* (Ten Speed Press, 1991), video, and vegan products at www.eco-cuisine.com. Ron Pickarski is a seven-time Culinary Olympics medal winner, whose dishes range from the everyday to the elegant. This superb cake with Coconut Squash Icing is a great way to introduce people to the delights of vegan cuisine. It is celebratory way of getting your day's supply of omega-3 fatty acids from the walnuts and canola oil!

1 H cup	Sucanat or brown sugar	375 mL
1 H cup	unbleached white flour	375 mL
1 G cup	whole wheat flour	310 mL
I cup	cocoa or carob powder	175 mL
2 tsp	baking soda	10 mL
H tsp	salt	2 mL
2 cups	water	500 mL
H cup	maple syrup	125 mL
6 tbsp	canola oil	90 mL
2 tbsp	apple cider vinegar	30 mL
2 tsp	pure vanilla extract	10 mL

Preheat oven to 180°C (350°F). In large mixing bowl combine Sucanat, flours, cocoa, soda, and salt and mix well. In another bowl combine water, maple syrup, oil, vinegar, and vanilla extract. Add wet ingredients to dry and mix well. Pour batter into two lightly oiled and floured 23-cm (9-in) round cake pans; springform pans are ideal. Bake for 30 minutes or until a toothpick inserted into the centre comes out dry. Cool completely. Turn one layer onto a serving plate so that bottom is facing up. Spread one-third of Coconut Squash Cake Icing (recipe, page 428) onto the surface. Place the other layer on top of icing and put remaining icing on top. Do not ice the sides. Makes 16 servings.

Coconut Squash Cake Icing

2 cups	almond milk	500 mL
G cup	coconut milk	60 mL
1 cup	dried unsweetened coconut	250 mL
3 tbsp	arrowroot powder dissolved in 45 mL/3 tbsp cool water	45 mL
1 cup	Sucanat or brown sugar	250 mL
H tsp	pure vanilla extract	2 mL
H cup	peeled, steamed, butternut squash	125 mL
2 cups	chopped walnuts, ground to a medium coarse meal	500 mL

In 2-L (2-qt) saucepan, combine almond milk, coconut milk, and dried coconut and bring to a simmer over medium heat. Remove saucepan from heat, add arrowroot-water mixture and stir vigorously with a whisk until thickened. Add Sucanat and vanilla, then transfer to a blender, add squash and walnuts, and blend until smooth. Chill for 1 hour before using.

Per slice (1/16 cake with Coconut Squash Cake Icing): calories 452, protein 6 g, fat 20 g, carbohydrate 67 g, dietary fibre 5 g, calcium 94 mg, iron 3 mg, magnesium 78 mg, sodium 270 mg, zinc 1.6 mg, folate 23 mcg, riboflavin 0.1 mg, vitamin B12 0 mcg, vitamin C 1 mg, vitamin E 3.4 mg, omega-3 fatty acids 1.8 g
% calories from: protein 6%, fat 38%, carbohydrate 56%

Super-Simple Chocolate Icing

This is a very classic chocolate icing is a simple alternative to Ron Pickarski's gourmet Coconut Squash Cake Icing above. It is perfect for a birthday cake that you wish to decorate in a traditional way with writing, grated chocolate, coconut, nuts or sprinkles, and candles. Put any decorations on before the icing sets, especially if you want to decorate the sides of the cake.

3 cups	icing sugar	750 mL
G cup	cocoa powder	60 mL
2 tbsp	non-hydrogenated margarine	30 mL
3 tbsp	fortified soymilk (or other "milk")	45 mL
1 tsp	vanilla extract	5 mL

In a medium bowl mix icing sugar and cocoa powder. Stir in margarine, soymilk, and vanilla. Beat until smooth and creamy. To reach desired consistency, it may be necessary to add another 15 ml (1 tbsp) or so of soymilk. Spread about one-third of icing on the first layer of the cake. Place the second layer on top. Spread another third of the icing on the top layer, and the final third on the sides of the cake (or you may use half of the icing between layers and half on top). Decorate immediately.

Per slice1/16 (German Chocolate Cake with Super-Simple Chocolate Icing): calories 316, protein 4 g, fat 7 g, carbohydrate 63 g, dietary fibre 3 g, calcium 37 mg, iron 2 mg, magnesium 47 mg, sodium 260 mg, zinc 1.1 mg, folate 6 mcg, riboflavin 0.1 mg, vitamin B12 0 mcg, vitamin C 0 mg, vitamin E 2 mg, omega-3 fatty acids 0.5 g
% calories from: protein 5%, fat 20%, carbohydrate 75%

Nutty Date Cookies

These cookies were developed in Brenda's kitchen and were originally featured in *Defeating Diabetes* by B. Davis, T. Barnard, and B. Bloomfield (The Book Publishing Co, 2003). They are delicious enough for the country fair—no one would even suspect they are free of sugar, butter, and eggs! The only sweetener used is cooked dates, yet they are very sweet. In place of canola oil, you may use another high monounsaturated fat oil such as high oleic sunflower or safflower oil, if desired. Instead of eggs, flaxseed is used as a binder. Be sure to use fresh walnuts (they shouldn't have any bitter aftertaste). For a low-fat version of this recipe see Variation #1. Enjoy!

2 cups	dates, packed	500 mL
H cup	water	125 mL
1 tbsp	lemon juice	15 mL
H cup	canola oil	125 mL
G cup	soymilk	60 mL
1 tsp	vanilla	5 mL
1 tbsp	ground flaxseed	15 mL
1 cup	whole wheat flour	250 mL
2 tsp	baking powder	10 mL
H tsp	baking soda	2 mL
H tsp	salt	2 mL
1 cup	walnut halves	250 mL

Preheat oven to 160°C (325°F). In small saucepan with a lid, bring dates and water to a boil, cover, reduce heat, and simmer for about 5 minutes or until dates are soft. Remove from heat and mash (a potato masher works well).

In a large bowl, combine lemon juice, oil, soymilk, vanilla, ground flaxseed, and mashed dates. In a 500-mL (2-cup) measuring cup or bowl, mix flour, baking powder, baking soda, and salt. Pour dry ingredients into wet ingredients and stir to mix (do not over-stir). Fold in walnuts.

Drop with a tablespoon onto an oiled cookie sheet. Bake for about 20-25 minutes or until nicely browned. Remove from the oven and cool on a wire rack or on the pan. Store in an airtight container. Makes 2 dozen large cookies.

Per cookie: calories 129, protein 1.8 g, fat 8 g, carbohydrate 16 g, dietary fibre 2 g, calcium 39 mg, iron 0.7 mg, magnesium 33 mg, sodium 132 mg, zinc 0.7 mg, folate 9 mcg, riboflavin 0 mg, vitamin B12 0 mcg, vitamin C 0 mg, vitamin E 1.2 mg, omega-3 fatty acids 0.8 g
% calories from: protein 5%, fat 50%, carbohydrate 45%

Variations

1. **Lowfat variation, with only 4 g fat per cookie:** Add 1 large grated apple or 125 mL (H cup) applesauce, decrease oil to 60 mL (G cup), and decrease walnuts to 125 mL (H cup). (Add apple or applesauce to the date mixture before adding flour.)

2. **Cranberry-pecan Variation:** Add 125 mL (H cup) dried cran-berries, and use pecan halves instead of walnut halves.

Chocolate Mint Nut Bars

These wonderful energy-packed chocolate candies are super-simple to make. Be creative—almost anything goes! Make a double batch for the holidays—they keep beautifully. To make these even more fudge-like or candy-like, cut back to 250 mL (1 cup) cereal. You can replace the chocolate with 70 g (2.5 oz) carob chips, if desired.

| H cup | syrup (corn, rice, barley malt syrup) | 125 mL |

G cup	tahini or other seed or nut butter	60 mL
2.5 oz	semisweet baking chocolate (2 H squares)	70 g
G tsp	mint extract	1 mL
1 cup	flaked cereal (such as millet rice cereal)	250 mL
1 cup	puffed cereal (such as puffed rice)	250 mL
H cup	chopped walnuts or other unsalted nuts	125 mL

Place syrup, tahini and chocolate in a medium-size saucepan, and cook on medium-low heat, stirring frequently until chocolate melts and mixture begins to bubble. Remove from heat and add mint extract. Stir in cereals and nuts and mix until they are coated with chocolate mixture. Spread in lightly oiled 10 × 23-cm (4 × 9-in) loaf pan, refrigerate for a half hour to set, and cut in squares. Keep refrigerated. Recipe can be doubled—use a 20 × 20-cm (8 × 8-in) pan for the larger batch. Makes 21 small bars.

Per bar: calories 87, protein 1 g, carbohydrate 11 g, fat 4 g, dietary fibre 1 g, calcium 7 mg, iron 0.4 mg, magnesium 7 mg, sodium 11 mg, zinc 0.2 mg, folate 6 mcg, riboflavin 0 mg, vitamin B12 0 mcg, vitamin C 0 mg, vitamin E 0.2 mg, omega-3 fatty acids 0.3 g
% calories from: protein 7%, fat 43%, carbohydrate 50%

CHEF'S TIP: *Ground Flaxseed Egg Replacer*

This flaxseed egg substitute works well to replace an egg or two in pancakes, muffins, and most cakes and cookies. As an easy way to prepare your own ground flaxseed, place 125 mL (H cup) of flaxseed in a blender and process for about 1 minute until all seeds are ground into a coarse powder. If you prefer a finer powder, blend until the desired consistency is reached. Ground seeds can be stored in a jar, in your refrigerator or freezer for several months; they will retain their omega-3 either way. When stored in the freezer, the flaxseed remains as a powder and need not be thawed before using. In recipes, use proportions below as replacement for each egg.

| 1 tbsp | ground flaxseed | 15 ml |
| 3 tbsp | water | 45 ml |

Place flax and water in a bowl. Stir, and add to wet ingredients when thick.

Nutrition Booster Variations

1. **Calcium booster.** Use almonds and almond butter.

2. **Zinc booster.** Use cashews and cashew butter.

3. **Omega-3 booster.** Use walnuts and flaked cereal with flaxseed.

4. **Protein, pocketbook booster.** Use peanuts and peanut butter.

Variations

1. **Cory's cranberry squares.** Replace mint extract with 5 mL (1 tsp) vanilla. Use a total of only 1 cup of cereal. Rather than flaked or puffed cereal, toasted oats may be used. Add 170 mL (2/3 cup) dried cranberries and 60 mL (G cup) coconut (optional) at the same time cereal and nuts are added.

2. **Chocolate mint nut balls.** Either the mint or cranberry squares can be rolled into balls. Spread 85 mL (N cup) fine, unsweetened coconut onto a plate or wide, shallow bowl. Take a spoonful of the chocolate mixture, form into a ball about 2.5 cm (1 in) in diameter, and roll ball in coconut. Store in refrigerator until used. (These freeze well.) Makes about 21-24 balls.

CHEF'S TIP: *Toasting Oats*

Oats can be toasted in the microwave on high for 2 minutes, in a frying pan on medium heat for 5 minutes, or in the oven at 180°C (350°F) for 10-15 minutes.

Berry Delicious Ice Dream

This creamy, sweet "ice cream" is sure to be a favourite with those who want to avoid dairy products, fat, or excess calories. You won't be disappointed; it is bursting with "real" fruit flavour. Put it in fancy sherbet glasses and serve to guests for a refreshing summer treat.

3	frozen bananas (See Chef's Tip, page 391)	3
1 cup	frozen berries (such as raspberries, strawberries, or blueberries)	250 mL
1 cup	fortified soymilk (vanilla or original) *or* vanilla soy or dairy yogourt	250 mL
2 tbsp	frozen juice concentrate (orange, citrus blend, peach, or mango)	30 mL

Place frozen bananas, berries and soymilk (or yogourt), and frozen juice concentrate in blender or food processor and blend or process on high speed until thoroughly smooth. A sturdy blender is ideal; many food processors work well too. (If your blender struggles to blend this, partially thawing the fruit, especially the strawberries, will help.) Serve immediately in bowls or in cups with a spoon. Top with nuts or fresh berries, if desired. Makes 3 servings (750 mL/3 cups).

Per 250 mL (1 cup): calories 200, protein 4 g, fat 2 g, carbohydrate 45 g, dietary fibre 6 g, calcium 126 mg, iron 1.3 mg, magnesium 67 mg, sodium 51 mg, zinc 0.6 mg, folate 73 mcg, riboflavin 0.2 mg, vitamin B12 1 mcg, vitamin C 37 mg, vitamin E 0.6 mg, omega-3 fatty acids 0.1 g
% calories from: protein 8%, fat 9%, carbohydrate 83%

Variation

Replace some or all of the berries with other frozen fruit such as peaches, kiwi, mango slices, or melon.

appendix

nutritional recommendations

TABLE 15.1: *Dietary Reference Intakes for Vitamins for Canada and the United States**

Life Stage/Age	Vit A[a] mcg	Vit C mg	Vit D[b,c] mcg	Vit E mg	Vit K mcg	Thiamin mg	Riboflavin mg	Niacin[4] mg	Vit B[6] mg	Folate[f] mcg	Vit B12 mcg	Pantothenic Acid mg	Biotin mcg	Choline mg
Infants														
0-6 months	400	40	5	4	2.0	0.2	0.3	2	0.1	65	0.4	1.7	5	125
7-12 months	500	50	5	5	2.5	0.3	0.4	4	0.3	80	0.5	1.8	6	150
Children														
1-3 years	300	15	5	6	30	0.5	0.5	6	0.5	150	0.9	2	8	200
4-8 year	400	25	5	7	55	0.6	0.6	8	0.6	200	1.2	3	12	250
Males														
9-13 years	600	45	5	11	60	0.9	0.9	12	1	300	1.8	4	20	375
14-18 years	900	75	5	15	75	1.2	1.3	16	1.3	400	2.4	5	25	550
19-30 years	900	90	5	15	120	1.2	1.3	16	1.3	400	2.4	5	30	550
31-50 years	900	90	5	15	120	1.2	1.3	16	1.3	400	2.4	5	30	550
51-70 years	900	90	10	15	120	1.2	1.3	16	1.7	400	2.4[h]	5	30	550
>70 years	900	90	15	15	120	1.2	1.3	16	1.7	400	2.4[h]	5	30	550
Females														
9-13 years	600	45	5	11	60	0.9	0.9	12	1	300	1.8	4	20	375
14-18 years	700	65	5	15	75	1	1	14	1.2	400[i]	2.4	5	25	400
19-30 years	700	75	5	15	90	1.1	1.1	14	1.3	400[i]	2.4	5	30	425
31-50 years	700	75	5	15	90	1.1	1.1	14	1.3	400[i]	2.4	5	30	425
51-70 years	700	75	10	15	90	1.1	1.1	14	1.5	400	2.4[h]	5	30	425
>70 years	700	75	15	15	90	1.1	1.1	14	1.5	400	2.4[h]	5	30	425
Pregnancy														
≤18 years	750	80	5	15	75	1.4	1.4	18	1.9	600[i]	2.6	6	30	450
19-30 years	770	85	5	15	90	1.4	1.4	18	1.9	600[i]	2.6	6	30	450
31-50 years	770	85	5	15	90	1.4	1.4	18	1.9	600[i]	2.6	6	30	450
Lactation														
≤18 years	1200	115	5	19	75	1.4	1.6	17	2	500	2.8	7	35	550
19-30 years	1300	120	5	19	90	1.4	1.6	17	2	500	2.8	7	35	550
31-50 years	1300	120	5	19	90	1.4	1.6	17	2	500	2.8	7	35	550

* Recommended Dietary Allowances (RDA's) are in bold type and Adequate Intakes (AI's) are in regular type.

Both RDA and AI can be used as goals for individual intake.

a Vitamin A—as retinal activity equivalents (RAEs). 1 RAE = 1 μg or 1 mcg retinol; 12 μg beta-carotene, 24 μg other pro-vitamin A carotenoids in foods.

b Vitamin D—1 μg or 1 mcg cholecalciferol = 40 IU vitamin D.

c Vitamin D—only required with insufficient sunlight exposure.

d Vitamin E—as alpha-tocopherol

e Niacin—as niacin equivalents (NE). 1 mg of niacin = 60 mg tryptophan; 0-6 months must receive preformed niacin, not NE.

f Folate—as dietary folate equivalents (DFE). 1 DFE = 1 μg or 1 mcg food folate = 0.6 μg of folic acid from fortified food or supplement consumed with food, or 0.05 mcg (0.5 μg) of supplement consumed on an empty stomach.

g Choline – although AI's have been set for choline, there is still uncertainly regarding its necessity throughout the lifecycle.

h Vitamin B12—10-30 per cent of people 50 years and above malabsorb vitamin B12, thus they are advised to meet the RDA using B12 fortified foods or supplements.

i Folate—due to concerns about neural tube defects in infants, all women capable of becoming pregnant are advised to consume 400 mcg (400 μg) of folate from supplements or fortified foods, in addition to folate from foods.

j Folate—women are to continue consuming 400 mcg (400 μg) folate from supplements or fortified foods until pregnancy is confirmed and they begin prenatal care.

Source: Food and Nutrition Board, The Institute of Nutrition, National Academies of Sciences. All Dietary Reference Intake reports can be accessed free at www.nap.edu (search for "Dietary Reference Intakes" and several books will be shown—all can be opened online and read free of charge).

TABLE 15.2: *Dietary Reference Intakes for Minerals for Canada and the United States**

Life Stage/Age	Calciums mg	Chromium mcg	Copper mcg	Fluoride mg	Iodine mcg	Iron mg	Magnesium mg	Manganese mg	Molybdenu mcg	Phosphorus mg	Selenium mcg	Zinc mg
Infants												
0-6 months	210	0.2	200	0.01	110	0.27	30	0.003	2	100	15	2
7-12 months	270	5.5	220	0.5	130	11	75	0.5	3	275	20	3
Children												
1-3 years	500	11	340	0.7	90	7	80	1.2	17	460	20	3
4-8 year	800	15	440	1	90	10	130	1.5	22	500	30	5
Males												
9-13 years	1,300	25	700	2	120	8	240	1.9	34	1,250	40	8
14-18 years	1,300	35	890	3	150	11	410	2.2	43	1,250	55	11
19-30 years	1,000	35	900	4	150	8	400	2.3	45	700	55	11
31-50 years	1,000	35	900	4	150	8	420	2.3	45	700	55	11
51-70 years	1,200	30	900	4	150	8	420	2.3	45	700	55	11
>70 years	1,200	30	900	4	150	8	400	2.3	45	700	55	11
Females												
9-13 years	1,300	21	700	2	120	8	240	1.6	34	1,250	40	8
14-18 years	1,300	24	890	3	150	15	360	1.6	43	1,250	55	9
19-30 years	1,000	25	900	3	150	18	310	1.8	45	700	55	8
31-50 years	1,000	25	900	3	150	18	320	1.8	45	700	55	8
51-70 years	1,200	20	900	3	150	8	320	1.8	45	700	55	8
>70 years	1,200	20	900	3	150	8	320	1.8	45	700	55	8
Pregnancy												
≤18 years	1,300	29	1,000	3	220	27	400	2.0	50	1,250	60	13
19-30 years	1,000	30	1,000	3	220	27	350	2.0	50	700	60	11
31-50 years	1,000	30	1,000	3	220	27	360	2.0	50	700	60	11
Lactation												
≤18 years	1,300	44	1,300	3	290	10	360	2.6	50	1,250	70	14
19-30 years	1,000	45	1,300	3	290	9	310	2.6	50	700	70	12
31-50 years	1,000	45	1,300	3	290	9	320	2.6	50	700	70	12

* Recommended Dietary Allowances (RDA's) are in bold type and Adequate Intakes (AI's) are in regular type.

AI's (Acceptable Intakes) are in regular font. Both RDA and AI can be used as goals for individual intake.

Source: Food and Nutrition Board, The Institute of Nutrition, National Academies of Sciences. All Dietary Reference Intake reports can be accessed free at www.nap.edu (search for "Dietary Reference Intakes" and several books will be shown—all can be opened online and read free of charge).

Index

notes:

notes: